THE JEWS IN
MODERN FRANCE

The Tauber Institute, established by a gift to Brandeis University by Dr. Laszlo N. Tauber, is dedicated to the memory of the victims of Nazi persecution between 1933 and 1945. The Institute is devoted to the study of European history since the Enlightenment, with a particular focus on the history and culture of the Jewish communities of Europe.

THE JEWS IN
MODERN FRANCE

EDITED BY

FRANCES MALINO

AND

BERNARD WASSERSTEIN

PUBLISHED FOR BRANDEIS UNIVERSITY PRESS
BY UNIVERSITY PRESS OF NEW ENGLAND
HANOVER AND LONDON, 1985

Printed in the United States of America

LIBRARY OF CONGRESS CATALOGING IN PUBLICATION DATA

Main entry under title:

The Jews in modern France.

(Tauber Institute series; 4)
Includes bibliographical references and index.
1. Jews—France—History—Addresses, essays, lectures.
2. Antisemitism—France—Addresses, essays, lectures.
3. France—Ethnic relations—Addresses, essays, lectures.
I. Malino, Frances.   II. Wasserstein, Bernard.
III. Series: Tauber Institute series; no. 4
DS135.F83J49   1985   944'.004924   84-40591
ISBN 0-87451-324-3

Contents

vi   *Contents*

BERNARD WASSERSTEIN

Preface

THIS BOOK focuses on the encounter between Jews and French society and culture in the period since the Revolution. The Franco-Jewish relationship has often been regarded, from several points of view, as a litmus test of the possibilities of emancipation. But the points of view (and therefore, not surprisingly, the conclusions) of writers on the subject have been disparate—so much so as often to appear to inhabit hermetically sealed universes of discourse.

Two developments in recent years have created a fertile soil for the growth of a new approach to French Jewish history. The first, and by far the most important, is the changed self-image of French Jewry. The trauma of Vichy, the unavoidable impact on French Jews of the State of Israel, and the immigration to France of hundreds of thousands of Jews from North Africa—these shattering events have transformed the community, within one generation, demographically, socially, and ideologically. The centripetal force of the Jacobin tradition remains strong enough to ensure that the ethnic particularism characteristic of Jews (and others) in North America is unlikely to take root in France. And yet the French Jewish community today presents an aspect of striking vitality and self-confidence—striking in contrast both to its own modern history and to the moribund or declining Jewish communities of all other European countries.

The second development has been the upsurge in recent years of monographic research in French Jewish history, drawing on archival resources of immense range and rich variety. Much of the most original work in this field has been conducted by Anglo-American historians, particularly by a new wave of young American historians who combine a rigorous training in history as a scholarly discipline with a sympathetic insight into the wellsprings of Jewish tradition.

Against this background the Tauber Institute at Brandeis University convened a conference in April 1983 whose purpose was to provide a forum for dialogue between specialists on the French Jewish community and scholars engaged in research in French history and civilisation. The conference was the first of its kind to be held anywhere, and we were fortunate in securing the participation of more than two hundred scholars from several countries, representing a variety of scholarly disciplines, and approaching the topic from what were sometimes sharply differing points of view.

At the outset Eugen Weber's keynote address (printed later in this book) posed a challenge to all of those present. If, as Weber suggests, the Jewish question "to most French during most of the nineteenth century and to many French in the twentieth century . . . was a minor question, or no question at all," were we, in effect, discussing a nonsubject? Weber's own paper, as well as the ensuing four days of discussion, demonstrated that this alleged nonquestion was capable of evoking some extraordinarily valuable responses.

Several underlying themes of debate emerged in the course of the conference: was the Jewish question central or peripheral to French politics and society in the postemancipation period? Is anti-Semitism an enduring, ineradicable, and characteristic feature of modern French behavior, or is it rather a fringe phenomenon occasionally emerging into lurid prominence in moments of acute crisis? What are the lessons to be drawn from the French Jewish experience during the supreme crisis of France in this century, the Vichy period? What has been the special impact on the Jews of the historic schism in the French political consciousness between the revolutionary tradition and its foes?

Some of our contributors come to strikingly different conclusions on many of these issues. Compare, for example, Stephen Schuker's scathing and thoroughly documented indictment of the Jewish role in the French left in the later Third Republic with the more charitable interpretation of the Communist party's role in these years offered by William B. Cohen and Irwin M. Wall. Zeev Sternhell's analysis of French anti-Semitism as a "crucial aspect of the revolt against the legacy of the Enlightenment and the Revolution" stands in stark contrast to Patrice Higonnet's suggestion that we must redirect the focus of our attention away from the problem of the Jews, qua Jews: "The crime of ordinary Frenchmen

in 1940–44 was not their anti-Semitism, but their passive conformity and their indifference to the plight of individuals—individuals who in this instance were Jewish." Pierre Birnbaum's stress on
the uses of anti-Semitism in left- and right-wing demonology in
contemporary France is usefully read in conjunction with Michael
Marrus's survey of the long-term trends in French attitudes toward
Jews as shown in public opinion polls since World War II. Shmuel
Trigano's onslaught against what he sees as the central features of
the French Jacobin tradition evokes an incisive retort from Stanley
Hoffmann, who rejects Trigano's postulation of a total incompatibility between the French republican system and "Jewish difference." David Landes's paper excoriates what he regards as the
"nuances, mitigations, reticences, exculpations, and misgivings" of
some other contributors whose interpretation of French conduct
toward Jews in the postrevolutionary period may occasionally
smack of the apologetic.

The reader searching for uniformity of approach among the articles in this book will therefore be disappointed. Our aim has
been to present a diversity of viewpoints and to seek to stimulate a
fruitful dialectic. French history and Jewish history have hitherto
been so compartmentalized that the mere encounter seems in itself
a salutary exercise. By the end of our conference, after vigorous,
sometimes impassioned debate, most participants could agree at
any rate on this: that the study of French Jewish history is worthwhile, not merely because of any paradigmatic utility it may hold
but in its own right and for its own sake. We hope that the reader
of this book may reach a similar conclusion.

Our aim has not been to produce a comprehensive survey of
French Jewish history, and there are several important aspects of
the subject that receive only passing attention here. For example,
recent valuable work on the sociology of French Jewry, drawing on
a variety of quantitative, anthropological, and other methodolo-
gies, could not fit readily into the structure of this book. Nor do
we pretend to have done sufficient justice to the implications for
France and for French Jewry of the special relationship, sometimes
intimate and at other times tortured, between the French and Jewish states. We intend this volume as a first rather than a last word.
Occasionally it may even seem a word in edgeways. This is deliberate. Our method has been spectroscopic rather than panoramic.

We have consciously sought to separate out and examine closely the areas of most intense color in our subject. By thus analyzing some parts we hope to shed illumination on the whole.

Most of the essays in this volume were first delivered as papers at our conference. A few of the conference papers that were somewhat peripheral to our central theme have not, however, been published here. On the other hand, in certain cases the essays, as printed here, were not presented as conference papers but were suggested by the discussions on that occasion and were written for this book at the special invitation of the editors.

A note on the organization of the book, which is thematic rather than chronological. Part 1 is concerned with situating the history of French Jews within the context of modern French history. Part 2 traces the origins of the enduring images and traditions of the two most significant immigrant groups among French Jews in this century. Parts 3 and 4 examine the ideological forces contending for supremacy in modern France as they affected Jews: the sources, nature, and degree of anti-Semitism of both left and right receive particular attention from a variety of viewpoints. In Part 5 we present three strikingly different perspectives on what is perhaps the central question in any discussion of the place of the Jews in a liberal society—the costs and benefits of emancipation. Finally, in Part 6, two essays survey the rich historiographical literature concerning the Jews in France.

The Tauber Institute, which was founded at Brandeis University in 1980, has laid special emphasis on research in European Jewish history within the larger context of general European history. It was therefore entirely appropriate that such a conference should have taken place under the Institute's auspices and that this book should appear as a volume in the Tauber Institute series published for Brandeis University Press by the University Press of New England.

The editors wish to pay particular tribute to Jonathan Mandelbaum, whose translations of several of these essays from the original French combine meticulous accuracy with a rare felicity. The number of others who have helped us at every stage of this enterprise is legion. We hope they will forgive us if we express our appreciation to them collectively rather than individually. It is no less heartfelt for that.

Abbreviations

AAIU	Archives of the Alliance Israélite Universelle, Paris
ACC	Archives of the Consistoire Central, Paris
ACIP	Archives of the Association Consistoriale Israélite de Paris
AEP	Archives of the Ministère des Affaires Etrangères, Paris
AI	*Archives israélites de France*
AIU	Alliance Israélite Universelle
AJDC	Archives of the American Jewish Joint Distribution Committee, New York
ANP	Archives Nationales, Paris
APP	Archives of the Préfecture de Police, Paris
BAIU	*Bulletin de l'Alliance Israélite Universelle*
CAHJP	Central Archives for the History of the Jewish People, Jerusalem
CCOJA	Commission Centrale des Organisations Juives d'Assistance
CDJC	Centre de Documentation Juive Contemporaine
CGT	Confédération Générale du Travail
CRIF	Conseil Représentatif des Israélites de France
FANG	Fédération d'Action Nationale Européenne
FSJ	Fédération des Sociétés Juives
IFOP	Institut Français d'Opinion Publique
JTS	Jewish Theological Seminary Archives, New York
LICA	Ligue Internationale contre l'Antisémitisme
MOI	Main d'Oeuvre Immigrée
PCF	Parti Communiste Français
SFIO	Section Française de l'Internationale Ouvrière
UGIF	Union Générale des Israélites de France
UI	*L'Univers israélite*
YA	*Der Yidisher Arbeter*
YIVO	Archives of the YIVO Institute for Jewish Research, New York
YVA	Yad Vashem Archives, Jerusalem

Contributors

MICHEL ABITBOL, *Hebrew University of Jerusalem*

PIERRE BIRNBAUM, *Université de Paris*

YERACHMIEL (RICHARD) COHEN, *Hebrew University of Jerusalem*

WILLIAM B. COHEN, *Indiana University*

NANCY L. GREEN, *Ecole des Hautes Etudes en Sciences Sociales, Paris*

PATRICE HIGONNET, *Harvard University*

STANLEY HOFFMANN, *Harvard University*

PAULA E. HYMAN, *Jewish Theological Seminary*

DAVID S. LANDES, *Harvard University*

FRANCES MALINO, *University of Massachusetts, Boston*

MICHAEL R. MARRUS, *University of Toronto*

STEPHEN A. SCHUKER, *Brandeis University*

ZEEV STERNHELL, *Hebrew University of Jerusalem*

SHMUEL TRIGANO, *Université Paul Valéry, Montpellier*

IRWIN M. WALL, *University of California, Riverside*

BERNARD WASSERSTEIN, *Brandeis University*

EUGEN WEBER, *University of California, Los Angeles*

GEORGES WEILL, *Directeur des Services d'Archives des Hauts-de-Seine; Conservateur de la bibliothèque de l'Alliance Israélite Universelle*

PART I

FRENCH HISTORY AND JEWISH HISTORY

FRANCES MALINO

Introduction

In life . . . there are no essentially major or minor char-
acters. Everyone is necessarily the hero of his own life
story. *Hamlet* could be told from Polonius's point of view
and called *The Tragedy of Polonius, Lord Chamberlain
of Denmark.*

> JOHN BARTH, *The End of the Road*

MODERN JEWISH historical scholarship, as Yosef H. Yerushalmi has so eloquently demonstrated in *Zakhor*,[1] is relatively recent and essentially problematic. Such scholarship demands at the outset a disregard of Divine Providence and a denial
of the intrinsic uniqueness of Jewish history. It seeks, nonetheless,
to remain culturally and spiritually connected to Jewry. General
historians who turn at one time or another to the Jews must equally
distance themselves from their own traditional, although not exclusively theological, assumptions and perceptions. For both Jewish and general historians, however, this marks a necessary but not
a sufficient condition of dialogue. There follows the demanding
task of avoiding an inhibiting parochialism or a universalism that
rejects the idea that Jews were different and simultaneously ignores
them in the general study of history.

All too often Jewish and general historians alike have been led to
exaggerate or diminish the meaning of an event, misread the intentions of the protagonists, and deny to the reader an accurate understanding of the historical distinctiveness of the place of the
Jews. Nowhere is this more obvious than in the history of the Jews
in modern France, whether revolutionary, Dreyfusard, or that of
Vichy.

[1] Yosef H. Yerushalmi, *Zakhor: Jewish History and Jewish Memory* (Seattle, 1982).

Rather than enter the controversies concerning the modern period, which readers have richly before them in the essays in this
volume, let us illustrate the problem with an example from the distance of the middle of the eighteenth century. On one level the episode appears to be quite simple. The Jewish community of Metz
struggled to retain its juridical autonomy against a competing judicial body, the Metz Parlement. Historians have presented the narrative accordingly, some emphasizing what they perceived as a threat
to Jewish survival, others stubbornly refusing to acknowledge any
threat. Both perceptions bear truth, but the events themselves defy
these constraints. What emerges is a complicated struggle significant not only for the evolution of the Jewish community in France,
but also for the history of the judicial bodies of the ancien régime.
The events themselves can be easily recounted.

Nothing protected the uniqueness of Jewish community life
more than the privilege of living under and according to Jewish
law and tradition. To abandon this juridical autonomy would entail abrogating the civil legislation of Judaism; to remove the
powerful weapon of excommunication would deny the sanction
necessary to ensure compliance. On 30 January 1759, the Parlement of Metz prohibited the use of excommunication against
those Jews who sought adjudication in royal courts, or by Jews
against Jews. The rabbi was personally answerable for any in-
fringement of the decree; the acts of those Jews who disobeyed the
Parlement would be rendered legally null and void.[2]

Almost two hundred years later, Rabbi Netter of Metz recalled
1759 as a time of great upheaval for the Jewish community. The
Parlement, he wrote, had long wished to deprive the rabbinate and
leaders of the community of their jurisdiction "to profit" the royal
courts.[3] Jewish historians since the mid-eighteenth century have
seen the Parlement's intentions exclusively in terms of an attack
upon the community. M. Gabriel, a distinguished Metz lawyer,
would agree. Why tolerate in a rabbi, he asked in 1787, what we
refuse to permit a bishop?[4] The Parlement's abrogation of Jewish
autonomy evoked a simple, but misleading, parallel between Jew-

---

[2] *Arrest de la cour de Parlement, qui fait défenses au Rabin de Juifs* . . . 30 Jan. 1759.
Houghton Library, Harvard University, FC7F844P8 759a.
[3] Nathan Netter, *Vingt Siècles d'histoire d'une communauté juive* (Paris: 1938), 115−16.
[4] M. Gabriel, *Observations détachées sur les Coutumes et les Usages anciens et modernes du Parlement de Metz* (Tome 1, 1787), p. 23−24.

ish powers of excommunication and the punitive authority of the Church.

The crown, on the other hand, continued to support Jewish juridical autonomy (including the weapon of excommunication) and angrily directed the Parlement of Metz to act accordingly. For good reason, then, the king was seen as the main defender of Jewish interests, especially when they involved chastizing a Parlement for its usurpation of royal authority. Jews and king served each other's purposes, not for the first time in French history.

The Parlement's decree of 1759 thus appears to be perfectly clear and consistent with what historians have generally assumed to be the nature of Jewish communal life in the ancien régime. In fact, however, the situation is far from clear. Closer examination reveals numerous cases of individual Jews rebelling against the discipline of the Jewish leadership, the "superstition" of the rabbis, and the economic constraints of a corporation. These Jews struggled to reach the sovereign courts of Metz. For them, the Parlement's decree offered freedom and protection.

Royal support of the Jews, moreover, was significantly qualified. The Parlement had requested from the Jewish community a compendium of Metz Jewish law and custom that was to serve as the basis for adjudicating cases between Jews. Toul and Verdun had already compiled similar compendia. Once the crown reinforced the Parlement's request in royal *lettres patentes*, the well-known rabbi of Metz, Jonathan Eybeschuetz, complied. Much to the chagrin of Parlement, however, the crown subsequently refused to recognize the compendium prepared by the Jewish community. Why had the king changed his position? Official endorsement, a royal counselor privately advised the crown, presumed giving the Jews a degree of establishment comparable to that of "actual citizens."[5]

The Parlement of Metz, therefore, had not only threatened Jewish juridical autonomy but had also suggested an avenue of potential integration—albeit on terms less far-reaching than those of 1789.

French historians might be surprised to discover that a Parlement defiantly supported the rights of individual Jews and then subsequently, as part of its defense of prescriptive liberties against royal absolutism, reinforced the authority (including that of excommunication) of the rabbis and Jewish leaders. For in a dra-

[5] "Sur les juifs," undated, unsigned ms., Archives Nationales K1194 no. 40.

matic about-face the Parlement of Metz issued its decree of 1782 explicitly recognizing the juridical power of the Metz Jewish community and giving executive force to its decisions. Jewish historians will learn, moreover, that this endorsement of Jewish juridical autonomy facilitated the Parlement's exclusion of Jews from the crown's edict of 1787 granting significant economic rights to non-Catholics.

By the end of the century, then, the Parlement of Metz defended the interests of the Jewish community but not those Jews who attempted to enter the economic life of the country. The crown, on the other hand, appears to have been committed to freeing the Jews from the discipline of their communities, thereby denying these communities their traditional authority.

But let us return to the decree of 1759.

French and Jewish historians alike have simplified the intentions of the Parlement and crown, overlooked the struggle within the Jewish community, and contributed to the use of history as a form of mythotherapy. In so doing, they have missed the significance of a lonely battle, in the middle of the eighteenth century in a garrison town on the outskirts of France, to resolve a conflict between individual and group freedoms—a recurrent theme in the Franco-Jewish relationship throughout the modern period.

In 1880, the first volume of the *Revue des études juives* appeared. Supported by the newly formed Société des Etudes Juives and influenced by the German *Wissenschaft des Judentums*, this scholarly quarterly was to provide a serious forum for the "discovery" and "reconstitution" of the entire Jewish past. No less overwhelming than this task were the proclaimed goals of the editors.

One has often stated, and with a feeling of regret, that our country is far from occupying one of the first ranks in the vast scientific and literary movement, which during the last forty or fifty years has successfully revived the study of Jewish antiquity. To raise France from the state of inferiority, which suits neither her past nor her present traditions, to enter freely into this remarkable movement where she was so wrong to have let herself be outstripped, to regain, if it is possible, *le temps perdu*, such has been the goal of some men of goodwill.[6]

We smile at this missionary zeal to revive and restore an intellectually undernourished (and thus also easily defeated) France. The

---

[6] "A nos lecteurs," *Revue des études juives* 1 (1880), v.

determination to establish a medieval-aristocratic pedigree for French Judaism or a French pedigree for "universal Judaism" justifiably finds little support. The alternative, however, is not to confine French Jewish history within a purely Jewish perspective but rather, while retaining its uniqueness, to integrate it into mainstream French history. Such is the purpose of this book.

EUGEN WEBER

Reflections on the Jews in France

—————————————

IF CLIO is the muse of history, Anna Kronista must be her first
cousin. It is natural, and it is easy, to think (without thinking)
that questions that preoccupy us, questions that loom large in the
consciousness of our time, were as apparent, and as evidently interesting, in other times. And even when we approach such questions with scholarly caution, our very thoroughness can produce
an unbalanced result: a study of anarchism, or of anticlericalism,
in nineteenth-century France can easily give the impression that
these issues had a quantitative significance, a visibility, that just
was not there much or most of the time. The same impression can
be created by the wealth of thorough, thoughtful, useful studies
that have been dedicated to the Jewish question in France. It is no
criticism of admirable works to suggest that their number, their
proliferation, may be liable to mislead—not about their subject,
but about the importance of their subject to the society in whose
midst it is situated. It is no depreciation of the Jewish question to
suggest that, to most French during most of the nineteenth century
and to many French in the twentieth century, it was a minor question, or no question at all.

The Jewish question was a *Jewish* question. It is well to keep
that in mind. And if we take modern France to begin with the great
Revolution, I should be inclined to say that the exceptions to this
rule cover only very brief periods, such as the later 1890s and
much of the 1930s. Which is not entirely surprising when we think
of the tiny numbers involved: around forty thousand at the time of

the Revolution, not many more in 1815 (0.16 percent of the population). And even though Jews grew in number, their proportion of the nation's population remained fairly slight: 0.20 percent in 1851, it had risen to 0.23 percent in 1866, before plunging back to 0.14 percent in 1872, after the loss of Alsace and Lorraine, where so many of them lived.[1]

Figures vary, all of them admitted to be rather inexact, but the best sources do not differ very much. So, always bearing in mind that we are talking about an *ordre de grandeur*, the Jewish population of France, which had been about seventy-four thousand in 1851, stood below that figure in 1897: perhaps at seventy-one or seventy-two thousand. Even if you prefer to count a few thousand more, as Michael Marrus does, at the century's end the Jewish community in France remained the smallest in any major country: less than half that of England, a lot smaller even than that of the Netherlands.

I think this is important, because it gives us a sense of proportion. Equally important is the fact that in lots of places there were no Jews at all. In 1815, forty-two departments had no Jews, which suggests that half the population of the kingdom had no truck with them at all; and things had not changed much a quarter of a century later. Only thirty-eight departments answered an official survey of 1840, and some of these reported ridiculous (but credible) figures: nineteen Jews in the Cher, six in the Creuse, two in Eure-et-Loire, seventeen in Somme, nineteen in the Yonne. . . . In 1851, still, forty departments had no Jewish residents, and the number of departments (out of a total of eighty-six) that counted a hundred Jews or more soared from twenty-four in 1851 to thirty-two in 1872. It need not surprise us, therefore, that—the Wandering Jew apart—Jews have left remarkably little mark on peasant folklore; and that, were it not for the same Wandering Jew, the four huge volumes of Paul Sébillot's *Le Folk-Lore de France*, would offer less than half a dozen mentions of them, and none that cannot be over-matched by other social groups.[2]

[1] For numbers, see Patrick Girard, *Les Juifs de France de 1789 à 1869* (Paris, 1976) pp. 102, 109; Doris Bensimon-Donath, *Socio-démographie des juifs de France et d'Algérie: 1867–1907* (Paris, 1976) p. 68 and passim; Bernhard Blumenkranz, ed., *Documents modernes sur les juifs* (Toulouse, 1979) p. 304. See also below p. 146.
[2] Sébillot, *Le Folk-Lore de France*, I (1904) p. 380: near Uchon (Saône-et-Loire), in the

We know that that is so because, outside Alsace (and perhaps Lorraine), the Jews were heavily concentrated in towns: by the 1870s, 94 or 95 percent of Jews lived in urban centers. But even there their small absolute number did not make them terribly obtrusive—at least, not statistically. Except for four or five towns, no city of the Second Empire seems to have boasted more than a thousand Jews. And the typical community ran from a few families to two or three hundred in places like St.-Etienne, Montbéliard, Besançon.[3]

More typical than the typical community, though, is the absence of one, as in the Indre, where, to the century's end, we count 5 or 6 Jews for a population around 280,000; and where in May 1870 the *commissaire de police* of Châtillon-sur-Indre reports that there is, indeed, one old Jew in Châtillon, but he got baptized a few days ago.[4]

Which leaves Paris, of course, whose Jewish population grows exponentially to the point where, at the end of the nineteenth century, 50 or 60 percent of all French Jews live there. No wonder that Paris is the center and the forge of French antisemitism. And, since French politics are conducted from Paris, and since French ideologies are made in Paris, and since French history is written in Paris, this makes antisemitism bulk large. Larger, I think, than it did for most people, in most places, most of the time.

Which is not to say that anti-Jewish sentiment did not exist and had to be invented. Far from it. Antisemitism as an explicit modern doctrine may have been imported from abroad (as Lazare Landau avers in his introduction to Doris Bensimon's book), even though Zeev Sternhell has shown its strong ideological roots in France. But anti-Jewish sentiment, in a diffuse sense, is as French as apple pie. There were Jews in France before there were Franks;

---

mountainous country west of Le Creusot, the rough shape of a cross in the rock passes for the trace of the body of a saint martyred there by Jews; but other such alleged imprints attributed to popes or devils make no mention of Jews. Ibid., 3 (1906) p. 141, cites satirical legends of Jews changed into pigs because of deceitful activities, intended to explain their refusal to eat pig's meat. But similar legends exist about non-Jews.

[3] P. Girard, p. 109; David Cohen, *La Promotion des juifs en France à l'époque du Second Empire (1852–1870)* (Aix, 1980), 1, pp. 86–89 and maps.

[4] Daniel Bernard, 'La Vie quotidienne sous le Second Empire dans les cantons de Buzançais et de Châtillon,' *Bulletin du groupe d'histoire et d'archéologie de Buzançais*, 10 (1978) p. 141. For confirmation, Adolphe Joanne, *Géographie de l'Indre* (Paris, 1879 and 1907) p. 36.

and persecution of Jews is well documented, especially for the twelfth, thirteenth, and fourteenth centuries, with popular hostility mostly connected with charges of ritual murder, profaning the host, and other abominations. In this context, we do well to remember that "the people" tends to ascribe its own hostilities to those whom it abhors, and that charges of poisoning, or arson, or plotting terrible things, were leveled against nobles, bourgeois, doctors, priests, and government agents well into the nineteenth century. It should not surprise us, therefore, to find lots of people in 1840, including apparently Thiers himself, believing the Jews capable of ritual murder; and quite a few still in the 1890s believing that they had real contact with real devils.[5]

Further, and in the same context, it is a platitude to say, but it has to be said because it is crucial, that the Christian Church prepared the ground for anti-Jewish hatred, even where there were no real Jews to hate; that growing up Christian meant the assimilation of sentiments of suspicion at best, more often obloquy and contempt, focused or unfocused, perpetually refreshed by catechism and liturgy right through the nineteenth century and a good part of the twentieth;[6] and that gradual detachment from the Church, and from religious beliefs, had little effect on prejudices that were largely assimilated as cultural traditions needing no more examination than the return of the seasons did.

On this rich and enduring compost, other cultural stereotypes were piled. The most familiar was that of the money-grubbing Jew, especially the usurer. In 1694, the Dictionary of the French Academy cites the word *jew* specifically for its figurative uses: it is used for usurers, it is used for the rich, and it is used for the wanderer—

[5] On Thiers and the Damascus ritual murder charges of 1840, see P. Girard, p. 149; and Henri Heine, *Lutèce* (Paris, 1861) pp. 58, 64, 75, where we sense the wider political implications of a complex affair. But it is well to place such beliefs in the context of times when cholera was attributed to doctors (when it was not blamed on nobles or priests); when some churches and castles were said to have been built with *mortier de sang*—a mortar mixed with peasants' blood; when fear of medical men avid for *graisse de chrétien* was widespread and villagers mounted special guard over the grave of a fat friend. See also Francis Pérot, *Folklore bourbonnais* (Paris, 1908) pp. 102–3, for *graisse de chrétien* and belief in its uses in a variety of situations, especially to avoid spells on animals or men. The legends that refer to Jews are mere adaptations of current beliefs.

[6] Annie Kriegel, *Les Juifs et le monde moderne* (Paris, 1977) p. 116, quotes Richard Wright's recollection of his youth, when "all the Blacks . . . hated the Jews, not because they exploited them but because we had been taught, at home and at Sunday school, that the Jews were Christ's murderers."

the *juif errant*—who has no home and no stability. In 1784, a Nantes official draws up a report against a certain Salomon, "*juif de profession*."[7] In 1863, the great positivist dictionary of Emile Littré does not offer a very different image: to be rich as a Jew, to lust for gold, to be a usurer. The Wandering Jew, popular with printmakers and balladeers, lasts into the 1880s and 1890s—and it is worth bearing in mind the negative connotations of the image, the strong suspicion of *all* strangers that relatively isolated communities maintained to the century's end.

But the Jew was not only a stranger. He was a very peculiar stranger in one respect among many others: for Jews, learning was and remains a crucial aspect of status. So the Jew was generally literate, and he was almost always more literate than those in whose midst he lived. For hundreds of years, the Jews were literates in an ocean of illiteracy, living in, or moving through, communities where possession of written material was associated with sorcery and spells. As late as the 1830s we hear of a schoolteacher (a normal, Christian schoolteacher, of course) stoned out of a village for reading a book out in the open. As late as the 1870s, peasants with books were quite possibly witches. No wonder that Jews seemed not only strange, but odd and threatening.[8]

And then there is the business of moneylending; and, more generally, the business of business, the business of trading. This too deserves to be put in perspective: the perspective of a country where, until the latter part of the nineteenth century, three people out of four made their living from the land, where exchange for most of them was the exchange of goods and services with little money changing hands, where cash was scarce and unfamiliar and credit hard to get, and costly when you got it. Business, in those circumstances, was nearly always small business, and those engaged in it were rather suspect and not particularly respected, because trading in horses or cattle was easily connected with dirty tricks, and peddling was an activity of the poor and strange, and dealing in grain was associated with forestalling and speculation. And even though Jews were not particularly prominent in any of

---

[7] Abbé J.-L-M. Noguès, *Les Moeurs d'autrefois en Saintonge et en Aunis* (Saintes, 1891) p. 65; Léon Brunschvicg, *Les Juifs de Nantes et du pays nantais* (Nantes, 1890) p. 22.

[8] Michel Rouche, *Histoire générale de l'enseignement et de l'éducation en France* (Paris, 1981) I, p. 275; Bensimon-Donath, pp. 131 ff; Paul Lorain, *Tableau de l'instruction primaire d'après des documents authentiques* (Paris, 1837).

these activities, they were semantically and stereotypically associated with them.[9]

This was even truer of usury, crucial when banks and savings institutions were practically nonexistent—as they remained for most French until pretty well the end of the century—and interest rates excruciatingly high. Most French peasants were in debt and suffered from it and resented it bitterly, generation after generation. And most of the usurers were neighbors, or small local notables likely to have a bit of cash: notaries, priests, millers, even the odd schoolteacher. But here too the semantic confusion worked to identify the enemy as "a Jew"; hence the Jew, generally nonexistent, with the enemy.

Of course, there was one area where the identification was broadly correct; and that was in Alsace—and to a lesser extent in Lorraine—where Jews were relatively numerous and scattered in small towns and villages, where they performed the functions of a typical trading class: dealing in crops and livestock, rags and junk, dry goods, old clothes (which means almost all clothes, in times when most French folk went about in other people's cast-off clothing), and also in small loans to peasants always short of ready cash to pay their rents or taxes, to buy seed or land, or livestock or bread, with the attendant accumulation of resentments and social strains.[10] The fact is that, even in Alsace, Jewish usurers were only a small proportion of the total, and Jews held only a limited proportion of total loans and obligations (less than half at most at the beginning of the nineteenth century, less than that as the century progressed). But precisely because the Jews were relatively poor and ill placed to go in for bigger deals, their loans were small, and they were made to fellow peasants who were just as poor as they were, though possibly less thrifty; hence more likely to default and to resent them.

So, again, it is not surprising to find Alsatian anti-Jewish senti-

[9]They seem also to have been associated with agencies to find substitutes for military service: "shameful traffic . . . odious trade." According to Cohen, 2, pp. 361, 670–74, Jewish *marchands d'hommes* were numerous all over France, especially in Alsace.

[10]On Jewish occupations, and their usury, see G. Cahen, "Les Juifs et la vie économique des campagnes (1648–1870)," *Revue d'Alsace*, 97 (1958) pp. 143–48; Zosa Szajkowski, *Agricultural Credit and Napoleon's Anti-Jewish Decrees* (New York, 1953); Freddy Raphaël and Robert Weyl, *Juifs en Alsace* (Toulouse, 1977) pp. 370–71; Cohen, 2, pp. 674 ff., 687–98; and Roland Marx, *La Révolution et les classes sociales en Basse-Alsace* (Paris, 1974, especially pp. 392, 401, 464, 469. Marx's *Recherches sur la vie politique en Alsace*

ment very lively, to find it reflected also in popular folklore, with special rocks (like the Spitzbergfelsen) known to denounce liars and Jews, or thieves and Jews; with ballads and rhymes that speak of the dirt, the stink, the hatred of the Jews (a hatred assumed to be mutual, so that when Jews put Zion soil in a coffin, the peasants believe that it is stones for the dead to throw at Jesus); and even a rhythm for threshing grain with the flail while grunting out "Itzig/Nathel/Gimbel." All of this connected with the good old Christian tradition of punishing the Jews at Christmas, and especially at Easter, when one burnt Judas, or the *Ewig Jud*, preferably on Good Friday, as late as 1928.[11] What the subprefect of Sélestat (Bas-Rhin) wrote in 1834 could just as easily be repeated in 1848, when the February Revolution brought widespread anti-Jewish riots in his area: "The Jews are always the excuse the agitators use for provoking uprisings in Alsace."[12]

The interesting thing is that Alsace and Lorraine, where Jews conformed most closely to the anti-Jewish stereotype, and where hostility against them was most alive, provided an important proportion of Jewish migrants into Paris; especially after 1871, when well over half the French-born Jews living in the capital turn out to have been born in those provinces. But they also provide a good number of non-Jewish migrants, who bring their native prejudices with them; and it is no coincidence that antisemitic leaders such as the Marquis de Morès found some of their most active supporters among the butchers of La Villette, behind the Gare de l'Est, where a lot of these people settled. Or that Pierre Biétry, the antisemitic

---

prérévolutionnaire et révolutionnaire (Strasbourg, 1966) suggests that even there the Jewish question played a very small role.

[11] Raphaël and Weyl, pp. 408–10. In Corsica, between the wars, children and adults still "killed the Jews" on Easter Saturday: P. Bonardi, *Le Retour à Jérusalem* (Paris, 1927), quoted in André Spire, *Quelques Juifs et demi-juifs* (Paris, 1928), 2, p. 183.

[12] Quoted in Zosa Szajkowski, *Jews and the French Revolutions of 1789, 1830 and 1848* (New York, 1970) p. 1031. A letter of July 3, 1832, written by a Saint-Simonian engineer after a month in Sélestat, "certainly the most backward little town in Alsace," puts things in perspective by blaming the previous month's serious anti-Jewish riots on the priests. The rioters are miserable pawns whom "misery, ignorance and demoralization place at the mercy of an infamous clergy" (Bibliothèque Nationale, *Nouvelles acquisitions françaises* 24613, no. 57). However, Camille Mauclair, one of the first Dreyfusards, explains that his parents, like normal Alsatian peasants, "haissaient les juifs parce que des accapareurs . . . excellaient alors à endetter les villageois" (*Servitude et grandeur littéraires*, Paris, 1922, p. 128), and another Dreyfus supporter, P.-V. Stock, that his father, born in Lorraine, was "naturally" anti-Jewish (*Mémorandum d'un éditeur*, 3e série, Paris, 1938, pp. 14–15).

creator of "yellow" unions, should have been born at Fesches-L'Eglise, in the territoire de Belfort, on the very border of Alsace.

These are the traditional roots, religious, cultural, socioeconomic, of French attitudes toward the Jews. Now let us look at more modern developments, also quite well known, also not to be ignored.

Under the ancien régime, Jews could live only in certain parts of France: the southwest (Bordeaux, Bayonne), the south or southeast (Avignon, Comtat Venaissin), the eastern provinces taken over from the German Empire, and as a semiclandestine group in Paris. The more relaxed conditions of the eighteenth century gave them a bit more latitude for movement and enterprise. On the eve of the Revolution, we even find a Jew of Alsatian origin, Monsieur Colmar, buying the signory of Picquigny, with which went the viscountcy of Amiens and the right to appoint the canons of Amiens cathedral—a right that the Parlement of Paris upheld against the indignant protest of that city's bishop.[13] More important than a bishop's ire, we learn that the appearance of Jews as competitors was beginning to rouse the middle and the petty bourgeoisie, who complained against Jewish competition with arguments that combined economic charges with traditional religious prejudice, in a very modern fashion. Lastly, the party of Enlightenment also joined in the fray, attacking the Jews as unenlightened (which they were), "ignorant and barbarous." It is well known that the best Voltaire could say for them was that, for all that, "il ne faut pourtant pas les brûler."[14] Is it mere coincidence that Voltaire's rural retreats were all in eastern areas where Jews were looked on with little sympathy?

More representative of enlightened attitudes is the prize essay that was set in 1787 by the Royal Society of Metz, and that concerned the means of making French Jews happier and more useful. The three prizewinning works, all very well intentioned, painted a depressing picture of social parasites in a state of physical and moral degradation, which they ascribed to the oppression inflicted by Christian society; of Jewish inertia and stupidity, caused by what amounted to slavery. It is well to remember that this sort of language, and the kind of analysis it carried, would also be used in

[13] Arthur Young, *Travels in France* (Cambridge, 1950) p. 8.
[14] Bernhard Blumenkranz, *Histoire des juifs en France* (Toulouse, 1972) p. 270.

the 1850s about French peasants, also in a well-intentioned sense, and also justified, at least in part, by fact.

The reformist position would come into its own in 1789, when the National Assembly, having decided that Protestants, actors, and executioners should be treated as full citizens, went on to discuss Jews; and the Comte de Clermont-Tonnerre declared, "We must refuse everything to the Jews as a nation, we must grant them everything as individuals."[15] Jews were to become individual citizens, shedding their particularism, their peculiarities, assimilating the culture and the patriotism of the new nation—France—and not least its language. Since this is a sore point with antiassimilationists, it may be worth setting enlightened hostility to Jewish obscurantism in the context of the larger battle against superstition and backwardness. The strongest advocates of emancipation were also the sharpest enemies of *patois* (local dialects) and of reactionary observances. Far from being anti-Jewish, men like Grégoire and Clermont-Tonnerre looked to the disappearance of all particularisms; and Jewish particularism mattered infinitely less than that of Bretons, Flemings, or Occitanians. All of these threatened not only national unity, not only the new regime itself, but also the battle for equality, and justice, and progress.[16]

One may not share such enlightened preconceptions; one can even point out that the road to Terror was paved with good intentions—and indeed, under the Terror, some Jews were hurt by the "lutte contre le fanatisme et la spéculation," though just how few proves how unimportant they were. But we cannot dismiss the concept of cultural, that is, national, assimilation, because it represents one more factor of tension between the Jews and a modern France that is quite consistently culturally imperialistic and assimilationist and lacks all sympathy for those who want to participate in the nation but not, or not fully, in its culture.

In the event, outside Alsace, it mattered little what Jews thought about all this, because the French thought about Jews hardly at all. They had other fish to fry. But let me say very quickly that true emancipation came only under the July Monarchy; that accultura-

---

[15] P. Girard, p. 51.

[16] P. Girard, pp. 30–31, is shocked by the hostility Voltaire and other men of the Enlightenment show toward Jews but makes no attempt to set it in context. The fact is that, from Napoleon to Bernard Lazare, the Jews are portrayed as unproductive and parasitic, a powerful image that took time to dim.

tion and assimilation, very slow at first, proceeded apace during the middle of the century; and that, as they advanced, with increasing (though still limited) numbers of Jews rising in business and finance and the administration, joining the professions,[17] being elected to municipal and national office, the problems of assimilation became increasingly clear.

For Catholics, a Jew had to be converted. For patriots, he had to have one definition and one commitment only. For opponents of the new financial and industrial forces, the Jew had to be opposed as a representative of the money power, incarnated not only by the Rothschilds but by the crucial role Jews played in the Saint-Simonian movement, and in the *Saint-Simonisme d'affaires* of the Second Empire. Even though Saint-Simon did not like Jews very much, we know that he had many Jewish disciples who made the movement, with all the financial and industrial implications attributed to it, into a "Jewish venture."[18] But some developments are less well remembered, such as the fact that, for Legitimists, their Catholic suspicion of the Jews was reinforced when, in 1832, the Duchess of Berry was betrayed by a Jewish convert, Simon Deutz, the son of the chief rabbi of France. Legitimists have long memories almost by definition, and things were not helped when Victor Hugo denounced Deutz in a nasty poem about the Jew who sold a woman for gold.[19]

For Progressives, on the other hand, Jewish religiousness was no better than Christian religiousness: both obscurantist, both detestable. It was alright to believe in God, but ritualistic religion was just another out-of-date practice good for the ideological junkyard, when there were plenty of more up-to-date ideologies that

[17] J. Félix, *Israël Bedarride* (Montpellier, 1870) p. 6, has a suggestive passage in this memoir that praises one of the most successful among the first generation of Jewish lawyers from the south, a great battler for social as well as religious equality, and all those who, in order to contradict unjust prejudices, "opposaient à de persistantes préventions le choix de ces carrières libérales, où la fortune ne se rencontre point, mais qui recompensent le travail par la considération." So, one might turn to liberal (or learned) professions in reaction against the money-grubbing stereotype.

[18] Saint-Simon spoke about "ce peuple sombre, concentré, dévoré d'orgueil." See Szajkowski, p. 1092. This stiff-necked image keeps recurring, from Agobard's *insolentia judaeorum* to General de Gaulle's "peuple d'élite, sûr de lui-même et dominateur." Bernard Lazare, who refers to the Jews' "immense pride," even suggests that the legend of the Jewish stench (*judaeorum foetentium*) is a misreading of Jewish turbulence (*judaeorum poetentium*). *L'Antisémitisme, son histoire et ses causes* (Paris, 1894) pp. 9, 183.

[19] Szajkowski, p. 1042.

had not yet been recognized as junk. We know that some masonic lodges rejected Jews to the end of the century.[20] This could have been for political reasons, but it could also have been on anti-clerical grounds. As for the left, if antisemitism is the socialism of fools, it is well to remember the preponderant weight of fools in all societies. It was only the Dreyfus Affair that condemned men of the left to giving up attacking Jews and permitted them to attack only Christians (at least in France!). On the other hand, those assimilated Jews who became like their French fellows and abandoned religious observance found it hard to take religion seriously enough to take the step of conversion that might have helped them to pass. Michael Marrus has quoted Mme Straus's remark, "J'ai trop peu de religion pour en changer."[21] It must have been hard to be a Frenchman of the Jewish confession, if you had no confession to confess.

But, of course, the greatest obstacle to national integration lay in the Jews themselves, most of whom proved reluctant to abandon their ritual separatism that looked remarkably like exclusivism, their dress, their practices, their tight little communities, the beards of the men, the wigs of the women. . . . In 1831, a member of the Consistory of Strasbourg talked about a regeneration that would carry the Jewish community to the level of their non-Jewish neighbors;[22] and, significantly, this would be encouraged by founding societies that were supposed to inculcate the work ethic (*Société des Amis du Travail, Société d'Encouragement au Travail*). But regeneration proved hard going.

Assimilation, welcomed by the better-off and by southerners, was resisted by the poorer groups, especially by the mass of Alsatians and Lorrainers whom I incline to compare with other French who resisted "civilization" at that time: the peasants, who also clung to traditional securities and solidarities, until they perceived a working alternative for ways of life that had long allowed them to cope with apparently inescapable miseries.

[20] Jacques Bidegain, *Le Grand Orient de France* (Paris, 1905) pp. 113, 119; Daniel Ligou, *Frédéric Desmons et la Franc-maçonnerie sous la IIIe République* (Paris, 1966) p. 193.

[21] *The Politics of Assimilation* (Oxford, 1971) p. 61.

[22] P. Girard, p. 115. More important, that same year, the Central Consistory prohibited the preaching of a sermon in any language other than French. Simon Debré, "The Jews of France," *Jewish Quarterly Review*, 3 (April 1891) p. 387.

For emancipated Jews, however, and for those few non-Jews who bothered, the picture must have been an exasperating one, of persistent primitivism and superstition, mulish stick-in-the-muddishness, stubborn refusal to come in out of the cold and the dark, to shed what Bernard Lazare calls the "abjection" of their condition.[23] This impression would be enhanced by the fact that a degree of assimilation came to different groups at different times, Parisians and southerners accepting civilization and regeneration long before the Alsatians; the latter flooding in during the 1870s, still unregenerate, to provide an unpleasant reminder of peculiarity-by-association; then being frenchified in their turn, and in their turn disgusted by the dirt, the ugliness, the beards and garb of the "Polaks," which they took as indications of idleness and dishonesty, exactly as three or four score years before a parisianized Jew found the Alsatians "ignorant, boorish, avid for money and without principles."[24]

This is the sort of cascade of contempt with which the historian of peasants and peasant migrations is quite familiar. But it also recalls that, in the 1880s and 1890s, just when assimilation seemed well on its way at last, a rising tide of immigrants from Eastern Europe reminded Jews—and this time not only Jews!—that maybe they were not quite or altogether like other Frenchmen and provoked Bernard Lazare to complain that French Jews were being identified with these eastern hordes: a lot of gross, predatory, churlish *tartars*, who made people forget that Jews had lived in France for nearly two thousand years.[25]

But the Tartars could not be halted, and their invasion came at a particularly awkward moment: on the one hand, because the economic depression of the *fin-de-siècle* made questions of competition very acute; on the other, because national and international politics after 1871 stressed the foreignness of Jews and their ap-

[23] *L'Antisémitisme* (1969 edition) p. 102. Orthodoxy posed certain problems: opening a shop, for example, could tempt one into breaking the Sabbath. Peddling was despised, but you could get home for Friday night.

[24] Raphaël and Weyl, p. 401; Paul Catrice, *L'Harmonie entre l'eglise et le judaïsme d'après la vie de Paul Drach* (Lille, 1978) pp. 21, 73.

[25] Quoted in Nelly Wilson, *Bernard Lazare* (Cambridge, 1978) p. 77. In 1913 still, and again, Baron Edmond de Rothschild would complain about the "new arrivals [who] remain among themselves, retain their primitive language, speak and write in jargon." Cited by Paula Hyman, *From Dreyfus to Vichy* (New York, 1979) p. 118.

parent kinship to Germans, hence their presumed sympathies for the national enemy.

The fact is that by now, and especially in Paris, a very large proportion of the Jews came either from Alsace-Lorraine, or from German and Austrian lands;[26] and many of those who did not seemed to speak a Germanic dialect—Yiddish—which could appear to substantiate suspicion and hostility in a period when xenophobia was riding high anyway (as it always does in times of economic crisis), when foreign workers all over France were being physically assaulted by French workers who accused them of taking their jobs and working for lower wages; when anti-Germanism was rife at every articulate level of society—and while the workmen who were attacked and sometimes killed in little local pogroms of the 'nineties were not Jewish but mostly Italian; and while the musicians, and the waiters, and the hotel employees attacked for unfair competition were mostly Germans and Italians.[27] The Jews were also involved in these frictions, because there were other poor, struggling, uncivilized immigrants in the cities now, and especially in Paris: Bretons, Auvergnats, southerners, who tried to work their way up in just the same poor jobs and small businesses as the Jews.

Before I come to that, however, another way of putting things in perspective is to compare the Jews with Italian immigrants to France, of whom there were over 112,000 in 1872 and nearly 300,000 in the 1890s—one quarter of all the foreigners in the country, and concentrated mostly in the southeast.[28] Edouard Drumont knows what he is doing when he denounces Gambetta as an Italian's son,[29] for he does it at the very time when grave xenophobic riots in Dauphiné (and in Provence, and in Lorraine) set local workingmen against Italians, so that at La Mure and at La Motte in one single day over 500 persons have to flee their pillaged homes. We are told that their attackers "fear unemployment and competi-

[26] Bensimon-Donath, pp. 96–97.

[27] See Roger Girard, Journal d'un Auvergnat de Paris (Paris, 1982), pp. 120, 246. Balzac tended to conflate Auvergnats, Normans, and Jews. The first were sometimes called "modern Jews." In December 1897, a court judging a man who had assaulted another for calling him "Auvergnat" rejected his plea of extenuating circumstances on grounds that the term could not be taken as insult or provocation. Girard, pp. 246–47, and p. 29.

[28] Anne-Marie Faidutti-Rudolph, L'Immigration italienne dans le sud-est de la France (Gap, 1964) I, pp. 19–20.

[29] La France juive (édition populaire, Paris, 1888) préface, p. xxvii.

tion" from the presence of aliens "more sober and thrifty than the French";[30] and these motives (and *motifs*) recur in anti-Italian commonplaces at least as late as the 1930s, along with equally familiar charges: dirt, cowardice, hypocrisy, particularism (failure to mix and drink with locals), readiness to accept low wages. . . . "Vous les Ritals, vous êtes comme les Juifs," a schoolmate at Nogent tells an Italian mason's son. "L'honneur, vous savez pas ce que c'est." And Cavanna concludes: "C'est nous qu'on éponge tout. La crise c'est de notre faute. Le chômage, c'est nous."[31] Which should help remind us that no minority has a monopoly of the scapegoat role, especially when it shows itself too sober, hardworking, and thrifty for the natives' comfort.[32]

In the same vein, the rich and complex record of the urban assimilation and social promotion of French rural populations shows that the Jews were not exceptional at all, indeed scarcely visible as one small minority among larger ones, during the decades when national cultural integration was running its course. They became so only when the integration was achieved or nearing achievement in the 1880s and 1890s, when two things happened almost simultaneously. On one hand the great mass of French Jews were becoming like other Frenchmen, which meant among other things that they mixed and competed with them, now, not just in a few particular cases, but on all professional levels. On the other hand, an unexpected wave of unregenerate Jews reminded everybody who wanted to be reminded (and more people now were ready to be reminded) that Jews were *not* like Bretons or Auvergnats, that they were different—as all latent prejudices suggested—and that, being different, they could be suspected and treated in ways that the growing degree of social and economic competition made very convenient.

[30] Faidutti-Rudolph, 1, p. 210. Economic tensions were enhanced by contemporary political friction between France and Italy (which was a member of the Triple Alliance). When, in 1893–94, some Italian families were harrassed in Chambéry, their lawyer referred to the "hostility that some seek to maintain between two peoples of the same race." *Gazette des Tribunaux,* 3 Jan. 1894.

[31] F. Cavanna, *Les Ritals* (Paris, 1978), pp. 14, 20, 35–39, 272–73.

[32] See Guillaume Enriquez, *La Main d'oeuvre rurale et le péril italien en Tunisie* (Paris, 1905) p. 14. With his usual perceptiveness, Bernard Lazare, *L'Antisémitisme* (1894), several times compares the Jews to the Chinese, as on p. 395: "tribu d'étrangers ayant conquis les mêmes privilèges que les autochtones et refusant de disparaître. On les sent encore différents et plus les nations s'homogénéisent, plus ces différences apparaissent." See *Interna-*

As long as Jews remained exceptional (rare for one thing, peculiar for another), the great mass of French folk had never abandoned their prejudices, but they had been largely indifferent to them. By the end of the nineteenth century Jews were no longer extraordinary: just competitors in a lot of different markets. And Captain Dreyfus may be said to have personified this competition, new in kind, in degree, in extent: a competition that is relevant and noticeable because it is no longer based on Jewish differences, but on Jewish presence on common ground. In the case of Dreyfus, the common ground was the Ecole Polytechnique, and then the rather exclusive milieu of the army, where there were quite a lot of Jewish officers already,[33] which is bad enough I suppose, but where Dreyfus's access to the General Staff would cause traditionalists to bristle.

In fact, Dreyfus was not the first Jew to enter the sanctum sanctorum. Colonel Abraham Samuel, a Saint-Cyrard, had worked in the intelligence branch there since 1871, and he was heading the *service de statistique* itself when he was eased out in 1880.[34] But if it is difficult to know the reasons for Samuel's disgrace, Dreyfus's disfavor is easy to conceive, for what we hear about him depicts him as the typical French *bête à concours*, still relatively rare in army circles: a *fort-en-thème*, with the characteristics of the type—humorlessness, rigor, dedication, a certain lack of sociability, something that might be taken for pushiness—and it is these characteristics, along with his success, that make him unattractive to comrades, who react by resorting to familiar stereotypes. Which is, of course, what stereotypes are for![35]

---

tional Herald Tribune, 13 Dec. 1982, "Anti-Chinese Riots Feared as Indonesia Economy Declines."

[33] [W.] Rabi, *Anatomie du judaïsme français* (Paris, 1962) p. 67, tells us there were some five hundred of them in the regular army; Bensimon-Donath, p. 166ff, indicates a constant 3 percent of Jews among regular army officers in 1867, 1887, and 1907, while in the reserve their numbers rise from 1 percent in 1867 to 4 percent in 1887 and 10 percent in 1907. This might be compared with the 815 Corsican officers, about 5 percent of the regular officer corps, not counting half as many again in the *gendarmerie*. *Petit Bastiais*, 14 April 1888, quoted in F. Pomponi, *Typologie des crises dans les pays méditerranéens* (Nice, 1977) p. 89.

[34] Cohen, 2, p. 420. Béatrice Philippe, *Etre Juif dans la société française* (Paris, 1979) pp. 181–82, reflects the *Libre Parole*'s campaign capitalizing on the "novelty" of Jewish presence in the army, and also the widespread sense that Dreyfus's penetration of the General Staff was exceptional, shared even by Jaurès, who thought him first of his race to get there.

[35] Which is not to minimize the contemporary concern over a spy threat highlighted by a

There are a few things that strike me about the Dreyfus Affair. The first is that, when so many officers were unusually prejudiced against Jews—some because of their origin in the eastern provinces, some because of Legitimism or Catholicism, but more I think because of service in North Africa—that when so many regular officers disliked and despised Jews, there should nevertheless have been, and there should have continued to be, hundreds of regular officers (and even ten generals) who were Jewish. Not to mention Dreyfus himself, who was an artilleryman, and we know that the artillery was the corps with the second highest number of Jewish conscripts (after the Infantry)—those Jewish conscripts who (class for class) tended to avoid military service rather less than other young men.[36]

This relative success, or at least advance, of Jews in heretofore protected territory would seem to call for trouble. But when the trouble broke out (and God knows that the antisemites worked hard and long to mount it![37]) the army was much more interested in settling things *en famille* than it was in persecuting Jews as such, even Dreyfus.[38] What you have between 1894 and 1899 is a very clannish institutional reaction, of the sort that any professional organization, any university for that matter, could produce. Anti-

---

series of scandals. After the Schnaebelé affair in 1887, *Le Petit Parisien* had even set up a special rubric: "Les espions allemands." For *l'espionnité*, see Maurice Baumont, *Au coeur de l'Affaire Dreyfus* (Paris, 1976), ch. 1. Alan Mitchell, "Contre-espionnage et mentalité xénophobe," *Revue d'histoire moderne et contemporaine*, (Jul. 29-Sept. 1982) p. 489, who attributes the Affair at least as much to xenophobia as to racism, quotes a secret memo of 1872 suggesting the recruitment as spies of "israélites allemands, presque tous achetables, mais tous à surveiller."

[36]Bensimon-Donath, p. 170. Blumenkranz, *Documents*, p. 210, lists Jewish general officers. Kriegel, pp. 147–48, makes the point that, for Jews, going into the army was an assertion of successful assimilation.

[37]The help they got from some Jews has been noted here and there. Thus, when the *Libre Parole* came out in 1892, its basic funding was provided by Gaston Crémieux, alias Wiallard, a converted Jew who also became its first, unsuccessful, manager; Morès borrowed money from Cornelius Herz; *La France juive* got a boost by serial publication in *Le Petit Journal*, which had been founded by the Bordeaux banker M.-Polydore Millaud and edited by his cousin from St.-Rémy, Alphonse Millaud.

[38]It is interesting to see that in the general press (as opposed to antisemitic publications) the first articles on Dreyfus's arrest do not mention that he is a Jew; and that, if one assumed his guilt, his treatment seemed lenient. This is why the *Petit Parisien*, 8 June 1895, in an editorial on the reform of the military code, could comment that "Dreyfus gets away with his life despite his frightful crime, yet a soldier at Rochefort is condemned to death for *bris de casernement*."

semitism plays a seminal role in the Affair, but the Affair is not really about Jews.

Second, while the Dreyfus Affair is the creation of antisemitism, and antisemites prosper in its heady atmosphere, these golden days are quite brief: really, only 1897 to 1900 or so. If you look at a newspaper like the *Auvergnat de Paris*, highly representative of a certain petty bourgeoisie of *parvenus*, in the best sense of the term, and of small businessmen, whose interests often bring them into conflict with Jewish competitors, a paper that makes a point of saying that it does not like Jewish capitalism, you will see that it begins (as many other papers did too) by reporting Dreyfus's arrest *not* as that of a Jew, but as the second case of an *Alsatian* officer betraying important secrets to the Germans. The *Auvergnat* has no sympathy for Dreyfus, but some Auvergnats are among the captain's supporters; and when *La Libre Parole* and its ilk begin to denounce these kin as Jews, to attack fellow Auvergnats for their Dreyfusard sympathies, then the *Auvergnat* turns against the anti-Dreyfusards. By February 1901, we find it supporting a Socialist, Allemane, against Max Régis, one of the great antisemitic figureheads, because Régis is the son of an Italian.[39] So there are degrees of chauvinism, and some of these give no priority to the Jews.

Third, the Dreyfus Affair remains largely a storm in an urban teacup. When you come across antisemitic slogans or gestures at the rural level, they have been funneled in from town. By and large the countryside, never specially sympathetic to Jews but never really interested in them either, simply does not echo the urban ruckus. When it does so, it is by way of urban migrants,[40] or else by

[39] R. Girard, pp. 265, 267, 287, 297.

[40] Thus, it is well to remember that when uncharacteristic cries are heard around the draft board sitting at St.-Chély-d'Apcher (Lozère) in January 1898, "Long live the Army! Down with the Jews!", this must have had something to do with the Auvergne's close contact with Paris and Paris politics. See R. Girard, p. 248. On the other hand, at Manheulles (Meuse) all the village was anti-Dreyfusard, but *not* antisemitic; and the Affair never divided the village, even from its Jews, as *combisme* would do a few years later. Georges Wolfromm, *Mon Enfance me suit* (Paris, 1970) pp. 37–38. At Roanne (Loire), where there had been no Jews at all until after 1871, and which now counted four families of Alsatian refugees and two of Yiddish-speaking "Poles" (whom the former regarded as foreigners), *les Jeunesses socialistes* attack "government and jewry" in January 1898; one month later, the priest of St.-Etienne demonstrates in the pulpit that the Dreyfus Syndicate is the fruit of a conspiracy initiated by Lord Palmerston (long dead!), the notorious Jewish freemason. And yet, "the Dreyfus Affair does not seem to have awakened strong feelings in the Roannais." Marcel Gouinet, *Histoire de Roanne et de sa région* (Roanne, 1977) 2, p. 276. Monique Lewi, *Histoire d'une communauté juive: Roanne* (Roanne, 1976).

recasting familiar local myths in a new antisemitic mold.[41] So, a large number of French electors pay only a distant attention to Dreyfus; and the moment the government shows itself really determined to settle the matter with justice, it pretty much gets settled. The incident is closed; and the Jewish community, like Dreyfus himself, asks only to forget that it ever happened. Since a lot of people had never paid much attention to it anyway (a lot more people than history books suggest), this is what happens.[42] The Dreyfus Affair is important because it occasioned a reversal of alliances, because it witnessed a significant political precipitation, and for a variety of other reasons. But it is only one incident in the history of Jews in France, and not the most significant.

This last, I am inclined to see in the period 1940–44, which Michael Marrus and Robert Paxton have so thoroughly covered.[43] And what strikes me there is not the imbecile and understandable politics of Vichy, which I do not regard as specially representative of modern France; but the high degree of public indifference to the plight of the Jews. Seen in the context of French first principles,

[41] Thus, Sébillot, 4, pp. 403–4, tells us that in 1898 a story circulated to the effect that Jews had bought large quantities of grain, loaded them on ships, and ordered them to be dumped into the sea. This should be compared with a report of the imperial attorney general at Rennes, dated 7 July 1856 (Archives Nationales, BB 30 386), of "persistent rumors that a party exists that wants to starve the people, that grains bought in the markets are brought to Nantes and thrown into the Loire, or charged on vessels and thrown into the water once at sea."

[42] Gradually, of course. See Pierre Abraham, *Les Trois Frères* (Paris, 1971), pp. 59–64, who makes very clear that being a Jew at school in Paris after 1896 was uncomfortable— even after the agitation had died down. Kriegel, pp. 172–73, tells the story of her maternal grandparents, who changed their name from Dreyfus to Simonin to save the trade of their small wineshop; and Paul Lévy, *Les Noms des israélites en France* (Paris, 1960) p. 18, confirms that after 1895 many Dreyfuses changed their name—as, in 1901, at Bourg, an Esterhazy family would do also. After 1914, names like *Deutsch* would likewise be abandoned, and not only in France: witness the Battenbergs turning into Mountbattens. Paula Hyman, pp. 118–19, who blames the Consistory for demanding an end to Yiddish sermons in the immigrants' synagogue of the rue Pavée when World War I broke out, ignores the chauvinistic tide of those days, turned far more against Germans (and Swiss) than against Jews.

[43] *Vichy France and the Jews* (New York, 1981). They have also explained the grounds (evident in Cavanna's *Les Ritals* as well) of a mounting antisemitism, which was only one aspect of the mounting xenophobia of those difficult and dangerous times. Significantly, the first two volumes, published in 1925 and 1928, of the Lorrainer Louis Bertrand's autobiographical novel, *Une Destinée*, hardly mention Jews and, when they do, are not particularly hostile. The third volume, published in 1932, opens with an antisemitic scene: *Hippolyte Porte-couronnes*, p. 8. Yet, even then, Jews continue to be of secondary importance compared to greater concerns, as can be seen from a careful reading of Jean Giraudoux's much impugned *Pleins Pouvoirs* (Paris, 1939).

everything falls into place: the official intention to discriminate between French and foreign Jews, the variety of private initiatives varying from denunciation to taking grave risks to shelter and to help. And we should not forget that, if 75,000 Jews were sent to their death, three in four were nevertheless preserved—a higher proportion than in any country besides Italy and Denmark. Above all, though, there stands out the massive self-concern of the vast majority of French folk, perfectly understandable if you remember the dire circumstances of those times; but also if one assumes from the beginning, as this paper suggests, that Jews never were a problem to the French, that the French had and have other problems—first among them those caused by other Frenchmen (which Jews are not quite, as Jean Paulhan and General de Gaulle agree). And anyway, the French are always ready to throw somebody to the wolves, provided they do not have to jump out of the sleigh themselves.

The fact that they may not particularly like the Jews is irrelevant in this context, because the French do not particularly like anybody; and, these days, not even themselves. The French are a very old people. They know that, contrary to received fiction, human beings are neither very attractive, nor very safe to handle. Nor are the French really racist, because their reservations on this score concern the whole of the human race. As for the Jews, most normal French, as usual, do not think of them and would thus find the Jewish question irrelevant. Which could be considered a step forward by those who think that, at other times, a significant portion of the French people paid more attention to them than it does now, and that such attention as was paid them was less than favorable.

On this, let me quote Tocqueville's words that "there is a natural prejudice that leads men to despise those who have been their inferiors, long after they have become their equals." Tocqueville, in this passage, is talking about blacks, "the memory of whose slavery dishonors the race, and the race perpetuates the memory of slavery." But, whether in the 1830s when he wrote it, or 150 years later, he could just as well be talking about Jews: still different in their history, and still different-by-association. And yet . . . and yet. . . .

Another look at the Jewish condition, in France as elsewhere, suggests that it *continues* to provide us with a sharpened reflection of the human condition in general: harrassed, under attack, insecure—only a bit more so, and given to excessive expressions of relief when catastrophe does not appear the immediate order of the day.

Deeper reflection might produce a more portentous conclusion. Just a little reflection, however, suggests that perhaps we could consider the Jew (that is, the perception of the Jew, for all history is about perceptions) less as a stereotype and more as an archetype. In this light, the Jews are simply humanity writ more clear, the Jewish question can be left to Jews and to antisemites, and we may shift from the Jewish condition to the human condition, which also constitutes, unbeknownst to him, the core of the antisemite's passion and of his ire. For, surely, antisemites cry out against mankind and revile it through the Jews, who share all mankind's faults, only more evidently when scrutinized in a magnifying (and distorting) mirror that reveals a human condition where danger lurks, where peace is a snare, security a delusion, and survival a question of living with your guard up and your bags packed.

PART 2

IMMIGRANTS AND NATIVES

MICHEL ABITBOL

The Encounter between French Jewry and the Jews of North Africa: Analysis of a Discourse (1830–1914)

THE FRENCH *israélites* in the first half of the nineteenth century were proud to be citizens of France, and happy to have been elected by Providence to a place in that "Palestine of liberty," where "all divine and human treasures" abounded. Since the Restoration, they had not only enjoyed a remarkable social promotion, but also seen the gradual disappearance of the vestiges of legal ostracism distinguishing them from their Christian neighbors.

As theistic and moralizing individuals, they had a fairly clear idea of what they rejected on the spiritual level: "superstitions" and certain Talmudic principles "expounded by suffering and mistreated men." But apart from certain general notions such as the central role of the Bible, no one had yet come up with the slightest coherent definition or content for the new message that French *israélitisme* prided itself on bringing.

And yet French Jews did not regard themselves any less as the "elite troops" or "the scepter of the entire tribe of Judah," convinced as they were that by their presence on French soil they embodied, in their relations with the rest of the Jewish people, something of the national genius, the spirit, and the heritage of "the first country in the universe." Thus they made up for the doctrinal and spiritual inadequacies of their own discourse by taking refuge behind the ideas of the eighteenth-century philosophes and the values embodied in the Revolution and in the Declaration of the Rights of Man, a document complacently presented as inspired by

Translated from French by Jonathan Mandelbaum.

"Mosaic" principles. While their rabbinical schools in Metz and later in Paris had hardly become renowned centers of Jewish learning and science, the *israélites* took solace at seeing to what extent Paris had become "the new Mecca" of civilization and the French people "the true savior of the world."[1]

From the French people as "saviors of the world" to French Jewry as saviors of the Jewish world, there was only one step. The French Jews felt that, on account of their numbers (there were between 60,000 and 70,000 Jews in France in the mid-1840s, a figure often rounded up to 100,000), they represented the strongest battalion of *sans-culottes* of the Jewish emancipation.

To be sure, the openly proclaimed harmony between the "French ideal" and the "Jewish ideal" strengthened the patriotic feelings of French Jewry—its "second nature." In its external repercussions, beyond the borders of *l'Hexagone*, this harmony also expressed a deep feeling of Jewish solidarity, whose persistence in official discourse was somewhat surprising, given the implications of the Napoleonic Great Sanhedrin's decisions.[2]

Oriental Jewry had impressed itself on the consciousness of French Jews in the wake of events abroad, the most important of which, prior to 1852, were the conquest of Algeria, the Damascus affair, and the fitful developments of the "eastern question."

The descriptions of oriental Jewry (whether in Algeria, the Ottoman Empire, or Morocco) that reached the French Jews were hardly encouraging. It was said to be a community as immobile "as the East" itself, whose members spoke corrupt idioms and had grown so accustomed to oppression as to be no longer aware of it; their "ignorant, superstitious and intolerant" rabbis were largely responsible for the community's "appalling" social condition.[3] The diagnoses made at the patient's bedside, however, were unanimous on three points:

1. Oriental Jews, "despite everything," were superior to their Arab, Moorish, Kabyle, Turkish, or even Greek and Armenian neighbors.

---

[1] French Jews not only regarded themselves as a "light" for world Jewry but were also fond of comparing themselves to the tribes of Gad and Reuben, which did not return home until they had taken part with their brothers in the conquest of the land of Canaan. See for example the sermon of Rabbi R. D. Wurmser of Soultz (Haut-Rhin), *Univers israélite* (hereafter *UI*) 4 (1847): 36–38; see also "Récapitulation—1846," signed "S. B.," ibid., 1.

[2] See for example *Archives israélites de France* (hereafter *AI*) 6 (1845): 259.

[3] See for example *AI* 1 (1840): 198–201, 249–51; 2 (1841): 216–22, 272–74.

2. The salvation and "regeneration" of these Jews could come only from the outside.

3. Once regenerated and civilized, they would serve as a link, an "electrical connection," between East and West.

An ideal observation ground, the Algerian community long remained the only oriental Jewish community with which French Jews were more or less fully acquainted. But this knowledge rarely transcended the ethnological or anthropological level. Much was known about these Jews' mores, accoutrements, professions, family and community institutions, as well as the taxes they paid and their relations with the authorities and with the Muslim "tribes." But little or nothing was known about the community's internal history—apart from its "oppression" and "decay"—or its culture.

Although cast in the same cultural mold, the many articles and "reports" offered to its readers by the Jewish press in France should not be viewed as a repetitive mass. The "vices," the virtues, and even the future of Algerian Jews were diversely evaluated and perceived according to whether such accounts were provided by unofficial or official emissaries of the Consistory, or by ordinary Jewish "tourists" whom the hazards of adventure, business, or military duty had brought in contact with these distant "brethren" of the southern Mediterranean. Thus, whereas an "*israélite* doctor" of the *Armée d'Afrique* and an "honorable schoolmistress" saw them only as a "despicable, cunning, avid, and ungrateful race,"[4] representatives of the Consistory praised their capacity for assimilation, their pro-French sympathies, and even—why not?—their religiosity.[5]

Until the founding of the Algerian consistories (1845), the general attitude that prevailed among French *israélites* and conditioned their campaign in favor of this African community involved one basic element: the refusal to regard the Algerian (and oriental) Jew as a truly distinct being—the open determination, on the contrary, to regard him as a being essentially identical to themselves or, more accurately, to what they, the emancipated Jews of

---

[4] *AI* 1 (1840): 269–72, 476–80, 537–48.

[5] J. Cohen, "Aperçu général sur les moeurs des Israélites algériens," *AI* 4 (1843): 23–35, 102–12, 230–38, 332–44, 418–27; see also, as additional evidence, the Altaras report published in S. Schwarzfuchs, *Les Juifs d'Algérie et la France* (Jerusalem: Ben Zvi Institute, 1981).

France, had been prior to the Revolution; in short, to regard him as an imperfect version of themselves. Such an attitude, which logically implied a projection onto the Other of one's own values and even of the phases of one's own history, necessarily led French Jews to an assimilationist approach to the Algerian problem. This approach was especially easy for them to adopt as the same state presided over the fate of the Jews in the metropolis and in the colony. Admittedly, it was quite obvious that differences of environment and "climate" existed between the two communities. But, in the event, this criterion of differentiation was used only to explain the past and the present—not to predict the future, which would of necessity be forged by the identical French spirit that prevailed from one shore of the Mediterranean to the other.

Arguing from their own experience, French Jews suggested to the authorities an emancipation of Algerian Jewry through the Law. As faithful disciples of the Enlightenment, they were convinced that by changing institutions—in this case, by setting up consistories as a first step—one would also change men.

Since the spark of Reason that would one day enlighten Algerian Jewry could come to it only from the outside, the only conceivable means of "moralizing" these Jews was to send French rabbis to the colonies. For it was out of the question for "natives," and even more so for native rabbis, to instruct or civilize other natives. This was true even if they happened to be of the calibre of Joseph Sebag, unsuccessful candidate for the post of first chief rabbi of Algiers in 1846. Although a doctor of the Faculty of Medicine of Montpellier and a minister of religion in Toulouse, Rabbi Sebag was turned down by both the war ministry and the Consistory because he had the misfortune of being of Moroccan origin. His twofold shortcoming of being a "native" and a foreigner, and, more important, his unconcealed sympathy "for the mores and habits of African populations" despite a fifteen-year stay in France, made him unfit to carry out "the civilizing mission that will be entrusted to the chief rabbi of the Algerian Consistory."[6]

Behind such language lay a peculiar concept—to say the least—of civilization and culture. Culture was seen not only as a matter of acquired knowledge, but also, and especially, as a matter of "birth" and, indeed, geography.

[6] Archives Nationales, Paris (hereafter ANP), F19/1143 (1846).

An individual's cultural background was of little or no account. If he was born to the north of a specific geographical boundary, the northern shore of the Mediterranean, he could not but possess as innate characteristics the qualities required to enter "the higher spheres of intelligence." Below that boundary, individuals remained "natives," and consequently, by definition, prey to "superstitions" and "extravagant beliefs." There remained the rather comical case of the natives of Gibraltar, like Messaoud Miguères, member and later president of the Algiers Consistory. As Gibraltar "straddled" Europe and Africa, Miguères himself was regarded as embodying the transition between the African spirit and the European spirit, or between barbarism and civilization.[7]

The mid-nineteenth century saw the emergence on the French Jewish scene of a new category of men, clearly too restless and still too "young" to accept the soft-spoken stiffness of the consistorial notables who presided over the affairs of the community. It was in this middle class of French Jewry—composed of academics, lawyers, doctors, engineers, and artists—that the idea of setting up the Alliance Israélite Universelle (AIU) took root.[8] Established in 1860, the Alliance eventually numbered among its members at least two barons, a count, a (Viennese) knight, and even two lords; but one unmistakable sign pointed to its true character: no Rothschild was ever an habitué of the establishment on the rue de Trévise.

Adolphe Crémieux,[9] one of the most virulent critics of that famous family, was indeed the first noteworthy president of the Alliance. A talented lawyer, former president (for a brief spell) of the Consistory and former government minister, Crémieux, a veteran of the Damascus affair and other noble causes, was no longer a "young blood" in 1863, the year of his appointment as president of

---

[7] On the Miguères case, see ANP, F 19/11147, letter from the Central Consistory to the minister of justice and religious affairs, 16 January 1895.

[8] The 142 founder members of the AIU included 30 wholesale merchants, 15 civil servants and office workers, 16 "artists and industrialists," 12 professors, 8 rabbis, 5 lawyers, 5 men of letters, 3 doctors, 2 engineers, 1 public prosecutor, 1 member of the Institut, 1 editor in chief of a newspaper, and 8 "bankers and rentiers." *UI* 15 (1859–60):663.

[9] In 1844, Crémieux launched a violent attack in the Chamber of Deputies on the Rothschild family, of which he was a lawyer. His diatribe earned him the congratulations of his colleague Alphonse Cerfberr: "Your hour-long exposition . . . will be of greater moment in the task of moral rehabilitation of French Jewry than the influence of the gilded client whom you have had the honor of losing," Cerfberr wrote to Crémieux (ANP, 365 AP 2, Crémieux papers, 17 July 1844).

the Alliance. But on account of his experience, temperament, and ideas, he was a bridge between the class of notables, who knew all the ins and outs of the official bureaucracy, and the men of the younger generation, who were more receptive to contemporary currents of thought and more concerned with social policy than with philanthropy.

In addition to sharing in the common worship of the ideals of 1789, men such as Jules Carvallo, Eugène Manuel, Narcisse Leven, and Isidore Cahen displayed a greater awareness than their seniors of the imperfections of legal emancipation. For not only had emancipation failed to overcome age-old "prejudice"—as was demonstrated once again during the anti-Jewish riots of 1848— but it had also failed to solve the acute social problems of a significant proportion of the Jews of Paris and Alsace.

The men who shaped the Alliance were spiritualists more than believers; liberals and moderates more than socialists or radicals. They combined to an astonishing degree a firm belief in science, its methods, and its empiricism with a Utopianism or indeed what was at times a very unrestrained variety of messianism.

Abandoning the provincialistic and Gallocentric discourse of their elders of the Restoration period, these men spoke freely of the existence of a Jewish "race" and of Jewish cosmopolitanism. "There is no such thing as *geographical Judaism*," wrote S. Bloch as early as 1850, in a study entitled "Judaïsme et socialisme," "that is, [a form of Judaism] confined to, and circumscribed by, certain countries, and influenced by certain local mores; but there is a cosmopolitan, universal, invariable, and independent entity called Judaism, above time, space, soil, and races." [10]

While this unity of the Jewish people was far from being self-evident to all, the strengthening of intercommunity ties, reaching beyond borders and regimes, was recognized as a necessity. Back in 1851, Jules Carvallo had suggested convening a "congrès israélite": "The unity of our dogmas makes for our strength. Isolation and dispersion make for our weakness," explained this graduate of the Ecole Polytechnique, a railroad builder for whom scientific progress would soon break down the barriers between nations.

From one end of the earth to the other, a wind has swept over the spirit of nations; the old world is collapsing, and its trembling leaders are seeking

[10] *UI* 7 (1850): 398–99.

shelter beneath the altars of their gods, whom they have caused by their teachings to be challenged and misunderstood; Israel, scattered amid these nations, will find itself standing alone with its immutable Decalogue and its unique, eternal, eternally beloved, eternally strong and protective God. It is in the midst of these vast social crises that persecution is the most violent, the most cruel, and the most relentless. Let us forestall it by our union.[11]

The other founders and future leaders of the Alliance preferred Isaiah's peaceful prophecy of the day when "the wolf shall live in peace with the lamb" to Daniel's terrifying vision of Gog and Magog. For them, the discovery of the Jewish universal undoubtedly involved another dimension: the immersion of this universal in the human universal. This was both a hope and a plan for action. "The union of all free *israélites* to emancipate oppressed *israélites* the world over" was thus but a step "toward the day of radiant light" when "all the world's peoples" would form a single people and "all religions [would] unite in a single religion."[12]

This vision, entirely centered on the future, also rested on a new concept of Jewish solidarity, no longer regarded as a vestige of the old "community of misfortune" but rather as a powerful means of action—both in respect of "oppressed" Jews, whom the Alliance wanted to aid and rescue, and in respect of the "oppressor" countries, which, so the Alliance hoped, might yet abandon their practices and prejudices. To this end, the Alliance did not content itself with recording the violations of its brethren's "human dignity," but, even as it strove to better their legal status throughout the world, it set up its famous "school charity" ("oeuvre des écoles"), so as to train "a generation of men capable of performing every function in society—useful citizens, who will be an honor to the religion they worship."[13]

By choosing to "change men" rather than "change institutions," the Alliance broke away on a crucial point from the Consistory's approach. It remained faithful to this basic idea even when, in later years, it was nominally in a position to promote the reform of Jewish community structures, for example in Tunisia and Morocco.

[11] *UI* 8 (1851):255–57.
[12] See for example L. J. Koenigswarter's address to the general assembly of the AIU on 10 April 1862, *Bulletin de l'Alliance Israélite Universelle* (hereafter *BAIU*), May 1863, 88; A. Crémieux used the same language in 1864, *BAIU*, July 1864, 23.
[13] "L'Oeuvre des écoles," *BAIU*, January 1865, 5.

On one specific point, however, the two institutions of French Jewry did agree: in addition to its human, religious, and social dimensions, the campaign to assist the oppressed was a patriotic undertaking, for how could one forget that such action would foster "love for France, a country of such great ideas and such fine achievements"? Above all, how could one forget that the *French israélites* were the first to wave the banner of "protection for all the *israélites* of the universe"? To this country, the first in the modern world to give the practical example of freedom of conscience, "*israélites* in all lands must be eternally grateful." [14]

Judging by the number of articles published in the Jewish press concerning oriental Jews between 1852 and 1880, never in any other period did French Jewry display so keen an interest in the fate of the communities in the Levant and in North Africa. The increasing number of visits made by notables or official travelers to these communities, the funds started in their favor, [15] the founding of the Alliance's first schools in Morocco, Turkey, Iraq, Syria, Lebanon, Tunisia, and Palestine, and, lastly, the Crémieux decree on the naturalization of Algerian Jews—all these developments were indisputable signs of the interest shown by the Jews of France in those of the orient.

A climate of remarkable idealism marked the inception of this solidarity movement. The "call of the orient"—possibly an echo of Saint-Simonian discourse—was understood by some as an opportunity for Western Jews to reconcile faith with civilization "by reciprocally exercising our distinctive influences on one another." Furthermore, was not the orient "the cradle of our religion" and "our ancestors' homeland"? This feeling became even more in-

---

[14] *BAIU*, May 1862, 67; 1st semester 1873, 26; on this whole question, see G. Weill, "Emancipation et humanisme," *Nouveaux Cahiers*, no. 52 (1978).

[15] In 1860, the Central Consistory started a fund in aid of Jewish victims of the Spanish-Moroccan War living in Tétouan (Archives du Consistoire Central [hereafter ACC], M. 4, "Souscription ouverte en faveur des Israélites marocains réfugiés en France," 15 January 1860). The relatively meager results of the appeal prompted the following criticism of French Jewry from Chaim Guedalla, a wealthy London businessman of old Moroccan stock: "We are very surprised in London [he wrote in a letter to the *Archives israélites*] at the slowness displayed by your central consistory. . . . I am surprised (allow a foreigner to reiterate the observation) that a community which equals that of London in wealth and wisdom has not more prominently manifested its spontaneous feelings of generosity. . . . I believe we are ahead of our French brethren; and the aim of this letter is precisely to rouse them" (*AI* 21 (1861):499–501).

tense when, in the early 1850s, following the international stir over the question of the Holy Places, highly alarming reports began to reach France as well as Germany and Britain concerning the state of the Jewish population of Jerusalem. While Albert Cohn set off on a charity mission to the Holy City—a mission compared by the Consistory to Abraham's departure from Aram-Naharaim for Palestine—a long debate took place in the Jewish press over the ways of saving the Jews of the Holy Land. But, leaving donors and benefactors to their hesitations, Rabbi Dreyfus of Mulhouse, for his part, discerned "God's finger" in the events taking place, which he saw as an opportunity to create a sort of Jewish Vatican in the Holy City: "Why could not Jerusalem become for the Jewish universe what Rome has become for Catholic Christendom?" he asked. The reader will not be surprised to learn that, for the rabbi of Mulhouse, this "Jewish pope" could only be a Frenchman. The French rabbinate, Dreyfus argued, was the most fortunate of all the rabbinates of the world, the only one with a strong hierarchical structure, the only one, too, with representatives "on African soil—as it were, on the borders of Palestine."[16]

In the mid-1850s, a wave of enthusiasm swept French Jewry at the news of the promulgation of the *Hatt-i-Humayun*, which proclaimed equality among all the peoples of the Ottoman Empire. Extolled by *L'Univers israélite*, Abdul Majid was glorified for having given a lesson in tolerance to many a European head of state.

At the same time, the Jews of Turkey were advised to show themselves worthy of their sovereign's goodwill. In a somewhat hasty analogy between the post-1855 Ottoman Empire and post-1791 France, they were also recommended to "tie themselves ever more closely to this blessed land where the divine sun of liberty shines, all the fruits of justice grow, and all the flowers of mankind blossom." Lastly, they were advised to bridge the "gap that exists between them and the Muslims, of whom they are more than fellow citizens, since Isaac and Ishmael are brothers, and the sons of Abraham."[17]

As it was soon realized, this emancipation hardly solved all the

[16]Rabbi Dreyfus, "La Question d'Orient sous le point de vue israélite," *UI* 9 (1853–54):546–56; S. Cahen, "Les Sympathies des Israélites de l'Occident pour leurs coreligionnaires d'Orient," *AI* 15 (1854):366ff.; "Manifestations en faveur du judaïsme oriental," *UI* 9 (1853–54):433–57.

[17]S. Bloch, "L'Emancipation en Turquie," *UI* 9 (1855–56):337–42.

problems of Ottoman Jewry. The increasingly frequent reports
from various sources, in particular those sent by the first schoolteachers appointed by the Alliance, were filled with details about
the sorry state of all the Jewish communities of Asia and Africa.
Even in Algeria, the negative effects of the conquest and of colo-
nization on Jewish economic structures persisted after the collective naturalization of 1870.

Misery and ignorance were the only spectacle that the Jews of
the orient continued to offer to their Western brethren. Rarely
"spiced" with exoticism, the reports reaching France about oriental Jews were starkly realistic.

Realistic, too, were the new solutions advocated for rescuing
these Jews from their predicament. Reviving a scheme published in
1854 by the editor of the *Allgemeine Zeitung des Judentums*,
Dr. L. Philippson, the *Archives israélites* suggested inviting to Paris
a number of younger members of these communities in order to
provide them "not with scholarly training" but rather with a general education that would allow them "access to any career." After
returning to their native country, they would, as a circle, constitute
"the seat of education and civilization." [18]

In the early phase of the conquest of Algeria, similar schemes
had been mooted by the Consistory, which eventually opted for
the solution of sending French rabbis to work on the spot. In contrast, and as if the better to underline its disagreement on this
question with the Consistory, the Alliance chose what might be
termed "indirect emancipation"—which later became its official
doctrine. The Ecole Normale Israélite Orientale, opened in Paris in
1867, had no other aim than to train young Orientals to become
teachers by educating them in the values of the Western world, by
freeing them from "verbal formalism, in which they indulge out of
habit and natural taste," and by opening their minds "to abstraction, which they are somewhat unwilling to understand," "while
respecting all the good, creative, and original features" of these
trainee teachers. [19]

Instructing its teachers to introduce change more by personal
"demonstration" than by "assertion," the Alliance was generally
careful "not to offend parents and rabbis" by being too eager to

[18] E. Cahen, "Les Israélites en Orient," *AI* 15 (1854):315–18.
[19] A. H. Navon *Les Soixante-Dix Ans de l'Ecole normale israélite orientale* (1935),
33–34.

"rid children's minds of the fantasies that inhabit them." It preferred the general education of the masses to the promotion of a
small elite and consequently rejected all scholarship schemes designed to give the most gifted students access to higher education.[20]

The Alliance was also pragmatic in its relations with community
notables. Although disdainful of them—except when they belonged to the Sassoon and Camondo families—the Alliance usually avoided clashing with or even circumventing them. The Moroccan *gvirim* were regarded as a sui generis bane, an outgrowth of
"Arab policy," which, it was said, "invariably aimed at placing the
common people under the sway of a small number of privileged
men." This tendency was alleged to have entailed "the emergence
of a fairly powerful oligarchy in the population of the Mellah
[Jewish quarter]—an oligarchy that enjoys the ostentatious support of the higher authorities and that, out of fear or gratitude, is
constantly conniving with the public administration in order to
stifle the voice and the complaints of the people."[21]

References to the cultural setting and to the environment became
more frequent as observers became convinced that they had a better understanding of these communities, and as the latter displayed
the full extent of their "difference" in respect of the European communities. As a result, even certain usages that were nothing but authentic features of religious life were promptly regarded as the reprehensible products of Arab or oriental influences.

This trend was especially perceptible in Algeria, where, paradoxically, the "indigenousness" of the native Jews had been most
"effectively" perceived and most strongly criticized by their French
brethren after the 1850s and even long after their naturalization—
whereas, in all likelihood, the Frenchification of Algerian Jews was
by then far more advanced than at the time of the Consistory's first
missions. The conflictual relationship between Ashkenazim and
Sephardim was totally absent from this display of ostracism, very
largely conditioned by the bitter struggle for control of the community that pitted religious and lay "Europeans" against religious
and lay "natives." It is no surprise, therefore, that the debate was
soon personalized and came to focus almost exclusively on the vir-

---

[20] Archives of the Alliance Israélite Universelle (hereafter AAIU), copies of correspondence, S 71, Central Committee to Morris Cohen (Baghdad), 21 January 1860.

[21] "Rapport adressé au Comité central par M. Joseph Halévy sur l'état des écoles dans les
communautés juives du Maroc," *BAIU*, 1st semester 1877, 54–55.

tues and failings of the leaders as well as on recommendations or criticism concerning their power over the masses.

In 1855, the chief rabbi of Algiers, Michel Weill, submitted to the Central Consistory what amounted to a full-scale treatise of political sociology. The occasion for this was discussion of a plan to link the Algerian consistories to those of the metropolis and to establish more democratic procedures for appointing and electing consistory members.[22]

In his "general remarks," Rabbi Weill began by observing that "in order to govern men one must know them, and in order to govern them well, one must adapt institutions to men and not attempt to shape men according to institutions." Without suspecting for a single moment that this wise principle could call into question the very establishment of consistories in Algeria, he went on to posit another "truth." "Human behavior . . . proceeds from two general principles that seem to have divided up the world between them: *authority*, which rests on tradition, and *reason*, which relies on personal awareness . . . each of these principles is now sun, now moon, occupying the first or second rank according to time and place, the character of a people, its temperament, and its national traditions. Until now, for instance, reason seems to have prevailed in the West, authority in the mysterious East."

What followed—"of the principle that must prevail in the government of the native *israélites*"—was obvious: by their mores, the Algerian Jews belonged to the orient. The principle that was to guide their "government" thus had to be authority—not, of course, the "inexorable, blind, and crushing" authority of the ancien régime but an enlightened authority that, while leaving considerable room for reason, had to take account of the age-old traditions of this population, for example by conferring "a certain prestige" on the authorities, for orientals would bow deferentially "only to what glitters and what strikes the imagination." This was all the more necessary as "it has been demonstrated that the oriental mind and, consequently, the natural character of our native subjects are hostile to the new spirit."

Thus the Algerian Jews, at first regarded—in the early days of the conquest—as beings "almost like us," were subsequently per-

[22] ANP, F 19/11144, "Rapport adressé au Consistoire central sur le projet de l'annexion des Consistoires algériens à l'administration israélite de la Métropole par Michel A. Weill, Grand-Rabbin du Consistoire algérien," 18 June 1855.

ceived by French Jews as individuals radically "different from us." This awareness of their difference would not have been peculiar in itself had it not been immediately expressed in terms of inferiority and superiority. In this respect, it is true, the language of the rabbis of the consistory was only a reflection of the prevailing colonial and anthropological discourse, with a single but substantial difference: whereas, with Bugeaud and Faidherbe, the French colonial doctrine had ceased to be assimilationist (if it ever had been), the Consistory's doctrine remained so at least in public pronouncements and at the political level. The ultimate proof of this was provided by the Algerian consistories' campaign in favor of the *senatus consultum* of 1865.

This doctrine was taken to its logical conclusion by Crémieux, a minister of the government set up in Tours in 1870, and a former "defector" from the Central Consistory. By 1871, he was back in Algiers to reap the electoral fruits of his decree and, either because of his "youthful liveliness" or on account of his "receptiveness to oriental flattery," the president of the Alliance Israélite Universelle became a prominent supporter of the "ex-native" notables against their French rabbis.[23] But Crémieux was not alone: there was also the Algerian colonial administration, which could not remain indifferent to the cause of these notables, who had, among their other qualities, the ability to deliver progovernment votes.

In a sermon delivered on 11 May 1889 to mark the centenary of the Revolution,[24] the chief rabbi of France, Zadoc Kahn, presented a sort of balance sheet of the progress of French Jewry since 1789, in which he highlighted for his listeners the spectacle of their successful integration.

No one criticized the chief rabbi for having forgotten to mention in his magnificent description the few dark clouds that were beginning to appear on the horizon of French Jewry: the tremendous success of Drumont's *La France juive*—published in 1886 and destined to play a notorious role several years later—and the misery of the hundreds of refugees from Eastern Europe, newly settled in the Marais, who were generally looked upon with disdain.

[23] ACC, 1 CC 38, "Le Grand-Rabbin de la Circonscription Israélite de Constantine à Messieurs les Président et membres du Consistoire Central israélite," 1 November 1863; letter from Chief Rabbi Abraham Cahen to Baron de Rothschild, 30 October 1878.
[24] Zadoc Kahn, *Sermons et allocutions* (1894), 3:177–80.

An examination of the Jewish press of the *Belle Epoque* shows that well before the Dreyfus Affair—and even more so after 1896—it was widely felt that, behind its facade of solid self-assurance, French Jewry, having lost a part of its vital forces since 1870, was in a very advanced state of decay.[25]

This awareness (one could also mention Bernard Lazare's well-known change of attitude during the Dreyfus Affair) should not mask the reality of the situation. As Michael Marrus has shown, in response to the difficulties arising from their emancipation and to each of the attacks against their identity as Jews and Frenchmen, French Jews continually strove for an ever greater assimilation into French society at large.

But French Jewry was not only weakened from within. In the late nineteenth century, it was faced with the challenge of Zionism, whose basic principles ran counter to all the values on which French Jewry had built its ideological edifice since 1791. While spontaneously rejecting "Dr. Herzl's fantasies," French Jewish newspapers followed with keen interest the activities of the young movement, the meetings of its congresses, and the hesitations and initiatives of its leaders: "We are not Zionists; we are not Zionists in any way whatsoever; but we are sorry not to be Zionists."[26]

This statement—an ambiguous one, to say the least—by the editor of *L'Univers israélite* and the public pronouncements of Zadoc Kahn suggest that the opposition to Zionism on the part of the French Jewish establishment was not as clear-cut as one might have supposed. If one goes beyond the slogan "Neither Jerusalem nor Basle," the criticisms regarding Zionism's "irreligiousness," and the observations concerning the anti-Semites' use of Zionist notions about the Jewish people and about the impossibility of Jewish assimilation, one can observe that French Jews were well aware of the speed with which Zionist congresses had become a magnet and a center of intense activity for a sizeable proportion of the Jewish people. Zionism had, in a sense, taken over the position hitherto occupied on the Jewish world scene by the Alliance and consequently by French Jewry.

[25] On this whole question, see Michael R. Marrus, *Les Juifs de France à l'époque de l'affaire Dreyfus* (Paris: Calmann-Lévy, 1972), 137–44, 323–27; see also H. Prague's editorials in *AI*, 8 December 1904, 18 March 1905, 22 June 1905, 17 and 24 June 1909, 17 February and 31 March 1910, 29 September 1911.

[26] *UI* 57 (1901–2): 613.

This realization was all the more unbearable as the Alliance by now had more than one "rival": not counting the Anglo-Jewish Association and the Austrian *Israelitische Allianz*, which behaved if anything like tame branches of the Alliance, there was the threatening *Hilfsverein der Deutschen Juden*, established in 1901, whose aim was precisely to copy, in the name of Germany and German culture, what the Alliance had achieved in the name of France and French civilization.[27]

French Jews were nevertheless lucid enough to treat these developments as more than just an expression of the wave of patriotism and nationalism that had gripped European Jewry. These events were interpreted no less as a sign of the new configuration of Jewish communities the world over and of the new "balance of power" among them. In this new configuration, French Judaism was indeed marginalized and its "great association," the Alliance, on the verge of becoming "a secretariat of a school inspectorate."

H. Prague was perhaps justified in taking solace at the sight of how "the Providence that watches over Israel's destiny" had fostered American Jewry, with its Oscar Strauses, its Schiffs, and its Sulzbergers, in order to "take over from an enfeebled Alliance the burden of managing the affairs of persecuted Jewry." The fact remained, however, that at the turn of the twentieth century the time was long since gone when French Jewry could regard itself as "the elite legion of Judah's tribe."

Similarly, owing to the changes both in French society and in the Jewish world, only a few scattered vestiges remained of the universalism proclaimed in the heroic days of Adolphe Crémieux. Just as, on the domestic front, French Jews had chosen to merge into the surrounding society the better to ward off threatening storms, so they were soon obliged, on the external front, to determine their behavior—either out of necessity or out of deliberate choice—in accordance with the foreign policy and the lines of expansion of their country and its empire.

Apart from obvious motives of a patriotic and national character, this withdrawal of French Jews into themselves was nevertheless still being justified by their total faith in their country's republican ideals. French Jews saw their country as the protector of the "weak and oppressed" to which the Jews—whether in Morocco,

---

[27] H. Prague, "L'Alliance Israélite et ses émules," *AI* 63 (1907).

Russia, Rumania, or Turkey—"instinctively turn when their pos-
sessions, their persons, their dignity, and their faith are attacked."[28]
The fact remained that not everyone in France interpreted these
ideals in the same manner. This was true of influential newspapers
no less than of senior officials at the Quai d'Orsay.

During the period 1880–1914, which saw Tunisian Jewry, followed by Moroccan Jewry, come under French rule, the attitude of
French Jews toward their North African brethren was neither entirely clear nor completely consistent. Indeed, it was a vivid reflection of their own internal changes. Expressed at various levels (diplomatic, political, and philanthropic) and on various linguistic
registers (official statements, articles in the press, "internal" reports), this attitude was an astonishing juxtaposition of ethno-
centrism and universalism, pragmatism and unrealism, secularist
intolerance and religious spiritualism—a surprising blend of expressions and gestures of deep-felt human and "brotherly" sympathy and instances of brutal rejection and ostracism.

Here, by way of example, are the cases of Rabbi Abraham Meyer
of Tlemcen and Rabbi Moïse Netter of Oran.

In 1902, Rabbi Meyer published at his own expense what pur-
ported to be a study on Ephraim Encawa, the famous fifteenth-
century "rav of Tlemcen." Dismissing the life and work of Encawa
in some twenty pages—insignificant ones, to say the least—Rabbi
Meyer, who was probably not up to tackling such a subject, was
unable to avoid the temptation of skipping over four centuries in
order to dwell in chapter after chapter on the laws and customs of
"our brothers of Tlemcen" and to show the "abyss" that divided
them from "our brethren in France." Rabbi Meyer's book caused a
scandal, and the Jewish community of Tlemcen, regarding itself as
having been libeled, requested the minister of religious affairs to
recall the author.[29]

---

[28] After the "commotion" of the Dreyfus Affair, the *Jewish* press made ample use of these
expressions in begging the government to come to the aid of Russian Jewry and later in
asking it to come to the rescue of Moroccan Jews.

[29] ANP, F 19/11153, petition addressed to the minister of religious affairs, 24 June 1906.
The title of Abraham Meyer's work (which runs to a mere sixty-odd pages) is, to say the
least, pretentious: "Zakhor la-Rav—A study of the present-day mores of the *israélites* of
Tlemcen, preceded by a full biographical note on Rebbenou Ephraim Aln'Caoua, known as
the Rab, founder of the community, and followed by brief notes on the Aln'Caouas (may
their souls rest in peace), accompanied by genealogical and chronological tables concerning

The Jews of Tlemcen reproached their rabbi not only for the inaccuracy of his ethnographical observations and their interpretation—these points could, admittedly, be debated—but also and especially for questioning their "Frenchness" and overstressing the "barbarism" and "Arab" character of their mores. This, it was argued, could only serve to endorse the allegations of the anti-Semites. Rabbi Meyer's initiative was thus regarded as a breach of the fundamental solidarity that ought to link a pastor to his flock. His transgression was all the more unforgivable as it came at a time when Algeria was just emerging from one of its most virulent anti-Jewish crises.

The affair involving Rabbi Moïse Netter of Oran, although more complex, was partly due to the same causes. Netter, who had taken up his post at Oran in 1892, told all comers that the local Consistory and its "ex-native" president Kanoui were guilty of electoral management for instructing the Jews of Oran on how to vote—an "accusation" that, however justified, could but reinforce anti-Semitic arguments.[30] But in the climate then prevailing in Algeria, when the worst insults involved accusations of unpatriotic behavior, Rabbi Netter was also accused by Kanoui's friends of playing into the hands of the "foreigners" by drawing on the support of the town's eight hundred Moroccan Jews against the Franco-Algerian "national party" in the Consistory. And the ultimate reproach was that "by acting in such a manner, M. Netter has not taken as his models the rabbis of France, who are so respectable and so respected, and are all incapable of such acts; rather, he has imitated the Muslim Cadis of yore; those of today are more urbane [*délicats*]."[31]

One could add indefinitely to this list of reciprocal recriminations by citing countless derogatory comments exchanged by the two sides, the most "amiable" of which, directed at North African Jews, often ran something like this: "But where have all the proud Sephardim gone?"

Nevertheless, when anti-Semitic passions broke loose in Algiers

this family and that of the Sultans of the Bani Zeyans, from the reign of Abu Hamu Musa II to that of Abul'Abbas Hamad, one of the latter's sons, 14th and 15th centuries."

[30] "Les Consistoires algériens et l'enquête parlementaire," *UI* 57 (1901–2): 169–70.

[31] ANP, F 19/11153, the Consistoire Israélite of the Oran *circonscription* to the minister of religious affairs, 18 July 1893.

and in the other towns of the colony, at no point did the Jewish press in France cease to proclaim its vociferous support of Algerian Jewry, despite the Central Consistory's calls for moderation. Furthermore, when, in the wake of these disturbances, the gravity of the Algerian Jews' social predicament and the extent of their endemic indigence became apparent, the second most important association of French Jewry, the Alliance, took it upon itself to assist the Algerian community by establishing various vocational institutes for it and also—a sign of the times—by providing it with religious instruction.[32]

Other examples of the ambivalence that characterized the encounter between French Jews and their North African brethren were provided when the Tunisians, followed by the Moroccans, heard what H. Prague, in an exceedingly pompous phrase, called the shofar of the French *geula* (deliverance).[33]

With the treaty of the Bardo (establishing the French protectorate in Tunisia) in May 1881, French Jewry began to relive the early days of the conquest of Algeria. The situation of the Tunisian community, of which the Alliance had been apprised only recently (1878), immediately reminded French Jewry of the fate of Algerian Jews prior to 1830. Accordingly, in the many articles that it devoted to the treaty, the Jewish press revived the same expressions, the same clichés, and the same solutions as those devised and advocated for Algerian Jews fifty years earlier.

The Tunisian Jews, "a large, active, and intelligent community," as Isidore Cahen observed in September 1881, "were superior to all the other inhabitants" of the protectorate by their "sagacity" and "industry." No less categorically, Cahen stated that they looked upon France as the "aegis" that would guarantee them "the enjoyment of the liberty and civic rights that [their] Algerian brethren possess."[34]

Two years later, the Alliance received a report on an inspection tour by Salomon Reinach, whose observations were totally at vari-

---

[32] No words were too harsh for the Alliance's first envoys to criticize the Consistory, "which has sinned grievously by sending to Algeria, for many years now, the most incompetent rabbis imaginable, not only to the provinces, but also to the capitals" (AAIU, Algeria I B1, Schuhl report, 12 October 1900). Later, the Alliance also contemplated taking part in a scheme to recruit Jewish working-class families from the Constantine area for resettlement in the Lille region (ACC, 1 E 2, 16 March and 20 April 1914).

[33] "La France au Maroc," *AI* 65 (1904): 122.

[34] *AI* 42 (1881): 176.

ance with those usually found in Parisian Jewish newspapers. In addition to glib comments such as "the Sfaxians are the worst breed of Tunisians and the Jews are not the best sort of Sfaxians," Reinach described in rather unpleasant terms the mores of Tunisian Jewry. "The rabbis are ignorant and superstitious; most of those who teach Hebrew in school do not understand the texts they assign for reading." While, generally speaking, he found no positive features in the "moral condition" of Tunisian Jews, that of the Jewish women, "with their ridiculous and indecent attire," seemed to him "utterly loathsome."

Although he paid tribute to the work of the Alliance's schoolteachers in Tunis, Sousse, Méhédia and Sfax, Reinach advised the Alliance not to enter into competition with the congregational schools of the *Pères Blancs* nor to prevent Jewish children from attending the schools run by Monseigneur Lavigerie, "the eminent prelate, who is a friend of mine."[35]

Neither the Alliance, of course, nor Chief Rabbi Zadoc Kahn shared Reinach's views. As early as 1882, the first scheme that occurred to the Central Consistory was to ask that Tunisian Jewry be formally linked to that of metropolitan France or, at least, that an organization "borrowed" from the French consistorial model be set up in Tunisia.[36] This Mediterranean Jewry, divided between the "rich, educated, and European-mannered" Leghornians and the "poor, superstitious, native-mannered" Twansa, seemed to French Jews somewhat reminiscent of an aspect of their own history prior to the Revolution and to the convening of the Great Sanhedrin. Accordingly, all joined wholeheartedly in an attempt to convince the authorities of the need to establish a local consistory. While, for obvious political reasons, this consistory could not be immediately tied to the Central Consistory, it ought at least to have, it was argued, "an eminent [French] fellow Jew" in Paris who would ensure its proper functioning and serve as the "representative" of Tunisian Jewry to the French government and the *grand rabbinat de France*. This "eminent fellow Jew" turned out to be Eugène Pereire, president of the Compagnie Générale Transatlantique and an immensely active figure in the protectorate.[37] But he

---

[35] AAIU, France VII A 56, report from S. Reinach, February 1884.

[36] AAIU, France IV A 19, letter from the Consistory to the AIU, 26 December 1882.

[37] This plan prompted a long exchange of letters between the two leading Jewish associations and between Chief Rabbi Zadoc Kahn and the foreign minister in Paris: Archives du

was no more successful than Zadoc Kahn or the Alliance in winning concessions from the authorities or in convincing the local
Jews themselves. In the event, only the Leghornians backed the
schemes put forward by French Jewry. Acting as though they did
not take the Leghornians' pro-Italian leanings seriously ("How
can one be a Persian?"), French Jews thought they could attenuate
the Quai d'Orsay's hostility by holding out the attractive prospect
that this community, which was so influential in the life of the protectorate, would "change sides." But all the efforts undertaken were
to no avail, and, following the outburst of anti-Semitism in Algeria,
the Quai d'Orsay's opposition became even more vehement.[38]

Nevertheless, and despite Isidore Loeb's advice to David Cazès
in 1887 ("When things are going wrong, you must know when to
stop"),[39] the Alliance and the Central Consistory, up to the eve of
World War I, continued to put pressure on the government to introduce the changes they had always advocated for Tunisian Jews.

When, from 1910 on, France finally adopted a more "innovative" policy in favor of Tunisian Jews—for example, by allowing
a certain number of them to be naturalized as French citizens—the
change was due not to pressure from French Jewry but primarily
to the threat posed by "Italian covetousness" to French prepon-
derance in Tunisia.

This divorce—however serene—between the policy of the French
government and that of French Jewish organizations can also be
observed in connection with Moroccan Jewry. On the eve of the
Madrid Conference (1880), all signs indicated that the campaign
launched by the Alliance to maintain the system of protection

---

Ministère des Affaires Etrangères, Paris (hereafter AEP), Correspondance Politique (hereafter CP), Tunisia, NS vol. 130, fos. 58–64, 100–114, 118–20, 185–200, 253–65. Other
parts of this correspondence are to be found in the AAIU, in particular France VII A 55
(Pereire Papers), as well as in the Zadoc Kahn Papers, a microfilm copy of which is deposited
at the Central Archives for the History of the Jewish People in Jerusalem.

[38] AEP, CP, Tunisia, NS vol. 131, 14 January and 4 March 1899.

[39] AAIU, S 141, Central Committee to David Cazès, 8 April 1887. The secretary general
gave the following advice to Cazès with regard to the nature of the "pressures" to be put on
the government: "In general, everyone should be told about the absolute need to keep to
legal means and to abstain from noisy demonstrations. Nothing will be obtained if legal
means are not kept to. These means are: official, written requests, to be submitted to the
proper authorities. Next, one must make sure, by friendly inquiries, that these requests are
not lying idle in some office or other; next, if justice is not obtained, new requests must be
submitted, still in writing, to the next higher authorities, and followed up by inquiries. I am
convinced that by following this course you will obtain justice on all counts."

in Morocco enjoyed the total support of the foreign ministry in Paris.[40] Indeed, the leaders of the Alliance did not conceal the fact from their correspondents in Europe when they announced their decision to dispatch Netter and Vénéziani to the Spanish capital.[41]

Nevertheless, the Alliance aligned itself with the Quai d'Orsay's position and backed the resolutions passed at the Madrid Conference, even though they fell distinctly short of its own expectations. In the event, the Alliance was primarily concerned that no major breach of the principle of protection should occur, for the figures available to it indicated that of the total of 503 protected persons in Morocco, 103 were Jews, of whom 25 were French nationals.

In the following years, and as the hour of the protectorate approached, the attitude of the French government toward the problem of protected persons changed. Both at the instigation of Charles Féraud, minister plenipotentiary in Tangier since 1885, and out of an obvious concern for political efficiency, France began to lose interest in Moroccan Jews—*protégés* included—and decided to pay exclusive attention henceforth to its Muslim *protégés*. With some reason, it was felt that these Muslims, being more firmly "established" in the area, would contribute more effectively to a stronger French presence in Morocco.[42]

Increasingly irritated by the "abuses" committed by protected and naturalized Jews, French officials in Morocco now received with only polite interest the many complaints lodged by the Alliance following the frequent attacks on Moroccan Jews. But despite the irritation provoked by its political action, the Alliance steadfastly refused to play the strictly humanitarian role to which the Quai d'Orsay wanted to confine it. The Alliance persisted in its policy even at the price of incurring the hostility of certain sections of metropolitan public opinion, in particular the right-wing press, which regarded its Central Committee as the very personification of the "Elders of Zion."

Neither the explanations of its officials nor the protestations of patriotism of Zadoc Kahn and the Jewish press in general put an

[40] See for example the letter sent by the Central Committee to the Foreign Minister, de Freycinet, AAIU, S 72, 5 March 1880.

[41] AAIU, S 72, 16 March 1880.

[42] On the changing policy of the Quai d'Orsay toward Moroccan Jewry, AEP, CP, Morocco, vol. 49, fos. 279–81, 284–88; vol. 50, fos. 21–25, 292–97; vol. 51, fos. 24–43, 59–64; vol. 53, fos. 278–303.

end to the malevolent innuendoes concerning its activity. Not even the argument often advanced by *L'Univers israélite* and the *Archives israélites de France* ever since the convening of the Algeciras Conference was of any avail. It was in France's own interest, so the argument ran, "to put back on their feet the hundred thousand Jews who, as we know, are languishing in misery and insecurity in Morocco"; this would be a most effective way of embarking on "the task of economic penetration that is Europe's goal." In a revival of the old refrain already used in connection with Algerian and Tunisian Jewry, it was stated that the Jews of Morocco were, "on account of their knowledge of the country and its languages, their commercial skills, and their business connections with the natives, the born pioneers of this vast undertaking aimed at regenerating the social fabric of the Moroccan Empire and at opening up the Empire to western civilization."[43]

Yet these "born pioneers" cut a very sorry figure indeed in the reports from the Alliance's schoolteachers, who described them as uncouth savages "in whose minds all the world's superstitions seem[ed] to have taken up residence," stubborn individuals who "refus[ed] to open up their tiny brains to let in some light," lived in filth, and wore dark "corkscrew curls" and skullcaps. Of course, it remains to be shown that the language of the Benchimols, Nahons, Ribis, Guérons, and other "neophytes" from Salonika, Constantinople, Smyrna, and Tétouan were part and parcel of the Alliance's "discourse" on Moroccan Jewry.

Verba volent, acta nolent: on the eve of the protectorate, some 5,000 Jewish children in Morocco attended schools run by the Alliance. In 1913, Narcisse Leven wrote to General Lyautey asking him to exempt Moroccan Jews from local jurisdiction and to apply French legislation to them. "This is what was done in Algeria," he explained to the résident général.[44] Yet Leven, who certainly did not fancy himself as another Crémieux, was nevertheless aware of the consequences of the legal assimilation of Algerian Jewry, the unrest it had provoked in Algeria, and the reaction of the French authorities to similar requests submitted "in the name" of Tunisian Jewry.

[43] H. Prague, "La Question judéo-marocaine à la conférence d'Algésiras," *AI* 67 (1906): 10.

[44] Letter of 14 February 1913 quoted in A. Chouraqui, *L'Alliance Israélite Universelle et la renaissance juive contemporaine* (1965), 440–42.

In actual fact, France was not alone in having changed since 1830. The Jews of Tunisia and Morocco at the time of the protectorate, for their part, bore no resemblance to the Algerian Jews encountered by the Comte de Bourmont in 1830. They formed larger and demographically more diverse communities; furthermore, during the seventy-five years of European penetration that preceded the arrival of the French, they had had the time to undergo social change, to choose a variety of political options (pro-Spanish, pro-Italian, pro-British, and so on), and even to work out plans for the future and develop a series of cultural models (ranging from active religious orthodoxy to Zionism) that differed from those suggested to them—in good faith—by French Jewry.

The letter addressed to Zadoc Kahn in 1900 by "a group of Jews in Tunis" gives a fairly accurate idea of the state of mind of a part of the North African Jewish population.

Each nation has a national education system that is the product of its national life, is imbued with its spirit and national traditions, proceeds from its historic past, and answers the present-day needs of its national life. . . . The Alliance Israélite . . . in violation of the most basic rules of conduct, is seeking to impose the French spirit, embodied by the French national education system, on the Jewish population of Tunisia. While the Jews of France can still pride themselves on partaking to a certain degree in the national life of the French, they will surely not venture to believe that the same is true of Tunisian Jews, whose past has nothing to do with France or the French, and whose traditions and mores have nothing to do with French civilization—a civilization, moreover, that appeared in Tunisia only yesterday. . . . In order to enlighten this population, to introduce it to modern life, one must not replace its traditions and historical memories by other traditions and other memories. One must not seek to replace one's own national spirit by that of another nation. On the contrary, the ingredients of a nation's progress must be drawn from its own historical past. It is in one's own intellectual and national field that one must sow those seeds of civilization and progress that belong to all nations and do not bear the stamp of any nation in particular.[45]

Clearly the tone of this complaint was quite different from that of the reprimands addressed many years earlier by Algerian Jews to their French rabbis on the subject of divorce, polygamy, the levirate, and other "superstitions." Indeed, this letter challenged the very principles of French Jewry's "mission" in North Africa.

[45] AAIU, Tunisia I G 3, 2 October 1900.

NANCY L. GREEN

The Contradictions of Acculturation: Immigrant Oratories and Yiddish Union Sections in Paris before World War I

W HEN ASKED WHY the Jewish immigrants from Eastern Europe set up their own mutual aid societies upon arrival in Paris, the secretary of the Société de Chevra Kadisha (burial society) de Varsovie replied without hesitation, "To have total independence."[1] To be independent from the existing French Jewish community's organizations, he further explained. What he did not add (it was so obvious as to go without saying) was the immigrants' need to be independent of French organizations as well.

Immigrant associations are one way of focusing on immigrant needs and on the often slow and halting process of acculturation. Acculturation combines continuity and change as immigrants' needs are confronted with those of the receiving society. A recent renewed interest in immigrant organizations reflects post–melting pot theories in the United States and the newly discovered "droit à la différence" for minorities, immigrants, and regional groups in France. For too long acculturation (or in its now outmoded formulation, assimilation) was seen to be an inevitable process of cultural exchange, all the more so in France, where cultural hegemony rather than cultural pluralism ruled the day.[2] Now, however,

I would like to thank the George Lurcy Foundation, the Memorial Foundation for Jewish Culture, and the National Foundation for Jewish Culture for helping finance various stages of this research.

[1] Abraham Uhafti, interview in Fontenay-sur-Bois, October 27, 1978.

[2] See the interesting comparison in Dominique Schnapper, "Centralisme et fédéralisme culturels, les émigrés italiens en France et aux Etats-Unis," *Annales E.S.C.* (October 1974), pp. 1141–59.

revised policies are admitting a certain politics of pluralism just as revised histories are examining immigrant organizations in order to explore the possibilities of cultural diversity within the nation state.

One could say that the process of acculturation is always successful in the long run. It is a necessary part of adaptation implicit in the migration process. It is usually, but not always, desired and generally bound up with perceptions of the future. To stay, one must adapt. If one plans to return to the home country, the desire to participate in the "temporary" country's culture may not be great. But even then, as the stay is prolonged, certain adaptations seem bound to take place.

Historically, acculturation may be examined from various perspectives: that of the individual; that of the group; over the short run of the first generation; over the long run of a foreign group's ultimate acculturation to a nation state while yet not part of the nation. All these cases, however, assume acculturation over the long term and basically ask the question of what form it will take. Recent migration scholarship has turned to questions of survival of ethnic identities and the form they take. It is in this respect that immigrant organizations are particularly important. The organizations created by first-generation immigrants reflect the options for acculturation that present themselves and the immigrant responses to them.

Acculturation may be seen as a multiform process implying both voluntary and involuntary adaptation to a variety of situations: economic, social, political, and cultural. Even when decidedly voluntary, from the purchase of that first symbol of frenchification, a beret, acculturation is halting at best, marked both by refusals and constraints that limit integration. By refusals we will see immigrants demanding separate organizations to cater to their specific needs. By material constraints to cultural adaptation we must keep in mind the geographic or economic environment that may limit contact between the old culture and the new: immigrant neighborhoods, compatriot-run shops and cafés, economic concentration in certain trades, piecework done in family workshops, social, economic, and even political networks that remain within the confines of the immigrant community.

But the acculturation process is halting not only because of explicit refusals or more implicit geographic or economic constraints

on cultural exchange. It is halting because of the nature of the
receiving society. The question must be asked: acculturation to
what? In the case of migrants such as the Jews, immigration means
a double confrontation, both with a foreign society (the indigenous population being just as "foreign" to the immigrant as vice
versa) and also with an important subset of that society: a preexisting Jewish community.[3]

In this paper I will examine immigrant adaptation within this
double referent: French society and the Jewish minority subset. By
focusing on two types of immigrant organizations, immigrant oratories and their relation to the Paris Consistory, and immigrant
trade union sections and their relation to the Confédération Générale du Travail (CGT), we can examine two modes of acculturation: one religious and one secular. We can also examine how two
aspects of the Jewish immigrants' identity, religion and class, were
mediated by the migration process. In both instances we can see
elements of acceptance and rejection, of change (acceptance of new
cultural forms) and continuity (persistence of old forms). Continuity and change are intertwined; separation from and integration
into the new societies exist side by side. From immigrant oratories
to Yiddish union sections, we can examine a first generation of immigrants coming to grips with two very distinct aspects of (the not-
so-hegemonic after all) French culture: French Jewry and French
workers' organizations.

Yiddish separated the Jewish immigrant workers from French
workers just as it separated them from French Jews. One could
ask, however, whether in another language, Hebrew, the Eastern
European and French Jews could find common ground. The Paris
Consistory may be said to have represented an option for immigrant acculturation particularly insofar as religious solidarity

---

[3] And that community may have its own problems of assimilation. See Michael Marrus,
*The Politics of Assimilation: A Study of the French Jewish Community at the Time of the
Dreyfus Affair* (Oxford: Oxford University Press, 1971), also published in French by
Calmann-Lévy in 1972. Paula Hyman and David Weinberg have both explored the problematic relationship between immigrant and native organizations and have shown that it
reflects as much about the French Jewish community's difficulty to adapt to the "immigrant
challenge" as about immigrant adaptation itself. Paula Hyman, *From Dreyfus to Vichy: The
Remaking of French Jewry, 1906–1939* (New York: Columbia University Press, 1979); David Weinberg, *Les Juifs à Paris de 1933 à 1939* (Paris: Calmann-Lévy, 1974), also published
in English by the University of Chicago Press in 1977.

could be postulated as the basic common denominator of Jewish solidarity when other cultural, economic, and even political differences separate immigrant and native communities. As the immigrants set about creating their own oratories and eventually a synagogue, their attempts at religious "independence" reflected the specificity of their linguistic, cultural, and ritual needs.

Even before the arrival of Eastern European Jews in France, the practice of Judaism had varied widely, resulting in often bitter struggles within the Paris Consistory during the nineteenth century over Sephardic or Ashkenazic rituals.[4] Then, with the immigration of Eastern European Jews at the end of the century, further ritual differences came to the fore, this time within the Ashkenazic branch of Judaism alone. Although French Jewry had not undergone a reform movement similar to that in Germany, concessions to "modernization" in the practice of certain religious rituals (for example, choirs, organs) had occurred. Consequently, as will be seen, synagogues, far from providing a meeting place for French and Eastern European Jews, became one more example of the distance between the two communities.

The Ashkenazic French Jews' attitudes toward the religious practices of the Ashkenazic foreign Jews were twofold. There were, on the one hand, the more orthodox French Jews who deplored the increasing secularization and indifference of so many of their coreligionists and who felt that the immigration of more orthodox Eastern European Jews could provide a needed support if not a savior for the religious foundation of French Judaism.[5] An article in *L'Univers israélite* of 28 June 1907 perhaps best expressed this (guarded) optimism. "Provided that we know how to win them over and lead them, that we do not oppose them with disdain and ostracism, who knows whether our foreign coreligionists are not destined to enrich French Judaism, at least morally, and give it new force?" Parenthetically it may be added that the implication is an important one that should be brought to all acculturation studies.

---

[4] See Phyllis Cohen Albert, *The Modernization of French Jewry: Consistory and Community in the Nineteenth Century* (Hanover, N.H.: Brandeis University Press, 1977); Patrick Girard, *Les Juifs de France de 1789 à 1860: De l'émancipation à l'égalité* (Paris: Calmann-Lévy, 1976).

[5] *L'Univers israélite* (Paris, hereafter cited as *UI*) noted that the proportion of immigrants among religious Jews had risen from 25 percent in 1896 to 60 percent in 1908. *UI*, 5 February 1909. See also *Archives israélites* (Paris, hereafter cited as *AI*), 28 June 1883.

Not only can we ask how immigrants adapt to a new environment, but we must also ask how that environment adapts to the immigrants. What are those cultural or religious traditions that the immigrants import to the receiving society? In the case of French Jewry the result has been that substantial and successive waves of immigrants have been grudgingly acknowledged as giving new life to a minority otherwise seemingly doomed to disappearance.

But in the period of initial confrontation with the immigrant challenge, attitudes are not always so appreciative, and the majority of the French Jewish community in the early 1900s could see only the "backwardness" of the immigrants, occasionally complimenting them on their "ardor" ("which we would do well to imitate"), but following such compliment by a description of the "crowd, a bit noisy" in the synagogue.[6]

The encounter between Western and Eastern Jews in this period must, however, be seen from another viewpoint. While the disdain of the emancipated Jews for their backward brethren from the East is no longer a new subject, much less has been said about the often similar antipathies felt by the Eastern European Jews for the pernicious effects of assimilation. From the viewpoint of Eastern Europe, the West and certainly Paris ("Babylon") was no place for any self-respecting religious Jew. As old Sarah, a character in *L'Epopée de Ménaché Foïgel*, complained, you couldn't even tell the Jews from the *goyim* in Paris anymore; they dressed like the French, ate like the French (including snails and frogs' legs) and prayed—or didn't—like the French.[7]

Indeed many who emigrated from Eastern Europe did so because of the attraction of "Babylon." For nonbelievers (*apikorsim*) or for those simply seeking a less traditional environment, the act of emigration was a break with traditions and origins that they considered the cause of their ills.[8] The most extreme expression of this antitraditionalism would be the Yom Kippur Balls organized as early as 1900 by immigrant anarchists, attracting as many as four hundred people.[9]

---

[6] *AI*, 11 June 1914; cf. *UI*, 26 October 1900, and 9 and 30 November 1900.

[7] André Billy and Moïse Twersky, *L'épopée de Ménaché Foïgel*, 3 vols. (Paris: Plon, 1927–28), 1:167.

[8] *UI*, 2 January 1903. See also my article in *Pluriel*, no. 27 (1981), "L'Emigration comme émancipation," pp. 51–59.

[9] Police report entitled "Les réfugiés révolutionnaires russes à Paris," F[7] 12894, Archives

Nonetheless, in comparison to the secularized traditions found in the West, the majority of Eastern European Jews transplanted there represented a totally different manner of "Jewishness." If only as seen externally, by clothing and habits, the Eastern European Jews were associated with religious orthodoxy (even fanaticism). The difference between Eastern and Western Jews (often poorly stated in terms of "religiosity," a term mixing faith and practice) was perhaps less one of faith (the ability of a Western Jew to identify an Eastern European *apikores* was no better than that of an immigrant to distinguish a *croyant* French Jew) than of ritual practice and traditional styles.[10] As J. Tchernoff, in his memoirs of this period, described the differences in style:

> When the Jews from Eastern Europe cross the threshold of a temple in Paris, they feel bewildered, out of their element, surprised by the attitude of the worshipers. The manner of these men, wearing top hats, ceremonious, proper, who speak in whispers of their business affairs during the service, which few of them understand, for whom the enactment of the rituals is part of a certain fashionable snobbery, surprises and shocks the persecuted Jews who, gesticulating wildly, swaying their bodies, put into their prayer the mystic ardor that devours them.[11]

The vivid juxtaposition described by Tchernoff in fact probably occurred rarely within one temple. To see the contrasts described so well by him one would have had to travel from the ninth to the fourth *arrondissement*, from the French synagogue on rue de la Victoire to the private Eastern European oratories of the Pletzl. For wherever the necessary *minyan* of ten men had been gathered for this purpose, the Eastern European Jews created their own places of worship. These *minyans* were often ephemeral and the lack of more religious activity among the immigrants was lamented by some, but insofar as religious life did remain important for a

Nationales, Paris, p. 5; J. Tchernoff, *Dans le creuset des civilisations*, 4 vols. (Paris: Editions Rieder, 1937) 4:279; *UI*, 19 October 1900; *AI*, 12 September 1901.

[10] See "Les réfugiés révolutionnaires russes," pp. 4–5, for the police department's evaluation that the Russian Jews were outwardly religious in order to receive philanthropic aid from the rich Parisian Israelites. Or, as Harry Golden put it, an Eastern European "freethinker" and Socialist may still have gone to *shul* regularly because "these people are my brethren, they are the people among whom I was raised, I love them. Dudja Silverberg goes to *shul* to speak with God, I go to *shul* to speak with Dudja." Isaac Metzger, ed., *Bintel Brief* (New York: Ballantine, 1971), p. 70.

[11] Tchernoff, 3:14–15.

segment of the immigrant community, it was in *immigrant* oratories—founded anywhere from an artist's loft to a shoemaker's
workshop—that their faith would be expressed.

Russian and Rumanian oratories appear as early as the first immigration and by 1900 the *Archives israélites* counted five oratories on Montmartre and seven in the Marais–St. Paul area, which
observed the *"Polish rite."* By 1914 some thirty had appeared (and
often just as quickly disappeared).[12] These small prayer groups
sometimes had no other designation than the name of the street
on which they were located. The oratories sometimes grouped
members of a particular trade (reminiscent of the "Tailors' Synagogue" in Eastern Europe); the officiating *ministres* were usually
themselves workers or merchants, the job of spiritual leader for
an oratory being hardly a full-time position. By tracing the oratories or their administrators through sporadic appearances in the
Consistory's archives their common characteristics soon emerge:
individually ephemeral but collectively persistent. The oratories were small and often underwent several address changes, yet
their tenacity was a clear testimony to the specific religious/ritual
needs of the immigrant community and a continuity of immigrant
traditions.

Contact between the immigrant oratories and the French Jewish
community did exist. Chief Rabbi Zadoc Kahn gave them his support, and, although private and independent, the immigrant religious organizations often turned to the Consistory for legal or financial help or even to resolve an internal dispute. Furthermore,
since places of worship were supposed to be authorized by the
Consistory (before 1905), many sought this formalization, although quite often after the fact. All other associations and societies were supposed to be authorized by the Préfecture de Police,
and it was often at that time that an immigrant group made itself
known to the Consistory, requesting the latter to be an intercessor
with the French authorities.

[12] Nancy L. Green, "Class Struggle in the Pletzl: Jewish Immigrant Workers in Paris,
1881–1914" (Ph.D. dissertation, University of Chicago, 1980), appendix F. For the following discussion of immigrant religious life see Paris, Association Consistoriale Israélite de
Paris Archives (hereafter cited as ACIP), AA19: Procès-verbaux, 1906–15; BB50–59:
Lettres envoyées, 1882–91; and the B series (*Lettres reçues*), from 1888 to 1917, particularly the files labelled "Sociétés," "Oratoires," "Commission du 4ème arrondissement," etc.
See also Paris, Consistoire Central Archives, I^cc77: Lettres du Ministère de l'Intérieur et des

One example is the tailors' society Ahavath Reim which, after fifteen years of existence as an oratory, decided to constitute legally a mutual aid society for which by-laws to be filed with the police were drawn up on 15 October 1896.[13] Article 29 of these by-laws even provided for a prayer to be said for France and for the president of the Republic during the morning service. Having thus drawn itself to the attention of the authorities, the society was closed the following March by the police. It was then that it turned to the Consistory, which commented on how, after having been without authorization for so long, this "groupement quelconque d'Israélites" seemed to be showing more responsibility than usual.

Faced with the continuing influx of immigrants from the East, the Consistory proffered an ideology of integration, but integration, as has been seen, "provided that we know how to win them over and lead them." And when the question arose of replacing a cantor at a Consistory-run oratory on Montmartre, there was some debate as to whether he should be replaced by someone of the immigrants' mentality or of "our own." The latter option was finally chosen for "the issue has to do with forming, educating in some way this population."[14]

The immigrants, too, turned in expectation to the French Jewish community. Just as direct appeals were made to the chief rabbi or the Rothschilds because of the spiritual or financial power that they held and even more importantly symbolized, the immigrants looked to the Consistory because of the institutional, moral, and religious weight it represented.

At first the immigrants demanded more representation on consistorial committees, through which their oratories would have a greater voice in religious affairs. At the same time the immigrants also began turning to the Consistory out of dissatisfaction with their private oratories. On the one hand the immigrants became increasingly dissatisfied with the poor material conditions of their places of worship. On the other hand tradition too was sometimes ripe for change. The move from oratories to a synagogue led to two opposite tendencies within the immigrant community: a move-

Cultes, 1899–1905; and Roger Kohn, "L'organisation de l'éducation juive chez les immigrés d'Europe orientale à Paris," *YOD*, vol. 3, fascicule 2 (n.d.), pp. 87–90.

[13] ACIP, B60.

[14] ACIP, B95, "Oratoire Ste. Isaure"; see also Hyman, "Who Shall Rule?", pp. 139–43.

ment toward a closer relationship with the Consistory on the one hand, yet also an opposite movement toward complete independence on the other. The contradictions and varieties of acculturation are evident in the immigrants' requests for relative religious autonomy.

In 1913 the president of the temple on rue Ste. Isaure, while petitioning the Consistory for better and larger quarters, explained how the settling-in process of the immigrant population presaged dissatisfaction. "For among this Jewish population on Montmartre, hardworking, serious and frugal, there are many who gradually attain a degree of economic security, and once the needs of their families are assured, their savings go first of all toward religion."[15] Religion was thus to a certain extent a luxury, but a luxury only insofar as a formal synagogue with its own building implied necessary dues to assure its upkeep. The private oratories, which required only ten men and an apartment or workshop in which to meet, had the clear advantage of being free or of requiring only minimal dues, and they were thus perfectly suited to the modest needs of a newly arrived and generally poor community. However, the premises in which worship took place were often "makeshift quarters, absolutely unworthy of the usage for which they are destined," as the Consistory described them.[16] By the second decade of the twentieth century it would seem that many immigrants agreed with this description.

A delegation of immigrants from the fourth and eleventh *arrondissements* went to the Consistory in July 1913 with a request for a temple of their own. A similar request came from the Bastille area (eleventh *arrondissement*) in November, and another petition representing the fourth, eleventh, and twelfth *arrondissements* was submitted in December. It was argued that "our young people, who have already gone through French schools, refuse to frequent our oratories, which are little appropriate to the dignity of a place of worship."[17] It was not only the smallness or insalubrity of the oratories but also tradition itself that was ripe for change as the older generation became sensitive (and were themselves not impervious) to the more rapid frenchification of the young. The Consistory de-

[15] ACIP, B95, "Oratoire Ste. Isaure."
[16] ACIP, B95, "Commission du 4ème arrondissement."
[17] Ibid.

spaired that the immigrants did not even know what they wanted. Earlier that year the Montmartre community, after requesting the installation of a special barrier for the women's section of the temple on rue Ste. Isaure (a necessity for the orthodox), had asked the Consistory to take it down "under the pretext that they were 'in France.'"[18]

The issue of change versus continuity came to a head most clearly with the creation of an immigrant synagogue. To transcend the outgrown oratories yet to maintain their separateness from the consistorial system, a group called the Agoudath Hakehiloth decided to build its own temple. This organization (with J. Landau as president and J. L. Herzog as rabbi) first appears in the fall of 1911 in a letter to the Consistory asking that an immigrant be named to the Consistorial Committee for the Supervision of Ritual Practices. The request was granted, but a second letter soon followed from another group of immigrants who contested the right of the Agoudath Hakehiloth to speak for the immigrant community. This second group claimed instead that it represented the larger and calmer element of the community in contrast to the few "agitated" followers of Herzog. A report on the situation by a (consistorial) committee called the Société Tipheret Israël described the Agoudath Hakehiloth in the following terms: "The supposed new rabbi of the Polish *israélites* is, in reality, but a *magid* (preacher), of inferior rank, brought to the fore by a handful of faithless and lawless [*sans foi ni loi*] charlatans, hypocrites and audacious persons who believe they have found a way to raise money."[19] The Consistory's Solomon-like decision was to expand its committee in order to permit one member from each immigrant group to be included, but the controversy did not end there. The ensuing struggle for control over the immigrant community reveals as much about the divisions among the immigrants themselves (and the differing options for or rejection of acculturation) as about the range of relations possible between the immigrants and the Consistory. It may be added that this first stage of the controversy in 1911 had the side effect of bringing another group to the Consistory with a request for help; several immigrant bakers, complaining of demands

---

[18] ACIP, B95, "Oratoire Ste. Isaure."

[19] ACIP, B90, "Union des Communautés." ACIP, B95, "Commission du 4ème arrondissement" and ACIP, AA19, pp. 190–93, 212–17, also deal with the Agoudath controversy.

being made on them by the two antagonistic factions, asked to be
put under the Consistory's protection.

On 6 April 1913, construction on a grand orthodox temple designed by Guimard for the Agoudath Hakehiloth de Paris began at
10 rue Pavée. In the face of this act, agitation among the immigrant
community was heightened. The anti–Agoudath Hakehiloth group
wrote to the Consistory requesting that the existing synagogue on
rue des Tournelles be turned over to the immigrant community or
that a new (consistorial) synagogue be built. In either case it was
stipulated that the ritual of such temple be orthodox, that administration of the temple be given to the delegation making the request
(i.e., immigrants) and that a rabbi from the Ecole Rabbinique de
France be chosen, but one of Russian-Polish origin.

The next day, however, the Consistory received yet another
letter, from the third party involved: the Alsatian Jews who fre-
quented the rue de Tournelles temple. The author of that letter
wrote that as a true *israélite* he was obliged to warn the consistory
that if the Tournelles temple were given to the immigrants, the
Alsatians of the Marais would "rise up in a quarrel against the
Consistory."

The quarrel over the Tournelles temple arose from the very essence of the need for private immigrant oratories in the first place.
The inadequacy of French temples for the Eastern European Jews
was evident in the temple on rue des Tournelles, which, as the bas-
tion of Alsatian Jews in the Marais, had among other things a
choir and an organ, which were contrary to the immigrants' traditions. Demographic changes in the Parisian Jewish community
had, by the early twentieth century, led to a population shift in the
Marais resulting in a gradual displacement of French (Alsatian)
Jews by the Eastern European immigrants. The result was a consistently declining membership at the Tournelles temple. The immigrant petitioners therefore also argued that if put at their disposal
that temple would once again be full, and that seven or eight hundred immigrants would thereby become dues-paying members
of the Consistory.

The consistorial response in this complex affair ranged from respect for the immigrants' conservative orthodoxy (and a regret that
not enough attention had previously been paid to these "exotic elements") to condemnation of the separatists as fanatics. Chief Rabbi
Dreyfuss suggested conciliation; but a consistorial delegate sent to

investigate the matter was outraged by the Agoudath's "extreme in-
gratitude" toward the French community's philanthropy and the
immigrants' insistence on "superannuated customs."[20]

Yet through this interimmigrant struggle the Consistory discovered the more assimilable element of the immigrant community,
which it perceived as a potential ally, on the condition that that ally
be correctly educated and organized. The immigrants who wanted
the Tournelles temple argued that they would help bring a veritable
religious and financial renaissance to Parisian Judaism.

But as far as the separatist Agoudath Hakehiloth was concerned,
the Consistory turned its back on them. In June 1914 the new
Russian-Polish synagogue, 10 rue Pavée, was dedicated: a "modern" temple, with seating for one thousand people, two spacious
galleries for the women, special rooms for weddings and meetings,
and plans for a *talmud torah* for four hundred children. The *Archives israélites* complimented the "pious initiative of our immigrant coreligionists" and chided the community representatives for
"pouting" instead of congratulating the immigrants for having
done it all on their own, without costing a cent to the Parisian Jewish community.[21]

Thus the immigrants' religious needs were multidimensional,
from freethinkers to "fanatics." The schism produced within the
immigrant community between the Agoudath Hakehiloth and
Tournelles factions exhibited the heterogeneity of needs within
the immigrant community as it adapted to its new environment.
Some immigrants turned to the established Jewish community as a
mode of integration within a subset of French society, although still
holding out for a rabbi of their own, while others chose a path of
independence representative of irreconcilable ritual and cultural
differences.

In both cases, however, the step from the creation of oratories to
demands for synagogues of their own reflected the progressive

[20] ACIP, B95, "Commission du 4ème arrondissement." "Orthodoxy is only a pretext for
justifying enrollment under the banner of a foreign, fanatical rabbi, maintaining among his
followers the ideas and prejudices of another civilization."

[21] *AI*, 18 June 1914. In an interesting article, "Hector Guimard's *Art Nouveau* Synagogue in rue Pavée, Paris," *Journal of Jewish Art* 6 (1979): 105–11, Carol Krinsky suggests that the architecture itself may have reflected both a desire to break with the usual
Romanesque style consistorial synagogues and an attempt to appeal, with a modern and
French style, to the immigrant young. (I would like to thank Yerachmiel (Richard) Cohen for
this reference.)

settling-in of the immigrant community. They were able to amass a small amount of disposable income for the luxury of moving religious worship out of multifunctional workshops into unipurpose synagogues. The immigrants' demands represent changing levels of adaptation along the time-scale of settlement. If at first oratories are enough to fulfill the needs of just arrived immigrants, once they are settled in, immigrant institutions themselves must take a firmer form. That may involve turning toward the preexisting native community for help or it may result in separate, reinforced immigrant organizations. In either case it shows a growing stabilization of the immigrant community itself.

The immigrants' relation to the French Jewish community was based on certain assumptions of Jewish solidarity that came into conflict with the French Jews' desire to educate and frenchify the immigrants after their own image. Even in the religious domain, ritual differences remained insurmountable. The foreignness of the French Jewish forms available for integration and disappointment over the attitude of the Consistory led the immigrants to insist on separate forms of organization. Those forms also manifested the diversity of immigrant acculturation patterns and their change over time. With the passage of time some immigrants were more ready to take down certain religious and other cultural barriers while others maintained a firm commitment to imported traditions and thus declared all the more stridently their independence from the French Jewish model.

A similar argument may be made for a quite different set of options: participation of the Jewish immigrant workers in the French labor movement. There too relations were based on an underlying ideology of solidarity, working-class solidarity, which, however, confronted with difficulties and disappointments, also led to the creation of separate immigrant forms of organization: Yiddish union sections. And it became the task of *Der yidisher Arbeter*, the Jewish workers' newspaper, to explain this existence *within* but not entirely *of* the CGT.

Jewish immigrants began to organize fairly soon after their arrival in France, and that organization first took the form of mutual aid societies. The cap makers (some of whom had emigrated from Poland after the 1863 revolution) founded a mutual aid society as early as 1879 and another in 1887. Jewish rubber workers, fur workers, tailors, and woodworkers also created self-help societies in the 1880s and 1890s.[22]

These mutual aid societies often reflected the paternalistic family-workshop nature of the crafts, with employees and their small-time bosses joining together in an attempt at mutual support. Purely workers' organizations soon evolved, taking the form of union sections attached to the pertinent CGT union. These foreign-language sections of the CGT were described either as the Yiddish section "by" (*beim*) the French union; the Yiddish section "under the direction" (*unter der leitung*) of the French union; or merely "the Jewish section" (either *section israélite* or *section juive*). The Jewish cap makers were important enough to have their own union rather than a section, but it too was basically a Yiddish affair. An umbrella organization called the Intersektzione Byuro (precursor to the CGTU Yiddishe Intersyndical Commission created in 1923) was founded on 18 December 1910 at a meeting of 109 Jewish immigrant labor leaders, and it represented the capmakers' union and all of the Yiddish-speaking union sections affiliated with the CGT.[23] In 1912 *Der Yidisher Arbeter* proudly proclaimed, "We have brought together in one stream the small forces that have been born and that have spread in all of the trades," and by 1914 the masthead of the newspaper listed, in addition to the cap makers, the following as all having union sections: fur workers, tailors, woodworkers, leatherworkers, shoemakers, barbers, and bakers.[24]

While thus declaring their independence from their immigrant bosses and their fundamentally opposed interests, the Jewish immigrant workers also remained distinct from, even while within, the French union organization.[25] For in spite of fervent and impas-

---

[22] See Green, pp. 219–26 and appendix F on mutual aid societies and chapter 9 for more detailed information on the history of the union sections.

[23] Zosa Szajkowski, *Di Profesionele Bavegung tzvishn di Yidishe Arbeter in Frankreich* (Paris: Frydman, 1937), pp. 30–31. For the interwar history of the Intersyndical Commission, see Hyman, pp. 103–8, and Weinberg, pp. 159–60.

[24] *Der Yidisher Arbeter* (Paris, hereafter cited as *YA*), 1 May 1912, and 4 July 1914.

[25] The formation of union sections as opposed to separate unions was undoubtedly due in part to legal restrictions. According to the law of 21 March 1884, which legalized unions, foreigners could not be members of a union's central committee. Therefore immigrant unions could not exist unless the son of an immigrant (automatically French according to a law of 1889), a naturalized immigrant or even a "front" was available to comply with the regulation. Much easier, however, was the formation of union sections within the French union, which was the choice of most of the Jewish immigrants. See Maurice Didion, *Les*

sioned appeals to class unity and workers' brotherhood regardless of race, religion, or nationality (as the Jews were variously defined), theoretical workers' unity had to confront the practicality of separate immigrant union sections. The problem of separate organization was not a new one for the Jewish labor movement; it was at the heart of the Bund's polemic with Lenin in Russia.[26] In France it would be crystallized in the union sections' relation to the CGT.

A theoretical option for acculturation thus existed for Jewish workers in the economic domain just as it did in the religious domain, this time in the form of the French labor movement. Several factors, however, would make unity with the French workers difficult. Labor protectionism, sometimes tinged with anti-Semitism, on the one hand, and the immigrant workers' specific organizational needs on the other both made separate Yiddish union sections as obvious to the immigrants as their own oratories or synagogue. The French labor movement, like the Jewish workers' paper, repeatedly stressed the ideological importance of unity of the immigrant workers' cause with that of French workers. In practice, however, certain tensions developed that would ultimately help lead the way toward separate immigrant organizations.

Already in 1898, during the Dreyfus Affair, disappointment with the French labor movement came to the fore in an open *Lettre des ouvriers juifs de Paris au Parti Socialiste Français* signed by a "groupe des ouvriers juifs socialistes de Paris" in which the Jewish workers expressed their keen disappointment with the French Socialists' weak stance on the Affair. That disappointment was all the greater because of the high hopes they had placed in the French Socialists. A particularly pointed criticism was aimed at Jules Guesde (who led the more intransigent stand against Socialist participation in the Affair). "We find our anger cannot be exhausted through the reasoned revolt of Marx and his disciples. They exert

---

Salariés étrangers en France (Paris: V. Giard et E. Brière, 1911), p. 97; Albert Matline, secretary of the Syndicat des Chapeliers, Modistes et Casquettiers, interview in Paris, May 12, 1977.

[26] See Henry J. Tobias, *The Jewish Bund in Russia from its Origins to 1905* (Stanford, Calif.: Stanford University Press, 1970); and Jonathan Frankel, *Prophecy and Politics: Socialism, Nationalism and the Russian Jews, 1862–1917* (Cambridge: Cambridge University Press, 1981).

their anger in too narrow a sphere, that of the class struggle; but our anger cannot stop there."[27] For the struggle of the Jewish immigrant workers would have to go beyond a strict bourgeois/proletariat analysis and address the issues of small-time bosses and exploitation *within* the immigrant community. In any case the Jewish workers ended their *lettre* with the hope and appeal that the French Socialists would come to their aid.

These high hopes, often tinged with disappointment, would characterize the relationship between the Jewish and French labor movements in Paris. The often difficult integration of immigrant labor within a national labor movement was problematic as ideological unity sometimes confronted labor protectionism in the workshop if not in ambiguous newspaper articles or congress resolutions. The "national question" within the labor movement was a microcosm of the problem of immigrant groupings within the nation state. When Marx wrote, "Working men of all countries, unite!" he did not know how pertinent that phrase would become as the increased migration of labor brought working persons of all countries together within one land.

The fundamental importance of unity among all workers and the necessity of organizing to effectuate that unity were repeated by the CGT leadership each time there was a strike in which the immigrants were involved. Jewish workers were often defended and even praised in the French labor press; an article in *La Bataille syndicaliste* of 10 April 1913, pointed to the example of a Jewish bakers' strike as a lesson for all French bakers. Racamond, secretary of the French bakers' union, wrote to *Der Yidisher Arbeter* of 8 February 1913, praising the solidarity of immigrant and French workers in a recent strike. "For us, union workers, there exist no nations . . . there exists only one nation—that of the exploited class."

Concrete support of immigrant strikes often took the form of providing premises, paying for leaflets, or giving financial aid. The Bourse du Travail headquarters in Paris was a common meeting place; publicity leaflets with the CGT stamp attest to its help for that important communication medium; and the French union occasionally helped out with strike funds enabling the strikers to

[27] Karpel and Dinner for the Groupe des Ouvriers Juifs Socialistes de Paris, *Le prolétariat juif: Lettre des ouvriers juifs de Paris au Parti Socialiste Français* (Paris: Imprimerie Typographique J. Allemane, 1898), p. 15.

hold out longer.[28] Beyond this, moral support from the French unions was also important.

All such manifestations of solidarity reflected the basic ideological premise of workers' unity. Yet institutional constraints of the French union structure, the disparity between the French leadership and the immigrant rank and file, disagreement over political involvement and dissensions between French and immigrant co-workers all created concrete obstacles to theoretical unity. Strains of anti-Semitism reveal the most basic contradiction of all, the issue of labor protectionism. The premise of ideological unity was threatened by the division of labor, which brought immigrant workers into conflict with their fellow workers. More generally it was threatened by the ambiguous position of the immigrant in French society. This latter, in the case of Jewish immigrants, often translated as anti-Semitism.

On numerous occasions strikes themselves provoked a conflict between immigrant and French co-workers. Divisions of workplace and function, overlaid by those of sex or nationality, were often reproduced within the strike movement itself. Thus in many cases those who struck were immigrants and those who did not were French(women). During a Galeries Lafayette strike in 1913, the company recognized the potential of such work force divisions and spread the rumor that the (immigrant) strikers' only real intent was to cause the firing of the French workers.[29]

Even within a strike movement tensions sometimes arose between immigrant and French strikers. In 1913 some French and Italian workers walked out of a strike meeting in anger that all of the speeches were in "Russian" (in fact, probably Yiddish). Similarly, during a 1916 strike at the Société Parisienne de Confection

---

[28] E.g., the hat federation's 1,000-franc grant and 4,000-franc loan at the time of the 1912 cap makers' strikes. Fédération des Syndicats Ouvriers de la Chapellerie Française, *15e Congrès national (Bort, Corrèze), 22–27 juillet 1912 et 8e Congrès international (Milan, Italie), 15–19 september 1912* (Paris: Imprimerie La Productrice, 1913), p. 63; cf. Jean Vial, *La Coutume chapelière: Histoire du mouvement ouvrier dans la chapellerie* (Paris: Editions Domat-Montchrestien, 1941), p. 343; and Michelle Perrot, *Les Ouvriers en grève, France 1871–90*, 2 vols. (Paris: Mouton et Cie. and Ecole Pratique des Hautes Etudes, 1974), 2:523, 525, on the hatters' union strike funds. For other instances of French union financial aid to Jewish strikes, see Szajkowski, *Profesionele Bavegung*, pp. 212, 230.

[29] Paris, Préfecture de Police Archives (hereafter cited as APP), BA1394, Files "Grève . . . British Tailors Ltd, Septembre 1912." and "Grève . . . Galeries Lafayette, Février 1913"; Szajkowski, pp. 190–96.

(production unit of Galeries Lafayette), a group of Frenchwomen threatened to leave the strike meeting and go back to work, saying, "We're not in Russia here and cannot understand what's going on."[30] Complaints about the use of Yiddish persisted in subsequent meetings.

The premise of ideological unity thus faced serious problems on the shop floor as at union meetings. And at times slogans of solidarity were even more gravely damaged by anti-Semitic incidents. In October 1910 an important railroad strike occurred against the Chemin de Fer du Nord, the shares of which were mostly owned by the Rothschild family. On 3 April 1911, at a meeting of the electric workers' union, Emile Pataud, secretary of the union, used the word "Jew" as synonymous with foe of the working class. Articles in *L'Humanité* and *La Guerre sociale* sharply attacked Pataud, and nearly two thousand Jewish workers showed up at a meeting organized by the cap makers', fur workers', and leatherworkers' unions and the Bund to protest Pataud's remarks. Alongside the Bundist speaker, Liber, there was the French socialist, Jean Longuet, who began his speech with "The French Socialist party is with you, Jewish workers!"[31]

Only eight months later, a tailor wrote to *La Guerre sociale* (the Socialist-revolutionary paper edited by Gustave Hervé) complaining that the competition of Jewish tailors had caused him to lose his job and that if there were an anti-Semitic movement he would join it.[32] As Bernard Lazare wrote in his work on anti-Semitism, it was not always the Jew but often the immigrant worker who was the butt of anti-Semitic attacks.[33] In effect, it was job competition, between indigenous and foreign labor, that characterized whatever rank and file animosity existed toward the Jewish immigrants.

Faced with this workers' competition, the French union more often than not supported the "protection of national work," i.e., protection of French labor. It was this protectionism that lay at the

[30] *APP*, BA1394, "Grève . . . Galeries Lafayette, Février 1913" and "Grève . . . Galeries Lafayette, Septembre 1916."

[31] *Forverts* (New York), 5 May 1911; see also *AI*, 20 April 1911, and Szajkowski, pp. 37–44, for the most extensive account of this affair.

[32] *La Guerre sociale* (Paris), 20–26 December 1911.

[33] Bernard Lazare, *Antisémitisme, son histoire et ses causes* (Paris: Leon Chailley, 1894), pp. 384–86; see also his comment in *Tribune libre* (Paris), 24 May 1896.

crux of the contradictions affecting relations between the French labor movement and the Jewish as well as all other immigrant workers in Paris. If on the one hand the unity of all workers, regardless of sex, race, nationality, or religion was idealized, on the other hand the protection of French workers' interests first and foremost sometimes led to ambivalent if not hostile opinions with regard to immigrant labor.

International solidarity continued to be the theoretical ideal to which the French labor movement subscribed as the necessary cure for the evil of labor competition. The imperatives of workers' unity and organization were repeated throughout all strikes. Yet in the face of contradictions arising from labor protectionism, in the face of the realities of the division of labor within the workshop, and perhaps in response to a certain "atavistic racial rancor" (as described by one contemporary labor writer), when it came to organizing, the immigrants felt the need to do so separately.[34]

Like the French labor movement, the Jewish labor movements' spokesmen proclaimed workers' unity as their primary goal. This meant a double task for Der yidisher Arbeter and the Intersektzione Byuro of organizing the Jewish workers in Paris and more specifically of organizing them within the CGT. To this end workers' solidarity and especially that between Jewish and French workers was emphasized in the paper's pages. Der Yidisher Arbeter served as an important communication medium to explain the "burning" issues of the French labor movement to the Jewish immigrants. The first two issues of the paper contained lengthy articles explaining the organizational structure of the CGT and the value of its revolutionary-syndicalist ideology. A series of articles by the Polish Socialist Sofia Posner examined French syndicalism, while French labor leaders such as Léon Jouhaux, A. Roux, Georges Yvetot, and A. Savoie contributed articles to the paper explaining various aspects of the French labor movement's struggles.[35] Der Yidisher Arbeter carried reports of the CGT congresses, and it supported the CGT's demand for the eight-hour day and the English work week. It urged participation in the French May Day celebrations and supported the CGT's call to a one-day general strike on

---

[34] Paul Gemähling, *Travailleurs au rabais, La Lutte syndicale contre les sous-concurrences ouvrières* (Paris: Bloud et Cie., 1910), p. 222.

[35] See, e.g., *YA*, 1 May, 3 August, and 2 November 1912, 8 February, 8 March, 1 May, and 7 June 1913, and 11 April 1914.

16 December 1912, to protest against war. *Der Yidisher Arbeter* (run by many who themselves had undoubtedly fled the tsar's military service) also published the CGT manifesto and several articles against the 1913 law increasing military service to three years.

Virtually every article in the three years of the paper's existence was an appeal to the benefits of solidarity and the strength in unity through which the Jewish workers could better their condition. Their organization, first in trade sections, further within the French union, was urged as the most important task of the Jewish proletariat. On the masthead of *Der Yidisher Arbeter*, alongside the motto, "Workers have nothing to lose but their chains" was the maxim, "In unity is strength," and the underlying theme of the paper was "hand bei hand mit unsere franzoyzishe chaverim . . . zeire tzores iz unzere tzores"; "zeier kampf iz unzer kampf; zeier tzukunft iz unzer tzukunft" (hand in hand with our French brothers . . . their troubles are our troubles; their struggle is our struggle; their future is our future).[36] In the second issue the editorial stressed the commonality of the Jewish workers' and French workers' oppression: Jewish workers are exploited like their French comrades (*chaverim*); the rising cost of living hits the Jewish workers just as it does the French. Are Jewish wages higher? No! Some say, Why should I protest? I am not French. No, but you are a worker. You are not a French citizen, but you are exploited by French capital.[37]

A sense of malaise often comes through *Der Yidisher Arbeter*'s proclamations of solidarity with the French labor movement, and the paper's insistence on workers' unity sometimes rings of "protesting too much." In fact the paper reflected the inherent contradiction implicit in those "by" or "under the direction" formulations describing the relationship of the union sections to the CGT. At either extreme there were the Bundists and the anarchists who wrote to *Der Yidisher Arbeter* to argue that the Jewish workers needed to be altogether independent of the CGT: for the Bundists, on the basis of greater autonomy for the Jewish labor movement; for the anarchists, because of their inherent dislike of any federative body.

[36] See *YA*, 17 November 1911 and 5 October 1912.
[37] *YA*, 17 November 1911.

The task of *Der Yidisher Arbeter*, the Intersektzione Byuro, and all of those Jewish workers who opted for integration within the largest representative organization of the French workers, was to explain why that integration had to take a special immigrant form. The contradictions inherent in the very medium—Yiddish—by which solidarity with the French workers was expressed underlay the often defensive posture of *Der Yidisher Arbeter*. Consequently the reasons for that separation had to be addressed, and they ranged from language to working conditions to the community character of the Jewish labor conflict.

First, the most obvious justification for separate immigrant organizations—and for the Jewish workers this was no exception—was language. Language represents the most basic level of immigrant difference from native workers while it also symbolizes the immigrant culture as a whole. Language was not only a barrier to a more complete understanding of workers' issues and to full participation in the French labor movement; it was also a factor isolating the Jewish worker.

In fact, the primary role of the (separate) Jewish labor movement, of the Intersektzione Byuro and of the Yiddish sections within the CGT, was said to be that of *agitatzie un propaganda*, of which *Der Yidisher Arbeter*, along with numerous Yiddish leaflets (sometimes stamped with the insignia of the CGT), was the crucial expression. Since French leaflets would be useless and the CGT clearly could not write Yiddish ones itself, it was up to the Jewish workers' sections to handle their own Yiddish media. *Agitatzie un propaganda* were seen to be *Der Yidisher Arbeter*'s and the sections' very raison d'être.

Justification of separateness based on language problems alone did not completely explain the immigrant situation, however. The Jewish workers did indeed need their own "propaganda" arm. This was a matter not only of form of expression (Yiddish), but also of content—the specific grievances resulting from the immigrants' role in the economy.

The "specific exploitation" of the Jewish worker, different from the conditions that obtained between French workers and their compatriot employers, was referred to on several occasions in *Der Yidisher Arbeter*. This specificity was in fact so apparent to the readers that it was rarely defined. When defined, these conditions were none other than those of the putting-out system: homework, piece wages, exigent demands of overtime and low pay.[38] For not only language but also the putting-out system isolated the immigrant worker and created unique conditions necessitating particular means of labor organizing. Economic concentration in immigrant neighborhoods and trades also served to isolate the immigrants from their French counterparts.

The result of this situation was a third interrelated factor that also impelled separate Jewish labor organization: the exploitation of the Jewish worker by the Jewish boss. Or, as Paul Pottier cried in astonishment in his article exploring the misery of the Marais, "Où est-elle la solidarité juive?"[39] The community character of the immigrant work context could not be allowed to mislead, as the Bonneffs warned in their examination of the Jewish cap-making trade. "Even though the workers and bosses are of the same origin and belong to the same race, the social conflicts are just as bitter, just as violent in this industry as in the others."[40] And for Yankel Mykhanowitzki, hero of the novel *Les Eaux mêlées*, the realization of the hypocrisy behind the boss's paternalistic offer of a cup of tea, before asking him to come in to work on Saturday, was a harsh disappointment. "These Jewish bosses whom he sought out in the belief that they would be more humane, more fraternal toward a compatriot, but they were the worst of the exploiters! They took advantage of the misery and ignorance of the poor immigrants in order to impose famine wages upon them. . . . A boss who was a compatriot and philanthropic, who spoke Yiddish and treated you as a comrade, offered you cups of tea and exploited you."[41]

The intracommunity nature of the immigrant conflicts largely defined the character of the Jewish labor movement. And it is for this reason, in addition to language and the particular character of domestic industry in which the immigrants were largely concen-

---

[38] Examples where the "specific exploitation" of the Jewish workers was mentioned but not defined are: *YA*, 1 May 1912, and 4 July 1914. For its definition see *YA*, 5 October 1912.

[39] Paul Pottier, "Essai sur le prolétariat juif en France," *Revue des revues*, 3d ser., 28 (March 1899): 486. See also ibid., pp. 491–92. Cf. Mlle. Schirmacher, *La Spécialisation du travail—Par nationalités à Paris* (Paris: Arthur Rousseau, 1908), p. 98.

[40] Leon and Maurice Bonneff, *La Vie tragique des travailleurs*, 3d ed. (Paris: Jules Rouff et Cie., 1908), p. 329.

[41] Roger Ikor, *Les Fils d'Avrom: Les eaux mêlées* (Paris: Albin Michel, 1955), pp. 154, 139.

trated, that a separate labor organization was necessary. In order to interpret and defend the Jewish immigrant workers' interests against their Jewish immigrant bosses, Yiddish-speaking union sections of the CGT were imperative.

Thus, although theoretical unity with the French working class never ceased to be the ideological basis of the Jewish labor movement in pre-1914 Paris, practical unity took the form of separate union sections. The specific nature of the Jewish immigrants' intra-community struggles and disappointment with certain attitudes of the French labor movement necessarily led to separate immigrant forms of organization. *Der Yidisher Arbeter* never ceased proclaiming the commonality of French and Jewish workers' interests, but it was difficult for the immigrants to work hand in hand with their French brothers when they lived in different neighborhoods, spoke different languages, and had different functions within the French economy.

For both immigrant oratories and Yiddish union sections a model of acculturation into a subset of French society existed, based on an ideology of solidarity; religious solidarity in one case, class solidarity in the other. Some immigrants turned expectantly to the Consistory while others turned just as hopefully to the CGT. The relative failure of those models of acculturation, in a first stage, manifests the immigrants' desire for (and the initial necessity of) continuity rather than change.

Both an external dynamic and an internal one are at work. The external dynamic was rejection by the immigrants of the proferred model of acculturation for negative reasons: due to disappointments in that model, due to disputes over institutional control or perhaps due to forms of rejection perceived from the very institutions into which the immigrants were supposed to integrate (anti-Semitism in the one case or even a type of Jewish anti-Semitism in the other). The internal dynamic leading to separate immigrant organizations has less to do with a negative rejection of French or French Jewish cultural forms than with the positive necessity for immigrants to express their own specific needs and their own cultural identity.

Finally, however, one could argue that even within this first stage of maintenance of cultural continuity rather than change, an important tendency toward integration into the host society may be discerned. Witness the move from oratories to a synagogue and the struggle for the betterment of conditions in the host country. In each case a certain amount of integration to French forms occurred, but it had to take place first in the immigrant language.

The acculturation process is a halting one, marked by desires for integration and refusals and constraints as to the actual possibility of learning a new culture. Acculturation is imbued with hopes and strewn with frustrations. Aspects of it are voluntary and others merely come with time. What must be particularly stressed, however, is that adaptation is a heterogeneous process. It is heterogeneous with regard to the cultural, political, and/or religious models chosen for integration. And it is heterogeneous to the extent that it is halting, marked by tendencies toward continuity just as well as toward change, toward separatism just as well as toward adaptation to the new environment. The question of acculturation of first-generation Eastern European Jews in France must be situated within the double context of French society and the French Jewish subset. And more particularly, it must be examined, as above, through those types of institutions close to the immigrants' and workers' preoccupations, institutions that offered the most immediate real possibilities for integration. Only then can we see how the ideology of integration is in fact replete with the contradictions of acculturation. Or, as Yankel Mykhanowitski complained about the migrant's lot, "a foreigner everywhere! I am no longer completely Jewish, yet I am not completely French. Stuck midstream." [42]

[42] Ibid., p. 299.

PART 3

LEFT AND RIGHT

WILLIAM B. COHEN

AND

IRWIN M. WALL

French Communism and the Jews

T HE FUNDAMENTAL EVENT in the history of French Jews was the Revolution of 1789, which brought about their emancipation, assuring them equal rights and making them into full citizens. It therefore was natural for Jews to identify their emancipation and indeed that of all mankind as coming from the left.

Revolutionaries and the left, however, did not always advance the cause of Jewish freedom. In the heady, unstable times surrounding revolutions, when law and order broke down, as in Alsace in 1791 and again in 1848, there were attacks on Jews. And from the left, mass popular antisemitism first arose; the left rather than the right was originally the home of antisemitic dogmas. In this connection the Utopian Charles Fourier might be mentioned, who saw in Jewish emancipation a sign of the dissolution of traditional communitarian society. For the emancipation of the Jews recognized people as individuals, and individualism, Fourier found, undermined traditional values. The emancipation allowed full and open economic competition, and if some Jews benefited financially from this situation, they became the symbol for Fourier of a society that valued profits above everything else. "The emancipation of the Jews," he declared, "[was] the origin of all the misfortunes of society." [1]

The Jews—although Protestants were as likely to occupy this

---

[1] George Lichtheim, "Socialism and the Jews," *Collected Essays* (New York, 1974), 417–21; Fourier, quoted in François Delpech, "L'Histoire des juifs en France de 1780 à 1840," Bernhard Blumenkranz and Albert Soboul, eds., *Les Juifs et la Révolution française* (Toulouse, 1976), 22.

position—became in the eyes of the left the symbol of the bankers or financiers. In a sense it was the medieval image of the Jew as usurer modernized. The 1813 edition of the *Dictionnaire de l'Académie Française* defined the word *Jew* with an exemplary phrase: "You are a real Jew, wanting to charge me 15% interest rate." Fourier's disciple Alphonse Toussenel, a popular writer on ornithology, known as the Balzac of the animal world, wrote vivid antisemitic prose in his two volume work, *Les Juifs, rois de l'Époque*; it first appeared in 1845 with a second edition in 1847, and it was republished in 1887 and 1888. The Jews personified all the terrors of capitalism and modernization for Toussenel and his readers. The Jews were a "horde of usurers and lepers, a burden on all mankind"; since the beginning of the ages Israel had been "the people of Satan, not the people of God: and the God of the Jewish people is no other than Satan."

Proudhon, that ambiguous figure hard to situate politically but belonging clearly to the left, wrote in his diary in December 1847: "The Jew is the enemy of the human race. One must send this race back to Asia or exterminate it." Commenting on Proudhon's antisemitism, George Lichtheim remarked, "On balance, Marx's characterization of Proudhon as a confused petit bourgeois seems to err on the side of charity. What he really represented was a fusion of backwoods barbarism with the mental chaos typical of the autodidact."[2] Syndicalism, which to some degree traced its intellectual pedigree back to Proudhon, also adopted a strong anti-Jewish bias. Emile Pataud, secretary of the electricians' union, in 1911 wrote that "Jew is synonymous with inhuman." Georges Sorel, sometimes regarded as the theorist of the movement, also went through an antisemitic phase.[3]

Within the more traditional forms of French Socialism, antisemitism also flourished; thus in 1883 a Socialist newspaper, *L'Antisémitique*, was founded, its subtitle "Les Juifs voilà l'ennemi." Benoît Malon, one of the leading independent Socialists in the 1880s, was a close friend of Drumont and opened the columns of his *Revue socialiste* to antisemites. When antisemitism had become also the tool of the right, as became clear in the early 1890s, the

[2] Lichtheim, 422–27; Edmund Silberner, "The Attitude of the Fourierist School towards the Jews," *Jewish Social Studies* henceforth *JSS* 9 (1947), 340–45.

[3] Edmund Silberner, "Anti-Jewish Trends in French Revolutionary Syndicalism," *JSS* 15 (1953), 198–202.

Socialists distanced themselves from antisemitism. The Dreyfus Affair was not for Socialists a Jewish issue. Jaurès was for revision of the case, but only after he had in his mind transformed Dreyfus into a proletarian, whose sufferings gave him an identity equivalent to the oppressed; Dreyfus only then became worthy of socialist solicitude. And, of course, it was the danger that antisemitism posed for French democracy and ultimately the achievement of social democracy that motivated Jaurès to join the Dreyfusard cause.[4]

The whole left was not antisemitic, and even in the earlier part of the nineteenth century there were examples of philosemitism; thus Saint-Simonianism was characterized by strong mystical elements of messianism, making the Jewish prophecy of the coming of a more perfect world its own. The ancient Hebrew prophets had, as it were, been foreseeing the new world the Saint-Simonians were trying to create. Some young Jews eagerly embraced the Saint-Simonian philosophy: among the master's closest disciples were Rodriguès, Halévy, the Pereire brothers, and Gustave d'Eichtal. In this small group of young men we see as if in a microcosm what the temptation of the left would be for later generations of young Jews wishing to break out of the circle of their immediate family. What was attractive in Saint-Simonianism was its universalist aspirations; it promised assimilation, the creation of a world in which all differences between peoples would be obliterated; thus at the end of the process that Saint-Simon foresaw there would be no Christians or Jews—all would be united in the worship of science and reason. D'Eichtal and Rodriguès tried to develop a syncretic religion between Christianity and Judaism, again a half-way house that would obliterate the separateness of Jewish existence.[5] Saint-Simonianism also exercised the attraction of dogma, a complex set of writings that need to be mastered and understood by the adepts, a tradition not foreign to young men raised in their homes and synagogues with Talmudic respect for the written word, used to

[4] Harvey Goldberg, "Jean Jaurès and the Jewish Question—The Evolution of a Position," *JSS* 20 (April, 1958), 67–94. The possibility that the visibly proletarian character of French Jewry, especially underscored by the immigration of poor Jews from Eastern Europe, helped undermine the image of the Jew as capitalist and exploiter is suggested in the interesting, as yet unpublished paper by Nancy Green, "Socialist Anti-semitism, Symptoms and Cure, Defense of a Bourgeois Jew and Discovery of the Jewish Proletariat."

[5] Barrie Ratcliffe, "Some Jewish Problems in the Early Careers of Emile and Isaac Pereire," *JSS* 34 (1972), 189–206; and "Crisis and Identity, Gustave d'Eichtal and Judaism in the Emancipation Period," *JSS* 37 (1975), 122–40.

the need to interpret texts and debate their deeper meaning, beyond the superficial first understanding that the text might impart. Saint-Simonians also were imbued with a special sense of mission and felt chosen by destiny to fulfill a historic role, helping to hasten the arrival of the end of historic times. The similarity of this vision with what had been Jewish self-understanding of being a chosen people is relatively clear.

Young men like Léon Blum, at the end of the century, saw in socialism a system of values that would ensure the spread of the sense of justice that the teachings of his home had assured him were also the bases of Judaism. Other prominent intellectual Jews also came rushing to the side of that proponent of Kantian ethics and fighter for the Dreyfusard cause, Jean Jaurès. Thus Marcel Mauss and Lévy-Brühl were among those helping sponsor the launching of Jaurès's paper L'Humanité. In Socialism they saw the possible fulfillment of universal aspirations; by expressing solidarity with the working class of the world they affirmed their belief in the equality of men; politically the proletariat became the exemplar of the outcast, a category Jews could identify with easily. Men were not different because of their birth; rather it was the environment, their situation, that mattered. That was the same message that Durkheim provided in his contribution to sociology.

French Jews on the whole identified with the Republic, which had provided them the full rights of Frenchmen. Politically Jews found themselves in the center or slightly to the left. As was the case until recently in the U.S., Jewry in France voted slightly to the left of the way their fellow citizens in similar socioeconomic environments voted; but on the whole they identified with groups to the right of Socialism. The small number of visible Jewish adepts of Saint-Simonianism, the activities of individuals like Gaston Crémieux, leader of the Marseille Commune—executed for his commitment to the revolutionary cause—and Léon Blum's role in the Socialist party, created the impression in some quarters of a Jewish community wedded to leftist causes. The real political opinions of native French Jewry were probably better reflected by the activities of men like Joseph Reinach, an Opportunist and aide to Gambetta, or later Georges Mandel, Clemenceau's right-hand man. Opportunism, and in later times a tamed form of Radicalism, represented the commitment both to the Republic and to the belief

that order and moderation in public affairs best ensured the interests of Jews.[6]

The immigration into France in the later nineteenth century and
then again after World War I of Jews from Eastern Europe, who
came from areas where socialism had flourished among Jews and
who essentially occupied positions of menial labor, divided the
Jewish community politically. A stolid bourgeois native Jewry identified with the various republican strains going rightward from the
Radical party; newer, migrant Jews reflecting the secular Yiddish-
Socialist tradition of the Bund, identified with the Socialist party,
Communism, and various strains of political millenarianism; their
offspring fed a leftist Jewish tradition in France that has persisted
to this day. The objective conditions of the 1930s, placing the anti-
semitic danger on the right, intensified this trend.[7]

In contrast, some right-wing tendencies manifested themselves
among native French Jews. The Consistory of Paris identified with
the nationalist right; a former general from World War I, Edmond
Bloch, created l'Union Patriotique des Français Israélites, which
grew to fifteen hundred members. In 1936, running as deputy
from the Pletzl, Bloch was only narrowly defeated, receiving sixty-
five hundred votes. This group argued that it was necessary to have
a strong Jewish showing on the right to give the lie to antisemitic
charges that Jews were anarchists, leftists, and revolutionaries.
One of the goals of the Union was to build a statue to Chief Rabbi
Abraham Bloch, who had lost his life in the trenches of World War
I while carrying a crucifix to a dying Catholic soldier. This story,
never authenticated, formed part of the mythology of the union.

In the synagogue of rue de la Victoire, the Croix de Feu held a
meeting blessed by Chief Rabbi Kaplan, chaplain during the war.
While manifestly antisemitic in Algeria, the organization was not
at the time perceived by the authorities in charge of the synagogue as antisemitic. There were indeed many Jews who seem to
have identified with the organization. Such manifestations were ex-

[6] Stephen Wilson, *Ideology and Experience—Antisemitism in France at the Time of the Dreyfus Affair* (Rutherford, N.J., 1982), 353; Laurent Bensaid, "Cent Ans de fidélité à la République," *Histoire* 3 (November 1979), 49–53.

[7] David H. Weinberg, *A Community on Trial—The Jews of Paris in the 1930s* (Chicago, 1977), 33, 113–15, 204; Paula Hyman, *From Dreyfus to Vichy—The Remaking of French Jewry, 1906–1939* (New York, 1979), 102–3, 107, 213.

treme examples of the extent to which Jews wished to assert their "Frenchness."[8]

Only within the Pletzl, essentially inhabited by immigrants, was Zionism a subject of debate. In part what made the inroads of Communism difficult there was its opposition to Zionism; later the Communists' attempt to create various front organizations had some initial successes, but when the members showed that they were equally torn between their Communism and Jewishness, the French Communist party (PCF) dissolved these organizations.

The weakness of democracy in the face of Fascism outside and inside France created empathy for the Communist cause among many Jewish intellectuals. The Communism of the late 1930s appeared to be different from that of the earlier period, which had been sectarian and antipatriotic. The Communism of the mid-1930s was patriotic, nationalist, and Jacobin; it supported the Popular Front, abandoned much of its revolutionary rhetoric, and instead emphasized the need to hold the line against Fascism. Under these circumstances it was natural for Jews to be attracted to Communism.

The defeat of France in 1940, the German occupation, and Vichy were brutal shocks to all Frenchmen, but to Jews particularly. The French sociologist Georges Friedmann has movingly described his life until 1940.

I was until then one of those whom practicing Jews would have called "marginal" or "peripheral" Jews. Born in Paris in a family that no longer practiced traditional Judaism . . . that was profoundly integrated into France, to its life style, its culture, to a group of friends and colleagues, none of whom asked me questions about my "ethnic" origins, or my religious beliefs. I had never, although marked as a Jew by my name, suffered from anti-semitism, I had never, even in school, felt discriminated against in French society.

And then in October 1940 "I received a shock in discovering the shattering importance that being labelled Jewish might have for me. I have kept the document issued by the secretariat of public instruction of Vichy informing me that henceforth I was subject to special laws."

While deprived of his full citizenship rights, Friedmann was de-

[8] Ibid, p. 226; Weinberg, *A Community*, pp. 77–82; Pierre Aubéry, *Milieux juifs de la France contemporaine* (Paris, 1957), 182–91.

termined to prove the veracity of a slogan he would repeat to himself: "Civis gallicus sum"—"I am a French citizen." He joined the Resistance under the nom de guerre Gaston Fromentin and used other pseudonyms with the same initials; joining in the Resistance group "made me rediscover a community in which all discrimination was swept away"; he came to know "the unforgettable experience of comradeship side by side with men and women from many provinces and professions, who came together overcoming their differences."[9]

Annie Kriegel at the age of 16 joined a Communist youth resistance group. Her family had been French for centuries, tracing its ancestry to Alsace. She was a fine student with a promising future, who suddenly found her plans for study and career stopped short by the antisemitic laws of Vichy. The Republic in which her family had believed since 1871 had betrayed Kriegel and her family. She now felt deprived of a fatherland; by joining the Communist resistance the young girl gave herself a new fatherland and assumed an identity that transcended national boundaries. She now could identify with all the suffering peoples of the world; the cause of the proletariat and of the Jews were at one. The USSR incarnated the hopes of both groups; its victory over Fascism would mean the liberation of both the workers and the Jews. As Kriegel was later to put it in an interview, "all those people who did not want us to be French, well, we had become stronger than they, we had compatriots all the way to Vladivostok!"[10]

While collaboration with Vichy was obviously not a possible option for Jews (although some tried it), it is nevertheless striking how large the Jewish participation in the Resistance movement was; it is estimated that it was as high as 15 to 20 percent of the entire Resistance. (The Jewish population made up 0.5 percent of the population.) Three out of the six founders of Libération in 1941 were Jews and so was the secretary general of Combat; in Clermont-Ferrand and Limoges the organization was headed by the great historian Marc Bloch. Many Jews joined Communist organizations, which were especially adept at winning over immigrants; especially important was the Main d'Oeuvre Immigrée (MOI), which suffered very high casualties during the Resistance.

[9] Georges Friedmann, *Fin du peuple juif?* (Paris, 1965), 7–9.
[10] André Harris and Alain Sédouy, *Juifs et français* (Paris, 1979), 140.

In those desperate years when being Jewish often meant death, Communism held up the possibility of life. It lent dignity and purpose to Jews while giving them a sense of community and welcoming them into its subculture. And for the long run Communism held out the hope for a solution by assimilation of what was called the Jewish problem; simply put, there would be no Jews in the future Socialist order. For Communism claimed not to recognize such differences between peoples; there were only class differences. Jews were to lose their particularity. The universalism of Judaism was at one with the universalist claims of Communism. And it appeared that belonging did not mean apostasy: one could enter as a Jew and join a universal cause in which one's Jewishness was not a problem—rather, it would become irrelevant with the success of world Communism. Pierre Abraham found in Communism the lifting of his "Jewish burden." André Wurmser thought the glorious goal of Communism to be the obliteration of all specificity as far as Jewish existence was concerned. So confident of this was Wurmser that he disdained to change his name.[11]

Once the war was over, Jews who had selflessly joined in the struggle were to find that their cause was not necessarily that of the Communist party. Thus the party celebrated those who had died fighting Fascism, but it did not pay homage to the deported Jewish civilians who had been gassed in the death camps. And in celebrating its heroes who had died with rifles at their side, the party sometimes forgot to mention that they were also Jews. The party failed to recognize the heroic achievements of the fighters in MOI who had fought and died to free French soil from Nazi occupation; to the party, these Jews were not Frenchmen; rather, they were described as Rumanians, Poles, Russians, or whatever their nationality of origin. The party further seemed embarrassed to celebrate men with foreign-sounding names such as Trzebucki or Wolf Burstin. To tap the nationalist strain it was important not to seem to be a party that had members with such names.[12]

In the liberation era the PCF's nationalism often appeared to have antisemitic overtones. In denouncing the banks and trusts,

[11] Pierre Abraham, "Mon Père, Juif," Europe (September 1953). Cited with the Wurmser remark by Aubèry, Milieux juifs, 192.

[12] Annie Kriegel, "Vérité historique et mensonges politiques," Commentaire 12 (Winter 1980–81), 551–58; Kriegel in interview with Harris and Sédouy, Juifs et français, p. 141; Kriegel, Communismes au miroir français (Paris, 1974), 190.

party propaganda occasionally underlined their Protestant and Jewish character, thus reviving an early tradition of the left. In replying to Léon Blum's characterization of the PCF as "un parti nationaliste étranger," Benoît Franchon, leader of the Confédération Générale du Travail (CGT), did not hesitate to point out that the PCF's leadership, at least, had its roots in the national soil.[13] In *La Libération Trahie*, Communist journalist Pierre Hervé condemned the confusion between "internationalism and cosmopolitanism in bourgeois Jewish circles prominent both in high finance and the politics of Socialism." To have one's roots in one's country, its history and its present and future aspirations, was the condition of efficacious political action for Hervé. "It is striking to note how the Jewish bourgeois intellectual element has become preponderant in the leadership of the SFIO," Hervé wrote, accusing the high cadres of the Socialist party of turning it into a "parti de l'intelligencia juive." Noting the ties of Jewish financiers to their Anglo-Saxon compatriots, Hervé raised the specter of a new Fascism, no less, spearheaded by "Jewish industrialists unable to console themselves that Nazi antisemitism prevented them from being at Vichy."[14]

Hervé would again become the spokesman of vitriolic antisemitic stereotypes during the 1952 hysteria over Zionism. Although on the latter occasion he claimed that Jacques Duclos ordered him to write the offensive articles, it is always important to distinguish the antisemitic expression of individual Communists from what may or may not have reflected the actual party line. Hervé's fall from grace during the Marty affair and his apostasy in 1956 bear noting in this regard.

In the interval between the Liberation and the 1952 hysteria the PCF, following Soviet foreign policy, rallied to the defense of the nascent State of Israel in its struggle against British and Arab "imperialism." Noting Ernest Bevin's alleged statement in the House of Commons that "there are no Arabs in this assembly," *L'Humanité* accused the British foreign secretary of questioning the right of Jews to sit there. Antisemitism and anticommunism go together, Communist journalist Pierre Courtade warned.[15] On 19 May 1948 the PCF warmly greeted the birth of the State of

[13] *Cahiers du Communisme* 10 (August 1945), 39. Article by F. Bonte.
[14] Pierre Hervé, *La Libération trahie* (Paris, 1945), 180–82, 194.
[15] *L'Humanité*, 27 and 30 April, 15–19 May 1948.

Israel and called upon the French government to recognize it. The CGT sent official greetings to the Histadrut (the Israeli labor federation), while the Communists protested the foot-dragging of the French government in recognizing the new state. Recalling the concentration camps and the recent suffering of the Jews, Pierre Courtade wrote that it was a shame and dishonor for France to delay recognition of Israel. In its theoretical justification of this position, *Cahiers du Communisme* conceded that Zionism was a "reactionary and chauvinistic" ideology.[16] But the British had incited racial hatred in Palestine, making the preferred binational state an impossibility. Partition, and the creation of a Jewish state, was the only solution. Responding to those comrades who recalled the PCF's support of Arab resistance to Zionism in the Hebron massacres of 1929 and the Palestinian Arab insurrection of 1936, Florimond Bonte pointed out that in the 1948 context the Israelis were engaged in a struggle for national independence; the Haganah must be considered comrades-in-arms of the Chinese Communists, the Vietminh, the Greek partisans, and the Spanish republicans, all engaged in just wars of national independence against British and U.S.-sponsored imperialism.

Throughout its history the PCF attitude toward the Jews continued to manifest itself in four different, often contradictory and ambiguous ways. The PCF rejected any charge of antisemitism and often campaigned against it, noting that antisemitism was outlawed in Socialist countries while officially tolerated and unofficially encouraged in the capitalist West. Communists had no difficulty distinguishing, on the other hand, between antisemitism and anti-Zionism. Despite the momentary warm support for Israel in 1948, and the continued insistence thereafter on its right to exist, the PCF condemned Zionism as a reactionary, chauvinistic ideology, and after the early 1950s its support for the Arab side in the Middle East conflict became unflagging. In its propaganda the PCF often reverted to overtones of the early nineteenth-century history of antisemitism on the French left, although it should be noted that this was occasionally on an unconscious level and most often may be seen as rather the style of individual Communists rather than of the leadership as a whole. Thus it may be no accident that Pierre Hervé again appeared as the central figure when

[16] *Cahiers du Communisme*, July 1948, especially the article by F. Bonte, and September 1948.

the PCF's antisemitism became overt in 1952–53. Finally there remained the question of how the PCF would deal with its own large Jewish constituency. On the one hand the PCF was ethnically blind, and many Jewish names have figured prominently in party leadership positions, while the party avidly made use of the talent of individual Jewish intellectuals and journalists. Yet it remains striking that not a single Jew was to be found on the Political Bureau during the Stalinist era, and when Jews did accede to high positions beginning in the 1960s alarm was occasionally expressed about their numbers. Always particularly prominent among party intellectuals, Jews perhaps inevitably became the occasional targets of the PCF leadership's overt *ouvrierism* and inherent distrust of the bourgeoisie. Finally it may be asked whether the unusually large number of Jewish names among the many Communist dissidents of 1978 was not the cause of some renewed anti-Jewish feeling, and whether it is to be taken as a sign that the Jewish romance with Communism is finally ending, notwithstanding the continued prominence of figures such as Fiterman and Krasucki in the party leadership.

In no case did the PCF's contradictory attitudes on the Jewish question manifest themselves so clearly as in the Rosenberg and Slansky affairs. To be sure, antisemitic overtones continued through the late 1940s and early 1950s in PCF propaganda. Thus *L'Humanité*'s continued reference to Schuman-Mayer-Moch in various ministries, names that "do not smell either of Beauce or Berry"; "we, Communists," Political Bureau member Arthur Ramette wrote in 1948, "have only genuine French names." As for Léon Blum, always a target since the blatantly antisemitic diatribe "Léon Blum tel qu'il est," written in Moscow and published under Thorez's name in 1939, Gaston Monmousseau did not hesitate to remind his readers in 1948 that "Blum, in Yiddish, means flower." [17]

The PCF's, and by extension world communism's preoccupation with the Rosenberg case was clearly a means of deflecting criticism away from the antisemitic aspects of the November 1952 Slansky trial in Czechoslovakia and then the absurd "Doctors plot" in the USSR in January 1953. [18] French readers were intro-

---

[17] Cited in Gideon Haganov, *Le Communisme et les juifs* (Paris, 1951).

[18] The Rosenberg case became a bigger political issue in France in some ways than in the United States. See Ronald Radosh and Joyce Milton, *The Rosenberg File: A Search for the Truth* (New York, 1983), 348–50.

duced to the Rosenberg case on 14 November 1952 in a *L'Human-ité* article by the American author Howard Fast; a week later the Slansky trial opened. The innocence of the Rosenbergs was at once contrasted to the "obvious" guilt of the Slansky group, and *L'Humanité* rejected the death penalty as a cruel barbarism in the one case while advocating it freely in the other.[19] The two cases became a means of educating Communists in the differences between anti-semitism and anti-Zionism. The "atmosphere of antisemitism" had convicted the Rosenbergs in the United States, while the Slansky case revealed the machinations of Israeli Zionist espionage in the interests of U.S. imperialism against "the enemy of antisemitism," the USSR. "The Rosenbergs are Jews," Jacques Duclos proclaimed loudly at a mass meeting on their behalf on 9 December, but neither Mayer, Moch, or Rosenfeld (three Socialists with visibly Jewish names), while busily protesting the fate of the traitor Slansky, were concerned with the fate of these real martyrs in the United States.

With the condemnation of Slansky *L'Humanité*'s interest in the Rosenbergs lessened for a period, only to resume in January 1953 with the "unmasking" of the criminal doctors' plot in the USSR. The doctors, largely Jewish, and all agents of U.S. secret services, Zionism, and the American Jewish Joint Distribution Committee, had murdered the beloved Soviet leader Zhdanov, according to *L'Humanité*, and were now engaged in a plot to kill Stalin and the rest of the Soviet leadership.[20] With the doctors' plot, under the impulse of Soviet example, PCF indulgence in antisemitic rhetoric reached a historic high. Roger Garaudy compared the Soviet doctors to those in Nazi concentration camps, many of whom, he charged, had also been Jews and nevertheless carried on their cruel experiments on their coreligionists. (Long after his exit from the PCF in 1970 Garaudy was still a vehement critic of Israel and regarded as an antisemite by many French Jews.) Once again it fell to Pierre Hervé to paint, in the most lurid details, the picture of an international Jewish conspiracy against Soviet power that began with Dora Kaplan's attempt on the life of Lenin in 1918, was carried on through the machinations of Trotsky and the participation of Jewish financiers in the rise of Hitler, and culminated in the at-

---

[19] *L'Humanité*, 14, 23, 25, 27, and 28 November 1952.
[20] Ibid, 14–17 January 1953.

tempts on the lives of Soviet leaders.[21] Hervé's rhetoric was notable for its indiscriminate use of the term *Judaism* interchangeably with *Zionism* despite disclaimers of antisemitic intent. Thus, Hervé wrote, charges of antisemitism were a diversion; the U.S. State Department "had made of Judaism [not Zionism] a banner of militarism" engaging in sabotage, murder, conspiracy, and espionage. The attack on Jews as a religious and ethnic group was also clear in Hervé's description of Israel as a petty bourgeois, parasitic, and colonialist warfare state without an indigenous Jewish working class.

The hysteria in early 1953 was undoubtedly compounded by the apparently enforced absence of Thorez and an internal struggle for power within the PCF leadership paralleling that believed to be under way in the USSR in the last months before Stalin's death.[22] Thorez remained silent during the affair. It is known that several of the accused doctors had treated him and he regarded them as friends. Internally the escalation of PCF rhetoric took its toll on the party's Jewish cadres. PCF doctors, the vast majority of whom were Jews, were mobilized and made to sign declarations of support for the Soviet leadership and denunciations of the "white-coated murderers." Jewish intellectuals like Annie Besse (Kriegel) were mobilized to defend the PCF from the charge of antisemitism, condemn Israel, and denounce the phantom of international Zionist conspiracy.[23] Jewish members in the PCF apparatus found their advancement blocked; and in one case a prominent figure in the women's movement was told to break her engagement to a Jewish Communist intellectual if she expected further promotion. A curious note was the appearance of a didactic "socialist-realist" novel by Bertrand Fontenelle entitled "M. Goldberg aimait Minet," in which the Jewish hero, Robert, turns away from Zionism as Fascism and struggles against exploitative Jewish capitalism to find salvation in the party and a common effort with non-Jews to build a better society.[24]

[21] Hervé's articles appeared in *Ce Soir*, 14 January–6 February 1953.

[22] See Irwin M. Wall, *French Communism in the Era of Stalin* (Westport, Conn., 1984) for a fuller discussion of these issues.

[23] See Pierre Daix, *J'ai cru au matin* (Paris, 1976), 315–29. Annie Besse also wrote that the accused in the Slansky case, by virtue of their treason, had stripped themselves of their Czech nationality, leaving them no defining quality except their Jewishness. *Cahiers du Communisme*, February 1953.

[24] Interview with Blanchette Gillet; Bertrand Fontenelle, *M. Goldberg aimait Minet* (Paris, 1952).

A Jewish undercurrent may have been present as well in the exclusion of the noted heroes of the Spanish Civil War and the Resistance, André Marty and Charles Tillon, by the PCF while the Slansky and Rosenberg cases were in full swing. Marty had close ties to the Curiels, Egyptian Jewish Communists and pro-Titoists according to some sources. Curiously, a number of Egyptian Jews were excluded from the PCF in 1955–56 when PCF policy became staunchly pro-Nasser.[25] Marty's brother-in-law, a Jew named Georges Beyer, hosted the alleged factional meeting between Marty and Tillon that led to the two leaders' exclusion. Beyer, implicated in a mysterious betrayal of PCF comrades during the Resistance, was forced to testify against Marty in the latter's "trial," while Marty's wife was also turned against him. Tillon had close ties to Arthur London, Slansky's Jewish codefendant, former Czech foreign affairs minister, and also an important figure in the French resistance. Finally Political Bureau member Raymond Guyot, who played an important role in the prosecution of Marty and Tillon, was the brother-in-law of Lise London, Arthur London's wife. Guyot bitterly denounced Tillon, London, and Slansky in a successful effort to save his own skin.[26]

The Jewish question retreated from the limelight after the return of Thorez in 1953, not really to emerge again in any other guise than "anti-Zionism" until the Darquier de Pellepoix affair in 1978, and then in radically different circumstances. There was never any public reference to Mendès France's Jewishness when the party supported him in 1954, and if he, like Blum, later became the acerbic target of PCF hostility, it was because he refused to count Communist votes in his majority in 1954, thus delivering the ultimate insult to PCF patriotism. Still, Laurent Casanova was heard to remark privately of Mendès France that "la France ce n'est quand même pas ce petit juif marchand de tapis," and a similar remark has been attributed to Duclos.[27] The PCF officially remained blind to the ethnicity of its members, and some Jewish Communists succeeded in forgetting their troubling Jewish identi-

---

[25] Gabriel Enkiri, *Militant de base* (Paris, 1971), 50. André Marty, *L'Affaire Marty* (Paris, 1955).

[26] On the Marty affair see Wall, *French Communism*, and Philippe Robrieux, *Histoire intérieure du Parti Communiste*, vol. 2, 1945–1972 (Paris, 1981), 297–353.

[27] Jean Recanati, *Un Gentil Stalinien* (Paris, 1980), 19.

ties in the general messianic enthusiasm. The wartime and postwar influx of Jews meanwhile moved up in PCF responsibilities, although not without some expression of concern by the leadership. When Gary Cohn-Bendit, older brother of Daniel of May 1968 fame, became overly zealous in struggling against the Algerian War, he was accused of lacking national roots and sensibilities in elevating Algeria above the struggle against German rearmament. A classic "Catch-22" situation, since had the policy of the party been the reverse and Cohn-Bendit too preoccupied with Germany instead of Algeria, he undoubtedly would have had his dissidence explained on precisely the same grounds. There was no evidence of any Jewish aspect to the Servin-Casanova affair of 1960–61; only one of the prominent dissidents on that occasion, Maurice Kriegel-Valrimont, was Jewish. Yet the suspicion of Jewish party members as potential troublemakers remained; Philippe Robrieux, a non-Jew, leader of the Communist students' organization, and a sympathizer of Servin and Casanova, was told there were too many Jews in the leadership of the organization. Robrieux protested, but to no avail.[28]

Periodic remarks with antisemitic overtones continued to surface in PCF propaganda into the Marchais era. There was Frachon's crude depiction of the Rothschilds at the wailing wall in the aftermath of the June 1967 war: "The presence of certain personalities of high finance conferred on the event another meaning than religious fervor. . . . The spectacle made one think that, as in Faust, it was the Devil who was leading the ball."[29] Frachon, an anarcho-syndicalist in his youth before World War I, clearly echoed a venerable tradition of antisemitism on the left. Similarly, in the 1967 war and then again in Jacques Duclos's campaign for the presidency, PCF propagandists suggested that France was faced with opting for either the national interest, or on the other hand, "Rothschild and Dassault."

Of all these manifestations of insensitivity, George Marchais' reference to Daniel Cohn-Bendit as a "German anarchist" during the May 1968 upheaval has precipitated the most comment. The characterization of Cohn-Bendit as a Jew was only implied, but

[28] Philippe Robrieux, *Notre Génération communiste* (Paris, 1977), 63
[29] *l'Humanité*, 24 May 1967.

French students were certainly alive to the issue when they adopted the slogan: "Nous sommes tous des juifs allemands."[30]

Citing this evidence, Bernard-Henri Lévy has accused the PCF of being a right-wing, nationalist, racist, and antisemitic party in his assault on the French intellectual tradition entitled *L'Idéologie française*.[31] Lévy's argument is vastly exaggerated. Even taking account of the vitriolic outburst against "le chacal Blum" in 1940 and the PCF's virtual collaboration with the German occupation prior to the Nazi invasion of the USSR in June 1941, it remains to be demonstrated that antisemitism was anything more than a minor element of PCF propaganda, periodically indulged in by individual Communists and, on occasion, the leadership under Soviet prodding. Given the voluminous daily outpouring of Communist propaganda in France, the Jewish question is most conspicuous by its relative absence—it is anything but central to the contemporary party's ideological scheme of things. That this is so became clear when Lévy offhandedly accused the PCF of antisemitism during the Darquier de Pellepoix affair in 1978.

The discovery that Vichy's commissioner of Jewish affairs was alive and well in Spain touched off a general discussion in the French press of which Lévy's reference to Marchais was a distinctly minor part. Lévy termed antisemitism a "discrete and familiar ghost prowling about in a certain declaration of Georges Marchais, a comment of Michel Droit, a cover of *Charlie-Hebdo*, or the doubtful humor of a daily of the extreme left."[32] This was a far cry from *L'Idéologie française*, yet Marchais jumped to reply, accusing Lévy of the "lowest possible insult," and of challenging "that which makes up the most profound element of my being [*ce qui constitue mon être le plus profond*]." Marchais, clearly on the defensive because of the repeated controversy over the charge that he was a volunteer worker in Germany during World War II rather than a deportee, challenged Lévy to find a single statement ever made by Marchais that was even tinged with antisemitism. Indeed, Marchais noted, Jews were to be found at every level in the PCF, and all could so testify, "except one: my best friend—Jean Kanapa— whom I have just lost and whom you covered with insults during

[30] *L'Humanité*, 17 June 1967, 17 May 1969. Marchais's attack on Cohn-Bendit was on 3 May 1968.

[31] Paris, 1981.

[32] *Le Matin*, 1 November 1978.

his whole life and even beyond to his death."[33] While Lévy listed the various antisemitic incidents that the PCF had been involved in, he was able to attribute only one to Marchais personally, his "German anarchists" quotation of ten years earlier. *L'Humanité* published a whole barrage of letters from indignant Jewish Communists who rallied to the support of their insulted leader.

Marchais's sensitivity to the charge of antisemitism could well have been a reflection of the PCF's crisis in the aftermath of the March 1978 elections. His very possibly sincere reference to the departed Jean Kanapa highlights the complexity of the Jewish question as it relates to the PCF in the recent period. Several observers attributed the PCF's apparent lack of homogeneity and its heterodoxy in the 1970s to the ferment of predominantly Jewish intellectuals. *Le Monde* reported that the Soviets had expressed dissatisfaction with the large number of Jews in the PCF leadership; Annie Kriegel suggested a tie-in between the Jewish presence and the Eurocommunist phase of the PCF from 1976 to 1979, during which the party felt a particular need for Jewish journalists and technicians.[34] It is more likely that the apparent Jewish ubiquitousness in the 1970s represented simply the maturing of the unusually large influx of the offspring of Bundist immigrants of the interwar period who were acculturated to the Communist countersociety or subculture in their youth. Jews were prominent throughout the left in the student movement of the 1960s both in France and in America as well, prompting an American political scientist to suggest the absurd thesis of a "Portnoy's Complaint" syndrome as the motive for American rebellion. Annie Kriegel remarked that the split between Trotskyites and Maoists in France seemed at times to boil down to a feud between Ashkenazim and Sephardim.[35] Within the PCF the fact remains that the principal animator of the party's flirtation with Eurocommunism was the ex-Stalinist Jewish intellectual Jean Kanapa, upon whom Marchais had come to rely, and who functioned very much as an éminence grise in the party, while the leading PCF intellectual historian, Jean Elleinstein, also of Polish Jewish origins, for a time appeared to be for Marchais what Aragon

---

[33] *L'Humanité*, 3 November 1978. Protests continued throughout the month.

[34] Annie Kriegel in Harris and Sédouy, *Juifs et français*, 152. Alleged Soviet objections to PCF Jews were referred to by many informed observers inside and outside the party in this period.

[35] Annie Kriegel, *Communismes au miroir français* (Paris, 1974), 222.

had been for Thorez and Garaudy for Waldeck Rochet: a friend, adornment, and bridge to the world of culture. While Kanapa charted the party's strategic independence of Russia, Elleinstein provided the membership with a new "realistic" view of the USSR's past. And perhaps not fortuitously, Kanapa's death and Elleinstein's dissidence marked the return of the PCF to the Stalinist fold.

The Jewish presence among the disaffected Communists prompts questions about whether the century's Jewish romance with Communism and the left in general might not be coming to an end. So many of the prominent dissidents were Jews that Louis Althusser, who comes from a Catholic family, was suspected by many party members of being Jewish when he joined the bandwagon of protesters. A more notable aspect of the dissidence is the theme of rediscovered Jewish roots that appears periodically in the literature along with revulsion against antisemitism. Thus Elleinstein has become preoccupied with Soviet Jewry, evolved to a rather sympathetic identification with Israel, and accused the Soviets of propaganda in the tradition of Goebbels.[36] Henri Fiszbin, founder of the dissident group Rencontres Communistes, reflects on his Jewish past in Belleville; Guy Konopnicki writes ironically of the left-wing attraction of his immigrant parents. Antoine Spire, grandson of the famous Jewish poet André Spire, himself the son of a convert to Catholicism, rediscovers Jewish values; and Maurice Goldring reacts viscerally to Soviet antisemitism.[37] Other prominent Communist dissidents such as Michel Barak and Jacques Fremontier have declined to comment on specific Jewish questions other than, in the case of Fremontier, to deny their relevance. But the Jewish complexion of much of the dissidence remains, and Elleinstein is convinced it has given rise to a new subcurrent of antisemitism within the party's Stalinist faction.[38]

The 1978 elections were also noteworthy in that the PCF tried overtly for the first time to appeal to the Jewish vote. Candidates such as Claude Klein and Henri Fiszbin ran in the third, fourth, and nineteenth *arrondissements*, and Communists like Henri Malberg and Fremontier were asked to make public appeals for Jewish sup-

[36] *Le Monde*, 6 October 1978.
[37] Henri Fiszbin, *Les Bouches s'ouvrent* (Paris, 1980), 27, Guy Konopnicki, *Vive le centenaire du PCF* (Paris, 1979), Antoine Spire, *Profession permanent* (Paris, 1980), Maurice Goldring, *L'Accident* (Paris, 1978).
[38] See the comments by Fremontier and Elleinstein in *Juifs et Français*.

port. Fremontier, unaware that his Jewish origins had ever previously been noted by the party leadership, indignantly refused, and asked why Political Bureau member (and currently minister of transportation) Charles Fiterman did not do the honors instead. Apparently at Fiterman's exalted level a parochial Jewish appeal was considered inappropriate. Sensitivity to Jewish concerns in Paris may have been present in the choice of Malberg to replace Fiszbin as head of the Paris federation of the PCF after Fiszbin fell into disgrace. The PCF leadership also conspicuously fêted the editors of the Paris Yiddish Communist newspaper, *Naie Presse*, on the occasion of its forty-fifth anniversary in 1979.

In any event the PCF would seem to have evolved to a recognition of the pluralistic nature of contemporary French society and an acceptance of a continued Jewish religious and cultural presence, toward which the party has appeared to make overtures even as it adheres to its staunchly anti-Zionist line. The frequent appearance of the Israeli Communist party in joint declarations and appearances with the PCF may be designed to ameliorate the party's image with the French Jewish vote. Etienne Fajon's remarkable article in *Cahiers du Communisme* in May 1979 gave a theoretical basis to the PCF's attitude to the Jewish question. This was significant since Fajon was a Political Bureau member of many years' standing and a principal actor in many of the worst excesses of the PCF's Stalinist past. Complaining that a certain Jewish anti-Communist press "had deformed PCF policies toward Jews and Judaism," Fajon asserted the neutrality of Communism with regard to Jewish religious practice, its acceptance of a Jewish community and culture nourished by a shared historical destiny shaped by persecution, in particular the Holocaust, and the PCF's recognition of the legitimacy of Jewish fears concerning the rebirth of antisemitism.[39] Deploring antisemitism as a "secular monstrosity of which it is incredible that we should have to speak close to the year 2,000," Fajon asserted the PCF's solidarity with Jews in the struggle against antisemitism while lauding the contribution of Jews to modern culture. The PCF's existence was based on the doctrine of Marx, a Jew, Fajon noted, while prominent Jewish Communists like Haim Cukiermann, Charles Fiterman, and Henri Krasucki

[39] Etienne Fajon, "Les Communistes et la population juive," *Cahiers du Communisme*, May 1979.

were targets of the right-wing press. Applauding the showing of the American film *Holocaust* on French TV (despite its "lack of class analysis"), Fajon asserted the pluralistic and democratic aims of the contemporary PCF and hoped for the continued full expression of Jewish culture and self-expression as a component of the richness and diversity of the contemporary French scene.

The PCF continues to balance its solidarity with Jews against persecution and its acceptance of Jews in prominent positions in its leadership with a staunchly pro-Palestinian foreign policy and regular condemnation of Israeli aggression. The party sent a small delegation to participate in a demonstration in favor of Anatoly Shcharansky in 1978, and a much larger one to join in the shared French revulsion after the synagogue bombing at the rue Copernic in September 1981. A year later, however, there was another attack with several dead in the heart of the Jewish quarter on the rue des Rosiers. This time the PCF was not as forthcoming in condemning the attack, instead snidely suggesting that the terrorism was intended as "a diversion" from Israel's invasion of Lebanon; by indirection the Party echoed East European news stories that the rue des Rosiers operation had been mounted by the Israeli secret service.[40]

It is arguable that to the extent that the PCF indulges in anti-Zionist propaganda it also contributes to antisemitism; to deny to the Jews alone an otherwise universally recognized principle of national self-determination clearly is discriminatory, while to advocate the elimination of Israel as a Jewish state is certainly to wish a disaster upon collective Jewish interests. But the PCF, despite its apparent obsession with the Arab-Israel issue, does not define its anti-Zionism in this way. For the French Communists Zionism is the doctrine that all Jews must one day come to live in Israel, with the corollaries that Jews of the Diaspora may not assimilate into the national societies in which they reside, and that Israel must expand territorially to accommodate world Jewish emigration.[41] The PCF asserts that it supports a peaceful Israel within the pre-1967 frontiers, and, as noted, it makes repeated overtures to the Israeli left. Within the parameters of the PCF's definition

[40] *L'Humanité*, 10 August 1982; statement by J. C. Gayssot, member of the Political Bureau, *Le Matin*, 11 August 1982.

[41] *L'Humanité*, 20 June 1967. The article in question asserts that Communists support Israelis and Arabs against the imperialist policies of Israeli leaders, but also that "Judaism is a religion, not a nationality or race."

one should perhaps accept the party's distinction between anti-Zionism and antisemitism, which has been intellectually satisfying for a generation of Jewish Communists. On the other hand it should be noted that with the new sectarian phase the party entered following the 1978 elections, which has continued to characterize the party even as it participates in the government under François Mitterrand, French Communists have become increasingly reluctant to criticize antisemitism in the USSR or otherwise discredit what they regard as the "globally positive balance-sheet" of the Socialist countries. And *Israel* and *Zionism* in party propaganda often appear to have become symbols of imperialism in precisely the same way that *Jew* meant capitalist to the early nineteenth-century left.

Indeed, some commentators have seen a revival of antisemitism in the violence of language used by the left in denouncing Israel, especially after Israel's invasion of Lebanon in 1982. Why is the left so "little preoccupied with other grave world problems," Jacques Givet asked in 1968, "for example Soviet Jewry; why is the left concentrating on the fate of Palestinian refugees while ignoring refugees in other parts of the world?" The French Jewish philosopher Alain Finkielkraut sees in the language of the left, especially the Communists who frequently depict Israeli actions as Nazi-like, a conscious attempt to obliterate the memory and meaning of the Holocaust.[42] For much of the left a Palestinian victory would symbolize the victory of the Third World and all revolutionary forces; the Palestinians are the symbolic vanguard of revolution, and Israel is painted in demonic colors as the symbol of world imperialism. Once depicted as capitalists by the left, the Jews are now, Bernard-Henri Lévy complains, being ostracized and typed as "fascists."[43]

The PCF has thus far been able to separate the Israel-Zionist issue from any concern with the Jewish origins of some of its members. Despite rumors that, as a Jew, Krasucki could never succeed to the leadership of the CGT, he did when Georges Séguy retired; and the choice of Fiterman as the party's ranking minister in the Mitterrand government lends a certain plausibility to the similar rumor that Fiterman is a candidate to replace Georges Marchais. Yet the Jewish romance with Communism is ending; the appear-

---

[42] Jacques Givet, *La Gauche contre Israël* (Paris, 1968); Alain Finkielkraut, interview in *Nouvelles littéraires*, 30 September 1982.

[43] Bernard-Henri Lévy, "Le Liban à Paris," *Le Matin*, 16 June 1982.

ance in French translation of the memoirs of Moshe Zalcman, a Yiddish-speaking veteran of the PCF's foreign section and Stalin's labor camps, gives a good overview of the reasons for the romance and its bitter end.[44] A Jewish presence on the left lingers, to be sure, and the history of the left, Communism included, remains marked by its encounter with Jewish culture. But the specific historical circumstances that nourished the Jewish fertilization of the left no longer obtain. On the other hand the ability of the left to accept Jewish specificity and tolerate Jewish cultural and religious expression remains a test of its ability to guarantee freedom when it comes to power. In this sense the Jews, as a litmus test of freedom, continue to perform a secular version of their calling as a "chosen people." And to the extent that the PCF has seriously evolved toward recognition and support of Jewish cultural expression, we may conclude that the party has really changed.

[44] Moshe Zalcman, *La Véridique histoire de Moshe, ouvrier juif et communiste au temps de Staline* (Paris, 1977).

ZEEV STERNHELL

The Roots of Popular Anti-Semitism
in the Third Republic

A S A POLITICAL FORCE, popular anti-Semitism dates unquestionably from Boulangism, for it was then that the first nationalistic Socialists discovered its mobilizing power and its revolutionary force. Rochefort, Granger, Ernest Roche, Barrès, Francis
Laur, the disciples of Proudhon and Toussenel, as well as certain
Blanquists and Communards, all played a crucial role in accredit-
ing the notion that anti-Semitism was a progressive and nonconformist ideology, an ingredient in the revolt against the established
order, in short, one of the facets of Socialism. Thus anti-Semitism
was primarily a feature of the Boulangist left. As proof of this, one
need only look at the nationalist party not just in terms of General
Boulanger, but also from the point of view of the men who waged
the struggle in the field. Admittedly, Boulanger himself was not
anti-Semitic. Men such as Barrès, Déroulède, and Thiébaud never
ceased to reproach him for being a man of the old school. He stood
firm against any form of alliance with anti-Semitism and refused to
endorse Drumont's candidacy in the legislative elections.

Drumont's insults directed at Boulanger's father and at Boulanger
himself certainly have something to do with the general's loathing
for the author of *La France juive* and for anti-Semitism. Boulanger
can hardly have appreciated being portrayed as a "timid and fac-
tious soldier,"[1] but that is not the crucial point. The head of the
nationalist party was a genuinely republican general, a conser-

Translated from French by Jonathan Mandelbaum.

[1] E. Drumont, *La Dernière Bataille: Nouvelle Étude psychologique et sociale* (Paris:
Dentu, 1890), 159; see also 156–58.

vative republican, whose views were deeply at variance with those of the troops he supposedly commanded. He was a man of order, the very model of a career officer, who had been thrust into the role of rebel leader by a conjunction of circumstances that he barely understood.

As Boulangism became an organized movement and a reality independent from its nominal leader, one can observe an infiltration of anti-Semitism down to its deepest strata. Important figures in the general's entourage, members of the national committee, and candidates in the legislative elections of 1889 soon made anti-Semitism a major political theme. During the campaign leading up to the election of 27 January in Paris, Maurice Vergoin, deputy for the Seine-et-Oise, launched a violent anti-Semitic propaganda campaign whose impact was considerable. He was imitated in this by Barrès and Gabriel in Nancy, and by Laur, Granger, Roche, and—of course—Rochefort in Paris.

At the same time, the nationalist party was joined by a choice recruit who, more than anyone, helped to combine Boulangism and anti-Semitism: the Marquis de Morès. By the month of August, he was battling alongside the members of the national committee. A personal enemy of the minister of the interior, Morès launched himself into the fray with characteristic ardor. In Toulouse, in the race against Constans, he campaigned unstintingly for Susini, a member of the national committee—a gesture that won him definitive acceptance by the Boulangist leaders.[2]

While Morès plunged into Boulangism, Eugène Mayer, manager of *La Lanterne*, resigned from the national committee, and Joseph Reinach became the head of the anti-Boulangist campaign. This naturally fueled the anti-Jewish feelings of the Boulangist leaders, especially as, the more they became acquainted with the state of mind of their potential following, the more they discovered that in certain circles "Socialism meant war on the Jews."[3]

The Jews were well aware of this. Amid the diversity of strains in Boulangism, they distinguished with ever greater clarity a number of alarming sounds. Admittedly, during a meeting with a Jewish delegation that had come to voice its concern, Boulanger took the

[2] Mermeix (pseud. of Gabriel Terrail), *Les Antisémites en France: Notice sur un fait contemporain* (Paris: Dentu, 1892), 54; see also 43.
[3] Ibid., 42.

trouble to disavow those of his supporters who had expressed anti-Semitic opinions. But these assurances were short-lived, for, a few days later, in an interview with Chincholles, Drumont announced that, after mass on 27 January, he would vote for General Boulanger. The Jews of Paris heeded the warning. On the night of 27 January, the third *arrondissement* was the only one where the government candidate outpolled the common candidate of all the opposition parties.[4]

The anti-Boulangist vote of the Jews of Paris, Eugène Mayer's betrayal, Reinach's campaign, and the lack of enthusiasm for the movement displayed by the Rothschilds (as well as by the other financial magnates, who never believed in Boulanger's success) helped to feed, in the aftermath of defeat in the legislative elections, the legend that Jewish subsidies were responsible for saving the parliamentary regime from the people's wrath.[5] This argument was immediately exploited by Rochefort: the Rothschilds, who backed Constans, not only put their wealth at the minister's disposal but also delivered voters to him. Had they not brought from the depths "of the Danubian provinces more than 35,000 Jews whom they . . . almost immediately had naturalized as French citizens," and "without whose votes Paris would have elected the entire Boulangist list?"[6] Rochefort gave his Boulangism a violently anti-Semitic tone, not hesitating to threaten the Jews with "a fearful anti-Semitic movement" along the lines of the one raging in Eastern Europe.[7]

Following the elections, the Boulangist national committee and parliamentary group were composed of a majority of anti-Semites. Only the resistance of Naquet, Laguerre, and a few others—as well as the refusal of the general himself, in exile since April—prevented official Boulangism from veering into anti-Semitism. Most of its members were in very close contact with Morès, and the influence of this anti-Semitic agitator only increased,[8] all the more so as anti-Semitism had just proved its effectiveness. It was the left-

---

[4] Ibid., 44.

[5] See, for example, the article by Paul Adam, one of Barrès's two running mates in Nancy: "The Last Elections Were Organized with Jewish Gold" ("La République d'Israël," *Le Courrier de l'Est*, 20 October 1889).

[6] H. Rochefort, "Le Triomphe de la juiverie," *Le Courrier de l'Est*, 20 October 1889.

[7] Ibid.

[8] Mermeix, *Les Antisémites*, 58, 66.

leaning wing of Boulangism—which had made abundant use of
this new theme—that had scored the greatest successes. Some of
the movement's leaders were therefore keen to launch the new war
machine during the municipal elections of 1890.

The alliance between Boulangists and anti-Semites followed
naturally when, in the words of Mermeix, the former discovered
"in anti-Semitism a new force to enlist in their cause."[9] As it prepared for its last effort in the municipal elections of April 1890,
the movement badly needed to win over the popular electorate,
disappointed by the government's compromises with the right. The
"social" anti-Semites constituted the plebeian, Socialist-leaning,
nationalist element that could yet save the nationalist party. But
this rapprochement was not only tactical. It was an integral part of
a return to sources—and of a sweeping turn to the left by the nationalist party in the wake of its defeat in October 1889. The fact
remains that anti-Semitism during these years became the rallying
point par excellence, even among those who, like the Ligue des
Patriotes, had never conducted anti-Semitic campaigns before.

The alliance of Boulangism and anti-Semitism materialized officially for the first time in January-February 1890 during the campaign for the reelection of Francis Laur, member of the national
committee. Laur, deputy for Neuilly (now removed from office), a
friend of Drumont, and a leading figure of the Boulangist left, was
formerly a radical. He was the first to have spoken in the National
Assembly in the name of the anti-Semites. The campaign for his
reelection was the starting point of political anti-Semitism, and the
great Boulangist rally in Neuilly marked the birth of the anti-
Semitic movement. Prepared and organized by the new Ligue Antisémitique de France (presided over by Drumont), the meeting at
the Salle Gallice was a rather effective symbol of what was expected
of anti-Semitism. "One could see" Drumont wrote, "mingling fra-
ternally with the workingmen, and drawn closer to the workers by
a love of patriotism and justice, a number of noblemen whose
names evoke the finest pages of our history."[10]

The meeting, chaired by Susini, was conducted by Morès, manager of Francis Laur's election campaign. Most of the more prominent leaders of the nationalist party were in attendance, some to

[9] Ibid., 56. In July 1892, *L'Eclair* conducted a survey in order to find out to what extent
anti-Semitism was a new incarnation of Boulangism ("Sous le masque," 7 July).

[10] Drumont, *La Dernière Bataille*, 38–39.

make speeches,[11] others to ratify by their presence the conjunction of anti-Semitism and the vast protest movement represented by Boulangism. Naturally, Naquet and Laguerre, targets of personal attacks by Drumont, had stayed away. but Déroulède himself, hitherto hostile to anti-Semitism, consented to address the meeting after Drumont. The hopes pinned on the new force must have been great indeed!

The Neuilly rally was a resounding success, and Francis Laur's triumphal election gave anti-Semitism a popular seal of approval. There was no doubt in anyone's mind that, in the municipal elections of April 1890, the Boulangist troops would choose to march into battle under the banner of the Ligue Antisémitique. The left wing of the Boulangist party was unquestionably the first to think of using anti-Semitism as an ideological plank for a mass movement. One could even add that the Boulangists were virtually the pioneers in the field, since the arguments later advanced by the anti-Dreyfusards had, without exception, been used by Boulanger's friends before them.

One of the first French politicians of stature—if not the very first—to exploit the upsurge of anti-Semitism of the 1880s for political ends, and with considerable success, was Barrès. Having come to the left wing of Boulangism with no political or emotional ties to the old republican and Jacobin left, Barrès represented a new generation, free of the complexes that burdened men like Boulanger. He advocated a vast rallying movement that would give birth to a new, national, social, and anti-Semitic Republic.[12]

After the electoral defeat of October 1889, *Le Courrier de l'Est*, the Boulangist paper in Nancy, devoted one column to a message to workers and three and a half columns, out of the five on the front page, to a long anti-Semitic diatribe by Paul Adam, "La République d'Israël." The second page was more evenly divided: one and a half columns for an article on "Lutte des classes," and a col-

[11] R. Viau, *Vingt Ans d'antisémitisme, 1899–1909* (Paris: Charpentier, 1910), 14–18; see also Mermeix, *Les Antisémites*, 54–55.

[12] M. Barrès, "M. le général Boulanger et la nouvelle génération," *La Revue indépendante* 8 (April 1888):60. See also M. Barrès, *Les Déracinés* (Paris: Fasquelle, 1897), 297, 301; "Lettre d'un antisémite," *Le Courrier de l'Est*, 26 May 1889; and *L'Appel au soldat* (Paris: Fasquelle, 1900), 466. In 1889, Barrès was already calling for special legislative measures aimed at instituting a category of second-class citizens—measures opposed by Boulanger (see Zeev Sternhell, *Maurice Barrès et le nationalisme français* [Paris: A Colin, 1972]).

umn and a half too for Henri Rochefort's "Le Triomphe de la juiverie." Together with antiparliamentarianism and Socialism, anti-Semitism was an essential ingredient of popular Boulangism, as well as of the ideological system that the radical right would adopt for over half a century. The synthesis of these three in-gredients succeeded remarkably in Nancy, where it accounted for the resounding triumph of an aggressive and modern variety of Boulangism.

From the inception of Nancy-style Boulangism, the slogans "Long live Boulanger" and "Down with the Jews" became two intimately linked and practically interchangeable election cam-paign themes. This dual creed served as a banner for the first major Boulangist demonstration in Lorraine, on 9 February 1889. Later, the same slogans punctuated every meeting of the Boulangist Comité Révisionniste and were used by Barrès in his election cam-paign. The basic themes of this campaign were a rehearsal of the main arguments advanced by Drumont in his books.[13] While Catho-lic imagery and a certain form of racist argument were also present, Barrès waged his battle chiefly on the theme of social anti-Semitism. Amid a chorus of "A bas les juifs," he opened his first large-scale public meeting by accusing "the lackeys, the servants of Semitic high finance who control France's liberty under the name of Op-portunists" of being the cause of the country's plight.[14] Through-out the election campaign, Barrès, Adam, and Gabriel harped on this causal relationship, on the natural collusion between the Jews, the liberal state, and bourgeois society. This theme, introduced by Barrès, was to be one of the key leitmotivs of anti-Semitic cam-paigns in the twentieth century. Its success in 1889 furnished evi-dence of public responsiveness to this type of argument.

A "Jewish party," Opportunism, was "enslaving" France to "the Semites."[15] Was it surprising that, in a regime where "most of

[13] Barrès duly refers to Drumont's work, which he finds "for the most part of the highest moral value as well as useful"; he stresses "the generous working-class propaganda to be found in it"; see "Interpellation sur le monopole Hachette," Le Courrier de l'Est, 22 June 1890.

[14] "La Réunion de Nancy," Le Courrier de l'Est, 12 February 1889. See also, on this theme, P. Adam, "La République d'Israël," ibid., 20 October 1889, and two articles by Barrès, "Le Juif dans l'Est," ibid., 14 July 1889, and "L'Opportunisme, parti des juifs," ibid., 21 July 1889.

[15] Barrès, "L'Opportunisme, parti des juifs," and a speech by Gabriel at an election meet-ing at Dombasle, Le Courrier de l'Est, 21 April 1889.

the government is Jewish," where those who were not Jewish were "afraid of weakening this already tottering government by moving away from the Semites," and where so many magistrates and high-ranking civil servants "come from the synagogue," the Jews had "managed to take over all our credit institutions"?[16] Their political ascendancy had made the Jews the masters of the country; moreover, "Semitic high finance," which controlled the country, hoarded "public wealth" and was driving "thousands of workers to starvation."[17] Consequently, the "stock-market speculators," "Hebrews crossed with Germans," were responsible for "suicides induced by poverty"; and, if "people are literally dying of hunger today in France," it was because "national capital is being rapidly soaked up by the same exploiters."[18]

The presence of the Jew, his grip on the country's economic activity, was the chief explanation for the plight of the working class, the economic recession, and financial difficulties. Whether in Algeria, where "the vile Yids" were organizing a vast currency speculation,[19] or in eastern France, where Jewish usurers, peddlers, and merchants were sowing ruin, the nature of the evil was the same. By dint of subterfuge and embezzlement, they would first drive "some hapless old lady, some stupid peasant" to bankruptcy and destitution, then entire communes and cantons. A whole region could be reduced to poverty "by an association of five or six Jewish merchants and usurers."[20]

The image of the widow and orphan as victims of the Jew was a commonplace of anti-Semitic literature. The tone was set by the early 1880s by the first anti-Semitic paper of the period. *L'Antisémitique*, run by a certain A. Vrécourt, a weekly sold at 40 centimes and published in Montdidier (Somme) in 1883–84, represents the first wave of popular anti-Semitism in the late nineteenth century. Most of the features of modern anti-Semitism were already present: social radicalism combined with certain forms of social Darwinism, supplemented by the oldest and most deeply rooted form of anti-Semitism, Christian—and essentially Catholic—anti-Semitism.

[16] Barrès, "L'Opportunisme, parti des juifs."
[17] Remarks by Gabriel at an election meeting at Saint-Nicolas, *Le Courrier de l'Est*, 7 April 1889.
[18] "Les Pères de 89," *Le Courrier de l'Est*, 10 August 1890.
[19] "Les Juifs en Algérie," ibid., 1 December 1889.
[20] M. Barrès, "Le Juif dans l'Est," ibid., 14 July 1889.

With the exception of Chabauty and Chirac, the contributors to the paper were unknowns who were never heard from again after it ceased publication in the summer of 1884. Abbé E. A. Chabauty, *chanoine honoraire* of Angoulême and Poitiers, was the author of a work entitled *Les Juifs nos maîtres*, which was talked about for some time after its publication in 1882. The book advances the theory of the great plot aimed at the mastery of Western Christendom hatched by "Judaic freemasonry," which was busily uniting all the "enemies of Jesus Christ and of his Church."[21]

L'Antisémitique, is of interest precisely because it was able to come into existence and stay alive. Clearly there was an audience for this type of literature. Founded by a few drudges in the provincial backwoods, *L'Antisémitique* also has the signal distinction of being the forerunner of mass anti-Semitic literature, and even of having said all that could be said in that vein. Sorel's *L'Indépendance*, Drumont's *La Libre Parole*, Guérin's *L'Antijuif*, Rochefort's *L'Intransigeant*, Barrès's *Le Courrier de l'Est* (followed by *La Cocarde*) and, finally, Emmanuel Gallian's *L'Anti-youtre* (Gallian later became one of Biétry's associates) never did more than rehearse the same themes. Just as in the Montdidier paper, anti-Semitism, in its effort to mobilize and integrate, took on a plebeian, Socialist-leaning, and Catholic appearance. That is why obscure pen pushers in *sous-préfectures* and members of the Académie Française alike invoked the eternal arguments about defending the worker against cosmopolitan capitalism, as well as the theory of the Jewish plot, not forgetting, of course, the theme of ritual murder.[22]

A few years later, Barrès, himself perfectly aware of the psychological and sociological tensions that contributed to anti-Semitism, showed how they could be usefully exploited. "Hatred, sheer hatred, is the first thing one sees in this anti-Jewish expression. . . . Hatred is one of the strongest feelings produced by our civilization, by our big cities. The violent clash between great luxury and poverty in our world engenders and intensifies it unceasingly. It will never be lacking for those parties that want to exploit it. . . . Lis-

---

[21] Abbé E. A. Chabauty, *Les Juifs nos maîtres! Documents et développements nouveaux sur la question juive* (Paris: Société Générale de Librairie Catholique, 1882), viii, x. In 1880, Chanoine Chabauty had already published, under the pseudonym of C. C. de Saint-André, a work entitled *Francs-maçons et juifs* (same publisher).

[22] *L'Antisémitique*, June to December 1883.

ten to the crowd that shouted 'Down with the Jews' during the meetings—what they were really saying was 'Down with social inequality'" And Barrès concludes with an extremely important comment: "State socialism" that is the indispensable complement to the anti-Jewish expression. . . . State socialism embodies all our hopes. A man firmly in command, a strong authority, could impose their will and breach the walls for the destitute."[23]

Barrès knew—and the example of Nancy was there to corroborate this—that he had just found in anti-Semitism a "popular expression" with an emotional potential far greater than that of all the other fashionable slogans. That is why, in *L'Appel au soldat*, he criticized Boulanger for refusing to engage in anti-Semitism. Barrès too saw as the key to the general's failure his refusal to redirect the movement toward an anti-Semitism tinged with Socialism.

In its political function, anti-Semitism was also expected to play another role—not only that of shaking the masses and casting them into action, but also that of overcoming the ideological differences linked to social cleavages. After all, in a country as deeply divided as France, where conflicting political and historical traditions as well as deeply antagonistic ideological systems lived in uneasy coexistence, anti-Semitism was sufficiently rooted and widespread to serve as an ideal factor of unity: "Boulangism," Barrès wrote, "must be anti-Semitic precisely by virtue of its being a party of national reconciliation."[24] An instrument for integrating the proletariat into the national collectivity, social anti-Semitism was the only theme capable of winning over to the "national" camp a sizeable proportion of the "ardent and suffering masses" whose outlook was "entirely social."[25]

Anti-Semitism had another, and quite exceptional, advantage. "A second following of the general was constituted by the petty bourgeoisie, a staunch defender of private property, but jealous of the very wealthy. It is a propitious terrain for anti-Semitism."[26] In 1898, in the thick of *l'Affaire*, when Barrès stood for reelection at

[23] M. Barrès, "La Formule antijuive," *Le Figaro*, 22 February 1890. *Le Courrier de l'Est* actually called for the massacre of Jews (see two unsigned articles, "Le Circoncis de Fourmies," 2 May 1891, and "Le Mariage religieux de Marianne et du juif errant," 5 September 1891).

[24] Barrès, *L'Appel au soldat*, 464.

[25] Ibid., 466.

[26] Ibid.

Nancy, he sought to win over this category of the bourgeoisie by conducting the same campaign as in 1889 against Jewish high finance and against "the barons." [27] In order to demonstrate the convergence of interests between the working-class world and the bourgeoisie, he revealed their "common enemy" [28]—a fashionable phrase in the days of Boulangism—the common source of their woes: the Jew.

In the days of Boulangism and at the time of the Dreyfus Affair, Barrès sought to lead these traditionally radical and Jacobin elements in an assault on parliamentary democracy. By appealing both to their patriotic feelings and to their hatred of privilege, by denouncing the Jew as the cause of their hardship, he thought he could cut them off from the bourgeois Republic. Barrès was fully conscious of the potential role of the petty bourgeoisie, a heterogeneous gathering of intermediate groups and of social strata that all shared a fear of proletarianization. Fundamentally dedicated to conservatism and not to development, the petty bourgeoisie felt a deep hatred toward the magnates of finance. Deeply conservative in its economic outlook, unadapted to industrialization, often ignorant of the workings of a modern economy, it accepted the notion of Jewish exploitation and competition, of the usurer as inventor and master of credit, "the terrible weapon invented by the Yid to increase his power tenfold, a hundredfold." [29] The Jew as responsible for economic insecurity was the basic theme of the Nancy program of 1898, in which one finds the same nostalgia for a golden age—already encountered in *La France juive* and subsequently revived first by Vichy, then by Poujadism—the longing for an agrarian and hard-working France where social classes lived in a harmony that had been shattered by the Jew and by industrial development. [30] To the industrious petty bourgeois, to the worker earning his living by the sweat of his brow, the Jew was portrayed as irrevocably hostile to manual work, to effort, to honest occupations: "he will be a merchant of men or goods, if need be a usurer," but never a workingman, peasant, or honest small shopkeeper. [31]

[27] M. Barrès, *Scènes et doctrines du nationalisme* (Paris: Plon, 1925), 2:182.

[28] "Lettre d'un antisémite," *Le Courrier de l'Est*, 26 May 1889.

[29] "Les Juifs et l'Internationale," *Le Courrier de l'Est*, 4 April 1891 (article signed "L'Anti-youtre").

[30] Barrès, *Scènes et doctrines*, 2:162–64.

[31] M. Barrès, "Lettre d'un antisémite," *Le Courrier de l'Est*, 26 May 1889; the same themes occur in "Les Parasites," *L'Antisémitique*, 14 July 1883.

From Boulangism to the Great War, these themes formed the essence of popular anti-Semitism. And, while anti-Dreyfusism triggered their explosion, giving them an opportunity to manifest themselves concretely in the riots of the very last years of the century, one is obliged to observe that neither Jules Guérin nor the Ligue Antisémitique—leaders of the street-fighting in popular neighborhoods—had invented anything. To be sure, Jules Guérin came up with striking catchwords and slogans that appealed to the working class. For example, it was Guérin who said, "The farther we are from the Jews, the closer we are to the people"; Guérin, too, who defined anti-Semitism as "a specific and formal grievance of national Labor against Jewish speculation"[32]—a definition supplemented by the following equation by Morin, which could have come out of *La Question juive*: "What enemy is socialism constantly pointing out to the proletariat? Capital. Who represents capital today in France? The Jew."[33]

By the end of the century, men such as Drumont and Guérin believed that the official Socialists, prisoners of the Rothschilds, had betrayed the cause of the proletariat.[34] That is why they argued that the anti-Semites—depicted as the last Frenchmen to share with "the socialist and revolutionary workers" the love of their homeland and a devotion to the people's cause—were the only force still capable of defending the interests of the proletariat.[35] This Republic, "founded by an entente among Jews, Protestants, and Freemasons," protected by the "intellectuals," compliant servants of "Judeo-German collectivism," could have but one single raison d'être, now that it had destroyed labor associations at the same time as it had toppled the monarchy: the aim of turning the French workers into "slaves of the Jews," of delivering them bound hand and foot into the hands of the *haute banque*, of international fi-

[32] "Premières Initiations au péril juif," *L'Antijuif*, 7 May 1899; "La Révision des créances juives," ibid., 9 August 1898.

[33] J. Morin, "Socialistes," ibid., 21 May 1899. See also two very characteristic texts: an appeal to voters published in *L'Antisémitique*, 8 September 1883, and a pamphlet by the future manager of *La Libre Parole*, J. E. Milot, *Aux prolétaires de France, à tous les travailleurs des villes et des campagnes* (Asnières: Imprimerie du Progrès, 1889).

[34] J. Guérin, "Le Système juif," *L'Antijuif*, 8 January 1899, and "Les Ouvrières à Paris," ibid., 26 March 1899; J. Morin, "Socialistes," ibid., 21 May 1899. On Drumont's view, see *Le Testament d'un antisémite* (Paris: Dentu, 1899): "In truth, there are not two political parties; there is a single regime, there is a system, the capitalist and Jewish system, to which are also affiliated the representatives of the parties contending for power" (p. 5).

[35] J. Guérin, "Les Dreyfusards rossés par le peuple," *L'Antijuif*, 9 October 1898.

nance, of the monopolies.[36] The liberation of the French proletariat therefore required the destruction of the Jew, which would entail the disappearance of "creditor Jewry," the *juiverie* that ran the monopolies and was grabbing public wealth.[37] The theme of Jews grabbing public wealth was one of the oldest to be found in social anti-Semitism. From Toussenel—who catalogued the means used by the Jews to achieve this end[38]—to *L'Antisémitique*, from Morès to *L'Antijuif* and the members of the Action Française, the same complaint cropped up time and again.[39]

The charge of conspiracy emerged only at the end of the century. Having "publicly laid hands on the State," the Jews "held France in something like a stranglehold"; to "avenge themselves for the sentencing of Dreyfus," they were seeking to "destroy our army, the only organized force that has hitherto been immune to their influence."[40] By virtue of the principle that the "Jewish nation" would always seek the destruction of the "Christian nations," the Affair took on the dimensions of a "race war."[41] Hence Jewish treason was not simply brought on by this particular set of circumstances. It stemmed from a far deeper reality, from the fact that the Jew, at all times and in all places, whatever he did and whatever the situation, was a foreign element. "A French Jew! The pairing of these two terms seems monstrous to me," Toussenel had written earlier.[42] In any case, Drumont added, "the Jew's brain isn't made like ours,"

[36] J Guérin, "La Question sociale et la tyrannie des intellectuels," ibid., 29 January 1899; "Le Système juif," ibid., 29 March 1899; "Une nouvelle banque juive," ibid., 21 May 1899; and "La Banque des coquins judéo-capitalistes," ibid., 18 September 1898.

[37] Guérin, "La Révision des créances juives," Marquis de Morès, *Le Secret des changes* (Marseille: Imprimerie Marseillaise, 1894), 83.

[38] A. Toussenel, *Les Juifs, rois de l'époque: Histoire de la féodalité financière*, 3d. ed. (Paris: Marpon et Flammarion, 1886), 1:148. See also 149: "The children of Lorraine are convinced that the Jews never greet each other without asking: 'How many Christians did you rob today?' And, for that matter, what can two Jews say to each other today as they leave the stock exchange?"

[39] "La Guerre et la juiverie," *L'Antisémitique*, 1 June 1883; "Comment Rothschild traite les ouvriers," ibid., 23 June 1883; Marquis de Morès, *Rothschild, Ravachol et Cⁱᵉ* (Paris: 38 rue du Mont-Thabor, 1892), 39; "Accaparements et accapareurs," *L'Antijuif*, 21 August 1898; "Comment les juifs s'emparent des maisons françaises," ibid., 28 August 1898; Albert Monniot, "Que faire? Réponse d'un antisémite," *L'Action française*, 15 January 1904, 106; see also Monniot's other articles in the 1 January and 1 February 1904 issues of *L'Action française*, and an article by H. Vaugeois, "Les Hypothèses de Drumont," ibid., 1 September 1904, 329–40; ibid., 1 March 1904, 351–70, for a commentary by Maurras.

[40] "Premières Initiations au péril juif."

[41] Ibid.; Barrès, *Scènes et doctrines* 1:41.

[42] Toussenel, *Les Juifs, rois de l'époque*, 1:xii.

and Henry Vaugeois explained that, far from being a purely ideological phenomenon, anti-Semitism was also grounded in "an instinctive, almost physical repulsion to the Jew and to his skin, a 'savage' feeling scorned by today's high-minded folk." [43]

For the Action Française, which was very close to Drumont's anti-Semitism, the Jew symbolized all the aggressions directed against France. A symbol of "foreignness," and even more of perversity and evil, the Jew could not escape from his nature and even less give the lie to it. Even if he repudiated his religion, his ethnic identity made him remain a Jew: thus he had to be tracked down wherever he was. [44] More than anyone else, the Maurrassians, by making anti-Semitism one of the pillars of *nationalisme intégral*, provided it with the arguments for a pseudorationalization. For the new right, the Jew was a methodological necessity; he filled a vacuum, thus ensuring its survival. This vacuum was where nationalism had found itself after the failure of Boulangism. "Everything seems impossible or frightfully difficult," Maurras wrote, "without the providence of anti-Semitism. Thanks to it, everything works out, everything is smoothed over and becomes simpler. If we were not anti-Semitic out of patriotic determination, we would become so simply out of a sense of opportunity." [45]

Incapable of defining itself except in terms of opposition, nationalism at the turn of the century found in racism and anti-Semitism the means of distinguishing all that was alien to it. The Jew symbolized the antination; he was the negative entity, the cosmopolitan, the figure against whom national feeling could at last determine and measure itself. Thus, in the eyes of the new right, the function of anti-Semitism was to substantiate its need for an identity. Anti-Semitism was not only politically profitable; it was a fundamental factor in the nationalists' search for identity and in their revolt against the liberal consensus. [46]

In the heat of the Dreyfus Affair, militant anti-Semitism was joined by a new recruit. In the spring of 1898, the Duc d'Orléans's top advisers decided to bail out the Ligue Antisémitique, which

[43] Drumont, *La Dernière Bataille*, xvi; H. Vaugeois, "Notre antisémitisme," *L'Action française*, 15 August 1900, 266–67.

[44] C. Capitan-Peter, *Charles Maurras et l'idéologie d'Action française* (Paris: Ed. du Seuil, 1972), 72–74.

[45] Quoted ibid., 75.

[46] On this subject, see Zeev Sternhell, *La Droite révolutionnaire 1885–1914: les Origines françaises du fascisme* (Paris: Ed. du Seuil, 1978).

was in deep financial trouble. The duke's entourage hoped that, by infiltrating the *Ligue*, the Orleanists would gain access to popular quarters and acquire a combat organization capable of controlling the streets when the time came.[47] Responsibility for the scheme was entrusted to the probable originator of the idea, the Comte de Sabran-Pontevès, who was in charge of Orleanist propaganda for popular consumption. A candidate in the quartier de la Villette constituency in the legislative elections of 1898, the count had tried, while Guérin was away in Algeria compaigning with Drumont, to win over recruits to his own cause. But he soon realized that he could not do so without the help of the leader of the Ligue Antisémitique. After a fruitless attempt to seek a rapprochement with the Ligue des Patriotes, Sabran-Pontevès gave up: Déroulède was not the sort of man who would allow himself to be maneuvered. The count therefore turned his attention to the Ligue Antisémitique and saw to it that popular anti-Semitism, one of the best means of making inroads into the *faubourgs*, was regularly subsidized by the House of France.[48] Attentive to currents of opinion, the Duc d'Orléans, seeing the rising tide of anti-Semitism, lost no time in issuing a violent proclamation known as the San Remo Manifesto: in the late nineteenth century, integration into the national consensus required anti-Semitism.

On 28 August 1898 the first issue appeared of *L'Antijuif*, accompanied by *L'Antijuif français illustré*. These two weeklies, which were soon to merge, owed their existence to a first donation of 100,000 francs from the pretender, followed no doubt by a comparable sum that enabled the *Ligue* to move into fairly luxurious premises at 56 rue de Rochechouart.[49] Subsequently, and until April 1903, Guérin received regular monthly grants of 20,000 to 30,000 francs. In addition, the payment of a sum of 300,000 francs[50] en-

[47] Archives Nationales, Paris (hereafter ANP), F 7/12459, 15 September 1898, 10 July 1899 (on royalists joining the Ligue Antisémitique), 21 April 1900.

[48] Archives of the Préfecture de Police, Paris (hereafter APP), B/a 1104, 24 November 1899; ANP, F 7/12459, 16 October 1898, 13 and 27 February, 24 and 27 March, 15 and 29 May, 26 August 1899; F 7/12883, 1 March 1904.

[49] ANP, F 7/12459, 19 August 1898, 16 January and 6 September 1899. According to a report of 22 July 1898 (APP, B/a 1104), Guérin could also count on the financial support of the very wealthy deputy of Poitiers, Dupuytren, who was said to be ready to put a sum of 100,000 francs at his disposal.

[50] ANP, F 7/12882, 25 May, 30 August, 23 September 1899; F 7/12883, 1 March 1904; F 7/12459, 2 February 1899. See C. Spiard, *Les Coulisses de Fort-Chabrol* (Paris: Spiard, 1902), 29, 46–63. On royalist subsidies, see also APP, B/a 1104, 24 May 1899.

abled the *Ligue*, which meanwhile had dropped its name and be-come—in opposition to the masonic Grand Orient de France—the Grand Occident de France,[51] to set up a genuine fortress right in the heart of Paris. The imposing, lavishly furnished building on the rue de Chabrol was protected by tall wrought iron railings, a huge carriage entrance with triple locks, metal-plated shutters on the windows, and an elaborate electrical alarm system. The headquar-ters of the Grand Occident housed not only the offices of *L'Antijuif* and the administrative department of the *Ligue*, but also a lecture room with a capacity of five hundred persons, an arms room, a gymnasium, a printing press, and a free medical center.[52]

It was obvious that, in the minds of Royalist staffers, the former lieutenant of the Marquis de Morès was indeed to have the honor of winning France's proletariat over to the House of France—a task that, after the failure of Guérin and the debacle of the first genera-tion of nationalists, was devolved upon Biétry's Jaunes.

Immediately upon receiving royalist subsidies, Guérin launched an active propaganda campaign. He published *L'Antijuif*, whose print run rapidly soared from 40,000 to 90,000 copies, reaching 120,000 in January 1899. Plans were then mooted for increasing the print run to 150,000 copies.[53] In August 1898, actual sales to-taled 65,000, and they do not seem to have risen any further.[54] *L'Antijuif* was an unquestionable success. In January 1899, it was learned that newsdealers were asking for more copies, as were the provincial chapters of the *Ligue*, which sold at least 500 copies each.[55] As for unsold copies, they were distributed free in the sub-urbs by special motorized teams.[56]

It is impossible to determine the precise role of the *Ligue* in the 1898–99 riots. As far as one can judge from the existing sources, its role seems to have been fairly important. We know today that

[51] J. Guérin, "Le Grand Occident de France contre le Grand Orient juif," *L'Antijuif*, no. 40, March 1899.

[52] R. Viau, *Vingt Ans d'antisémitisme*, 192–95; ANP, F 7/12459, 10 September 1898, 15 and 20 March, 5 and 10 April 1899; F 7/12882, 25 May, 30 August 1899. See also APP, B/a 1104, 10 and 18 April 1898: Boni de Castellane reportedly paid Guérin 100,000 francs for the purpose of setting up his headquarters in the rue de Chabrol.

[53] APP, B/a 1104, 1 and 5 July, 22 September, 16 December 1898, 11, 19, and 30 January 1899. It is interesting to compare the print run of *L'Antijuif* with the 2,000 issues printed of *Le Bulletin officiel de la Ligue antisémitique de France* (APP, B/a 1107, 3 February 1898).

[54] APP, B/a 1104, 23 August 1898.

[55] Ibid., 21 August 1898, 19 January 1899.

[56] ANP, F 7/12882, 3 October, 3 November, 6 December 1898.

these riots occurred on a very large scale[57] and were taken with utmost seriousness by the specialists at the Préfecture de Police. Stationed in populous neighborhoods, these men were attentive to the state of opinion and admirably knowledgeable about the local inhabitants. Thus, on 14 January 1898, an official of the Préfecture de Police sounded an urgent warning to his superiors. According to him, Paris was on the verge of experiencing "what Algiers, Oran, and Vienna went through a few months ago"; "exasperation is rife"; in Clignancourt and Montmartre, among the unemployed and "les gens des faubourgs," but also among students, "a movement is clearly brewing" that would inevitably lead to "the looting of Jewish shops."[58]

On balance, the riots of January-February 1898, as well as the demonstrations that preceded and followed them, were nothing but an implementation of the entire span of anti-Semitic ideology from Toussenel and Proudhon to Drumont, Barrès, Rochefort, and Maurras. Every single word of the slogans shouted by the men who looted and vandalized Jewish stores, bodily assaulted Jews in the streets, or killed them (as in Algiers) had been uttered, written, and printed every day, year after year, in hundreds of thousands of copies. These words and slogans were eventually brought together and presented as bills at the Palais Bourbon. The successes scored by the anti-Semitic deputies were no less resounding than those of Jules Guérin's shock troops. In this respect, anti-Semitism was a crucial feature of the rightist, national, and social revolution. The anti-Semites aimed quite simply to destroy both the conceptual and the political structures of Jacobin democracy. This truly revolutionary undertaking would have been unthinkable without the long period of ideological preparation that preceded it and without the legitimation won by anti-Semitism both on the far left and on the far right. It is beyond dispute that, in its campaign to take hold among—and mobilize—the popular classes, plebeian anti-Semitism not only enjoyed the support of the most renowned publicists of the time but also benefited from the humming and hawing of the Socialists as well as the timidity of Jewish notables and politicians.[59]

[57] See S. Wilson, "The Anti-Semitic Riots of 1898 in France," *Historical Journal* 16 (1973):789–806, which, however, deals only with the first two months of 1898.

[58] APP, B/a 1043, 14 January 1898.

[59] "Is it too much to ask of the Jews not to insult those who defend them?" wrote

Of all the leaders of the left, Jaurès was the first to understand the function of popular anti-Semitism. In January 1898, he pitched into the battle with fervor, but it was now an uphill struggle, for he had to overcome the considerable weight of the old anti-Semitic tradition of French socialism. This tradition, now voiced in the Socialist press and by labor militants, paralyzed the Socialist movement at a crucial moment. If the Socialist deputies, in January 1898, could afford to be hostile to the review of the sentence pronounced against Dreyfus, it was because they were on solid ground. Until 1898, Claude Willard observes, the Dreyfus Affair provoked openly anti-Semitic reactions in certain Guesdist federations.[60] The militants did not always understand that the public meetings where Guesde and Lafargue had spoken in the company of Drumont, Morès, and Guérin were open debates. The presence of these men on a same platform had given cause to suppose that this was a confrontation between two branches of a single ideological family, particularly as *La Libre Parole* had consistently supported Jaurès and the workers of Carmaux.[61] The great Socialist leader himself, on his return from Algeria, had displayed an attitude toward the Jews that could have been construed as ambiguous.[62] This explains why, in early 1898, Clemenceau felt obliged to remind Millerand once more that it was a mistake to think that anti-Semitism had positive aspects simply because it "delivers the Rothschilds into our hands."[63]

In January 1898, after the bombshell of "J'accuse," Jaurès launched into the fray. *La Libre Parole* counterattacked on 19 and

---

Clemenceau in *L'Iniquité* (Paris: Stock, 1899), 375, citing as examples the anti-Dreyfusard statements issued by two Jewish candidates in the legislative elections of 1898, Fernand Crémieux and L. L. Klotz. Both men stigmatized in an identical text "the odious campaign against the army of the Republic" and "explicitly undert[ook] to vote against the review of the Dreyfus trial" (375, 352).

[60] C. Willard, *Le Mouvement socialiste en France, 1893–1905: Les Guesdistes* (Paris: Editions Sociales, 1965), 410–11.

[61] See "Réponse du citoyen Jules Guesde à MM. Drumont, Morès et leurs amis au meeting de la salle des Mille-Colonnes, le 8 juillet 1892," quoted in A. Zévaès, *Histoire du socialisme et du communisme en France de 1801 à 1914* (Paris: France-Empire, 1947), 258; H. Goldberg, "Jean Jaurès and the Jewish Question: The Evolution of a Position," *Jewish Social Studies* 20, 2 (April 1958):75–76; and *Jean Jaurès: la biographie du fondateur du parti socialiste* (Paris: Fayard, 1970).

[62] C. Ageron, "Jaurès et la question algérienne," *Le Mouvement social*, no. 42 (January-March 1963):3–29.

[63] G. Clemenceau, *L'Iniquité*, 147.

26 January. But Drumont's paper was not alone. Liebknecht believed in Dreyfus's guilt, even after the Rennes trial, and he said so in the purest anti-Dreyfusard style: he thought it impossible that a member of the governing class could have been unjustly sentenced.[64] Jaurès was not followed by the working class until it realized that "there was . . . a danger," in Rouanet's words, "not only for the bourgeois Republic, but for the social Republic."[65] Only then, with Kautsky's backing, but in opposition to Rosa Luxemburg and Liebknecht, did Jaurès define the position that was henceforth adopted by the French proletariat. "That the bourgeois Republic, as it struggles against the military conspiracy that encircles it, should itself proclaim its need for socialist energies is a momentous event; whatever the immediate outcome, this will go down in history as a major date, and a bold, conquering party must not, in my opinion, pass up these offers of destiny, these opportunities of history."[66]

Not until the *ligues* demonstrated their control of the streets did the Socialists become convinced that they were losing their grip on the urban crowds and intervene forcefully. This decision was reached only after eighteen months of unrest, riots, and an attempted coup d'état. And even then, after the formation of the Waldeck-Rousseau government, the representatives of the Parti Ouvrier Français, the Parti Socialiste Révolutionnaire, and the Alliance Communiste Révolutionnaire published a violent condemnation of this "so-called socialist policy, made of compromises and deviations, which for too long was being tried as a substitute for the class-based, and consequently revolutionary, policy of the militant proletariat and of the Socialist party."[67] Signed in particular by Lafargue, Guesde, and Vaillant, the appeal "à la France ouvrière et socialiste" suggested that the polemics about the innocence of Dreyfus pitted two sections of the bourgeoisie against one another. The proletariat, the authors concluded, should remain an "opposition party" in order to "wage . . . the right battle up to the final triumph—the necessary battle of the working class against the

[64] *L'Action française* (revue), December 1899.
[65] G. Rouanet, "La Crise du parti socialiste," *La Revue socialiste*, no. 176 (August 1899):212.
[66] Quoted in ibid., 202.
[67] Ibid., 207.

capitalist class, of the revolution against the coalition of all the reactionary forces."[68]

The class policy of French socialism, as we know, did not resist
the shock of the Affair. In this sense, popular anti-Semitism played
a very important, if not decisive, role in the political evolution of
the labor movement. It was during the Affair that the famous "defensive republican reflex" was forged—that the groundwork was
laid for the republican consensus that would hold fast against
the pressure of the radical right until the great debacle of 1940.
The Dreyfus Affair vividly demonstrated in France a truth that was
gradually becoming evident throughout Europe: the subversive
character of Socialism remained primarily theoretical. The various
Socialist movements, each in its own time and in its own way, took
the path of social democracy, which implied a de facto acceptance
of the established order. The Dreyfus Affair confirmed this trend
by sealing the alliance between socialism and the bourgeois center.
The various factions of Socialism reached the conclusion that the
interests of the proletariat and of the liberal bourgeoisie henceforth
converged on one crucial point: both needed democracy.

Thus the emergence on the political scene of the radical right—
of which social anti-Semitism, as a mass movement, constituted a
basic ingredient—created an unprecedented and unexpected situation: the interdependence of the bourgeoisie and the proletariat.
This community of interests paved the way for the Bloc and for
various forms of tacit cooperation between the bourgeois center
and the social democratic left. But at the same time, these new relationships between political parties representing conflicting ideologies and social classes, this de facto acceptance of the democratic
consensus, provoked a violent critique of democracy soon to be ar-
ticulated by revolutionary trade unionism.

From the end of the Affair until the Great War, anti-Semitism
was a weapon used exclusively for the forces attacking the republican consensus. Until 1914, anti-Semitism survived on the left only
in the ranks of the nonconformist wing of Socialism, the wing that
refused to play the game of liberal and bourgeois democracy. It
constituted one of the elements of the revolt against that selfsame

[68] Ibid., 208. See also R. Luxemburg, "Une question de tactique," *Le Mouvement socialiste* (1 August 1899):132–37; K. Kautsky, "Jaurès et Millerand," ibid. (15 August
1899):209–10.

liberal democracy, which had been saved by a fool's bargain in which the proletariat, in the minds of a great number of militants, had once again been the victim.

In many respects, the Dreyfus Affair came to be seen by some labor militants as a gigantic hoax. For all those who had accepted the common front between the workers and the liberal bourgeoisie in order to stem the nationalist tide, the Affair had ended in a debacle. The only tangible result of their hard-won victory seemed to be the rise of radicalism and the transformation of Socialism into another conduit for bourgeois democracy. This variety of Socialism was very soon personified by its "renegades": Millerand, Briand, and Viviani: no less rapidly, radicalism was associated with Clemenceau's repressive policy.

All the attacks on liberal democracy—from the insults uttered by Hervé and Janvion to Sorel and Berth's theories about proletarian violence as a necessary instrument for rescuing Marxism from the slough of reformism and Dreyfusism, as well as Robert Louzon's violent diatribe in *Le mouvement socialiste*—proceeded from a single, dominating concern: the determination to counter the wave of Dreyfusism that threatened to engulf the working class. Anti-Semitism was one aspect of this campaign against the established order, a campaign directed not only against Clemenceau and his methods, but also against the political and social system that made them possible and against the Dreyfusard alliance, which gave them a long lease on life. Thus, in the struggle waged by the far left of the Socialist party and by certain elements of the confédération Générale du Travail (CGT) backed by Lagardelle's *Le Mouvement socialiste* and Hervé's *La Guerre sociale*, anti-Semitism once again performed its classic function, that of acting as the best war machine ever invented for demolishing the established order.

Robert Louzon's "La Faillite du dreyfusisme ou le triomphe du parti juif" dates from July 1906, that is, just a few days after the ruling of the Cour de Cassation (appeal court). The article, published in *Le Mouvement socialiste*, harked back to the old tradition of left-wing anti-Semitism in its rehearsal of the classic arguments of pre-Dreyfusard anti-Semitism. On the Affair itself, it went as far as to espouse the basic arguments developed by the Action Française. Louzon's article, which appeared in the best revolutionary periodical of its time (perhaps the best ever produced in France), was like a bridge spanning the entire experience of the Affair. For the members of the Maurrassian movement, it raised the hope that it might now be possible, by casting aside ten years of Dreyfusism, to renew the old alliances of nationalist Socialism.

With Louzon, it was henceforth—or once again—possible to cease regarding Socialism as incompatible with anti-Semitism. "Like Drumont, we believe that clericalism exists, that Semitism exists. Semitism and clericalism constitute the two poles of the vast bourgeois alliance, and it is their struggle for influence that is increasingly becoming the dominant feature of the internal history of the bourgeoisie."[69]

For men like Louzon and Sorel, in the war between the two factions of the bourgeoisie, the ruling of the Cour de Cassation symbolized the unquestionable "triumph of the Jewish party," but not that of Dreyfusism. On the contrary, they saw the judicial coup d'état that rehabilitated Dreyfus as "the supreme failure of Dreyfusism," from which the working class had to draw the necessary lessons.[70] For Louzon, there was no reason why the working class should have "more faith in the Jew's proclamations in favor of Law and Justice than in the priest's virtue." Having understood that it would be absurd to "deny the existence of a party of which Jewry, thanks to its financial power and its commercial and intellectual activity, is the leader," the French proletariat now realized that "it should have nothing to do with such a business."[71] Carrying this logic a step further, *La Guerre sociale* quite naturally accused *L'Humanité* of having been founded by capitalist Jews and of actually defending the Rothschilds.[72] Admittedly, Hervé did not indulge, as Louzon did, in active anti-Semitism, but he thought it advisable to stand aloof from Jaurès's compromising friends, such as Blum, Lévy-Bruhl, and Bernard Lazare. This measure would be important in preventing the mistake committed during the Affair from ever being repeated, in preventing the popular masses from ever rising again to act as a shield for democracy. On the contrary,

[69] R. Louzon, "La Faillite du Dreyfusisme ou le triomphe du parti juif," *Le Mouvement socialiste*, no. 176 (July 1906): 197–98.

[70] Ibid., 197. See also G. Sorel, *La Révolution dreyfusienne* (Paris: Rivière, 1909), 46–48.

[71] R. Louzon, "La Faillite du dreyfusisme."

[72] See "Les Rothschild et la grève," *La Guerre sociale*, 14–20 September 1910; "Ma visite à *L'Humanité*," ibid., 16–23 November 1910.

Louzon added, "when Marianne has her crisis, we shall be there to administer the Extreme Unction to her."[73]

The same arguments were used by other contemporary far-left socialist militants for whom Dreyfusism became synonymous with Clemenceau's policy of repression. For Lagardelle, the spectacle of the minister of the interior, once a professional defender of justice and truth, arbitrarily throwing the secretary general of the CGT and its treasurer in the prisons of the Republic as an administrative measure—to cries of approval from "the alarmed cohort of Dreyfusards"—was the perfect symbol of "triumphant democracy."[74]

For André Morizet too, Clemenceau's repressive measures symbolized "Dreyfusism in power,"[75] while, for Alphonse Merrheim, Dreyfusism proved "that the Republic is not a better social system than the others." Following the terrible 160-day strike at Hennebont, Merrheim was led to conclude "that the priest, the squire, the factory manager, and the Republic, in their common complicity, are all the Masters who must be eliminated."[76] This idea comes up time and again in the writings of militants, and it is almost always accompanied by a feeling of deep regret, that of having "been so naive as to defend" a Republic where "there is less freedom than in neighboring monarchies."[77]

[73] "La France s'ennuie," La Guerre sociale, 8–14 July 1908. The same themes had already appeared in the editorials by "Sans-patrie" of 5 and 26 February 1908. At the same time, Hervé published an article very characteristic of the tone and spirit of the campaign he was then waging.

"Not much chance we'll go out again and get killed for your 25 francs," said a worker—remembering June 1848 and the night of 2 December 1851—to a bourgeois republican deputy who begged him to run off to the barricades.

"Not much chance we'll go out again and get killed for your 42 francs" is what the revolutionary proletariat would reply today if the radicals came to it for assistance against the reactionary monarchist bourgeois ("Le Ministère malade," La Guerre sociale, 11–17 March 1908).

Translator's note: the sums mentioned (25 and 42 francs) were the daily allowance paid to deputies in 1848 and 1908 respectively.

[74] H. Lagardelle, "La Démocratie triomphante," Le Mouvement socialiste, nos. 174–75 (May-June 1906): 187.

[75] A. Morizet, "M. Clemenceau ou le dreyfusisme au pouvoir," ibid., 129–36.

[76] A. Merrheim, "La Grève d'Hennebont," Le Mouvement socialiste, no. 181 (December 1906): 365. See also N. Papayannis, "Alphonse Merrheim and the Strike of Hennebont: The Struggle for the Eight-Hour Day in France," International Review of Social History 16 (1971): 159–83.

[77] See the harangue by the construction workers' representative, Mathieu, a member of the workers' delegation that sought—unsuccessfully—to obtain permission from the minis-

An attentive observer of changing attitudes in the working-class world, the Action Française hailed Louzon's article. The revival of an anti-Semitic current in the ranks of the labor movement acquired an exceptional significance for the Maurrassians. Valois saw it quite simply as the sign that "the infamous pact of 1898 had been torn up."[78] Once again one could dream, as the young Maurras already had, of the immense possibilities that would open up the day when nationalism would be paired with a popular concept, "that of Socialism for example," "a Socialism freed from the democratic and cosmopolitan element."[79] Thus anti-Semitism constituted a major aspect of the theoretical alliance between nationalism and trade unionism that was being forged on the eve of the war. The junction between the left wing of the Maurrassian movement and certain elements of revolutionary trade unionism occurred on two levels: that of ideology and intellectuals, with the founding of the Cercle Proudhon; that of trade union activism, with the formation of the editorial team of *Terre libre.*

One of the driving forces behind this synthesis was undoubtedly the nationalist revival that marked the four years leading up to the war.[80] The new upsurge of anti-Semitism occurred in a context of nationalist renewal and trade unionist reaction. On 15 November 1909 the first issue of the bimonthly *Terre libre* appeared. The periodical was launched by Emile Janvion, secretary of the municipal workers' union, with the assistance of Georges Darien, author of *Biribi*, Marius Riquier, later one of the founders of the Cercle Proudhon, and a small group of trade union militants.[81] A former Dreyfusard militant[82] dismissed under Clemenceau for participat-

---

ter of the interior for a May Day demonstration ("La Reculade," *La Guerre sociale*, 4–10 May 1910).

[78] G. Valois, *La Monarchie et la classe ouvrière* (Paris: Nouvelle Librairie Nationale, 1914), 216.

[79] Quoted in T. Maulnier, "Charles Maurras et le socialisme," *La Revue universelle* 68, 19 (1 January 1937):169; C. Maurras, *Dictionnaire politique et critique* (Paris: Fayard, 1931–33), 5:213.

[80] See E. Weber, *The Nationalist Revival in France, 1905–1914* (Berkeley: University of California Press, 1958), 93–119.

[81] *Terre libre* was published from 15 November 1909 to 15 March 1912, running to 56 issues. A second series, published from 1 December 1913 to 1 May 1914, totaled only 11 issues. Janvion's bimonthly led a precarious existence; in October 1911, it was even on the verge of folding. There is no question that if, as was believed in socialist circles, the staff of *Terre libre* was "in cahoots with the reaction," it was not receiving reactionary funds.

[82] See for example APP, B/a 1108, 8 January 1899.

ing in strikes, Janvion had made a name for himself when, at a meeting held in the lecture hall of the Bourse du Travail on 1 May 1908, he denounced masonic activity in the trade unions. His notoriety had increased when, immediately afterward, *La Guerre sociale* published a long series of articles by him between 27 May and 29 July on freemasonry and the trade unions.

Freemasonry was the daily bread of Janvion's bimonthly. A great proportion of the periodical's editorial space was regularly set aside for denouncing freemasonry as the chief agent of corruption among the trade unions and of the intoxication of labor organizations by the "Judeo-bourgeois government."[83] The failure of the great strikes, the defeat of the socialist and anti-Semitic deputy of Boulogne, Myrens, and the infiltration of the trade unions by agents provocateurs were all attributed to masonic machinations, to the organized power of freemasonry, and to the special position it occupied in the republican State.[84]

In reality, Janvion's group was campaigning against "la défense républicaine" and social democracy. For them, the cult of secularism in all its guises was designed solely to dodge the real problems; it was "a relaxation for the nerves of the people, who are happy to drown their economic woes in the Judeo-masonic font" of "the Panamist and trigger-happy Republic," the Republic of "the Judeo-Dreyfusian revolution," an "ideal sauce for seasoning the proletariat à la Millerand-Gallifet."[85] Finally, "by a century-long practice of masonic priest-eating, to the gradual benefit of the rabbis, now the high priests of Jewish France,"[86] the "Judeo-republican bourgeoisie," allied with parliamentary socialism, government officials, and CGT staffers, had succeeded, after trampling on the bodies of assassinated workers, in laying hands on the coun-

[83] See a letter from Janvion to *La Libre Parole* summarizing his speech at the Bourse du Travail, quoted and commented upon in *L'Accord social*, 21 May 1908.

[84] See for example "Les Jésuites rouges," *Terre libre*, 1–15 June 1910; "Notre programme et les événements," ibid., 1–15 November 1910; "Avant le congrès," ibid., 16–31 January 1912; and "La Foire aux vestes," ibid., 1–15 May 1914. On 3 April 1911, Janvion gave a long antimasonic lecture at the Sociétés Savantes hall, which took up a full three pages in *Terre libre* (15 April–1 May 1911) and was hailed by all the right-wing press. In addition, every issue of *Terre libre* contained an antimasonic column entitled "Les Macaques."

[85] E. Janvion, "Les Derniers Piliers de la République," *Terre libre*, 1–15 December 1909 (see also E. Laurent, "La Diversion nourricière," ibid., 15–31 March 1911); "Les Derniers Piliers" and "Notre Programme," *Terre libre*, 1–15 November 1910.

[86] Damoclès, "Le Porc et le rabbin," ibid., 1–15 June 1911.

try.[87] This led Janvion to the conclusion that "the Republic is a hoax,"[88] and that since it was "a hypocritical version of the monarchy, the real thing would be preferable to the hypocritical version of it."[89] To which Marius Riquier added, "However hard Marianne and the working class try to love each other, too many corpses lie between them."[90]

As time passed, the tone hardened, and Janvion's paper asserted ever more vigorously its nationalistic and anti-Semitic Socialist character. By late 1910, the anti-Jewish campaign had become so violent that anti-Semitism became the central ideological theme of this new form of trade unionist revolt. *Terre libre* rehearsed all the classic arguments of anti-Semitism, from the conquest of France by twelve foreign tribes to the assassination of French workers on strike.[91] It eventually issued the following warning, aimed more particularly at the Jewish proletariat: "Try to behave as men and not as Jews. Otherwise, by your outbursts of unseemly nationalism, you will hasten the explosion you fear."[92]

Socialism, nationalism, anti-Semitism, direct action—this ideological corpus was elaborated on by Sorel's *L'Indépendance* in all its forty-eight issues, published between March 1911 and July 1913. *L'Indépendance* did not hesitate to dwell at length on ritual murder or to resort to gross provocations, clumsy forgeries, and most of the themes and devices used by Drumont, Guérin, and Biétry.[93]

It is worth recalling that anti-Semitism was a basic ingredient of

[87] "Pourquoi ce journal," B. Broutchoux, "Le Syndicalisme doit être extra-corporatiste," and J. S. Boudoux, "Sur les fonctionnaires syndicalistes," ibid., 15–30 November 1909.

[88] "Réponse de M. Emile Janvion," in G. Valois, *La Monarchie et la classe ouvrière*, 223. Valois had conducted a survey on the monarchy and the working class, to which Berth and Louzon, among others, had replied.

[89] E. Janvion, "Il pleut des misères," *Terre libre*, 16 May–1 June 1911, as well as "Vive la République," ibid., 1–15 September 1911.

[90] M. Riquier, "Les Aliborons de foi laïque," ibid., 15–30 November 1909.

[91] Long anti-Semitic disquisitions abounded. See for example M. Riquier, "La Race persécutée," ibid., 15 November-15 December 1910; G. Sarda, "Antisémitisme?" ibid., 15 March-1 April 1911; M. Riquier, "La Peur des mots," ibid., "Le Nationalisme juif," ibid., 16–31 August 1911, and "Le Complot juif," ibid., 16–30 November 1911.

[92] "Aux prolétaires juifs," ibid., 15 April-1 May 1911.

[93] See in particular the series of articles on ritual crimes in Russia (*L'Indépendance*, 1 July and 1 September 1911, 10 October 1912), two long articles by Sorel, "Urbain Gohier" and "Quelques Prétentions juives," and the "Notes de la quinzaine" and "Echos" in the April 1912 and February and April 1913 issues. See also a statement purportedly sent to the magazine by one Isaac Blümchen, "Paroles juives sur les Français," ibid., 1 July 1913.

l'idéologie jaune (the "blackleg ideology"). There was nothing new in the arguments developed by Biétry's movement, but it is important to emphasize the significance of anti-Semitism for the proletarian right, which came into being in the ferment of the large-scale strikes that broke out in many leading industrial centers at the turn of the century. It was no accident that, in early 1903, the blackleg militants put themselves under the aegis of a political organization founded on the same occasion, the Parti Socialiste National. Later, when this party had disappeared, the old Boulangists and former anti-Dreyfusards were instrumental in launching the Fédération Nationale des Jaunes de France and its newspaper, *Le Jaune*, in January 1904. Popular anti-Semitism duly made its appearance: Rochefort, Henri Granger, Drumont, and Lionne, the former aide of Max Régis in Algiers, all took part in this new adventure. A year later, Biétry enrolled his movement in the Fédération Nationale Antijuive sponsored by Drumont.[94]

From then on, the anti-Semitic campaign forged ahead relentlessly. At the time, a Dr. Graveline lent the prestige of his profession to the statement that anti-Semitism was a "scientific theory par excellence" and was "related to the evolutionist hypothesis, which grows more probable each day." And, drawing the implications of the natural law according to which "of two races confronting each other, one must absorb, annihilate, or expel the other," Graveline added:

By the poison of Manchester liberalism yesterday, and the plague of collectivism today, the Jew has sought to take control of the French mind in the boldest manner imaginable, even as his stock market speculations made him the master of our finances, and his intrigues disorganized our army. The Jaunes, who spread the true social doctrine and build progress on tradition, the anti-Semites, who stigmatize speculation, the nationalists, who cherish their homeland's greatness—all are therefore carrying out the same task, since, in their various ways, they are fighting the same enemy.[95]

Later, Biétry himself unleashed his fury, regretting the not-so-distant time when Jews "paid the same tax as swine at village

[94] ANP, F 7/12793, 10 April and 6 October 1905.
[95] Dr. Graveline, "Les Jaunes en province," *Le Jaune*, 22 April 1905. It was on the strength of this natural law that *Le Jaune* informed readers that "Jews are smelly" (19 June 1909, 1), and that one of its editors might conceivably own a penholder consisting of "a magnificent Yid nose" (23 January 1909, 1).

gates," and when the "vile race" was forbidden to bathe "in the rivers where Christians bathed." And lo and behold, within less than a century, "the Jews have become the masters of Europe. In France, they make and unmake governments, they have closed down Catholic churches, they have grabbed the country's entire wealth, the press, the professions, our children's education—they own everything." [96] Biétry went on to applaud the wave of pogroms raging in Russia against "the cursed race," "these hook-nosed microbes." "Carry on, Russian brothers," the leader of the Jaunes exhorted, "scatter their bones across the fields." [97]

Socialism, "that microbe," was a Jewish phenomenon; it was one of the manifestations of the Jewish world conspiracy designed to strip the Christians of land and of the instruments of production. The Socialists, "guard dogs of the Jews," had only one assignment: to "dissolve property, corrupt the idea of homeland, defile religion; where Socialism passes, they make a clean sweep for the Jews." [98] Consequently, if "'Long live the Republic!' means 'Long live the Jews,' then we shall be antirepublican. . . . If that is what their Republic is all about, then down with the Republic." [99]

Thus did anti-Semitism at the turn of the century come into its own and take on the function that it would perform until the last days of the Third Republic. It was an essential feature of the revolt against the liberal consensus and the social democratic consensus. For this very reason, the anti-Semitic movement between the wars added nothing original to the themes of its late nineteenth-century forerunner. In the course of that half-century, neither the fundamental problems nor the function of anti-Semitism changed significantly.

Anti-Semitism was a crucial aspect of the revolt against the legacy of the Enlightenment and the Revolution, of the war against the decay and decline of France. The rebels of 1890, like those of 1930, had a very keen perception of decadence, which, in their view, affected the whole of political and cultural life and pervaded mores and life-styles. Their thinking was dominated by the feeling

[96] P. Biétry, "Les Propos du Jaune," *Le Jaune*, 30 November 1907.
[97] P. Biétry, "Les Propos du Jaune," ibid., 11 November 1905.
[98] Biétry, *Le Socialisme et les Jaunes*, 1; and "Les Propos du Jaune," *Le Jaune*, 24 August and 5 October 1907. In its 28 May 1904 issue, under the heading "*L'Humanité* juive," *Le Jaune* published the list of shareholders of the socialist daily and reached the conclusion that a majority of shares were in Jewish hands.
[99] P. Biétry, "Les Propos du Jaune," *Le Jaune*, 23 January 1909.

that an entire civilization was collapsing. Toussenel already be-
moaned "the wholesale ruination of public mores," and an age
"where blood seems to coagulate in the heart."[100] Morès never
ceased repeating that "the crisis is at hand"; Drumont harped on
"the final catastrophe."[101] Maulnier, Drieu, Jouvenel, and Doriot,
the worthy heirs of these "great ancestors," went back to the same
idea time and again.

"Will we escape from French abjection?" asked Maulnier in November 1936 in an article devoted to "French degeneracy."[102] The
answer was not at all obvious, for, in the view of the future acade-
mician, France was the issue, and not only bourgeois society or the
democratic system. The sad fact was that the France of Saint Louis,
the Crusades, and Versailles had become "a nation of swindlers,
eunuchs, and thugs."[103] "Certain irrefutable truths," the editor of
Combat went on, had to be properly stressed.

France, now withdrawn into its baseness, prides itself on this by a sort of
villainous bravado . . . [it is] incapable of playing any further role in the
world [and regards] as enemies of civilization those who do not take its
own decadence as a model—that France, which trumpets the challenge of
Democracy and Law the world over, but sweats with fear at its neighbors'
slightest move and disturbs the sleep of the mighty by vain insults with a
sort of provocative cowardice—that France is the France of today.[104]

These themes cropped up time and again in the utterances of all
the revolutionaries. The image "of a certain France acting as hotel-
keeper and pimp" as well as "the easy-going atmosphere" prevailing in "the French marshland"[105] were invoked by the rebels to justify their movement. Perhaps unwittingly, Doriot too came up with
the same expressions as Barrès. He deplored "the decadence" of a
"socially . . . disjointed" country.[106] Barrès had described a "dis-
sociated and decerebrated" France.[107]

---

[100] Toussenel, *Les Juifs, rois de l'époque*, 1–3.

[101] Morès, *Le Secret des changes*, 79; Drumont, *Le Testament d'un antisémite*, 2.

[102] Such was the title of his article in *Combat* ("Sortirons-nous de l'abjection française?").

[103] Ibid.

[104] Ibid.

[105] P. Drieu La Rochelle, *Socialisme fasciste* (Paris: Gallimard, 1934), 201; B. de Jouvenel,
Le Réveil de l'Europe (Paris: Gallimard, 1938), 229 (see also 12–13, 227–28); J. de
Fabrègues, "Les Nouveaux Bellicistes et la vraie dignité de l'homme," *Combat*, April 1938.

[106] J. Doriot, *Refaire la France* (Paris: Grasset, 1938), 53; see also 10, 93; see also
R. Loustau, *Un Ordre social français* (Paris: Ed. du PPF, n.d.), 25.

[107] Barrès, *Les Déracinés*, chap. 9.

The gravity of the illness—"the triumph of materialism"[108]—could not make one forget the direct responsibility of democracy, liberalism, and the bourgeoisie. "The regime has corrupted the country to the bone. . . . Democracy has degraded us."[109] "Capitalist democracy" was killing the country; democracy and capitalism were but "the two sides—economic and political—of a same evil," and the ravages of liberalism, an ideology imported from abroad, were "practically limitless."[110] Democratic institutions betrayed the highest values of civilization, parliamentarianism debased the country and hastened its decay, and the bourgeois spirit governing the nation had produced "a civilization made of pretense and plywood, of stucco and plaster."[111] Bourgeois culture, therefore, had to be done away with, but at the same time it would be absurd to expect to build a new France on the "unbridled vulgarity" of the people: French civilization had to be prevented at all costs from being dominated by proletarian values.[112] Consequently, another civilization had to be founded, and this meant carrying out a revolution.

The revolution that would save the nation and civilization would be a total revolution—a cultural revolution, an antibourgeois revolution, "a communal revolution,"[113] a "spiritual revolution"[114] that would be "a response to the dramatic predicament of our age and of our souls,"[115] an anti-Marxist revolution "that will overtake

[108] De Jouvenel, *Le Réveil de l'Europe*, 147.

[109] Editorial in *Combat*, April 1936, entitled "Une France qui nous dégoûte." See also Charles Mauban, "Les Bons Sentiments," ibid., December 1937.

[110] P. Drieu La Rochelle, "Congrégations," *La Lutte des jeunes*, 22 April 1934 (see also B. de Jouvenel, "La Crise du capitalisme et la fin des démocraties," ibid., 1 April 1934); T. Maulnier, "Un régime ennemi des arts," *Combat*, April 1936; G. Blond, "Liberté de presse et réalisme politique," ibid., December 1937 (see also D. Bertin, "Notes politiques," ibid., February 1939).

[111] T. Maulnier, "Les Nouvelles Conditions imposées à l'action politique en France," ibid., July 1937; J. Chaperon, "Pour ou contre Stavisky," ibid., 25 March 1934; B. de Jouvenel, *"L'Economie dirigée* (Paris: Valois, 1927), 177–80; Maulnier, "Un régime ennemi des arts."

[112] T. Maulnier, "A bas la culture bourgeoise," *Combat*, October 1936.

[113] *Chantiers coopératifs*, June 1932; Norgeu, "L'Esprit bourgeois," *La Lutte des jeunes*, 22 April 1934; B. de Jouvenel, *Après la défaite* (Paris: Plon, 1941), 191.

[114] J. Roumanès, "Rèvolution marxiste ou révolution spirituelle," *La Lutte des jeunes*, 20 May 1934. See also P. Andreu, "L'Opinion du groupe l'Assaut," ibid., 8 April 1934: the fascist splinter group "l'Assaut" had adopted as its slogan Charles Péguy's "La révolution sociale sera morale ou elle ne sera pas."

[115] J. de Fabrègues, "Une révolution justifiée," *Combat*, January 1938.

Marxism in the destruction of the regime."[116] This revolution would be carried out by "all the men of the 'Right' who have understood the shamefulness of capitalism" and "all the men of the 'Left' who have understood the shamefulness of democracy."[117] Because the prevailing social and political systems had "stultified and degraded this people,"[118] there was nothing to do but replace them with new structures. "What must be established," wrote Maulnier, "is an authority, a hierarchy, an order, a harmonious, coherent, and noble society."[119] Such a society could be achieved only through a "national revolution"—an idea that recurred continually in the writings of all the Fascist-leaning figures of the period.[120] The notion of a "national revolution," that is, a revolution at once antiliberal and anti-Marxist, was thus widespread several years before it became the motto and objective of all the movements that set out to reconquer France under the protection of Nazi Germany. Only the national revolution could found a society capable of integrating the proletariat into the nation even while purging the national body of all foreign elements, most notably all the materialist doctrines that contributed so powerfully to the nation's decay.

The Jew mirrored the nation's decadence, which he both hastened and aggravated. There would have been no Dreyfus Affair, no Bloc, no Popular Front, had France not been, for many years already, on the downward path. Thus anti-Semitism was one aspect of the great revolt against materialism—against liberalism and Marxism—against the core of the intellectual heritage on which Europe had been living since the eighteenth century.

[116]T. Maulnier, "Pour un complot contre la sûreté de l'Etat digne de ce nom," ibid., December 1937. See also Marcel Péguy, "Révolution," *L'Assaut*, 2 May 1935. Only three issues appeared of this magazine, whose staff consisted of Marcel Péguy, Roumanès, and Andreu.

[117]T. Maulnier, "Le Seul Combat possible," *Combat*, July 1936.

[118]T. Maulnier, "Sortirons-nous de l'abjection française?" ibid., November 1936. See also ibid.: democracy and capitalism must be destroyed "for capitalism is nothing but the social shape of democracy."

[119]T. Maulnier, "Désobéissance aux lois," *Combat*, January 1937.

[120]For the "neosocialists," see M. Déat, "Epreuve de la démocratie," *La Vie socialiste*, 10 March 1934, and the editorial in *Néo* by "Néo," ibid., 19 December 1934; de Jouvenel, *Le Réveil de l'Europe*, 62, and "Mes cinq points," *La Lutte des jeunes*, 27 May 1934. See also the articles in *La Lutte des jeunes* by Jean Roumanès, Philippe Boegner, Claude Maldor, and B. de Jouvenel, 15 and 22 April, 24 June, and 6 May 1934. For the *Combat* group, see the following articles in that magazine by J. de Fabrègues and Thierry Maulnier: "Où sont nos principes?" April 1936; "Une révolution justifiée," January 1938; "Désobéissance aux lois," January 1937; "Sortirons-nous de l'abjection française?" November 1936.

This very revolt against materialism brought about a convergence between antiliberal and antibourgeois nationalism and the variant of socialism that, even while rejecting Marxism, remained revolutionary. This brand of socialism too, by definition, was antiliberal and antibourgeois, and its opposition to historical materialism made it the natural ally of radical nationalism. This synthesis symbolized the rejection of a certain type of civilization, of which liberalism and Marxism represented but two facets; it proceeded from a total rejection of the eighteenth century, to which liberalism and Marxism were the heirs; it was grounded in a totally different vision of the relationship between man and nature, and between man and society. But above all, this synthesis was informed by an antimechanistic explanation of human nature and by a new concept of individual motivation.[121]

It is in this sense that anti-Semitism constitutes such an important element of the Fascist revolt that began its career in France in the late nineteenth century. It is not that this revolt necessarily implied the brand of biological determinism that would serve as the basis of Nazism (but not of Fascism); rather, it is because this revolt posed a radical challenge to a certain type of civilization. The new civilization had no room for the Jew, not only because he conveyed a certain form of cosmopolitanism, but above all because he was seen as the prime agent of every form of materialist evil.

To be sure, not all forms of antimaterialism are to be equated with Fascism, but Fascism was one of those forms, and it channeled all the major currents of twentieth-century antimaterialism. In this respect, Fascism was an authentically revolutionary movement. This revolution of the mind, of the will, and of instinct formed a whole. It set out to create a new breed of man, bodily linked to a new society. Society would no longer be a battlefield for conflicting individuals or social groups, but a collectivity where all strata and all classes of society would be perfectly integrated. The natural framework for this harmonious and organic collectivity would be the nation—a purged and revitalized nation, where the individual would count only as a cell of the collective organism; a nation enjoying a moral unity that liberalism and Marxism, being causes of dissociation and war, could never provide for it. The em-

[121] See Zeev Sternhell, *Neither Right Nor Left: Fascist Ideology in France* (Berkeley, Calif.: forthcoming).

anation of such unity would be the state, whose power rested on the spiritual unanimity of the mass.

The notion of the primacy of the collectivity over the individuals that compose it is essential here. It would be the precondition for the moral unity of the nation as a natural organic collectivity and would require new modes of social organization and cultural expression. In order to mount the assault against the capitalist citadel, against a society fragmented into antagonistic classes, against the nation's decadence, against the withering away of an entire civilization, the nation had to be freed not only of the impediments of universal suffrage, parliamentarianism, committees, and parties, but above all of the entire philosophical and ethical complex that allowed the Jew to be regarded as a full-fledged member of the French collectivity.

STEPHEN A. SCHUKER

Origins of the "Jewish Problem"
in the Later Third Republic

WHEN FRANCE declared war on Nazi Germany in 1939, between 300,000 and 350,000 Jews resided within the limits
of the hexagon. Five years later, more than a quarter of them had
perished. These Jews figured as the victims not of Nazi extermination policies alone, but also of Vichy government collaboration
amid the indifference of much of the French population. How can
this complicity be explained?

The war came at an inauspicious moment for the French nation.
The country had not yet recovered from a half-decade of latent
civil war. A defensive bourgeoisie and an increasingly numerous
and militant proletariat faced each other across the chasm of class
at a time when parliamentary institutions no longer functioned
well. The unstable governments of the 1930s—whether of the center or the left—had not coped effectively with the Great Depression. They had imposed successively the rigors of deflation and the
losses of devaluation without achieving the economic recovery now
manifest across the Channel and the Rhine. Even more important,
they had failed to rearm France quickly enough for the test of
battle that lay ahead. In the first autumn days of the war, no one
who observed the dispirited *poilus* as they mustered at the Gare du
Nord for the train trip out to the Maginot Line could sustain much
optimism about the prospects.[1]

In view of the brutalities already visited on German, Austrian,

[1] For a striking description of the scene, see Robert Murphy, *Diplomat among Warriors*
(Garden City, N.Y., 1964), pp. 27–28.

and Czech Jews, the fate that lay in store for Jews in France in the event that the French army met defeat seemed plain enough. Hitler had prophesied openly in the Reichstag in January 1939, "If international finance Jewry within Europe and abroad should succeed once more in plunging the peoples into a world war, then the consequences will not be the Bolshevization of the world and therewith a victory for Jewry, but on the contrary the destruction of the Jewish race in Europe."[2] Yet who would have predicted at this time that the Nazi authorities, in the worst of cases, would find large numbers of Frenchmen prepared to acquiesce and even to cooperate in that endeavor?

In Eastern Europe, where the majority of world Jewry still lived, popular prejudice against them might form an integral component of national self-identity. But France was not Poland. Nor was it Rumania. The virulent antisemitism that had surfaced at times during the ancien régime seemed to have little place in its mainstream contemporary culture. Indeed, the opposite case obtained. The public schools of the Third Republic had for sixty years inculcated in the minds of every young citizen the egalitarian ideals of the French Revolution and the Enlightenment values embodied in the Declaration of the Rights of Man. Thus the indifference of Frenchmen to the persecution of the Jews under the Nazi occupation so contravened the professed ideals of the dominant stratum in their society that it invites special attention.

The most congenial explanations have to do with moral deficiencies and strategic miscalculations among the particular men who held power under the Vichy regime. Robert Paxton has framed the indictment in terms that command assent both among survivors of the period and historians who study it. The decision makers at Vichy, he charges, exploited the 1940 defeat for narrowly partisan purposes. Consumed by enmity against the Popular Front and by fear of social upheaval, they blinded themselves to the impossibility of carrying through a truly conservative national revolution under Nazi auspices. Not only did they initially misjudge who would win the war, but they continued to deceive themselves about the chances of shielding France from the worst Nazi depredations through limited collaboration. In the end they sacri-

[2]Speech of 30 Jan. 1939, in Max Domarus, ed., *Hitler: Reden und Proklamationen, 1932–1945*, 2 vols. (Neustadt a.d. Aisch, 1962), 2:1058.

ficed interest as well as honor. The betrayal of the Jews figured as one of numerous squalid compromises that brought no recompense.[3]

The argument rings true—as far as it goes. Yet hostility to the Jews under Vichy extended far beyond the circles of those whom Resistance adherents stigmatized as the "anti-France." The historian who takes for granted the moral lessons of the period can now afford an uncongenial line of inquiry. Did the political behavior of both native and immigrant Jews in the later Third Republic contribute to the equanimity with which, at least until 1942, many French citizens regarded their suffering?

About the facts little doubt now remains. Michael Marrus and Robert Paxton, Georges Wellers, and other historians who have studied the issue reach analogous conclusions.[4] The Vichy authorities imposed an indigenous antisemitic program in 1940–42, and the French bureaucracy furnished much of the manpower that enabled the Germans to pursue their more extreme plans for identification, expropriation, and annihilation of Jews in the occupied northern half of the country. The process that took place in the occupied zone resembled what happened elsewhere in Nazi-ruled Europe. The Reich Security Office or Gestapo (which carried out Jewish policy with the collaboration of the Foreign Office and Wehrmacht) first mandated a census of Jews in September 1940. It then moved forward step by step. It seized and aryanized Jewish property in October 1940; excluded Jews from most occupations in April 1941; incarcerated those who had violated regulations during the rest of that year; forced the wearing of the yellow star in February 1942; and began the next month to deport the Jews from the Drancy detention camp to Auschwitz. Between that time and August 1944, the Germans despatched more than 75,000 men, women, and children to the extermination camps simply for being Jews. Perhaps another 10,000 Jews—an astonishingly high percentage of total casualties—met death as members of the Resistance.[5]

[3] Robert Paxton, *Vichy France: Old Guard and New Order, 1940–1944* (New York, 1972), esp. pp. 165–85, 380–83.

[4] Michael Marrus and Robert Paxton, *Vichy France and the Jews* (New York, 1981); Georges Wellers, *L'Etoile jaune à l'heure de Vichy: De Drancy à Auschwitz* (Paris, 1973); see also the splendid colloquium summarizing new research, Georges Wellers, André Kaspi, and Serge Klarsfeld, eds., *La France et la question juive, 1940–1944* (Paris, 1981).

[5] Marrus and Paxton, *Vichy France and the Jews*, p. 363, after reviewing various estimates, endorse the conclusions of Serge Klarsfeld, *Le Mémorial de la déportation des juifs*

The impetus for extermination came from the Germans. But French officials directed the census. Frenchmen stepped forward—all too eagerly—to serve as trustees for the 38,000 confiscated Jewish businesses and properties. And French police carried out the roundups of foreign and stateless Jews in 1942. They served as the intermediaries who watched over the hapless victims at the Vélodrome d'Hiver, and they mounted the guard until mid-1943 at Drancy, Pithiviers, and Beaune-la-Rolande.

Of course historians ought not to exaggerate the consequences of this collaboration. Vichy sympathizers frequently claimed after the war that through their participation they had slowed or moderated the process, on the model of the forest ranger who sets a backfire to control the flames. Marrus and Paxton assert on the contrary that the Germans would have accomplished far less in the north without local assistance.[6] Most probably, the positions taken by Frenchmen in the occupied zone made little difference either way. Where German forces administered a territory directly, their success in exterminating the Jews depended principally on the resources they were prepared to devote to the task. That explains why they proved almost as successful in the Netherlands as in Poland. Obstruction by the native population might sustain national honor, just as resistance by the Jews themselves might help maintain their self-esteem. Such heroics could affect the outcome but marginally.[7]

Still, putative diplomatic allies of the Nazi regime or indigenous governments that preserved some degree of independence could, and did, make a difference—particularly if they avoided direct control by German troops. Italy constitutes the most obvious example, although the cases of Bulgaria, Rumania, Hungary, and Finland all prove instructive in their separate ways. Mussolini, despite his ostensible conversion to racialism, shielded Italian Jews from the worst effects of Nazi extermination policy until his fall in

---

de France (Paris, 1978), who identifies 75,721 specific deportees and lists 2,000 more who died in detention. Wellers, L'Etoile jaune, p. 257, points to a minimum of 86,119 deportees. Lucy Dawidowicz, The War against the Jews, 1933–1945 (New York, 1975), p. 363, lists all deaths including those of Jews in the Resistance as totalling 90,000. The figures advanced by David Caute, Communism and the French Intellectuals, 1914–1960 (New York, 1964), p. 161, suggest the conclusion that perhaps half of those executed as Communists were also Jews.

[6] Marrus and Paxton, Vichy France and the Jews, p. 9.
[7] See especially Dawidowicz, War against the Jews, p. 359.

1943. (Some 84 percent of them survived the war.) The Italian authorities, often demonstrating remarkable local initiative, extended this protection to all Jews in the eight departments of southern France that their forces occupied in 1942–43.[8] The leading figures in the Vichy regime, like others who acknowledged the realities of power after 1940, uneasily walked a tightrope as they sought to make a place for themselves in Hitler's New Order. Yet, as the Italian model suggests, their margin for independent maneuver on the Jewish question remained far from negligible up to November 1942, and it did not wholly disappear thereafter even though German soldiers moved across the zonal demarcation line. Here again, the record speaks for itself. The Vichy government moved to circumscribe the social role of the Jews without German prompting. Its first measures commanded substantial popular support, for the humiliation attendant on defeat worked as a profound shock upon public opinion. The majority of Frenchmen, however confusedly, aspired toward a national renewal along lines quite different from the *République des camarades*. The popular mind lumped the Jews with Communists, Freemasons, anticlerical schoolteachers, and left-leaning corrupt politicians—all of them, according to conservative publicists, sources of the moral decadence responsible for the country's collapse.[9]

Within days of taking office the first Pétain cabinet sealed the borders. Shortly thereafter, Vichy cancelled the April 1939 decree-law that had forbidden antisemitic statements in the press. A panel to review naturalizations of foreigners was established. A fundamental statute of 3 October 1940 excluded Jews from major public offices, banned them from teaching and the mass media, and established a *numerus clausus* in the liberal professions. Supplementary legislation facilitated the internment of foreign Jews and withdrew citizenship from the Jews of Algeria.[10]

Nor did the disabilities visited on the Jews in the autonomous

[8] Meir Michaelis, *Mussolini and the Jews: German-Italian Relations and the Jewish Question in Italy, 1922–1945* (London, 1979). On policy in the Italian zone in France, see Philippe Erlanger, *La France sans étoile: Souvenirs de l'avant-guerre et du temps de l'occupation* (Paris, 1974).

[9] Henri Amouroux, *La Grande Histoire des français sous l'occupation*, vol. 5, *Les Passions et les haines* (Paris, 1981), pp. 149–50.

[10] The process is described in Marrus and Paxton, *Vichy France and the Jews*, pp. 3–21, and in Wellers, *L'Etoile jaune*, pp. 50–64.

southern zone stop here. The Germans continued to dump dispossessed Jews over the border. The harsh measures taken in the north motivated many Paris Jews to traverse the demarcation line. Soon, according to official estimates, 180,000 crowded into the southern zone.[11] Even forced labor battalions set up by Vichy could not handle the inflow. The economic burden on localities grew. Vichy then took the initiative in setting up a General Commissariat for Jewish Affairs in March 1941. The first commissioner, Xavier Vallat, was a Royalist deputy who, like most of his colleagues in Action Française, held anti-German views. But Vallat expressed willingness to cooperate with the Germans in so far as their mutual policies ran along parallel lines.[12]

Vallat sought to eliminate the role of foreign Jews in France entirely pending their emigration and to erect a legal barrier that would circumscribe the influence of the sort of native Jews whom conservatives held to have poisoned public life in the 1930s. Vallat promulgated a new fundamental law in June 1941. Vichy lawyers now sought to define who counted as Jewish. (Anyone with three Jewish grandparents or with two such grandparents who could not prove membership in another religion qualified.) A series of decrees between June 1941 and June 1942 then limited Jewish participation by quota in most professions and excluded them entirely from finance, the media, and agriculture. Only Jews resident in France for five generations and families of some war veterans received exemption from these stipulations. A census of Jews and their financial holdings then took place in the unoccupied zone. Finally, the General Commissariat won authorization to seize Jewish property and assets. Vallat intended to use this authorization in the first place mainly against foreign Jews. But the process got out of hand. The Germans forced the creation of a central communal organization—the Union Générale des Israélites Français (UGIF)— and through it levied a tremendous fine on the community's assets. This required liquidation of Jewish property in a more disorderly fashion than even Vallat had contemplated.

Gradually in 1942 the Vichy regime lost control of its Jewish policy. The Germans forced Vallat out and imposed the fanatic

[11] Amouroux, *Les Passions*, p. 159.
[12] For a revealing description of Vallat, see Pierre Pierrard, *Juifs et catholiques français: De Drumont à Jules Isaac (1886–1945)* (Paris, 1970), pp. 301–5.

Louis Darquier de Pellepoix, a rabble-rousing journalist who had lived off German subsidies before the war, as his successor.[13] From the summer of 1942, the Germans made increasing demands for the roundup of Jews for deportation in the southern zone. The Vichy authorities, beset by difficulties of higher priority, consented to the deportation of foreign Jews (including their French-born children) and attempted to save native Jews alone. Yet at this point the public mood began to change. The Catholic church hierarchy found its own breaking point with the brutal roundups of children in the summer of 1942. The harshness of direct German occupation after November 1942, the removal of young Frenchmen to forced labor service in Germany during 1943, and the increasing difficulties of everyday life thereafter fostered a turnabout in French attitudes.[14]

The events of 1943–44 made manifest the limits to Vichy's hostility against the Jews. Earlier Laval and the circle around Marshal Pétain had banked on German victory. Although Laval's postwar apologia provides a defense of his actions by no means devoid of logic, historians have treated him uncharitably.[15] Political heir to Aristide Briand, the "apostle of peace" in the 1920s, Laval was no more lacking in moral integrity and just marginally more slippery than many Third Republic politicians who did not end before a firing squad. Yet his experiences as premier in 1931 and 1935 left him with deep-rooted convictions about Russia's perfidy and Britain's unreliability. His assumption up to the battle of Stalingrad that France had somehow to come to terms with the Nazis followed from these experiences. Devoid of personal antisemitism, Laval bent with the winds of Nazi racism where necessary to safeguard France's other interests. He acquiesced in the deportation of foreign and stateless Jews to their deaths, but by avoiding discussions of principle managed by tactical delay to shield most French Jews from the worst. As for Marshal Pétain, who never spoke publicly on Jewish policy, he seemed to share the prejudices of his con-

---

[13] For a somber-hued portrait of Darquier, see Jean Laloum, *La France antisémite de Darquier de Pellepoix* (Paris, 1979).

[14] This account follows the careful description of the process in Marrus and Paxton, *Vichy France and the Jews.*

[15] Pierre Laval, *The Diary of Pierre Laval* (London, 1948). For a negative evaluation, see Geoffrey Warner, *Pierre Laval and the Eclipse of France* (London, 1968). My judgments rest also on consultation of Laval's diplomatic papers for 1931 and 1935 at the Archives Diplomatiques, Ministère des Affaires Etrangères, Paris.

servative, Catholic milieu. Presumably he did not differ fundamentally from his homologue in the Free French movement, General de Gaulle, who a generation later would still castigate Jews as a self-assured people eager for domination. For both Laval and Pétain, then, Jewish policies were instrumental, not matters of ideology.

In evaluating Vichy's Jewish policy one can largely discount the fanatic antisemitism expressed by *Je suis partout*, *Au pilori*, and *Le Cri du peuple*. These collaborationist sheets appeared in the shadow of the Hotel Meurice and reflected the sentiments of the German authorities far more than they did the French.[16] Nor need one tarry to explain the mentality of Darquier de Pellepoix or his sinister henchman, Joseph Antignac, for marginal individuals who would do the Nazis' bidding appeared in all countries in occupied Europe. The genuine popularity of Vichy's indigenous antisemitic legislation of 1940–42 appears far more interesting—and frightening. These measures, it is clear, corresponded to what large numbers of Frenchmen (not merely at Vichy, but also some who later sympathized with the Resistance) considered reasonable.

The area governed by Vichy corresponded to the departments that had voted to the left under the Third Republic. Yet the prefects' reports leave little doubt about the tremendous anger that welled up against the Jews there in 1940–41.[17] The desperate Jews fleeing German rule in Paris overtaxed the resources of the south. In areas like the Côte d'Azur (where cynics began to talk "Kahn" instead of Cannes), wealthy Jews were accused of using their resources to monopolize the black market and hence of raising prices charged to others. Poor Jews, critics argued on the other hand, had become a burden in the localities on which they imposed themselves.[18] Marrus and Paxton conclude that "the Jews became a kind of lightning rod for generalized urban-rural tensions, merchant-consumer tensions, fears about future scarcities and price increases, envy at certain not clearly specified 'others' who were rumored to have it easy, and even guilt about practices widespread within the general public."[19] Much can be said for this explanation. Undoubt-

---

[16] On Robert Brasillach, Jean Lestandi, and Jacques Doriot, the publishers of these sheets, and their milieu, see Bertram M. Gordon, *Collaborationism in France during the Second World War* (Ithaca, 1980).

[17] Marrus and Paxton, *Vichy France and the Jews*, pp. 179–214.

[18] Amouroux, *Les Passions*, pp. 303–4.

[19] Marrus and Paxton, *Vichy France and the Jews*, p. 185.

edly specific economic grievances generated great hostility to these hapless refugees. And yet resentment against the Jews touched circles far beyond those suffering from privation. As the writer Paul Léautaud put it typically if unfairly, the Jews had constituted themselves a "privileged class" when they were on top some years before. Now the wheel had turned.[20]

Antisemitic measures of the Vallat stamp won surprisingly broad political support. On both sides of the spectrum Léon Blum and his Popular Front became the object of opprobrium. Months after the Allied landings in North Africa, for instance, the governor-general there still cited Blum's misdeeds as a reason why citizenship should not be restored incautiously to the Jews.[21] Attacks on Blum from the extreme left had their origins in the period of Nazi-Soviet collaboration, when Maurice Thorez denigrated his character in language on which Vallat himself would not have wished to improve.[22] Thorez's charges had a resonance in the working class that endured long after the party line had changed. It is no wonder that the clandestine *L'Humanité* discussed anti-Jewish measures only abstractly most of the time and relegated reports of Nazi deportation policy to special publications like *L'Université libre* targeted at Jewish intellectuals. Despite the thousands of sabotage actions launched by the Communist resistance against the Nazi rail network in 1941–44 and the prominent role of Jews in these operations, never did the party hierarchy seek to block one of the eighty-five convoys that carried Jewish deportees from Drancy to Auschwitz. This circumspection suggests how fearful party leaders were of testing the patience of the militants by diverting priorities even temporarily from the welfare of the Soviet Union and the class struggle against Vichy.[23]

Nor did the noncommunist Resistance wish to make a crusade out of protecting the Jews. Prevailing sentiment in the clandes-

---

[20] Paul Léautaud, *Journal*, 31 Oct. 1940, quoted by Amouroux, *Les Passions*, p. 301.

[21] For the views of Governor-General Marcel Peyrouton, see Marrus and Paxton, *Vichy France and the Jews*, pp. 195–96.

[22] For excerpts from Thorez's remarkable 1940 pamphlet, *Blum tel qu'il est*, see Philippe Robrieux, *Histoire intérieure du parti communiste, 1920–1945* (Paris, 1980), pp. 510–11.

[23] See Annie Kriegel, "La Résistance communiste," in *La France et la question juive*, pp. 348–51, 359–60; also comments by former militants Abraham Rayski and David Avram in ibid., pp. 382–83 and 397–98. Kriegel notes that *L'Humanité* did publish nine articles, all limited to the one period May 1941–Sept. 1942, touching on persecution of the Jews.

tine Socialist party, according to its Jewish secretary, was at best "asemitic," and mild expressions of antisemitism surfaced frequently. Many in the Maquis who lacked clear knowledge of German policy professed not to consider the Jews more at risk than other Resistance groups.[24] Those who joined de Gaulle in London covered the whole political spectrum, and consequently Free French views on Jewish policy also varied. The general himself behaved correctly toward Jews who rallied to his side, but his entourage held decidedly mixed views. Georges Boris, a thick-skinned financial journalist who had shown few scruples as a propagandist for the Cartel des Gauches or the Front Populaire, found it expedient to remain in a position of restricted visibility running a press review because as a Jew he did not want to compromise the cause. His intimate Pierre Mendès France similarly opted for a low profile at first.[25] The political analyst Raymond Aron, who helped run Gaullist radio, later explained why he and his fellow Jews working for *Ici Londres* remained quiet about Vichy policy right up to the roundups of August 1942. "As Frenchmen we obviously opposed all these antisemitic measures," he recalled. "But a sort of tacit agreement obtained to speak of them as little as possible." Precisely because he felt himself a Frenchman before being a Jew, Aron considered it a necessary emotional precaution to "think as little as possible about what certain Frenchmen were doing to the Jews."[26]

In short, Jews appeared unpopular among their fellow citizens for various reasons, some of which had nothing to do with the specific privations endured by Frenchmen after the 1940 defeat. While relatively few condoned the brutality of Nazi methods, a larger number wished to reduce the numbers of Jews in France and to circumscribe their place in French life. Yet after the successive waves of immigration in 1919–39 Jews still totaled less than 1 percent of the population. The refugees who arrived from Spain in the single month of February 1939 outnumbered them by a considerable margin. What motives could possibly justify such virulent hostility against them?

Marc Gerschel, a regional leader of the partisan movement Franc-

---

[24] See the testimony of Daniel Mayer and Claude Bourdet in *La France et la question juive*, pp. 375, 380–81.

[25] Georges Boris, *Servir la république* (Paris, 1963), pp. 285–99; Jean Lacouture, *Pierre Mendès France* (Paris, 1981), pp. 142–46.

[26] Amouroux, *Les Passions*, pp. 308–10.

Tireur, would later comfort himself with the notion that large sections of the population—especially in rural central and southern France—had never met a Jew and possessed but a hazy notion of the Jewish "problem." That, he maintained, enabled unscrupulous Vichy propagandists to fill the void with caricature.[27] In light of the close-knit intracommunal social ties that Jews cultivated in some provincial centers, the argument may have considerable merit even where they lived in significant numbers. Pierre Pierrard, later to become the leading historian of Jewish-Catholic relations in France, recalled that middle-class adolescents growing up in his clerical milieu in Lille during the 1930s had no contact whatever with Jews. Comments dropped by their teachers at the local *collège* led them vaguely to conflate Jews and Socialists and to associate the hated "Blum-Blum" with the equally despised Roger Salengro ("sale en gros et en détail"), the Lille mayor and Popular Front interior minister. Yet for these youngsters the soot-blackened synagogue on the rue Auguste-Angellier remained as mysterious a place as the nearby masonic lodge, the rumored scene of sacrilegious rites that shocked the imagination.[28]

Nevertheless, a good deal of evidence suggests that most adult Frenchmen in urban areas had considerable contact with Jews. Their dislike of Jews in the late 1930s did not rest primarily on ignorance. Members of the conservative bourgeoisie who embraced what they called a "reasoned antisemitism"[29] rooted their feelings in politics. They perceived the Jews as taking one side in a convulsive social struggle. While Jewish confessional leaders remained resolutely nonpolitical, the Jewish political class in the late Third Republic stood overwhelmingly on the side of the left. Those who held the left responsible for the economic and military decline of the nation blamed these developments in part on the Jews. Moreover, recent Jewish immigrants, to a far greater extent than natives, belonged to Communist-affiliated groups that appeared to be sapping the state from within. It goes without saying that, in a society based on the rights of the individual, the sociological distribution of opinion in a subgroup provides no logical warrant for reproach against any individual. But logic played less of a role in French

[27] See Dominique Veillon, "Franc-Tireur et les juifs," in *La France et la question juive*, pp. 315–28; also Gerschel comments in ibid., pp. 384–85.

[28] Pierrard, *Juifs et catholiques français*, pp. 297–98.

[29] For the genesis of the phrase, see ibid., pp. 262–63.

politics during the 1930s than passion. It is therefore a useful exercise for the historian to explore to what extent prevailing stereotypes about the Jews conformed to reality.

The more closely one examines French antisemitism in the 1930s, the more different it appears in inspiration and character from the type of Jew-hatred that had marked public life in France during the late nineteenth century. Hostility to the Jews has assumed such a variety of forms that historians have often found it heuristically more useful to focus on persistence rather than on changes in the phenomenon.[30] Even those who distinguish clearly between the medieval Christian hostility to the Jewish religion and the secular nineteenth-century ideology that ascribed to the Jews an inner nature different from that of other people tend to treat the period 1880–1945 as a bloc.[31] In this view the nationalist awakening of European peoples heightened their perceptions of Jews as unassimilable outsiders precisely at the time when Jews were first beginning to assimilate; the antisemitic parties of the 1880s are frequently pictured as forerunners of the antisemitic political movements of the interwar era. Yet whatever the truth of this model for Central Europe, it clearly has limited applicability in France.[32]

Antisemitism flourished as an ideology on both the right and the left in nineteenth-century France. But outside Alsace-Lorraine (and Algeria) the movement had only a tangential connection to the presence or social role of actual Jews. Paradoxically, at the height of Edouard Drumont's campaign against *la France juive*, fewer flesh-and-blood Jews inhabited that country than any major nation in the Western world.

France had indeed figured as the first continental state to grant the Jews full citizenship. Yet the community released from the ghetto's bonds by the Constituent Assembly in 1791 was small. Two sequential expulsions had left only a few thousand Marranos

---

[30] See, for example, Léon Poliakov, *Histoire de l'antisémitisme*, 3 vols. (Paris, 1968), and James Parkes, *Antisemitism; A Concise World History* (Chicago, 1968). The semantic analysis by Ben Halpern, "What is Antisemitism?" *Modern Judaism* 1 (1981), pp. 251–62, proves most helpful in facilitating a clear definition.

[31] See for example Paul W. Massing, *Rehearsal for Destruction: A Study of Political Anti-Semitism in Imperial Germany* (New York, 1949), which examines the antisemitic parties of the 1880s as forerunners of the political movements of the interwar era.

[32] See Hannah Arendt's incisive analysis in *Antisemitism*, part 1 of *The Origins of Totalitarianism* (New York, 1951), pp. 48–50.

within the Bourbon realm proper by the mid-seventeenth century, and the growth of the Jewish population derived thereafter from peripheral annexations by the French state in Lorraine, Alsace, and the Comtat-Venaissin. Napoleon's consistorial census of 1808, the first really reliable count, turned up only 46,663 Jews—a bare 0.16 percent of the French population. To be sure, this tiny minority (which subsequently experienced a demographic expansion more characteristic of the general European than the French pattern) increased to 89,047 persons by 1866. Almost half that number, however, lived in parts of Alsace and Lorraine ceded to Germany after the Franco-Prussian War. A mere 49,439 remained in France in 1872. Although 15,000 Alsatian Jews moved back within the country's truncated borders during the next decade and a few thousand Eastern Jews joined them after the Russian pogroms of the 1880s, the Jewish population in 1897—just before the Dreyfus Affair engaged public passions—had climbed back to just 71,249, still under 0.19 percent of the total population.[33]

By the turn of the century the Jewish community had amassed nothing like the power imputed to it by *La Croix* and *La Libre Parole*. Still, in the three generations that had passed since Napoleon convoked the Great Sanhedrin and recognized Judaism as a religion deserving state support, this group had made considerable strides toward integration in the body politic. In 1808, four-fifths of French Jews still lived in Alsace-Lorraine. Isolated in small villages by ancient restrictions, the Alsatians eked out a precarious living as horse and cattle dealers, peddlers, and small-time moneylenders. With the exception of a few score Bordeaux merchants who had grown rich in the Atlantic trade, Jews elsewhere in France stood on but a marginally higher financial plane.

The end of legal disabilities, however, led to a remarkable evolution in the economic status and the mental outlook of the Jews. Barred from most cities under the ancien régime, the Jews now urbanized quickly. Increasingly they moved to Paris—which grew to contain two-thirds of the community as a consequence of the loss of Alsace. The first generation became storekeepers. The second

---

[33] Doris Ben Simon-Donath, *Socio-démographie des juifs de France et d'Algérie, 1867–1907* (Paris, 1976), pp. 19–91; Béatrice Philippe, *Etre juif dans la société française: Du Moyen Age à nos jours* (Paris, 1979), pp. 69–177; Zosa Szajowski, "The Growth of the Jewish Population of France: The Political Aspects of a Demographic Problem," *Jewish Social Studies* (July and Oct. 1946), pp. 179–96, 297–315.

often established itself in the garment, fur, or furniture business. And the most talented representatives of the third aspired to the liberal professions or joined the state bureaucracy. Social integration proceeded apace. The Jews adopted Western modes of dress, adopted French as their mother tongue, and took advantage of the educational opportunities offered by successive school reforms at a faster rate than the population at large. In gratitude for their emancipation, Jews characteristically exhibited a perfervid patriotism, and the majority expressed ostentatious loyalty in turn to the Orleanist monarchy, the Bonapartist empire, and the Opportunist plurality of the early Third Republic. In short, no Jewish community in any major nation made more rapid progress toward assimilation. None adopted more wholeheartedly the ethos of its host society.[34] In view of the decline in religious practice, some advanced thinkers like Théodore Reinach went so far as to predict the eventual disappearance of any Jewish particularity or identification in France.[35]

The currents of modernization that drew the Jews steadily into the mainstream of French life during the nineteenth century also undermined traditional social structures. Yet the connections between these two phenomena appeared only circumstantial. Those on the left who deplored the injustices accompanying urbanization and industrialization, like those on the right who anathematized the chaos of a social order based on wealth instead of hierarchy and religious sanction, frequently demonized the Jew. For utopian socialists in the 1840s, as for opponents of the lay Republic in the 1890s, the Jew served as a convenient symbol—the emblem of the grasping financier, the subverter of the social bond. But did hostility to the mythical Jew also involve as a practical consequence active prejudice against individual Jews? The evidence cuts two ways.

Most early French socialists taxed the Jews with responsibility for the excesses of finance capitalism. Proudhon, Leroux, Fourier,

---

[34] See the statistical data by Ben Simon-Donath, *Socio-démographie des juifs*, pp. 19–201, and the analysis in Robert F. Byrnes, *Antisemitism in Modern France: The Prologue to the Dreyfus Affair* (New Brunswick, N.J., 1950), esp. pp. 95–102, 253–61.

[35] Michel Winock, *Edouard Drumont et Cie: Antisémitisme et fascisme en France* (Paris, 1982), p. 88; see also the description of the community in Michael Marrus, *The Politics of Assimilation: A Study of the French Jewish Community at the Time of the Dreyfus Affair* (London, 1971).

and Toussenel vied in casting imprecations on them. "The Jew is the enemy of humanity," Proudhon wrote in 1847. "This race must be sent back to Asia or exterminated." [36] Yet the shock value of such statements diminishes when one considers that Jewish socialists such as Karl Marx and Moses Hess also flayed Hebraic egoism and materialism in unmeasured terms and that Alexandre Weill and Dr. Terquem attacked the Rothschild family from within the Jewish community as vigorously as other radicals denounced them from without. [37]

In fact, certain Jews or ex-Jewish converts did possess a mental outlook that prepared them to embrace the business opportunities of the July Monarchy and the Second Empire. If the Rothschilds amassed the only outsized fortune, a dozen other families joined the new financial elite; and Jews, like Protestants, continued to play a disproportionate role in merchant banking down to the end of the Third Republic. But the success of individuals, most of whom had severed any formal communal connections, scarcely affected the mass of their coreligionists. Significantly, only 124 Paris Jews felt wealthy enough to contribute to the Comité de Secours et d'Encouragement in 1840, while a quarter of the community received alms from that organization. [38] It is at least arguable that the Jew qualified as the ideal symbolic representative of the evils of modernity not because he stood at the center of the new society, but because he remained peripheral to it.

The French, after all, have long maintained an inward-looking culture. They show interest chiefly in themselves. Under the ancien régime, however, the censorship had frequently impelled intellectuals to make points about their own society obliquely. They put their criticisms in the mouths of foreigners, projected their hopes and fears on outsiders, and discoursed on other peoples' social arrangements to cast veiled aspersions on their own. Postrevolutionary literary practice perpetuated this convention. A direct line links Montesquieu's Persian travelers and Voltaire's anthro-

---

[36] Quoted by Stephen Wilson, *Ideology and Experience: Antisemitism in France at the Time of the Dreyfus Affair* (Rutherford, N.J., 1982), p. 334.

[37] George Lichtheim, *The Origins of Socialism* (New York, 1969), pp. 176–78; Philippe, *Etre juif dans la société française*, p. 204.

[38] On the role of Jewish bankers, see Theodore Zeldin, *France, 1848–1945*, vol. 1, *Ambition, Love, and Politics* (London, 1973), pp. 77–86; on the Comité de Secours, Philippe, *Etre juif dans la société française*, p. 179.

pophagous Indians with twentieth-century theatrical depictions of spiritual impoverishment in industrial America.[39] Given the limited number of Jews in France, antisemitic rhetoric at times served an analogous function. The stereotypical Jew—the miser, the money-lender, the social climber, the parvenu—who emerges from the pages of Vigny, Balzac, or Hugo exemplified traits that the French did not comfortably acknowledge in themselves as they passed through the strains of early industrialization.[40] Significantly, some antimodernist writers employed the terms *Jew* and *usurer* inter-changeably, without a specific "racial" connotation.[41]

Of course the wave of ideological antisemitism that engulfed the country in the last two decades of the nineteenth century seemed real enough to its victims—particularly to those who suffered in the Algerian pogroms and the less violent anti-Dreyfusard riots that coursed through thirty French towns in 1898.[42] But most Jews in the *métropole*, if we can believe the testimony gathered by Paula Hyman, felt nothing more than temporary anxiety. They never doubted the solidity of the political institutions that protected their rights. Nor did they experience much discrimination in their per-sonal or professional lives.[43] Indeed, not all political antisemites—however virulent their rhetoric—exhibited active prejudice against Jews as individuals. As Charles Péguy later put it, "the antisemites talk about the Jews, but the awful truth must be told: The anti-semites know nothing about the Jews."[44] Increasingly, historians have come to interpret the events of these decades as a many-sided conflict among opposing political forces vying for control of the state. The principal issue was the fate of the Republic, not the sta-tus of the Jews. Much to the frustration of ardent republicans, Jew-ish communal institutions kept a deliberately low profile in the

[39] For an instructive reading of eighteenth-century Utopian thought, see Frank E. Manuel and Fritzie P. Manuel, *Utopian Thought in the Western World* (Cambridge, Mass., 1979), pp. 413–52; for analysis of French theatrical preoccupation with the United States before World War I, consult Charles William Brooks, "America in France's Hopes and Fears, 1890–1920" (Ph.D. diss., Harvard Univ., 1974).

[40] See the sensitive reading in Philippe, *Etre juif dans la société française*, pp. 206–17.

[41] See Jeannine Verdès-Leroux, *Scandale financier et antisémitisme catholique: Le Krach de l'Union Générale* (Paris, 1969).

[42] Wilson, *Ideology and Experience*, pp. 106–24.

[43] Paula Hyman, *From Dreyfus to Vichy: The Remaking of French Jewry, 1906–1939* (New York, 1979), pp. 9–10.

[44] In *Notre jeunesse* (Paris, 1910), quoted by Wilson, *Ideology and Experience*, p. 666.

battle, as did the mass of individual Jews outside intellectual circles. Léon Blum would later ask acidulously whether, under other circumstances, the proper, bourgeois Captain Dreyfus would have become a Dreyfusard.[45]

Stephen Wilson's survey of the geographical sociology of antisemitism at the peak of the Dreyfus controversy confirms how difficult it is to fix the movement's etiology. In Paris and some eastern departments traces of apprehension about Jewish economic competition appeared. In certain strongly Catholic areas the laity and lower clergy held the Jews partly responsible for secularizing education and loosening divorce restrictions. But elsewhere antisemitism's strength did not correlate either with the presence of Jews or with objections to concrete political views attributed to them. Instead, it reflected displaced grievances relating to agricultural distress, diminished regional autonomy, and strains occasioned by depopulation in the countryside and unbalanced growth in the towns. It also mirrored the unfocused resentment of those who felt that economic and social changes promoted by the republican political class had worked against them.[46]

Given the large symbolic component in turn-of-the-century Jewhatred and the diffuse nature of the practical complaints involved, it is scarcely surprising that antisemitism dissipated as a mass movement as rapidly as it had arisen. The years 1899 to 1905 saw the final defeat of the army, the church, and the rural notables of *la vieille France*. They marked the consolidation of the anticlerical Republic dominated by the social classes and political forces to which native Jews increasingly belonged. The smart set in the faubourg St.-Honoré might still engage in antisemitic banter (like the joke about the Jewish heiress, "as beautiful as Venus, as rich as Croesus, and as innocent . . . as Dreyfus"), but worse could be heard in the drawing rooms of London or New York.[47] While racialist thinking did not disappear, lethal admixtures of integral nation-

---

[45] Léon Blum, *Souvenirs sur l'affaire* (Paris, 1935). For an elaboration of this interpretation see Douglas Johnson, *France and the Dreyfus Case* (London, 1966), and Marcel Thomas, *L'Affaire sans Dreyfus* (Paris, 1961). On the Jewish response, Marrus, *Politics of Assimilation*, remains the most incisive study.

[46] Wilson, *Ideology and Experience*, pp. 655–70. Pierre Sorlin, *"La Croix" et les juifs (1880–1899): Contribution à l'histoire de l'antisémitisme contemporain* (Paris, 1967), p. 221 offers another geographical mapping of antisemitism according to slightly different criteria.

[47] Philippe, *Etre juif dans la société française*, p. 254.

alism and social radicalism appealed mainly on the political fringes during the Belle Epoque. Only in retrospect would they appear as precursors of "fascism."[48] It certainly seemed at the time that World War I had brought the final step in acceptance of the Jews. Their battlefield ardor won general recognition; three figured prominently in the Clemenceau ministry that achieved victory in 1918; and even Maurice Barrès acknowledged them as one of the "spiritual families" of France. As a further augury, La Libre Parole, flagship of the antisemitic press, foundered ignominiously in 1924 because of lack of subscribers.[49]

François Goguel's now familiar typology interprets French politics since 1789 as a cyclical conflict between a party of order and a party of movement.[50] Until the early twentieth century, the Jews had always had reason to favor the party of movement. From the Revolution onward, every step forward for that party had fostered new advances for the Jews. The outcome of the Dreyfus Affair, however, freed the Jews from having to take a defensive position on the "left." And the same generation that witnessed the consolidation of the Republic also confirmed the embourgeoisement of the various strands in native Jewry. Thus the material interests of most French Jews lay increasingly with the center—that is to say with the parties of order.

One might have expected these developments to facilitate a more normal distribution of the community across the political spectrum. But such a realignment proceeded slowly. The Jews continued to exhibit distinctive political characteristics and to stand, as a voting bloc, predominantly on the left. Two factors joined to produce this result. The predilections of Jewish intellectuals, and of the Jewish political class that came to consciousness during the Dreyfus period, still reflected the struggles of the past. Even more significant, the demographically static native community was submerged by a new immigration, which tripled the number of Jews in France within twenty-five years.

[48] Zeev Sternhell, in Maurice Barrès et le nationalisme français (Paris, 1972) and La Droite révolutionnaire, 1885–1914: Les Origines françaises du fascisme (Paris, 1978), provides a brilliant exposition of this ideology but does not always escape the peril of reading history backward.

[49] Hyman, From Dreyfus to Vichy, pp. 49–62; Marrus and Paxton, Vichy France and the Jews, pp. 31–32.

[50] François Goguel, La Politique des partis sous la IIIe République (Paris, 1958).

The new arrivals from Eastern Europe brought with them the chiliastic outlook and radical politics of the shtetl. Moreover, they bore the stigmata of "underdevelopment" characteristic of their homelands, and that would confine at least the first generation to the lowest rungs of French society. Although the cultural gap between the two subgroups grew ever wider in the 1930s, each faction found reasons to support the Popular Front. If antisemites in the 1890s had known little about the Jews, their successors in the 1930s perceived them much more clearly. Of course extreme elements among the new antisemites drew on an irrational xenophobia rich in conspiratorial fantasy as well as on the crude racism in vogue across the Rhine. Yet for moderates who considered that the Popular Front meant social upheaval and economic disaster at a time when France faced the greatest foreign menace in its history, dismay at certain manifestations of "Jewish influence" also represented a pragmatic response to a not wholly imaginary threat.

To speak of Jewish influence is to venture admittedly onto perilous ground. In the absence of scientific polling, one cannot ascertain with precision the normative sentiments of Jewish citizens in particular social categories. Inevitably one falls back upon the views of those identified as Jewish spokesmen. But who, in the later Third Republic, could claim to speak for the Jews? Certainly not the rabbinate: by the 1930s assimilation had progressed so far that less than 4 percent of the Paris Jewish community remained even nominally affiliated with a consistorial synagogue.[51] In practice, those who represented French Jewry in the eyes of the larger public were politicians, intellectuals, journalists, and cultural luminaries.

Yet since the turn of the century, leading intellectuals—men such as the sociologists Lucien Lévy-Bruhl and Emile Durkheim, the philosopher Henri Bergson, the social critic Julien Benda, the historians Daniel Halévy and Marc Bloch, and the legal scholar and civil libertarian Victor Basch—had almost all abandoned religious observance and severed their ties to the ethnic community.[52] At most, like Bloch, they felt "neither pride nor shame" in their origins, but insisted that their intellectual development drew nourish-

[51] Hyman, *From Dreyfus to Vichy*, p. 30.

[52] For a consideration of the religious identification of these and other French Jewish intellectuals, see H. Stuart Hughes, *Consciousness and Society: The Reconstruction of European Social Thought, 1890–1930* (New York, 1958), and *The Obstructed Path: French Social Thought in the Years of Desperation, 1930–1960* (New York, 1966).

ment exclusively from Gallic roots. Others, like Bergson, flirted with Catholicism. For a surprisingly large number, socialism came to represent the true and only church. The occasional younger scholar like Raymond Aron, who spoke of his personal reactions as a Jew to Nazi antisemitism in lectures at the Ecole Normale Supérieure, quickly learned that deviations from universalist values buttered no parsnips in the academy; and few, in any case, felt tempted to follow Aron's example.[53]

In the light of these cultural discontinuities, one can sympathize with Paula Hyman's sense of injustice that the marginal Jew who pontificated in the chic biweeklies received more attention than the Jewish corner merchant, minor state functionary, or consistorial leader. The latter might embrace the ordinary values of family, property, and patriotism as fiercely as the next bourgeois. But that scarcely registered with those disposed by ideology to regard the Jews as an alien race. For such people, the more unconventional and radical the Jewish publicist or intellectual, the more authentically Hebraic.[54] Still, the preoccupation of the extreme right with the importance of Jewish opinion makers in the 1930s did not entirely miss the mark. After all, the French have always accorded more notice to intellectuals than most peoples. And in the interwar period, print journalism did exert a decisive influence on the nation's moral climate.[55]

Why did Jewish political figures, like assimilated Jewish intellectuals, stand disproportionately on the left in interwar France? All over Europe, Jews had obviously taken part in the great nineteenth-century movements for social and scientific "progress"—ranging from socialism to psychoanalysis—out of proportion to their numbers. A small minority everywhere, they had nevertheless played a

---

[53] For discussion of Bloch's Jewish origins see his *Strange Defeat: A Statement of Evidence written in 1940* (New York, 1968), pp. xiii, 3; the perceptive interpretation by the editor in Marc Bloch, *Memoirs of War, 1914–15*, ed. Carole Fink (Ithaca, 1980), pp. 15–73; and Carole Fink, "Marc Bloch: The Life and Ideas of a French Patriot," *Canadian Review of Studies in Nationalism*, 10 (Fall 1983), pp. 235–52. For Bergson's consideration of deathbed conversion, see Hughes, *Consciousness*, pp. 119–20; for the socialist loyalties of Lévy-Bruhl, Halévy, and their circle, see Harvey Goldberg, *The Life of Jean Jaurès* (Madison, 1968). For Aron's atypical outlook and consequent difficulties, see his *Mémoires: Cinquante Ans de réflexion politique* (Paris, 1983).

[54] Hyman, *From Dreyfus to Vichy*, p. 22.

[55] On the significance of the interwar press, see Raymond Manevy, *Histoire de la presse, 1914 à 1939* (Paris, 1945).

notable role in stretching the limits of existing academic disciplines and creating a host of new ones. Did some specific feature in Jewish culture predispose members of the group to intellectual ferment and to an irreverent disregard for traditional ways of doing things? Did some fundamental element in Jewish eschatology incline even those who had forsaken religious precepts to sympathize with the economically downtrodden and the socially oppressed? A simple answer appears impossible. If Hannah Arendt is right that the process of emancipation transformed the Jewish intelligentsia into a social group whose members shared psychological attributes and reactions transcending national boundaries, no clear consensus has emerged about the precise content of the psychology to which she refers.[56] At least in France, however, one can account for the majority political preferences of the Jewish leadership class without dealing with issues on this level of abstraction.

The mass of native Jews had secured economic and social mobility for their children in the course of a single generation, namely 1871–1905. The political processes that opened doors for the Jews during this period also brought the cultural homogenization of the French people. The public school emerged as the crucible of social change. In a process that began with the Ferry laws of 1879–86 and culminated with banishment of the Catholic teaching orders in 1902–5, the government imposed exclusively state-run educational institutions at every level from the primary school through the university. Because education became increasingly hierarchical, it afforded predictable mobility to the academically gifted. Jews of modest origins thus found a way to penetrate the elite. But along with the opportunities came considerable ideological baggage. With clerical competition vanquished, a highly indoctrinated teaching corps preached a secular religion of the Republic, and young Jews embraced this secular faith as eagerly as any segment of the population. Moreover, those who reached the pinnacle of the scholastic system—the Ecole Normale Supérieure—often fell under the spell of its remarkable librarian, the socialist Lucien Herr. The doctrines of Jean Jaurès exerted an attraction on idealistic youth at the universities as well (particularly before the cultural shift that set in around 1905). No wonder, then, that the bulk of the Jewish intelli-

---

[56] See Arendt's insightful but elusive discussion in *Antisemitism*, pp. 56–68.

gentsia developed left-republican, anticlerical, and even socialist sympathies, and that they maintained these values long after they had ceased to be fashionable in other circles.[57]

In view of this background, the prominence of Jews in radical politics during the 1930s should occasion no surprise. Yet historians sympathetic to the left have persistently sought to minimize Jewish involvement in the Popular Front. Marc Bloch, so scrupulous in his medieval scholarship, initiated the exculpatory process shortly after the 1940 collapse. "It is the fashion to say that the Jews were behind the Left-Wing movement," he observes in *Strange Defeat*. "Poor Synagogue—always fated to act as scapegoat! I know, from what I saw with my own eyes, that it trembled even more violently than the Church."[58] Bloch's disingenuousness seems the more peculiar because he elsewhere acknowledges how utterly marginal religious institutions had become for educated Jews of his generation.

Joel Colton, the distinguished American biographer of Léon Blum, engages in similar special pleading. Colton finds "not the shadow of justification" for charges that the first Blum cabinet of 1936–37 had a predominantly Jewish complexion, and he taxes the journalist Raymond Recouly with "complete inaccuracy" for having asserted that five Jews sat in it as ministers or undersecretaries.[59] As a matter of fact, the first Blum cabinet contained only four Jews (Blum, Cécile Léon-Brunschwicg, Jules Moch, and the militant freemason Jean Zay—who by some reckonings counted as a Protestant atheist rather than a Jewish atheist because his father alone was Jewish). But the second Blum cabinet did have five

[57] On the general processes, see Mona Ozouf, *L'Ecole, l'église et la République, 1871–1914* (Paris, 1963); Antoine Prost, *Histoire de l'enseignement en France, 1800–1967* (Paris, 1968); Eugen Weber, *Peasants into Frenchmen: The Modernization of Rural France, 1870–1914* (Stanford, Calif., 1976), esp. pp. 303–38; and Katherine Auspitz, *The Radical Bourgeoisie: The Ligue de l'enseignement and the Origins of the Third Republic* (Cambridge, 1982). For a concrete description of educational integration for the Jews, see Julien Benda, *La Jeunesse d'un clerc* (Paris, 1936). For the connection between republican ideology and the new orthodoxy in a representative discipline, see William R. Keylor, *Academy and Community: The Foundation of the French Historical Profession* (Cambridge, Mass., 1975). On the influence of Lucien Herr see Hughes, *Consciousness*, pp. 60–61; and Robert Smith, "L'Atmosphère politique à l'Ecole Normale Supérieure à la fin du XIXe siècle," *Revue d'histoire moderne et contemporaine*, 20 (1973), pp. 248–69.

[58] Bloch, *Strange Defeat*, p. 165.

[59] Joel Colton, *Léon Blum: Humanist in Politics* (New York, 1966), p. 144.

Jews (Blum, Moch, and Zay again, plus L.-O. Frossard and Pierre Mendès France).[60]

Finally, Jean Lacouture, the latest Blum biographer, concedes that his subject moved personally in "a very Jewish milieu" but tries to demonstrate that *Le Populaire*, the party newspaper, possessed an interdenominational staff. Yet after identifying Louis Lévy, Georges and Charles Gombault, Salomon Grumbach, and Daniel Mayer among the obviously Jewish contributors, Lacouture takes refuge in the improbable claim that chief editor Oreste Rosenfeld was not Jewish after all; aside from that, he finds but three certifiable non-Jews to balance the scales (one so obscure that he cannot discover his Christian name). Considering the percentage of native Jews in the age cohort from which these journalists were drawn (under 0.25 percent), this clearly amounts to less than perfect equilibrium.[61]

Of course, prevailing attitudes in an ethnic subgroup do not necessarily coincide with the views expressed by individual politicians or journalists. A scientific investigation must begin the other way around. Significantly, however, a prosopographical survey of all Jews who served in the 1936–40 legislature confirms in striking fashion the impression that elected officials from this background supported the Popular Front en masse. Henri Amouroux identifies ten Jews who remained members of the Chamber of Deputies in 1940 (after the exclusion of the Communists) and five such members of the Senate.[62] Perhaps Amouroux missed one or two other legislators with Jewish antecedents (for politicians of anticlerical orientation rarely admitted to religious affiliation). He has, in addition, overlooked Jules Moch and misidentified one deputy who, his name notwithstanding, seems to have come of Breton stock. As revised, the list includes the following ten deputies (along with the departments that they represented): Léon Blum (Aude); Jean Pierre-Bloch (formerly Pierre Bloch, Aisne); Ludovic Oscar Frossard (Haute-Saône); Max Hymans (Indre); Charles Lussy (formerly Charles Ruff, Vaucluse); Georges Mandel (formerly Louis Rothschild, Gironde); Pierre Mendès France (Eure); Jules Moch

---

[60] Jean Jolly, ed., *Dictionnaire des parlementaires français, 1889–1940*, 8 vols. (Paris, 1960–78), 1 : 140–47.

[61] Jean Lacouture, *Léon Blum* (New York and London, 1982), pp. 526–27.

[62] Amouroux, *Les Passions*, p. 166.

(Hérault); Raymond Vidal (Bouches-du-Rhône); and Jean Zay (Loiret). In this company, nine supported the Popular Front fully; the tenth, the Clemenciste maverick Georges Mandel, stood generally with the center on economic and social issues but drew increasingly close to Blum after 1936 on matters of foreign policy.[63]

The list includes men with some variation in social background. Yet one can generalize with fair accuracy that the typical Jewish deputy was a solidly middle-class, Paris-born Jew of Alsatian origin who had risen in the Socialist party hierarchy and won assignment to a safe seat in the left-leaning section of the country below the Loire river. Six were born in Paris; seven held seats on or south of the Loire. Eight could trace their ancestry to Ashkenazic origins; the exceptions were Vidal, who came of a family long established in Marseilles, and Mendès France, the grandson of a Sephardic fertilizer salesman who had migrated from Bordeaux to the capital. The political homogeneity of the Jewish deputies mirrored their social similarities. Blum, Pierre-Bloch, Hymans, Lussy, Moch, and Vidal all held membership in the Section Française de l'Internationale Ouvrière (SFIO). Frossard left that party so that he could serve as labor minister in 1935–36 and considered himself henceforth an independent socialist, but his failure to anticipate the sitdown strikes of June 1936 made him nevertheless a bogeyman of the right. Mendès France and Zay both stood on the extreme left of the Radical-Socialist party that had advocated the Popular Front with the Socialists and Communists.[64] (The one identifiable Jewish Communist deputy, incidentally, seemed out of place among his proletarian party comrades but fit the Jewish Socialist social profile precisely.[65])

Admittedly the Jewish senators formed an older and more conservative group than the deputies, but that reflected the relationship

[63] Biographical data are taken from Jolly, *Dictionnaire*. On Mandel's political evolution and rapprochement with Blum, see John M. Sherwood, *Georges Mandel and the Third Republic* (Stanford, Calif., 1970), pp. 165–221.

[64] This material derives from prosopographical analysis of the material in Jolly, *Dictionnaire*. For the genealogy of Mendès France, see Jean Lacouture, *Pierre Mendès France* (Paris, 1981), pp. 27–41. On Zay, see his *Souvenirs et solitude* (Paris, 1946); for Frossard's rightward evolution from Communism to moderate Socialism, see his *Sous le signe de Jaurès: De Jaurès à Léon Blum. Souvenirs d'un militant* (Paris, 1943).

[65] The Alsatian-born medical doctor Georges Lévy, deputy for the Rhône and PCF public health specialist, was one of three Communists of bourgeois origin among the twenty-six legislators expelled from the Chamber in January 1940. For the complete list, see Jacques Fauvet, *Histoire du parti communiste français*, 2 vols. (Paris, 1964), 2:41–42.

between the Senate and Chamber as a whole. Alexandre Israël, the most radical among them until his death in 1938, had helped animate the Cartel des Gauches in 1924 and 1932. Four of the remaining five—Moïse Lévy, Pierre Masse, Abraham Schrameck, and Georges Ulmo—belonged to the large, amorphous center-left grouping known as the *gauche démocratique*. Schrameck, as interior minister under the Cartel in 1925, had used the prerogatives of his office for party purposes (as interior ministers often did) and incurred the wrath of Action Française; and Masse, who had served as Painlevé's undersecretary of war in 1917, also retained a vaguely left coloration in the public mind. But by the 1930s Schrameck and Masse, like Lévy and Ulmo, had really become local notables and left active politics behind. That was a fortiori true of the more conservative Maurice de Rothschild, who avoided the rostrum and devoted himself to charities and the fine arts. Interestingly, while Rothschild fled the country in July 1940, all four of his confreres voted to grant Pétain full powers (compared with only two out of ten Jewish deputies). The moderation of the Jewish Senate contingent should have served to soften the public perception of Jews as uniformly radical. That it failed to do so testifies to the political passions aroused by events in the Popular Front era.

Pierre-Bloch figured as the only one among the ten deputies to espouse Jewish particularist causes during his parliamentary career.[66] But most of the others displayed themselves prominently on the left side of the barricades during the ideological and political struggles of the mid-1930s. In retrospect it seems fairly well established that the February 1934 Paris riots involved no "fascist" plot to overthrow the Third Republic. Rather, these disturbances reflected primarily the frustration of numerous uncoordinated groups at the somnambulent maneuverings of the Chautemps and Daladier cabinets in face of the deepening financial crisis. They mirrored also the public's dismay at the extent of parliamentary corruption revealed by the mysterious death of Serge-Alexandre Stavisky, a swindler and confidence man who happened to be Jewish. In fact

---

[66] Pierre-Bloch coauthored a sympathetic book on David Frankfurter, a Jew who in 1936 had murdered a Nazi official in Switzerland. The Ligue Internationale contre l'Antisémitisme tried unsuccessfully to turn the case into a cause célèbre. See Pierre Bloch and Didier Meran, *L'Affaire Frankfurter* (Paris, 1937). In his postwar career as a journalist, Pierre-Bloch returned frequently to Jewish themes. See, e.g., his *Les Causes politiques de l'antisémitisme en France* (Paris, 1954).

neither the riots, nor the subsequent activities of the larger extra-parliamentary leagues in 1934–36, posed a serious threat to republican stability.[67] But that was not how matters appeared to the left in those years.

As Socialists, Communists, and left-wing Radical Socialists moved toward formation of a Popular Front, the rhetoric of the left grew increasingly violent. At the same time, anti-Jewish sentiment revived on the extreme right on a scale unparalleled since the Dreyfus era. But which phenomenon was cause, and which merely effect? It is at least arguable that antisemitic outbursts in the right-wing press—however offensive in tone—constituted one element in an essentially defensive reaction by conservatives in the face of the vituperative campaign mounted by the left against the Doumergue, Flandin, and Laval cabinets.

Numerous signs bear witness to this change in mood. For example, in the pre-Depression years elderly clericals had often nurtured an obsession about Jews as progenitors of Freudianism, nudism, the cocktail, jazz, cubism, and other aspects of modern life that they abhorred. But more or less active philosemitism had also made significant headway among the adherents of Social Catholicism and among younger Catholics generally. Now the balance reversed itself.[68]

In the Royalist Action Française, which spawned most of the far-right *groupuscules* that emerged in the 1930s, the older leaders had manifested prior to the advent of the Popular Front what Eugen Weber calls a pragmatic or incidental antisemitism—largely aimed at increasing visibility. After Léon Blum aligned his SFIO

---

[67] See most recently Serge Berstein, *Le 6 février 1934* (Paris, 1975); also René Rémond, *The Right Wing in France: From 1815 to de Gaulle* (Philadelphia, 1969), pp. 254–94; Peter Larmour, *The French Radical Party in the 1930's* (Stanford, Calif., 1964), pp. 140–54; and Eugen Weber, *Action Française* (Stanford, Calif., 1962), pp. 319–40. Max Beloff's older view of a military plot in 1934 no longer seems plausible ("The Sixth of February," in James Joll, ed., *The Decline of the Third Republic* [London, 1959], pp. 9–35). Larmour, p. 150, minimizes corruption in the Radical party and rejects André Tardieu's charge that 14 deputies were involved. But Lord Derby, the usually well-informed former British ambassador, reported to London that up to 160 deputies had taken money from Stavisky. See Neville Chamberlain Diary, 3 Feb. 1934, NC 2/23A, Neville Chamberlain Papers, Birmingham University Library.

[68] For a discussion of the turning point from a different point of view, however, see Lazare Landau, *De l'aversion à l'estime: Juifs et catholiques en France de 1919 à 1939* (Paris, 1980), pp. 162–202. On Catholic sentiment, Pierrard, *Juifs et catholiques français*, pp. 245–85, also proves very helpful.

with the foreign-controlled Parti Communiste Français (PCF) a metamorphosis took place. In early 1936 the government dissolved Action Française and the paramilitary Camelots du Roi (whose strength the Ligue Internationale contre l'Antisémitisme [LICA] had always ludicrously exaggerated) after a mob no longer connected with either organization had roughed up Léon Blum. Charles Maurras, the revered elder statesman of the movement, would shortly suffer trial and imprisonment under a hastily drafted press law for having verbally menaced Blum and other supporters of sanctions against Italy. Subsequently, right-wing newspapers increasingly conducted their vendetta against Blum and the Popular Front in antisemitic terms.[69] Yet the essentially political nature of this campaign appeared patent from the outset.

Georges Mandel, for instance, had won the repeated plaudits of the far right for his no-nonsense treatment of the postal union as posts and telephones (PTT) minister in 1934–35. Only after he deserted his long-time ally Pierre Laval over the Ethiopian issue and became the linchpin of the center-left Sarraut combination that guided France through the elections did the right begin to dwell on his ethnic origins. *Le Canard enchaîné*, the satirical weekly, commented with suitable irony: "When Georges Mandel was a Lavalist, he was called an Israelite. . . . But now that he has become a Sarrautist, he is a dirty kike. . . . Soon [the right] will admit that the telephones worked even before he came to power."[70]

After 1936, anti-Jewish sentiment came to focus increasingly on the person of Léon Blum. As premier in 1936–37 and again in 1938, Blum could not escape ultimate responsibility for the economic stagnation and social disintegration attributable to Popular Front policies. Quite apart from this, moreover, Blum emerged as a symbol of everything that conservatives disliked about the Jewish intelligentsia. Representatives of the Jewish community had feared such a development. Indeed one prominent spokesman for the Paris Consistory reportedly appealed to Blum to abjure office in order to spare his coreligionists from reproach.[71] But the Socialist

[69] Weber, *Action Française*, pp. 194–201, 360–74. For a surprisingly favorable view of LICA and its president, the intemperate Bernard Lecache, by Jewish historians, see Hyman, *From Dreyfus to Vichy*, pp. 205–6 and 227–30; and David H. Weinberg, *A Community on Trial: The Jews of Paris in the 1930s* (Chicago, 1977), pp. 26–27, 164–65, and *passim*.

[70] *Le Canard enchaîné*, 29 Jan. 1936, quoted by Sherwood, *Mandel*, p. 178.

[71] Weinberg, *Community on Trial*, pp. 81–82.

leader, who had recently castigated the Jewish bourgeoisie for pu-
sillanimity at the time of the Dreyfus Affair, brushed this appeal
aside.[72] Probably he did not fully realize how close the tradition
of political civility had already come to breaking down.[73] When
Xavier Vallat told the Chamber in June 1936 that to govern this
"peasant nation" it would be better to choose someone whose origins sprang from French soil than to select a "subtle Talmudist,"
Blum exploded in anger. Yet far worse would follow. The right continued to propagate the story (which had originated as political
satire) that Blum was really a Bessarabian named Karfunkelstein.
By 1938 the Royalist historian Pierre Gaxotte would call him a
man accursed: "He incarnates all that revolts our blood and makes
our flesh creep. He is evil. He is death."[74]

Foreign observers, while conceding that Blum possessed an unfortunate manner, often expressed puzzlement at the depth of bit-
terness that he evoked. Both American and British diplomats taxed
the bourgeoisie with stupidity for failing to realize that he had
kept a social revolution within bounds.[75] Yet in truth Blum contributed mightily to the escalating rhetoric of which he became a victim. During the election campaign he spoke repeatedly of the
"military fascism" of the leagues and the "Jesuitical fascism" of
Doumergue and Tardieu. Reasonable men might well question the
republican credentials of a politician who denounced his centrist

[72] In 1899 Blum had summoned his fellow Jews to be brave and ignore the pinpricks of
discrimination; in his 1935 memoir of the Dreyfus period he explicitly attacked middle-
class Jews who thought that they could deflect antisemitism through political neutrality. See
his Nouvelles Conversations de Goethe avec Eckermann, in L'Oeuvre de Léon Blum,
1891–1905 (Paris, 1954), 1:262–68; and Souvenirs sur l'affaire, pp. 24–27.

[73] After Munich, Blum changed his mind and stated publicly that a Jew should not increase the international difficulties of his country by serving as premier. See Sherwood,
Mandel, p. 214.

[74] Colton, Léon Blum, p. 144, quotes the Vallat speech of 6 June 1936. On the origin of
the Karfunkelstein story, see Weber, Action Française, p. 375. Gaxotte's article in Candide,
7 Apr. 1938, is quoted among others by Weber, Action Française, p. 411, and Winock,
Drumont et Cie, p. 125.

[75] The American ambassador, who was sensitive to such matters, described Blum as having "the little fluttery gestures of the intellectual queer ones," but deemed him as conservative as anyone who could hold the situation together. (See Bullitt to Roosevelt, 24 Oct.
1936, in Orville H. Bullitt, ed., For the President, Personal and Secret: Correspondence between Franklin D. Roosevelt and William C. Bullitt [Boston, 1972], pp. 173–74.) Sir Orme
Sargent of the British Foreign Office similarly could account for the hysteria of his friends in
the Paris beau monde only by reflecting that a Frenchman "is always more frightened for his
pocket than he is for his skin." (Sargent to Phipps, 29 Dec. 1936, Sir Eric Phipps Papers,
PHPP I 2/10/90, Churchill College Archives Centre, Cambridge.)

colleagues as "fascist" while continuing—even in after years—to number the Communists among the "democratic forces" and "defenders of freedom."[76] In retrospect Blum has become a cult figure; his principal biographers accept his professions of humanistic socialism at face value and portray him as a visionary.[77] Those, however, who grappled with Blum in the political arena during the 1930s became conscious of his less attractive attributes. They perceived him as a rigid doctrinaire, an economic innocent, and a vainglorious phrasemaker for whom the betterment of mankind coincided unerringly with the dictates of factional interest. Blum's otherwise vacuous personal papers indicate that the enveloping flattery of his party comrades buffered him from real-world choices, and the recollections of dissident socialists make clear that he encouraged, even required, adulation.[78] Hence those on the right—in 1936 or later during the Riom trials—who targeted Blum as the "gravedigger" of the regime could point to more than policy misjudgments. Did not some fundamental defect in personality or outlook contribute to the man's willful, almost arrogant, refusal to come to grips with the diplomatic and financial constraints on France in time of crisis? Was it not then a short step for those who already thought in racial categories to associate Blum with his fellow Jews?

At his trial in 1941 Blum would seek to justify his record by claiming that he had "carried out the will of universal suffrage—the supreme authority."[79] This was a curious argument. In a democracy, a leader is supposed to lead, not merely to gratify the demands of his most benighted followers. By any objective mea-

[76] See Blum's retrospective discussion of the Popular Front, written in 1941, in *For All Mankind* (London, 1946), pp. 84–85. Blum's ambivalence toward the Communists is all the more remarkable in view of the abuse that the party lavished on him. See Annie Kriegel, "Léon Blum et le parti communiste," in Pierre Renouvin and René Rémond, eds., *Léon Blum, chef de gouvernement, 1936–1937* (Paris, 1967), pp. 125–36.

[77] See, e.g., Colton, *Léon Blum*; Lacouture, *Léon Blum*; Gilbert Ziebura, *Léon Blum: Theorie und Praxis einer sozialistischen Politik* (Berlin, 1963); James Joll, *Three Intellectuals in Politics* (New York, 1971). Most of the contributors to Renouvin and Rémond, *Blum, chef de gouvernement*, also take a favorable view.

[78] See the congratulatory letters scattered through sections 1 BL and 2 BL of Léon Blum Papers, Fondation Nationale des Sciences Politiques, Paris; also the devastating portrayal by Marcel Déat in "Mémoires, Ière partie: Le Massacre des possibles," ch. 13, MS. at Bibliothèque Nationale.

[79] Henri Michel, *Le Procès de Riom* (Paris, 1979), p. 112. In view of Michel's partisan defense of Blum and the other Riom defendants, it is worthwhile reading Blum's notes for his defense and the whole of this extraordinary testimony in 3 BL 5–6, Blum Papers.

sure, the economic and defense policies championed by Blum (whatever their attractions in another time and place) set France on the road to catastrophe. How could Blum (and with him virtually the whole of the Jewish political class) fail to understand that, in the circumstances prevailing in 1936, inflated wages, reduced hours, paid vacations, and disorder in the workplace would push up costs and price French goods out of world markets unless accompanied by drastic devaluation? It took no great foresight to predict that this program would lead—as it did—to diminished production and a disabling inflation just as Nazi Germany was gearing up for war.[80]

On national security matters Blum and his epigones gave proof of even greater folly. For years Blum had voted against the defense budget and championed unilateral disarmament in the hope of setting a moral example (even for Nazi Germany).[81] In 1936 he acquiesced in some modest rearmament. Yet during his second ministry (it did not pass unnoticed that he acted on the advice of his coreligionists Mendès France and Georges Boris), he sought to make a major rearmament program dependent on confiscatory capital taxation.[82] Meanwhile, he promoted belligerence against Italy and appeasement of Germany—the opposite of what prudent calculation would dictate. In 1938, he indulged the naive hope that the Soviet Union would save Czechoslovakia.[83] Proponents of realpolitik might well despair of ideological posturing such as this. There was much to be said in favor of the resolute defense of French interests against Nazi aggression. There was something to

[80] For a sensible survey of the economic consequences of Popular Front policies, see Jean-Marcel Jeanneney, "La Politique économique de Léon Blum," in Renouvin and Rémond, Blum, chef de gouvernement, pp. 207–32, and the index graphs in ibid., pp. 298–304. For a revealing display of the Popular Front mentality, see Pierre Mendès France's spirited reply in ibid., pp. 233–40. For evidence that leading industrialists considered the Matignon accords "pure madness" and foresaw all their consequences, see Jean-Noël Jeanneney, François de Wendel en République: L'Argent et le pouvoir (Lille and Paris, 1976), pp. 793–96.

[81] Edouard Daladier, who served as Blum's war minister but loathed him, maintained an extensive file documenting his chief's attacks on preparedness from 1930 onward. See "Prophéties de Léon Blum," in 2 DA 6, Dr. 1, Edouard Daladier Papers, Fondation Nationale des Sciences Politiques.

[82] Robert Frankenstein's skillful Le Prix du réarmement français (1935–1939) (Paris, 1982) makes out the best possible case for Popular Front rearmament policy. For the 1938 capital taxation program, see ibid., pp. 183–87; and Lacouture, Mendès France, pp. 95–101.

[83] For Blum's unrealistic view that the Soviet Union, after its army purges, would still intervene to help Czechoslovakia, see Procès-verbal, Comité Permanent de la Défense Na-

be said, perhaps, in support of realistic defeatism (as advocated, for example, by the pacifist Socialists under Paul Faure). But the most skillful dialectical prestidigitation could scarcely excuse those who had labored to undermine the national defense for almost two decades and then, as the cataclysm approached, summoned the nation to stand to its guns. However unfair *L'Action française* was to the security-minded Mandel and Reynaud, its thrust at Blum during the Munich crisis struck home.

> S'ils s'obstinent, ces cannibales,
> A faire de nous des héros,
> Il faut que nos premières balles
> Soient pour Mandel, Blum et Reynaud.[84]

The dismal truth is that most French Jews took positions—if not with the unanimity ascribed to them by right-wing publicists— roughly analogous to those of Blum. As internationalists, they had embraced a fashionable antimilitarism through the mid-1930s. They had, oblivious to diplomatic consequences, supported the social reforms of 1936. They did come to believe, particularly after Munich, that only through the destruction of Nazism could European Jewry find its salvation. Jewish communal leaders felt acutely sensitive to charges of "warmongering," and their press organs spoke elliptically and often with great embarrassment. In the nature of things, however, Nazism could be destroyed only through war.[85] In short, French Jews, despite their patriotism, found that their outlook and interests diverged from those of other Frenchmen. Their fellow citizens would not forget this after the 1940 debacle. When the search began for scapegoats, the consciousness of these differences would remain. Here we have not a rationalization but at least a partial explanation of the widespread indifference to the anti-Jewish legislation of 1940–41.

The anti-Jewish animus that engulfed most sections of French

---

tionale, 15 mars 1938, in Carton 2N 20, Service Historique de l'Armée de Terre, Château de Vincennes. For his equally illusory notion that Belgium remained loyal to the French alliance in 1936, see the note on the Blum–Delbos–Van Zeeland–Spaak conversation of 17 Dec. 1936 in Carton 11, 179–3, Ministère des Affaires Etrangères et du Commerce Extérieur, Brussels.

[84] *L'Action française*, 29 Sept. 1938, quoted in Sherwood, *Mandel*, p. 212.

[85] See Weinberg, *Community on Trial*, pp. 178–88; and Hyman, *From Dreyfus to Vichy*, pp. 229–32.

opinion in 1940 derived in part from the political stands of highly visible native Jews. But this irritant figured largely as a backdrop for the most proximate cause of public feeling—the presence on French soil of some 200,000 recent Jewish immigrants or refugees from Eastern and Central Europe. Between 1914 and 1939 the newcomers overwhelmed the demographically static native Jewish community. The number of Jews in the country tripled. Yet only a small minority of the new arrivals had achieved French citizenship by the time World War II broke out. Fewer still had genuinely as- similated. A substantial number of the newest refugees had settled in France illegally, simply because the nation did not maintain effective border controls; they had evaded expulsion on a variety of pretexts. The politics and culture of the Eastern Jews rendered them highly unpopular in conservative circles. The French people generally felt neither an affinity with them nor a responsibility for them. Why, then, the Vichy authorities might well have asked themselves, should they sacrifice their limited bargaining power with the Nazis in order to safeguard people who neither in fact nor in law were wholly French?

The answer may seem at first glance obvious to those whose humanitarian sensibility reflects a retrospective knowledge of the Jewish Holocaust in all its horror. And yet the question deserves examination in context—as it presented itself to political authori- ties at the time. Pierre Laval would argue before his execution that the government had one primary duty: "to protect French Jews." It could not hope also to guarantee the wider right of asylum in a country occupied by the German army.[86] No doubt, Laval made concessions that he did not have to make.[87] Still, the distinction that he drew between French and "foreign" Jews remained funda- mental—not least for the Jews themselves.

The Jews, to be sure, divided further along the axes of class, reli- gious belief, political affiliation, and degree of assimilation. A scru- pulous sociologist would undoubtedly prefer to speak of a con- tinuum rather than a sharp split and would note that correlations of belief and ethnic origin are never perfect when individuals think

---

[86] Laval Diary, pp. 91, 99.

[87] See the review of the evidence in Fred Kupferman, "La Politique de Laval, 1942–1944," in La France et la question juive, pp. 31–56; and in Marrus and Paxton, Vichy France and the Jews, esp. pp. 261–69 and 343–46.

for themselves.[88] But on a political level, the distinction between natives and immigrants manifested itself clearly. Between the wars social divisions between the two groups actually widened, and the resentment of the one and the jealousy of the other frequently surfaced in public hostility. The native-dominated consistorial organizations distanced themselves sharply from the extremist politics of immigrant Jews in the 1930s, just as the accommodationist Jewish notables who ran the Union Générale des Israélites de France followed a wartime strategy entirely opposed to that of the foreign militants who enlisted in the Communist-affiliated Main d'Oeuvre Immigrée (MOI).[89] Characteristically, some natives responded to the restrictive legislation of October 1940 by railing at the injustice of measures formulated so that "Frenchmen of old stock find themselves mixed up with those recently naturalized." Immigrants reacted by deriding the natives as PIAFs—Patriotes-Israélites-Antisémites-Français.[90]

The perpetuation of these quarrels even in the face of Nazi persecution should alert the observer to the presence of long-standing grievances. Yet many French writers have drawn a discreet veil over the subject, preferring like Béatrice Philippe to treat these tensions with lighthearted delicacy, like Anny Latour to dwell on the heroism of all Jews, or like Georges Wellers to rehearse the villainy of the Nazis and their Vichy accomplices.[91] David Weinberg and Paula Hyman, the most distinguished American students of Jews in twentieth-century France, do focus frankly on native-immigrant differences. Both, however, embrace wholeheartedly the immigrant point of view.[92] Those sympathies may seem perfectly natural to historians whose roots lie in a culture that celebrates "immigrant gifts" and romanticizes the experience of Eastern Jews making

[88] This view is expressed persuasively by Pierre Vidal-Naquet in his introduction to Maurice Rajsfus, *Des juifs dans la collaboration: L'UGIF (1941–1944)* (Paris, 1980), p. 17.

[89] Compare the account in Rajsfus, *Juifs dans la collaboration* (which after a third of a century still exhibits raw hostility to the native community) and the nostalgic discussion of MOI by Annie Kriegel, "La Résistance communiste," pp. 345–47, 354–70.

[90] For native Jewish reaction to the 1940 legislation, see Amouroux, *Les Passions*, pp. 166–68, and Rajsfus, *Juifs dans la collaboration*, pp. 59, 63–67; for the term *PIAF*, see Rajsfus, p. 14.

[91] Philippe, *Etre juif dans la société française*; Anny Latour, *La Résistance juive en France (1940–1944)* (Paris, 1970); Wellers, *L'Etoile jaune.*

[92] Weinberg, *Community on Trial*; Hyman, *From Dreyfus to Vichy.*

their way in a new land.[93] But the French have little notion of immigrant gifts. They hold no brief for pluralism. In the best of times
they maintain a relentlessly assimilationist culture. In a period
of tension like the 1930s such attitudes could easily shade into
xenophobia. We cannot hope to see the immigrants as native Jews
perceived them—still less to appreciate how ordinary Frenchmen
felt about their presence—unless we acknowledge the cultural assumptions of French society.

France had remained largely outside the turbulent population
movements of nineteenth-century Europe. Few potential Jewish
migrants from the Romanov and Hapsburg empires even thought
of going there. Why should an observant Jew from the shtetl want
to enter the cross fire between intolerant Catholic clericals on one
side and antireligious republican zealots on the other? And since
France industrialized slowly, it offered in any case little employment
opportunity to newcomers without skills.[94] Between 1881 and 1914
almost 2 million Jews immigrated to the United States, and 120,000
went to Great Britain. Scarcely 30,000 arrived in France, and
Sephardic refugees from parts of the Ottoman Empire or North
Africa touched by Gallic cultural influence made up fully a third of
these.[95] Paris could not compete with New York as the "promised
city." Any number of New York neighborhoods boasted more Jews
from the Pale of Settlement than peopled all of France.[96]

After World War I, however, conditions governing both the push
and pull of population movements changed. The United States followed Britain's lead in restricting immigration. At the same time
France, because of its frightful battlefield losses, experienced a labor shortage that grew most acute during the industrial spurt of

[93] As a measure of the romanticization of the immigrant experience, note the popular
response in the United States to Irving Howe and Kenneth Libo, World of our Fathers (New
York, 1976). On the beginnings of the American notion of immigrant gifts, see John
Higham, Strangers in the Land: Patterns of American Nativism, 1860–1925 (New York,
1973), pp. 116–30.

[94] Louis Chevalier, La Formation de la population parisienne au XIXe siècle (Paris,
1950); A. Armengaud, La Population française an XIXe siècle (Paris, 1971); G. Mauco,
Les Etrangers en France (Paris, 1932).

[95] Hyman, From Dreyfus to Vichy, pp. 63–64; Weinberg, Community on Trial, pp. 2–10;
Michel Roblin, Les Juifs de Paris (Paris, 1952), pp. 52–73. The several estimates made in
the absence of firm census data do not coincide perfectly.

[96] Moses Rischin, The Promised City: New York's Jews, 1870–1914 (Cambridge, Mass.,
1962).

the later 1920s. Meanwhile, Poland, Rumania, and the Austrian succession states once more made life difficult for Jews. The Eastern Jews who arrived in France during the interwar period joined a stream that included in all almost a million foreign workers. The newcomers initially found work in the mines and factories as well as in certain "preindustrial" crafts and the ethnically traditional clothing and textile trades. But when the Depression struck, their presence became unwelcome. The Laval government succeeded in placing quotas on the employment of aliens in 1934–35, yet the Popular Front repealed those measures, and the renewed tightening of employment regulations in 1937–38 came too late to discourage additional migrants (many of them Eastern Jews long resident in Germany and Austria who now moved on for political reasons). A discontented Jewish subproletariat developed, reduced to eking out a living on the margins of society.[97]

About three-quarters of the immigrant Jews eventually found their way to Paris. There they lived, often packed six or eight to a room in scarcely imaginable squalor, concentrated in the Pletzl section of the Marais, the area behind the Bastille, and especially in the Yiddish-speaking ghetto located in the *bas quartier* of Belleville. A large number did not even try to assimilate into French society. The representative shtetl Jew who emigrated to America before the war had carried with him the institutional supports of small-town life—the *landsmanshaftn*, the burial society, the synagogue—that cushioned his acculturation. By contrast, the characteristic emigrant in this later cohort had undergone urbanization and a degree of deracination in Poland. Frequently he had become radicalized in the Polish trade union movement and arrived in France with an identity forged in the heat of class struggle at home. (Indeed, the typical Paris militant of the 1930s had suffered expulsion from Poland in his youth for underground activity.) Yet whatever their background or skills, Jews who had not already obtained a residence permit in the prosperous 1920s could not aspire to industrial employment in France. Most new arrivals found themselves relegated to home labor under exploitative conditions in the clothing trades, while others survived as rag merchants, tinkers, or

[97] For an account of general migration and employment trends, see Colin Dyer, *Population and Society in Twentieth-Century France* (Sevenoaks, Kent, 1978). For the Jewish perspective see Weinberg, *Community on Trial*, pp. 14–19; and Hyman, *From Dreyfus to Vichy*, pp. 65–68.

repairmen of second-hand goods. Under the circumstances, the chiliastic element in traditional Judaism could easily resurface as a chiliasm of despair. Although the immigrant community remained segmented into a welter of competing organizations riven by ideological animosities and personal rivalries, one common denominator united virtually all: a radical approach to the issues of contemporary French politics.[98]

Immigrant Jews typically adhered to some variation or permutation of Zionism, socialism, or communism. Traditional Jews often belonged to one of the seven Zionist parties, while their secularized coreligionists transferred their enthusiasm to one or another of the socialist faiths. To French conservatives in the 1930s, all of these doctrines seemed pernicious. Native Jews had earlier won acceptance by acknowledging the unitary quality of French culture and ostentatiously repudiating any notion of dual allegiance. During World War I they had opposed the Balfour Declaration so vigorously that the Zionist leader, Nahum Sokolow, declared in despair that "talk of Jewish nationalism in France was like attempting to win converts for Luther at the Vatican."[99] The immigrant Jews, by contrast, went well beyond verbal sympathy for Zionism. In the 1930s they actively campaigned for a boycott against goods from Nazi Germany and proselytized in favor of various forms of intervention to aid their persecuted brethren abroad. Their mounting sense of urgency proved wholly realistic. All the same, their expressions of concern and outrage fanned the flames of suspicion among xenophobes that persons with a shaky legal right to stay in France at all sought to embroil the nation in foreign quarrels.[100]

The Ligue Internationale contre l'Antisémitisme, headed by the former communist Bernard Lecache, linked the militant defense of Jewish interests abroad to what it defined as the struggle against "fascism" within France. In practice this degenerated into an attempt to align the pro-Zionist forces in the immigrant community with the extreme left in politics. A petty but revealing contretemps over the holding of an interfaith ceremony to commemorate

[98] This analysis draws heavily on Weinberg, *Community on Trial*, pp. 11–44, but the material in Weinberg's notes often proves more helpful than his text.

[99] Florian Sokolow, "Nahum Sokolow's Paris Diary: Some Extracts," *Zion*, Nov. 1952, pp. 44–48. The diary covers Sokolow's negotiations with native Jews in February 1918.

[100] Weinberg, *Community on Trial*, pp. 45–148.

France's war dead illustrates LICA's tactics and its long reach in the immigrant community. A small organization of moderate native Jewish veterans, the Union Patriotique des Français Israélites, sought to undercut LICA's propaganda and to revive the spirit of the *union sacrée* by inviting Colonel de la Rocque's Croix de Feu to participate in its annual ceremony, held in the synagogue on the rue de la Victoire. A prominent consistorial rabbi presided over this ceremony for several years in the mid-1930s, but LICA's oft-repeated, albeit wholly spurious, charges of antisemitism against La Rocque forced abandonment of the practice after 1936.[101]

Political sentiments among immigrant Jews clustered in the part of the spectrum running from the democratic far left to the revolutionary extreme left. Admirers of the French SFIO, adherents of the Polish Bund (Medem-Farband), anarchists, left Zionists, Stalinists, and Trotskyites distinguished themselves sharply from each other. Yet bourgeois Frenchmen who did not care to analyze matters closely might well perceive in the positions of these sects, so hotly debated in the Yiddish press, an array of nostrums all equally dangerous to the health of the existing social order. The Fédération des Sociétés Juives, a loosely structured umbrella organization for Jewish mutual aid societies and cultural groups, represented moderates and religious traditionalists. Its leaders possessed socialist leanings, but their exposure to Communist and Bundist tactics in Eastern Europe had impressed upon them the perils of cooperation with the hard left. On the whole they preached political neutrality and concentration on ethnic issues. At the other extreme stood Polish and Rumanian militants who considered the Parti Communiste Français insufficiently revolutionary and decried its apparent petty bourgeois aversion to violence. In this peculiar context, the PCF assumed what looked like a centrist stance, particularly after the Comintern, for its own cynical reasons, sanctioned the tactics of the United Front. The new reformist orientation of the PCF Yiddish-speaking subsection and its concentration on bread-and-butter issues won it much sympathy among homeworkers in the clothing trades. Building on this success, the party seized the lead-

---

[101] The accounts of this question in Weinberg, *Community on Trial*, pp. 77–81, and in Hyman, *From Dreyfus to Vichy*, pp. 203–28, take the LICA point of view and reflect the partisanship of the sources on which these authors rely. For a demonstration that La Rocque was not antisemitic, see Philippe Machefer, "La Rocque et le problème antisémite," in *La France et la question juive*, pp. 95–100.

ership in creating the Mouvement Populaire Juif in 1935–36. If the Communists never commanded majority support among the immigrants in a strict numerical sense, they capitalized on their organizational skills to dominate the community's politics in the Popular Front era—even to the extent of making inroads on the normal constituency of the Fédération.[102]

In the 1936 elections, Jewish voters provided the margin of victory for at least ten Popular Front candidates—including seven Communists—in the Paris region alone. In a particularly revealing contest in the Pletzl, the Jewish voting bloc cast its second-round ballots overwhelmingly for the hard-bitten proletarian apparatchik Albert Rigal in preference to the centrist native Jew, Edmond Bloch, founder of the Union Patriotique des Français Israélites. The result seemed the more extraordinary because the normally pro-Socialist Yiddish daily, *Parizer Haint*, and Israël Jefroykin of the Fédération, who was fighting to stem Communist infiltration of his organization, had issued categorical warnings about Rigal's extremism.[103] (The irony of the outcome would become fully manifest only in September 1939, when Rigal signed the Communist manifesto for immediate peace with Nazi Germany while still sitting for his Jewish constituency.[104])

The striking electoral successes of the Jewish Popular Front gave only a partial indication of the drift to political extremism within

---

[102] Weinberg, *Community on Trial*, pp. 103–47. For the crucial shift in Comintern policy in 1934–35 and a clear demonstration of its purely tactical nature, see Julius Braunthal, *History of the International, 1914–1943* (New York and Washington, 1967), pp. 415–46; and Edward Hallett Carr, *Twilight of the Comintern, 1930–1935* (New York, 1983). This account of Communist power holds most true for Paris. The PCF apparently achieved dominant standing in provincial Jewish centers with some lag. Monique Lewi suggests in her path-breaking local study of Roanne, for example, that the 35–40 Jewish families in that community included only a dozen "virulent" Communists in the 1930s, not counting the large number of fellow travelers who had belonged to the Marxist-Zionist youth movement Hashomer Hatzaïr in Poland but never formally joined the PCF. Lewi's local data indicate that the Communist-front Union des Juifs pour la Résistance et l'Entraide (UJRE) did not become the predominant force among Roanne Jews until after the Liberation. Nevertheless, her account does not at all substantiate Weinberg's contention (pp. 156–57) that, as of 1936–37, the Jewish left had "little or no influence among Jews outside of Paris." See Monique Lewi, *Histoire d'une communauté juive: Roanne. Etude historique et sociologique d'un judaïsme* (Roanne, 1976), esp. pp. 64–72.

[103] Weinberg, *Community on Trial*, pp. 114–16, 141–42; Hyman, *From Dreyfus to Vichy*, pp. 214–15.

[104] On Rigal's later role, see Jacques Fauvet, *Histoire du parti communiste français*, 2 vols. (Paris, 1964–65), 2:41; and Stéphane Courtois, *Le PCF dans la guerre* (Paris, 1980), pp. 60, 439.

the immigrant community. The illegal newer migrants, many of radical persuasion, could not seek citizenship at all, and the number of Jews who adopted French nationality under the 1927 legislation facilitating naturalization turned out to be less than half the number commonly assumed.[105] Yet lack of civic enfranchisement did little to dampen political ferment among immigrants. Native Jewish spokesmen admonished them repeatedly that their activities contributed to the recrudescence of antisemitism. Robert de Rothschild, head of the Paris Consistory, issued a pointed warning in 1934 and 1935. If his coreligionists from Poland and Rumania were not happy in France, asserted Rothschild, "let them leave." "One does not," he added, "discuss the regime of a country whose hospitality one seeks."[106] The expression of such sentiments, however, had a counterproductive effect. Among the sorely tried foreign residents of the Pletzl and Belleville, they merely exacerbated feelings of frustration and alienation.

In 1937, disappointment with the economic achievements of the Popular Front drove Jewish militants further to the left. Meanwhile the PCF dissolved its Yiddish subsection as a response to the growing xenophobia of the party's mainstream working-class constituency, and this too augmented the prevailing sense of isolation. In the last two years before the war the immigrant community became increasingly factionalized and demoralized. While a further Communist endeavor to seize the leadership of Jewish cultural organizations and to group them in the Farband fun yidishe gezelshaftn in 1938 fell somewhat short of success, no constructive political alternative emerged. The months after the Munich conference witnessed the expression of various forms of despair. Some urged an impractical "return to the ghetto"; others argued that, as far as Jews were concerned, little remained to choose between the democracies and the totalitarian states. The Daladier government began for the first time to imprison illegal immigrants or to force them to volunteer for the army as an alternative to peremptory deportation.[107]

---

[105] The Vichy denaturalization commission concluded in 1943 that only 23,648 Jews had won citizenship from 1927 through 1940. This compared with the 50,000 who the Germans earlier estimated had taken out papers from 1927 through 1932 alone. See the discussion in Marrus and Paxton, *Vichy France and the Jews*, pp. 323–28.

[106] See the differing renditions of these speeches in Hyman, *From Dreyfus to Vichy*, p. 203; and Weinberg, *Community on Trial*, p. 76.

[107] Weinberg, *Community on Trial*, pp. 131–211.

While the plight of the immigrants worsened distressingly as war approached, the situation inevitably looked different from the point of view of the French government and people than it did from the vantage point of the Jews. When a social reaction to the Popular Front, accompanied by a justified panic about the state of French defenses, took hold in 1938–39, beleaguered conservatives were not disposed to overlook the actual role played earlier by immigrant, or native, Jews. Meanwhile, the Nazi invasion of Austria and then the German *Kristallnacht* pogrom brought two new waves of desperate Jewish refugees fleeing westward. This time the French government remained stonily unsympathetic. Though it could not deter a certain amount of infiltration, Paris declared itself "saturated."[108] American officials who at the Evian Conference and afterward argued that, with a modicum of goodwill, the nations of the world could absorb the German refugees expressed dismay at the refusal of the French and other states bordering on the Reich to do their part. "Whatever one may think individually about Jews," wrote the responsible State Department official, "the suffering that these people are going through cannot but move the humanitarian instincts of even the most hard-hearted."[109] The posture adopted by the French government seemed all the more hypocritical because, in February 1939, Paris admitted willy-nilly almost half a million Spaniards who came pouring over the Pyrenees as a result of Franco's victory.[110]

And yet French hard-heartedness, however reprehensible in moral terms, possessed a certain logic. For the Nazi propaganda minister Goebbels, the assassination of a German embassy secretary in Paris by a Polish Jew served as a mere pretext for launching the November 1938 pogrom.[111] In view of the ethnic tensions of which Paris had become the scene, however, it is scarcely surprising that most Frenchmen drew a perverse conclusion. Even Radical-Socialist newspapers now joined the clamor that the government deal sternly with refugees who sought to carry on the struggle against their persecutors from French soil. The incident lent an

---

[108] See Joseph Cotton memorandum for the president, 3 Sept. 1938, U.S. State Department (US) file 840.48 Refugees/809½, Record Group 59, National Archives.

[109] T. C. Achilles memorandum, 15 Nov. 1938, US 840.48 Refugees/900½.

[110] Louis Stein, *Beyond Death and Exile: The Spanish Republicans in France* (Cambridge, Mass., 1979), pp. 5–54.

[111] Helmut Heiber, *Goebbels* (New York, 1972), pp. 246–47.

appearance of verisimilitude to charges made by the right after Munich that the Jews, even if they denied it, secretly wanted war.[112]

Moreover, despite the Americans' optimistic prognostications, the refugee problem did not really admit of a solution. Poland demanded to be relieved of its Jews on a basis of parity with Germany; Rumania and Hungary watched its maneuvers with undisguised interest; and the millions of potential emigrants from all those states could not be placed anywhere.[113] The French knew that the mass expulsion of Jews from Central Europe, with its inevitable confusion, provided Germany with an easy opportunity to infiltrate agents into France. Although the Nazi "fifth column" never became as grave a problem as some anticipated, French leaders had no wish to become the victims of "war by refugee" while preparing belatedly for armed conflict.[114] That the fear of such infiltration did not entirely lack substance received unhappy confirmation during the war, when the Nazis employed the Viennese Jews Léo Israélowicz and Wilhelm Biberstein to monitor the activities of the Union Générale des Israélites de France.[115] But the greatest danger to national security in 1939 came from the Communist side, particularly after the signing of the Nazi-Soviet pact. The disorderly roundup of enemy aliens (many of them Jews) that took place when war broke out in one sense reflected French paranoia; in another it represented a confession of inability to control the vast number of refugees of various provenance now resident in the country.

The historian's evaluation of French government policy in this period must depend on the individual historian's reading of later

---

[112] See the superb analysis by Edwin Wilson of the American Embassy on the growth of antisemitism in France after Munich: Wilson to State Department, 8 Nov. 1938, US 862.4016/1809.

[113] For Polish representations and direct threats to foment antisemitic outbursts, see Messersmith memoranda, 3–19 Nov. 1938, in US 840.48 Refugees/884, 949, 952, 1056; on attitudes of the other Eastern European states, see Truman Smith report, 16 Dec. 1938, US 862.4016/2064.

[114] For discussion of "war by refugee" and evidence that American officials suspected Germany of taking advantage of the refugees' continued plight after the fall of France to send agents on to the United States, see Fred I. Israel, ed., *The War Diary of Breckinridge Long: Selections from the Years 1939–1944* (Lincoln, Neb., 1966), pp. 114, 133–35, 154, 174 (26 June, 28 Sept.-3 Oct., 20 Nov. 1940, 28 Jan. 1941).

[115] For the role of Israélowicz, Biberstein (incorrectly identified by Marrus and Paxton as Bigerstein), and Kurt Schendel, see Rajsfus, *Juifs dans la collaboration*, pp. 69, 145, 151–52, 265–83; and Latour, *La Résistance juive en France*, p. 46.

events. The role played by immigrant Jews in the armed struggle against Nazi Germany after 1939 remains, even today, a sensitive question. The dispute centers on the policies of the Communist party and its affiliate, the Main d'Oeuvre Immigrée (MOI), which coordinated the resistance activity of most Eastern Jews. By all accounts younger Jews from this background gave proof of extraordinary heroism once Germany had turned against Russia; according to Annie Kriegel, they may have undertaken half of all urban guerrilla actions against the Nazi invader in 1941–42. But despite the evocative force of her recollections, Kriegel views the stirring events of those years through the astigmatic lens of nostalgia.[116]

The Gaullist resistance, both for security and social reasons, did not, Kriegel maintains, accept foreign adolescents like herself. The MOI offered to immigrant Jews a way out of their isolation and the single realistic alternative to the negative identity thrust upon them by the Nazis. The Jews thus enlisted under the Communist flag out of special motives of their own.[117] But did the shock troops of MOI do battle for patriotic reasons or to further the interests of the Soviet Union and the internat·onal working class for which it claimed to stand? The anecdotal evidence suggests that some young Jews, at least, considered themselves engaged in a class war against the French and German bourgeoisie and hesitated, for example, to take action against "working-class" German enlisted men.[118] Moreover, as Kriegel herself concedes, a goodly number of MOI leaders departed after the war to carry on the struggle for "socialism" in Poland, Hungary, and Rumania, and returned only in the 1960s when antisemitism drove them out of their leadership positions in these East European utopias.[119]

The acid test of loyalty for Jewish and other Communists came

[116] Kriegel, "La Résistance communiste," pp. 358–60; for detailed evidence on MOI operations, see also Adam Rutkowski, ed., La Lutte des juifs en France à l'époque de l'occupation (1940–1944) (Paris, 1975).

[117] Kriegel, "La Résistance communiste," pp. 360–65. Kriegel has promoted the theory in other publications also that the Jews, despite their social isolation, were really patriotic and merely "duped" by the Communists. (See for example her French Communists: Profile of a People [Chicago, 1972], pp. 129–35.) That interpretation has provided great comfort to Jewish historians. See, e.g., the use made of it by Lewi, Histoire d'une communauté juive: Roanne, pp. 68–69.

[118] See the revealing testimony in Robrieux, Histoire intérieure du parti communiste, pp. 530–31.

[119] Kriegel, "La Résistance communiste," p. 347.

in 1939–41, during the period of the Nazi-Soviet alliance. Thirty years later the majority of Jewish Communists interviewed by David Weinberg recalled that, after a moment of confusion, they had decisively repudiated the new Moscow line.[120] But the recent research of Stéphane Courtois into this murky era suggests a more nuanced conclusion. While a substantial number of militants quietly disengaged from the PCF in 1939–40, the central party apparatus held firm. It endorsed the explanation that the security of the Soviet state figured as the precondition of socialist triumph everywhere. In a party where the Comintern overseer Eugen Fried called himself Clément, the Paris leader Ginsburger went by the name Pierre Villon, and the party treasurer Michel Feintuch cast himself as Jean Jérôme, it is impossible to isolate "Jewish" positions with any assurance. Apart from university spokesmen like Georges Politzer, however, the party leadership as a whole promoted sabotage in 1939–40 and turned to collaboration after the national collapse. Individual regional leaders—Charles Tillon of Bordeaux, Auguste Havez of Brittany, and Georges Guingouin of Haute-Vienne, for example—who took a patriotic line in the crisis never won the full trust of the party high command again. Indeed a special party execution squad under a "Colonel" Epstein subsequently carried out the murder of some who had shown unacceptable independence of thought in these years.[121] Given the orthodoxy of the party structure that emerged from this agonizing period, Jews who rallied to the MOI after 1941 should—if they possessed any political sophistication—have had little doubt about the moral quality of the organization for which many of them made the supreme sacrifice.

These dismal undercurrents in the history of the left provide no shred of justification, of course, for the persecution of immigrant Jews by Vichy. No government worthy of the name would hold an entire class of people responsible for the actions of individuals. Still, the paranoia of Frenchmen in 1940 rested on the perception

---

[120] Weinberg, *Community on Trial*, pp. 203–5.

[121] Courtois, *Le PCF dans la guerre*, esp. pp. 11–202, 473–554; cf. also the earlier study by David Caute, *Communism and the French Intellectuals*, pp. 112–61. For an illuminating account of the Epstein murder squad and its victims, see Courtois, *Le PCF*, pp. 254–55, and Robrieux, *Histoire intérieure du parti communiste*, pp. 498–500, 542–44. Jean Jérôme's memoir, *La Part des hommes* (Paris, 1983), recalls the milieu of the immigrant Jewish militants of the 1930s with characteristic discretion.

that events had thrust them into an extreme situation, and extreme situations often lead to the crumbling of the thin crust of civilized behavior. One final group of refugee Jews remains to be considered in explaining the growth of paranoia on the French right. Some fifty-thousand German Jews passed through Paris from 1933 to 1939, but only ten thousand remained in 1939, and most of these escaped in 1940.[122] France served largely as a way station for Jews from the Reich awaiting admission to Britain, the United States, or Palestine. What anecdotal evidence we possess about this population suggests that it included most prominently a self-selected group of left-wing professionals who, for political reasons, could not secure visas or did not relish going to the United States.

The former Kommunistische Partei Deutschlands (KPD) youth leader and self-described "humanist Communist" Henry Pachter, for example, comments in his frank memoir of exile that when faced with imminent arrest he chose exile in Paris because it figured as "the birthplace of all European radicalism" and "the probable center of any international action against Hitler."[123] For seven years Pachter lived in a Kafkaesque world carrying on "guerrilla warfare with the French authorities." While he tried to keep a low profile as an illegal, many of his fellow refugees deliberately sought an expulsion order because to be expelled meant to be recognized, and in the process of protesting the injustice they hoped to wangle a permit to stay. In this world of Marxist émigrés few people did sustained work. Most disdained the menial jobs that they could obtain without papers and preferred to live on grants and donations. As the Socialist former finance minister Rudolf Hilferding once asked Pachter with a sigh, "Did you ever have to work for a living?"[124] The ex-Spartacist Heinrich Blücher, then the intimate of Hannah Arendt and the husband of Natasha Jefroykin (sister of the head of the Fédération des Sociétés Juives) picturesquely described his occupation as "stringpuller."[125]

In this world of endless waiting in hotel rooms for a counter-

---

[122] Weinberg, *Community on Trial*, p. 8; Roblin, *Les Juifs de Paris*, p. 73.

[123] Henry Pachter, "On Being an Exile: An Old-Timer's Personal and Political Memoir," in his *Weimar Etudes* (New York, 1982), pp. 312–13. On Pachter's political loyalties, see also "Empire and Republic: Autobiographical Fragments," in ibid., pp. 3–92.

[124] Pachter, "On Being an Exile," pp. 314–18.

[125] See Elisabeth Young-Bruehl, *Hannah Arendt: For Love of the World* (New Haven, 1982), p. 135.

revolution that never came, politics and literature became the chief preoccupations. Not all émigrés saw eye to eye, of course. The Zionist proselyte Hannah Arendt, who moved in a circle of Brandlerite opposition Communists that included Blücher and Erich Cohn-Bendit (later the father of Daniel), distinguished sharply between her crowd and those who directed German Communism after 1924, when, as she put it, "the gutter opened, and out of it emerged . . . 'another zoological species.'"[126] Pachter complained acidulously about the herd of independent minds in the German Exile Writers' Club who followed every twist and turn of the Soviet line and cooperated with their French confreres in the "anti-fascist" writers' conferences orchestrated by the Comintern agent Willi Münzenberg.[127] But whatever their differences, all the German Jewish émigré intellectuals thrilled to the excitement of the Popular Front in France and Spain. "Never again was I to feel so close to the masses," Pachter later recalled sententiously, "never again did I experience a similar unity of thought and action. Here was the great cause that allied the future of European culture, the achievement of social justice, the rise of the masses to a share in power, and the fight against the evil dictators and usurpers."[128] One can imagine how French conservatives reacted in 1936 or in 1940 when asked to offer hospitality to people who talked like this.

This study has dealt with a familiar subject from an unusual point of view. It presents the terrible tragedy of French Jewry at the end of the Third Republic as a problem of rights in conflict. Specialists generally agree about the fearsome difficulties under which the majority of immigrant Jews labored in the 1930s; the affiliations of native Jews, perhaps, offer greater scope for dispute. The literature, however, does not examine the matter from the optic of conservative Frenchmen who, however mistakenly, cherished "a certain idea of France." Does a nation have the right to control its own borders? Can a refugee minority invoke moral imperatives in seeking to proselytize for a social or a foreign policy that may

---

[126] Young-Bruehl, *Arendt*, p. 126.

[127] Pachter, "On Being an Exile," pp. 321–22. On Soviet manipulation of French and German intellectuals and the mutual contacts of the latter, see also Herbert R. Lottman, *The Left Bank: Writers, Artists, and Politics from the Popular Front to the Cold War* (Boston, 1982).

[128] Pachter, "On Being an Exile," p. 323.

not lie in the interest of the native majority? To what standard of tolerance can one hold an imperiled nation in a crisis? These questions remain apposite in many historical situations. It is well known that first- and second-generation Jews, for example, made up a large proportion of U.S. Communist party membership during the 1930s.[129] But such was the solidity of American institutions that this fact never became a burning public issue when indications of Soviet infiltration of the U.S. government came to light in the late 1940s. France in 1940, however, experienced not merely a lost war and the collapse of a regime, but a social crisis perhaps without parallel since 1789. In these circumstances the Jews came to play, as so often in history, the scapegoat's role. In this civil war, sadly, no one emerges with an unblemished record.

[129] See Harvey Klehr, *The Heyday of American Communism: The Depression Decade* (New York, 1984), pp. 378–85; also Melech Epstein, *The Jew and Communism* (New York, 1959).

YERACHMIEL (RICHARD) COHEN

The Jewish Community of France
in the Face of Vichy-German Persecution:
1940–44

T HE HISTORIAN Marc Bloch had by 1942 resolved against
emigrating to America. Bloch rejected an idea that he had
himself initiated, optimistically casting his fate with his fellow
Frenchmen.[1] It was in this spirit of optimism and total devotion to
France that he, together with two other well-known Jewish figures,
declared the leaders of the Union Générale des Israélites de France
(UGIF) to be illegitimate representatives of the Jews of France. The
indivisible nature of the "spiritual family" of France remained for
Bloch the central credo.

The France that we have served to our utmost, as so many of us have
done and for whom we would again tomorrow sacrifice voluntarily our
blood and that of our children, is our country. In the same vein as our compatriots of Catholic and Protestant origin, among whom are many very
dear friends, and fellow comrades at arms, we feel ourselves to be loyal
and grateful children of this one mother. The hopes like the sorrows of
France are ours. The values of the civilization to which we remain pas-
sionately attached are those that France has taught us. The French people
is our people. We do not value any other.[2]

These words expressed the dilemma of innumerable French Jews
during the war period: whether they were associated with a particular French Jewish organization or were unaffiliated as was Marc

[1] Peter M. Rutkoff and William B. Scott, "Letters to America: The Correspondence of
Marc Bloch, 1940–1941," *French Historical Studies* 12 (1981), pp. 277–303.
[2] Centre de Documentation Juive Contemporaine (henceforth CDJC), CCXIV–75, 1
May 1942. The other two individuals were Benjamin Crémieux and René Milhaud. UGIF

Bloch, there lay a chasm between their revulsion from Vichy's racial laws and their motivation for opposition to the Vichy regime. Bloch's optimism that France would return to her historic tradition of brotherhood and national unity was a basic psychological postulate that much of French Jewry struggled with in assessing its stance toward Vichy. Native French Jews' enthusiasm was not dampened by the growing disenchantment with foreigners, refugees, and Jews, and others that characterized the late thirties in France,[3] and they continued to see themselves as an integral element in the French mosaic.

While Marc Bloch was considering the possibility of leaving France, Elias Tcherikower, a Russian Jewish historian, was on his way to New York (September 1940) after having spent some seven years in the French capital. Tcherikower had been one of the editors of the Yiddish journal *Oyfn Scheidveg* (*At the Crossroads*) in which Eastern European Jews gave vent to their despair with Western society and argued for a return to the ghetto values and mores of Eastern Europe. The "return to the ghetto" trend was a peripheral intellectual movement, but it encapsulated a growing current among Eastern European Jews in France: though Jewish existence was being challenged by Fascism, Europe (including France) was closing its doors and reducing the Jew to his historic role as a nomad.[4]

In his private diary, written during the summer of 1940, Tcherikower viewed the fall of France within the microcosm of Jewish life and the macrocosm of Europe: both seemed to him bankrupt with no hope in the future, while the future of Palestine was cloudy, completely conditional on the outcome of the war between Britain and Germany. The traditions of French culture were hardly able to combat these bleak developments, thus intensifying Tcherikower's deep-seated pessimism. The last entry in his diary, written in mid-September 1940 on board the ship that brought him to America,

became the official representative body of the Jewish community by virtue of a Vichy law of 29 November 1941.

[3] Timothy P. Maga, "Closing the Door: The French Government and Refugee Policy, 1933–1939," *French Historical Studies* 12 (1982), pp. 424–42; Michael R. Marrus and Robert O. Paxton, *Vichy France and the Jews* (New York, 1981).

[4] Zosa Szajkowski, *Jews and the French Foreign Legion* (New York, 1975), pp. 62–63; David H. Weinberg, *A Community on Trial* (Chicago, 1977), pp. 193–94; Elizabeth Young-Bruehl, *Hannah Arendt: For Love of the World* (New Haven, Conn., 1982), pp. 147–48.

was a poignant conclusion to Tcherikower's life in Europe. "And now something of history: how the ugly defeated and tormented France twists itself and enters the school of Hitlerism and Fascism and quickly learns the sin of official anti-Semitism. A most instructive fact." [5]

It was the plight of Jewry in Europe that Tcherikower and East European Jews sensed deeply, the frightening thought that the exodus from Egypt would be relived in the "exodus from Europe"— the "exodus from Poland, from France, etc." [6]—during the war against Fascism.

Bloch and Tcherikower had dedicated their historical studies to different fields of interest: they represented the two contrasting worlds of French Jewry on the eve of World War II, and the focus of their research indicates the profound gap that separated native French Jews from East European Jews. French Jewry, it is true, contained other elements (North African, Greek, and Turkish Jews) and more joined its midst in the wake of German victories in 1940 (Dutch, Belgian, and Luxembourg Jews); yet it was these two communities that dominated the life of French Jewry, and their attitudes and responses to Vichy's policies will be at the center of this discussion.

Historians of Vichy are in general agreement as to the submissive and sometimes even enthusiastic nature of French response to the fall of the Third Republic and to Pétain's installation as chief of state in the summer of 1940. They concur in the view that only insignificant opposition to Vichy existed prior to 1942, whether in the occupied north or the unoccupied south, maintaining that the figure of Pétain constituted a cohesive factor for most Frenchmen. [7] For the Jewish community, on the other hand, the fall of France wrought immediate havoc. More than 150,000 Jews joined the massive exodus from the occupied north, fleeing the Germans and seeking a new haven abroad or in the relatively free southern zone. An undetermined number of Jews—possibly reaching the thousands—returned to the north during the turmoil of the summer of 1940, after encountering the severe economic and social dislo-

---

[5] Tcherikower Diary, Tcherikower Collection, YIVO Institute for Jewish Research (henceforth YIVO), p. 35 (Yiddish).

[6] Ibid., p. 34.

[7] H. R. Kedward, *Resistance in Vichy France* (London, 1978), Chs. 1–3.

cation in the south and encouraged by fellow Jews to believe that the Nazi threat was exaggerated.[8] In returning to the north, they presumably believed, as did German Jews who returned to Germany in 1934–35 from other European countries, that French law would uphold its traditional liberal policies even in the face of National Socialist pressure.[9] Thus, prior to the first *Statut des juifs* of 3 October 1940, confusion reigned within the Jewish community, and in this uncertain atmosphere a wide spectrum of attitudes emerged ranging from outright acceptance of the German victory to clandestine efforts to sabotage the occupation. Yet, as is so often the case in historical reality, one could find the majority of opinion, with or without a clear formulation of its position, somewhere between the two extremes.

The Jewish Communist circles in Paris, generally of Eastern European origin, broke ranks with the French Communist Party as early as September 1939 when they actively advocated France's participation in the war, despite the Molotov-Ribbentrop agreement. For the Jewish Communists the fight against Fascism had a distinctly Jewish slant that could not be denied by the ideological détente reached by Germany and Russia. During the "phony war" they published an illegal newspaper, *Unzer Vort*, which after temporary closure resumed publication a month after the fall of Paris. The intrepid slogan of the Jewish Communists that the Jews of France must unite with the French proletariat to free France from German occupation was expressed unequivocally. The occupation and the Fascist threat that accompanied it were uppermost in their minds and overrode any minor considerations, such as the personality of Pétain or the revival of France. Their anti-Nazi stance preceded the later resistance activity of the French Communists, and it would seem that it was their particular sensitivity to the plight of European Jewry that was at the basis of this divergence.[10] Other elements in the Eastern European community organized clandestinely in June 1940 with the purpose of coming to the aid of

---

[8] YIVO, RG 116, file 56; H. Sinder, "Lights and Shades of Jewish Life in France, 1940–1942," *Jewish Social Studies* (henceforth *JSS*) 5 (1943), pp. 367–82.

[9] M. Jarblum to A. Marquet, 21 July 1940, CDJC, CCXIII–46.

[10] A. Raysky ed., *The Word From the Resistance and Victory* (Paris, 1946), (Yiddish); David Diamant, *Les Juifs dans la résistance française (1940–1944)*; Jacques Ravine, *La Résistance organisée des juifs en France (1940–1944)* (Paris, 1973); A. Kriegel, "Résistants communistes et juifs persécutés," *Histoire*, 3 (1979), pp. 93–123.

immigrant Jews in Paris. They too saw themselves as an avant-garde opposition to the Nazi occupation. Indeed, from this clandestine group, rue Amelot, which brought together various immigrant aid groups, emerged an important arm in the community's self-help organization during the war.[11]

These embryonic expressions of opposition are hardly coterminous with what appears to be the prevailing feeling among native French Jews. Unfortunately, our sources for the period of the summer of 1940, both private and public, leave much to be desired; they do, however, point in similar directions. Native French Jews saw beyond the cataclysmic events of the summer and bestowed trust in and allegiance to Vichy, seemingly echoing the sentiment of their fellow Frenchmen. They maintained the hope that France would emerge rejuvenated from the defeat and found solace in the apparently synonymous principles of Vichy and Judaism—service to the country, stress on family values, and respect for work. It would seem that alongside this outlook French Jewish leaders held strongly to their xenophobic sentiments vis-à-vis the immigrant Jews and clearly envisioned that relations with Vichy must be undertaken by responsible native French citizens.[12] All in all, the diversity of the community's response to the defeat and to the New Order in its early stages characterized the cleavages that had made a united stand during the prewar period impossible.

The *Statut des juifs* and the law of 4 October 1940 "concerning foreigners of the Jewish race," diminished somewhat the significance of the division between the occupied north and the free south and intensified the precarious status of the foreign Jews. Native French Jewry's response to these laws and those of early 1941 proceeded along two distinct courses: one characterized by the leaders of the Central Consistory and its circle of associates and another expressed by individuals involved in the various welfare organizations of the community. For the former, the impact of the *statut* was primarily psychological, and it was in this spirit that they directed their protests to Pétain. The *statut* was seen as con-

[11] J. Jakoubowitch, *Rue Amelot* (Paris, 1948), (Yiddish); Z. Szajkowski, *Analytical Franco-Jewish Gazetteer, 1939–1945* (New York, 1966), pp. 39–40.

[12] S. Hamel to J. Weill, 1 September 1940 (Hammel's private papers); Jewish Theological Seminary, New York (henceforth JTS), box 15, 10 August 1940, report of Scout movement; Y. Cohen, "A Jewish Leader in Vichy France, 1940–1943: The Diary of Raymond-Raoul Lambert," *JSS*, 43 (1981), pp. 293–95; Y. Bauer, *American Jewry and the Holocaust: The American Jewish Joint Distribution Committee, 1939–1945* (Detroit, 1981), pp. 159–60.

tradictory to the French tradition of liberalism and as seriously jeopardizing France's position among the nations of the world. German pressure upon Vichy appeared to be the only plausible explanation for France's deviation from her historic traditions in accepting a racial definition of Judaism. In their protests, the Consistory leaders rejected outright the new racial definition while they upheld the religious definition that went hand in hand with loyalty to France. In this vein, they emphasized apologetically their unique contributions to France on the battlefield, in public service, and in transmitting French culture abroad. The chief rabbi of France, Isaïe Schwartz, strengthened his argument on the virtues of French Jewry by quoting Barrès and pointing to the similarity in principles of the New Order and Judaism. He stressed the intrinsic spiritual connection between Judaism and France in the following terms: "French Jews (israélites) have accepted as a motto: Religion-Fatherland. Always devoted to this ideal, we draw our courage and hope from the love of God and the lessons of the Bible, the sources of the spiritual life of the French people."[13]

These French Jews avoided any public protests, expressing their wounded soul in the form of private communications to Pétain.[14] Pétain's mystique carried the day for these Jews, who believed that if anyone could save them from their predicament it was he. They too were part of the trend of *attentisme*, and as anti-Jewish legislation broadened in 1941, they elected to avoid any conflict with the Vichy government and with the occupying power. They called upon the community to suffer quietly, to respect the law, and to show undiminished loyalty in every possible respect. Such self-denial on the part of the community would, so they conjectured, have a healthy effect on French society: the French government would recognize that it had tragically erred in ousting the Jews from French society. In a sense, one could say that these French Jewish spokesmen saw themselves as the bearers of the "true France."

The Consistory leaders held no illusions concerning Jewish im-

[13] Schwartz to Pétain, 22 October 1940, in E. Tcherikower ed., *Yidn in Frankraykh* (New York, 1942), 2:295−97, (Yiddish); on the background to this appeal see Schwartz's report, JTS, box 13; Pétain's response 12 November 1940, CDJC, CCXIX−14. An earlier letter of Schwartz to Pétain 10 October 1940, Central Archives for the History of the Jewish People, Jerusalem, (henceforth CAHJP), F-350.

[14] E.g., see Pierre Masse to Pétain, 20 October 1940 in Adam Rutkowski, ed., *La Lutte des Juifs en France à l'époque de l'occupation (1940−1944)* (Paris, 1975), pp. 45−46; former war veterans to Pétain, 15 October 1940, YIVO RG 116, file 33; Rabbi Julien Weill in

migrants in France. They believed that even in normal times a special status for the immigrants, including the immigrant Jews, would be required; thus they opted to refrain from protest in this regard during 1941. The arrests of foreign Jews in the occupied zone in May and August 1941 took place without a single Consistory appeal to the Vichy authorities. In the atmosphere of national revival these native Jewish leaders wished to emphasize their French attachments and to minimize their identification with the foreign elements of the community. The *attentisme* of the Consistory circles and their call for conciliatory action within the Vichy system exacerbated their already strained relations with the immigrant community.[15]

This portrayal does not adequately describe the attitudes of various native Jewish leaders who were involved in the welfare organizations, both in the north and south. Here we find much greater concern for the future of French Jewry as a whole and much more intensive activity in this regard. The situation in the north was far more complicated and necessitated special caution in dealing with the authorities, German and French. The Comité de Coordination was established in Paris in January 1941 after concerted efforts on the part of the Nazi *Judenreferat*, Theodor Dannecker. At the outset, the *comité* included both native and immigrant welfare organizations (among the latter the rue Amelot group) and represented a high point in Jewish solidarity. The *comité* saw its role as an intermediary between the community and the German authorities, maintaining a low profile with regard to communal organization.

Dannecker obtained little satisfaction from the *comité*; his intention to establish a tightly knit community through the *comité* was stymied, and he subsequently intervened in two distinct ways. In March 1941 he brought two Jews from Vienna [16] to serve as his lackeys in the *comité* and at the same time withstood both German and French pressure to create a Commissariat for Jewish Affairs. This was a turning point for the Jewish welfare organizations in the north: it was to bring about the eventual resignation of most

---

the name of the Paris Jewish community, 23 October 1940, ibid.; General André Boris to Pétain, 10 November 1940, in Rutkowski, *Lutte*, pp. 44–45.

[15] See Y. Cohen, "Problems of Western European Jews in the 20th Century: A Comparative Study of Danzig and Paris," to appear in the proceedings of Harvard University Center for Jewish Studies symposium, *Danzig: Between East and West*.

[16] It remains unclear how and why these particular Jews (Israelowicz and Biberstein) were chosen.

of the influential Eastern European elements and the inclusion of native Jews, the most prominent being André Baur.

Thirty-seven years of age, a wealthy and respected banker, a former president of the reform congregation in Paris, Baur was to become the dominant figure in the *comité* from May onwards.[17] Baur was the nephew of Rabbi Julien Weill and was obviously impressed by the arguments of his uncle that Dannecker's actions must not lead to the dismemberment of the *comité* and that the appointment of Xavier Vallat as commissioner for Jewish affairs could be taken as a reason for hope.[18] Indeed, for Weill as for Baur and other Jewish leaders, there developed a clear division between Vallat and the German authorities: Vallat was a known anti-Semite, but he was a Frenchman, and within this framework it was felt that the Jews would be better off. For Baur the issue was clear. In a meeting of the *comité* after the second *Statut des juifs* of June 1941 he spoke of the pressing need for reorganizing the *comité* to face the serious challenges that threatened French Jewry. The social needs of the community were growing, and it was necessary to coopt individuals who shared a common sense of responsibility.[19] Baur presents a different paradigm from what has been described so far: a well-established French Jew who would have had no difficulty whatsoever in crossing the demarcation line and in joining his family in the south, but who opted to remain in the north, believing that French Jewry needed an umbrella organization to coordinate the welfare organizations and to generate a sense of solidarity within the community. Baur's position finds a parallel in the activity of Rabbi René Hirschler of Strasbourg.

Evacuated with the Jewish community to southern France, Hirschler took issue with those native Jewish leaders who spoke of maintaining the leadership of the community in the hands of the French Jews. Hirschler saw the October *statut* as opening a new era in the history of the Jews of France, one that would entail great hardship for all. He was convinced of the need to overcome the

---

[17] For biographical information on Baur, see Raymond Lindon, *Hommage à André Baur* (n.p., n.d. [Paris (?), c. 1981]).

[18] On Xavier Vallat see W. D. Irvine, *French Conservatism in Crisis: The Republican Federation of France in the 1930s* (Baton Rouge, La., 1979), passim; Marrus and Paxton, *Vichy France*, ch. 3.

[19] Report of meeting between Dannecker, Weill, and Baur, CDJC, CCXVII–4; protocol of *comité* special session, 9 June 1941, ibid.

differences within the community in order to mobilize efforts on the common behalf. In discussions with other welfare leaders, Hirschler recalled striking historic analogies. Jewish suffering in the contemporary period, he suggested, possibly surpassed that of the Jews expelled from France and Spain during the Middle Ages, and only by rising above the egoism inherent in emancipation could French Jewry emerge victoriously from its abyss. Like German Jewish leaders in the early thirties, Hirschler called for a rejection of the negative aspects of emancipation—sanctification of the individual's goals over the community's needs—and proclaimed the historic virtue of "common destiny." For Hirschler, a continuation of the negative attitude of French Jewish leaders to the immigrant Jews would bring disaster to French Jewry.[20]

Baur and Hirschler presented an important alternative to the Consistory circles to which they themselves were attached. Their demand for a response to the anti-Semitic legislation broke new ground within the community. They opened up new possibilities for coordinated efforts by being responsive to the needs of the entire community and by recognizing that occupation and Vichy entailed a major challenge for French Jewry. On the spectrum from collaboration to daredevil resistance, they and others like them adopted a centrist position that tried to salvage a sense of community in the rapidly deteriorating situation of mid-1941.

For the Eastern European Jews the anti-Semitic laws of October 1940 had an immediate disastrous consequence in the legal internment of thousands of foreign Jews in French camps in the south. Thousands of others were left without means to maintain a basic standard of living and became a major burden for the welfare organizations. This predicament was at the root of the response of Eastern European Jewish leaders to the Vichy legislation. Concrete action to alleviate the misery of their constituents took first priority, while protests to Vichy were obviously considered fruitless. During the first year of the Vichy regime, the Communists, the rue Amelot group and its associates, and the Fédération des Sociétés Juives (FSJ), both in the north and the south, galvanized their efforts in the direction of welfare of one sort or another. With very limited financial resources they established soup kitchens in Paris, "solidarity" groups in the internment camps, clinics, and children's

[20] See Yad Vashem Archives (henceforth YVA): 09/30–31, CAHJP, F–355.

homes. For these organizations, Pétain held little attraction and in-stilled no confidence in the future. On the contrary, the persistence of xenophobic attitudes on the part of the French only deepened the chasm between the Eastern European Jews and the French authorities.

It was this feeling of isolation, of being cast aside, that led im-migrant leaders (including the Communists) to initiate a modus vivendi with the French Jewish leadership. David Rappaport of the rue Amelot group turned to Rabbi Julien Weill in September 1940 with a concrete proposal for unity. Although Weill turned down the offer, claiming that the time was not yet ripe for joining ranks, Rappaport continued to favor joint deliberations with the consis-torial leadership in Paris.[21] Eventually Rappaport was to be the in-strumental figure in persuading the rue Amelot group to enter the controversial *comité* in January 1941. After the appearance of the two Viennese Jews, however, Rappaport's position became dif-ficult to maintain, and the group left the *comité* by summer 1941. Interestingly enough, problems of a similar nature arose in the un-occupied zone.

In the closing months of 1940 negotiations were under way to reconstruct the welfare organizations. The FSJ under the lead-ership of Marc Jarblum renewed its call of the thirties for the estab-lishment of an organization that would deal with all the refugees and would be neither under the tutelage of the Comité d'Assistance aux Réfugiés (CAR) nor under the FSJ. The paradoxical conse-quence was that the moment the umbrella organization, the Com-mission Centrale des Organisations Juives d'Assistance (CCOJA), was established under the auspices of Rabbi Schwartz, Jarblum feared that it would deal unjustly and inequitably with the Eastern European Jews and would fail to serve them in the ways required. By December 1940, Jarblum was already threatening to secede from the organization and to establish a parallel operation run by FSJ in the interest of the immigrant Jews alone.[22] This threat was not implemented, but it served notice that unity, even when

---

[21] YIVO, RG 343, file 3; YVA, 09/11–13. Jakoubowitch, *Rue Amelot*, pp. 29–30.

[22] See CCOJA protocol, 12 December 1940, YIVO, RG 245.5, II, France–70; ibid., France–67, 15 January 1941. This was confirmed in Herbert Katzki's letter to Joseph Schwartz, 8 May 1941: "The foreign Jews, despite the goodwill expressed by the French, do not think that they can rely 100 percent upon the assurances they give them. In conse-

achieved, could not overcome the differences in perception of events and the way to deal with them. Rappaport and Jarblum proposed unity, trusting that the Vichy laws and German occupation had driven home to the native Jews the necessity for cooperation. Both, however, had difficulty living with this cooperation, for it entailed political sacrifices, moral compromises, and official recognition. They rejected the political implications of a community in 1941 and became the staunch opponents of a German-Vichy concoction—the Union Générale des Israélites de France (UGIF).

In the establishment of the UGIF resides one of the most interesting paradoxes of Jewish life during the war. The UGIF was established by French law on 29 November 1941. All Jewish organizations, save purely religious bodies, were coerced into the union, which had a separate council for the north and south. Three months had elapsed from the time the Germans called upon Vallat to establish this body until the promulgation of the law. During this time, lengthy negotiations took place among the German and Vichy authorities and the Jewish community.[23] Nowhere in all of Europe was the publication of such a decree prefaced by such thorough discussions, uniquely revealing the internal deliberations of the Jewish leadership.

In the north, the process went smoothly. André Baur and Lucienne Scheid-Haas examined the proposed German law together with Vallat, trying to find points that could be removed and that would allow for the organization to fall under French authority as opposed to German. Vallat gained the respect of these Jewish leaders, who saw in him a Frenchman whose personal antagonism toward the Germans led him to endeavor to alleviate the Jewish tragedy. Indeed, the Jewish documentation is complimentary about Vallat, and in one instance he is even referred to as a possible "philosemite."[24] It was this trust in Vallat (or in the French in general) that softened the blow for the UGIF leaders and led them to accept

---

quence, they will continue taking whatever steps they deem proper through their representatives to protect themselves." American Jewish Joint Distribution Committee Archive, France, General (12–42), 1941.

[23] For the general outline of these developments, see Szajkowski, *Gazetteer*, pp. 46–52; Bauer, *American Jewry*, pp. 164–69; Y. Cohen, "The Jewish Leadership in France during World War II" Ph.D. diss., Hebrew University of Jerusalem, 1981, Ch. 3 (Hebrew).

[24] Special meeting between northern council members and representatives of immigrant welfare organizations, YVA, P7/8. For other sources on Jewish attitudes to Vallat see Y. Co-

nomination to an organization that negated the principles in which they believed, in the hope that it might allow them to work toward "ameliorating the fate of our coreligionists, native or immigrant living in France."[25] Yet on 28 January 1942 the leaders of the immigrant groups strongly criticized the UGIF council for cooperating with the Germans. Rappaport and Eugene Minkowsky rejected the possibility of working with UGIF, claiming that "now we are placed before a fait accompli and we cannot accept the slightest portion of responsibility for what will be done."[26] For them, neither Vallat nor Pétain offered much hope.

This dilemma of how to respond to the German-Vichy organization touched on all the central issues—evaluation of French motives, assessment of collaboration with the Germans, the nature and future of the Jewish community and its welfare organizations, and concepts of moral responsibility. The issue was vigorously debated in the south. What emerges from these discussions can be summarized as follows: the unprecedented nature of the law truly staggered the Jewish leaders. For the first time during the war the Consistory leaders were jostled out of complacency, and the Consistory president, Jacques Helbronner, interceded time and again with Pétain in an effort to change the basic tenets of the law. The Consistory saw the enforced legislation as a travesty of the French Jewish experience. The Consistory's position received the support of welfare leaders, especially Marc Jarblum. Jarblum condemned the law for its political implications, fearing the implication of the Jewish community in the anti-Semitic policies of Vichy and Nazi Germany. Native and immigrant Jews stood together in resisting the law and seeking to prolong the negotiations until a satisfactory solution could be reached.

But once again a mediating position appeared among the leaders of the welfare organizations, one that saw the preservation of the organizations as the highest priority. The leading figure in this regard was Raymond-Raoul Lambert. From the outset of his meetings with Vallat, Lambert was convinced that "it was not sufficient

---

hen, "Towards the Establishment of the UGIF in Northern France," *Yalkut Moreshet* 30 (November 1980), pp. 153–54 (Hebrew).

[25] Protest of northern council to Pétain, 20 January 1942, YVA, 09/6–1, published in Rutkowski, *Lutte*, p. 77.

[26] YVA, P7/8.

to say that one must protest and abstain. One must, on the contrary, in a strictly technical order, make useful propositions."[27] Lambert succeeded in persuading eight other prominent Jews to join the UGIF council, dispensing with the blessing of the Consistory for which they all waited. The nine were all aware of the momentous nature of their decision, feeling together with René Hirschler the call of history. "Just as the deliberations of the Sanhedrin continue to weigh upon us, after more than 130 years, for better or worse, so the decisions that the responsible figures of French Judaism must take in these grave hours . . . will weigh upon us, our children, and our grandchildren."[28] Hirschler's historical paradigm aptly expressed the view of the council designees—they saw their struggle still very much within the parameters of French Jewish relations, with Vichy alone, with no compelling sense of the Nazi conquest of Europe. They, after all, believed that they were part of "free France."[29]

The creation of the UGIF openly split the organized community, provoking more distinct attitudes to Vichy. The Consistory, the apotheosis of officialdom, was now clearly at odds with Vichy, encouraging individuals to refrain from participating in the UGIF, in direct contrast to its call for conciliation through much of 1940–41. The FSJ, under Jarblum's influence, became further disenchanted with the concept of communal unity, declaring forthrightly its intention to influence other agencies against UGIF.[30] Within the community at large the establishment of the UGIF antagonized individuals such as Marc Bloch, who called upon its leaders to avoid any action that would result in "morally isolating" them from the "national community [*la communauté nationale*]."[31]

[27] At CCOJA meeting 24 October 1941, CDJC, CCXIII–73.

[28] 22 October 1941, CDJC, CCXIII–72; YVA, P7/8.

[29] Hillel J. Kieval came to similar conclusions in his study "Legality and Resistance in Vichy France: the Rescue of Jewish Children," *Proceedings of the American Philosophical Society* 124 (1980), p. 354.

[30] See YVA, P7/12; CDJC, CCXIII–54, 57, 61 (all from late June 1942). It should be pointed out that within the FSJ there was far from unanimous support for Jarblum's position, both before and after the establishment of UGIF. After the departure from France of his foremost antagonist, Israel Jeffroykin, Jarblum and the FSJ become almost synonymous. This further shows that on the issue of UGIF, the origin of the leaders was of minor significance to their respective positions. See verbatim protocol of FSJ meeting on 17 January 1942, CDJC, CCXIII–49.

[31] See Bloch to UGIF council, early February 1942, CDJC, XXVIIIa–22; correspondence between Bloch and other Jewish personalities, ibid., early February 1942.

It took the events of spring and summer 1942 to bring about a more serious reevaluation of the community's perspective on its relations with Vichy and the German occupying power.

The months that followed the creation of the UGIF were ominous for the Jews of France. Vichy anti-Semitic legislation had reached its peak and henceforth French Jewry had to deal with the more aggressive policy of National Socialism toward the Jews—the implementation of the Final Solution. As has been conclusively shown, Vichy leadership actively cooperated with Nazi officials in many aspects of the Final Solution,[32] eliminating Vichy's apparent role as intermediary between the Nazis and the Jews. The Vichy entanglement multiplied the hardships of the Jews, and it is thus imperative in adumbrating the Jewish response during these years to deduce the extent to which Jews actually sensed Vichy's voluntary commitment to the new phase of anti-Semitism and how their perception affected their action. Put in other words, was Jewish perception of Vichy a salient factor in determining the direction of Jewish activity?

In mid-March 1942, Dannecker ordered the UGIF North to supply a large quantity of diverse products (among them shoes, blankets, food) to the German authorities. In the background loomed the Nazi preparations for the first deportation from France to Auschwitz. The UGIF council knew nothing of these implications. On 26 March 1942, André Baur filed a complaint to Vallat, claiming that the German request was contradictory to the statutes of the UGIF, and opposed to the armistice agreement between Germany and France.[33] Vallat, however, was already persona non grata in the north, thus making Baur's objections worthless. Although the UGIF did not meet the date required for delivery of the goods (set for 27 March, the day of deportation), it eventually fulfilled the German demand.[34] This incident is instructive of the UGIF North's predicament and behaviour: on the one hand, it relied on a new French law that in fact it rejected because of its racial nature, while on the other hand it faced an occupying authority that made

[32] See Marrus and Paxton, *Vichy France*, passim.

[33] Baur to Vallat, CDJC, XXVIII–20. See J. Billig, *Le Commissariat général aux questions juives (1941–1944)* (Paris, 1955–60), 1:94.

[34] See telegrams between Dannecker and Hoess, commandant of Auschwitz, and between Dannecker and Baur, CDJC, XXVb–24, 25, 25a.

havoc of French law. When it became clear to UGIF that there was no point in resorting to law, the demand was fulfilled as requested. The March episode would recur often in the following years, for the Nazi authorities intended to turn the UGIF into a purveyor of supplies for Jewish inmates or deportees. A case in point was the role of UGIF in the deportations of summer 1942.

In May-June 1942, Vallat and several of his cronies were replaced by a circle of Frenchmen who vigorously sought to comply with Nazi demands. This development enabled Dannecker to rely upon the French officials to carry out his policy with regard to the UGIF, while minimizing the need for Nazi intervention. Subsequently, a fortnight before the Vélodrome d'Hiver roundup (the mass arrest of thousands of Parisian Jews and their assembly in a huge stadium prior to their deportation to Drancy), the commissariat implored Baur to arrange for a supply of clothes and blankets for 7,000 people, in order to meet an "urgent need." The commissariat offered the UGIF its services in securing the implementation of this extensive demand while emphasizing that it held the "entire Jewish community" responsible for carrying it out.[35] Baur replied a week later. It was clear to him that a mass arrest was in store for the Jewish community and that the commissariat was sharing with him the disturbing information. Baur was deeply troubled. He raised the legal and technical difficulties involved in amassing the required quantity but was more disturbed by the psychological impact. Could he publicly call for such a recruitment of goods from the community without arousing concern and without creating needless panic? Feeling that he was corresponding with a Frenchman who shared a common understanding, Baur remarked that such a move entailed "grave responsibility," and he added, "We cannot assume it and publicize your information, unless you so request us in writing, with the permission of the occupying authorities."[36] Baur added, however, that the UGIF—and not the Jewish community—would carry out the request "with the same competence and the same diligence that it has shown until now." Once again, after expressing his opposition in principle, Baur promised to comply.

[35] Galien to Baur, 1 July 1942, YIVO, RG 210, CVIII–9; cf. Galien to Puech, 4 July 1942, CDJC, XXVIII–111.

[36] Baur to Galien, 6(8?) July 1942, YVA, 09/6–1; cf. Billig, *Le Commissariat*, III, p. 317; Galien to Baur, 15 July 1942, CDJC, XXVIII–37.

The UGIF council apparently resolved its dilemma by refraining from officially disseminating its information, opting to forewarn individuals of the impending events on an unofficial basis—this too on a minor scale. During the days of Vélodrome d'Hiver roundup, the UGIF willy-nilly went about the limited tasks the commissariat had accorded it—social and medical assistance to the arrested— priding itself on the efficient and capable execution of its role.[37] This particular situation offers an important insight into the presence of mind of the UGIF leaders during the critical moments of July 1942. The UGIF leaders, still oblivious to the ultimate goals of the Nazis, had not dispensed with their ingrained trust of their fellow Frenchmen and their penchant for legalism.

Was the response of UGIF North typical of the Jewish community during the tragic summer months of 1942? UGIF South found itself in a similar situation at the end of July. It was then that two of its leaders accidentally got word of the impending deportations that were to encompass the internment camps, labor battalions, and major southern cities. The UGIF leaders immediately called on various individuals to intercede with the Vichy government, although they themselves declined to do so out of deference to the Central Consistory.[38] The Vichy leaders were hardly disturbed by the interest taken by the U.S. chargé at Vichy nor by the various welfare organizations. The deportations, coordinated by Nazi and Vichy officials, proceeded without any major obstacles.

UGIF South worked on several different levels during August and September. Contact with Vichy authorities and underlings in the camps was organized by several of its council members, while the welfare agencies incorporated into UGIF handled the manifold social problems that emerged. Although the council members rejected the proposal that they present a complete alternate list of deportees against that prepared by the prefects, they pressed Vichy to protect certain categories of Jews against deportation. They especially emphasized the importance of granting to the

[37] The UGIF's role in the deportation process can be deduced from German and French documentation. See CDJC, XXVb–6, 55, 58, 60; XXVIII–36. See S. Klarsfeld, (hrsgb.), *Die Endlösung der Judenfrage in Frankreich. Deutsche Dokumente 1941–1944* (Paris, 1977), pp. 84, 87. C. Lévy et P. Tillard, *La Grande Rafle du vel d'hiv (16 juillet 1942),* (Paris, 1967), pp. 14–15, 77–78, 137–38.

[38] Bauer, *American Jewry,* pp. 174–77. The UGIF leaders declined to meet with Laval on technical grounds. See Cohen, "Lambert" pp. 299–301; Y. Cohen, "French Jewry's Dilemma on the Orientation of its Leadership", *Yad Vashem Studies* 14 (1981), pp. 178–80.

UGIF full authority over children between the ages of two and fifteen. These official requests did not go unheeded in the first series of deportations. Utilizing the UGIF entry permit into the internment camps, various welfare agencies entered those camps that were destined to supply the deportees and devised legal and illegal means of releasing children and dispersing them in private and public homes. These acts, undertaken under the guise of a legal, state-created institution, were directly designed to subvert the deportation.[39]

What needs to be clarified in this context is, of course, the relationship between the legal and the illegal. Were there, in the summer of 1942, two perceptions of Vichy working simultaneously in UGIF? What explains the fact that, while Lambert and the UGIF president Albert Lévy were frantically sending off telegrams to leading Vichy personalities demanding their intervention to stop the horrible deportations that are "unworthy of the French tradition and capable of harming the reputation of our country among all neutral and Christian countries,"[40] their subordinate agencies were circumventing Vichy policy?

The duality within UGIF stems from its basic structure and orientation. On the one hand, there was the UGIF council's amorphous nature. Throughout the summer months the council never met, and policy decisions were often on-the-spot responses, usually made by Lambert himself, and only months later did these decisions receive an airing in the council. Moreover, the individual member of the council preserved his loyalties and ties to a particular welfare agency. On the other hand, there was the relationship between the council and its agencies. The council had promised to preserve the independent activity of each of these organizations, and they were rarely called upon to answer to the council for a particular action. Aside from the bureaucratic necessities of a state organization, these agencies were able to develop fully their independent work, infusing it with their distinctive ideologies. UGIF South was anything but a monolithic body.

As the deportations occurred only several months after UGIF

[39] See Kieval, "Legality and Resistance," pp. 355–59.
[40] See Lévy to Pétain, 4 September 1942, YIVO, RG 210, XCII–10; Lambert to Guérard, 4 September 1942, YIVO, RG 210, XCII–10; Lambert to Bousquet, 13 September 1942, CDJC, CDXVI–139.

South had actually begun to function, a cohesive pattern of action had yet to emerge. Thus what transpired within UGIF South in summer 1942, the apparent rupture between UGIF and the agencies—the emphasis of the former on legality and of the latter on illegality—was merely symptomatic of the organization's inherent heterogeneity. Nevertheless, their perceptions of Vichy were not wholly at odds with each other: leading council members were not oblivious to the illegal action taken and in certain cases encouraged it or at least condoned it,[41] while prominent figures in the agencies recognized the important role that the council had played in securing certain concessions from Vichy through legal procedure.[42] It would seem that nobody within UGIF South had decided by the summer of 1942 to abandon trust in Vichy, although concrete indications of mistrust had begun to appear.

The Central Consistory maintained a low profile during the summer deportations, resorting to its traditional strategy. The Consistory, now located in Lyon, submitted two strongly worded protests against the deportations calling upon the Vichy government to return to the French tradition of humanity by protecting its Jewish citizens with the utmost diligence.[43] Between these two protests, the Consistory filed a further complaint against a Vichy law of June 1942 that excluded Jewish children from participating in the youth service corps (Chantiers de la Jeunesse).[44] This protest reflects upon the nature of the other two. Indeed, the Consistory was jolted by the events of the summer, as is clear from the two protests, but it nevertheless continued to view the world through the prism of the French Jews and the violation of their status. This had been at the root of their adamant stand against the UGIF in 1941 and the basis of their rejection of a joint delegation with UGIF to Pétain or Laval in August 1942. For the Consistory, neither the deportations nor the German occupation of the south in November 1942 necessitated a reassessment of their legalistic, patriotic, and iconoclastic attitude. It was not until the arrest of some

[41] I am referring here not only to Robert Gamzon, a leading figure in the resistance activity of the Scout movement, but also to Wladimir Schah, Raphaël Spanien, and possibly even to Lambert.

[42] See Kieval, "Legality and Resistance," p. 362.

[43] Rutkowski, Lutte, p. 102, pp. 115–17; Cohen, "French Jewry," pp. 178–80. Protests dated 28 July and 25 August 1942.

[44] Marrus and Paxton, Vichy France, p. 127; Consistory protest of 28 July 1942, YIVO, RG 116, file 33.

two thousand French Jews in Marseille in January 1943, by combined forces of the French police and the Gestapo, that the true
face of Vichy was driven home to them.[45] Months would pass before the Consistory actively threw in its lot with the Resistance
movement, but beginning in January 1943 it slowly amended its
position.

The deportations were a solidifying factor for those splinter
groups within the community, of leftist and Communist orientation, that had begun armed resistance in spring 1942. Nothing any
longer stood in their way. The Nazi invasion of the Soviet Union
had united almost all Communist elements against Vichy, while
the continual harassment of foreign Jews and leftist leaders put an
end to any fantasies of a change of heart at Vichy. Within these
Jewish groups, there developed a strong representation of young,
Eastern European immigrants. This concentration suggests that
alongside their ideological premises, a sensitivity to the plight of
foreign Jews was a significant factor in their original motivation
for joining underground activities.[46] The deportations strengthened these feelings and intensified the sense of attachment among
the various groups. It would still take close to a year before several
Communist-oriented groups were able to overcome their ideological differences sufficiently to join an umbrella resistance organization;[47] they began to establish contacts after the summer of 1942.

Those participant groups intensified their feud with native
French Jewry after the deportations. In the growing number of
underground pamphlets and clandestine tracts that were distributed, in Yiddish and in French, native French Jewry became the
butt of fierce criticism. French Jewry and its apparent representative, the UGIF, were called upon to recognize the true nature of
Vichy's anti-Semitic ideology and to prepare for a tragedy analogous to that of the immigrant Jews. This theme became even more
popular after the events in Marseille in January 1943 had shown
the vulnerability of French Jews.[48] From the critique of French
Jewry there reemerged the notion of the "common fate" of the Jew-

[45] Marrus and Paxton, *Vichy France*, pp. 302–7; Cohen, "French Jewry," pp. 182–85.

[46] Raysky, *The Word*, passim; D. Knout, *Contribution à l'histoire de la résistance juive en France 1940–1944* (Paris, 1947), pp. 91–103; Diamant, *Les Juifs*, passim; Ravine, *La Ré-sistance, passim*; Kriegel, "Résistants," pp. 116–21.

[47] This refers to the establishment of the Union des Juifs pour la Résistance et l'Entraide (UJRE) in May 1943. For the participant organizations see Knout, *Contribution*, pp. 93–94.

[48] See Rutkowski, *Lutte*, passim; Raysky, *The Word*, passim.

ish people, which was to set the tone for the rapprochement between Communist and Consistory leaders in January 1944.[49] It appears then that the deportations not only magnified the scope of
Communist resistance activity but also instilled a deep sense of involvement with the Jewish tragedy.

What is the general significance of the specific developments
described here? How did the deportation of 27,000 Jews from
Drancy to Auschwitz affect Jewish-Vichy relations? The impact
lies in the new image of Vichy being formed among Jews. No
longer was Vichy seen as the guardian of French tradition, but
rather at best as an impotent symbol, at worst as a wilful per-
petrator. Jews actively sought new alternatives to their precarious
status in France—escaping to Switzerland and Spain, taking on
a false identity, going into hiding—sometimes with, sometimes
without the encouragement of Jewish organizations. The impression of the deportations upon Jewish life was to grow as the arrests
and deportations continued, but they had already pushed more and
more Jews into that twilight zone between legality and illegality.

Finally, how does the response of French Jewry fit into the general scheme of French society at this period? Scholars of resistance have claimed that by the summer of 1942 strong inroads into
French society had been made by the resistance movements, both
ideologically and organizationally. They contend that Pétain's attraction had dwindled considerably and Laval became the object of
growing criticism. It was not until the demand for French forced
labor had become a major issue of contention that mass opposition
to Vichy emerged. So too with regard to the attitude of French society to the Jews. The monolithic hold of Vichy on French society
was waning, and new pockets of dissent were stirred up by the deportations, constituting "the first significant break . . . between
Vichy and major parts of the establishment."[50] But a rupture with
Vichy over the Jewish issue was nowhere in sight. Seen within these
perspectives, the developments within the Jewish community tend
to mirror the evolution within French society. The "first significant
break" had come, but this was only the beginning.

[49] As a result of these deliberations, the Conseil Représentatif des Institutions Juives de
France (CRIF) was set up. See Cohen, "French Jewry," p. 194. Cf. Kriegel, "Résistants,"
pp. 121–22; Bauer, American Jewry, p. 242.

[50] Marrus and Paxton, Vichy France, p. 279.

The closing two years of the war witnessed a serious transformation in Jewish responses to the persecutions. The organizations that were affiliated with UGIF, but not dismantled, showed increasing resilience in combatting German and Vichy initiatives. In this regard, the German occupation of the south in November 1942 was a turning point. It not only closed the door against all legal attempts to escape from France but signified the end of "free France." Even the existence of the "Italian Zone" in southern France, which loomed as a possible oasis from November 1942, could not dispel the impact of the German occupation. This is not to say that from that moment on the community went underground, but rather that from then on it became a common occurrence for organizations to participate in both legal and illegal activity. The process by which they developed this dual existence and in certain cases later shed all legal appearances was a long and arduous one. In those latter instances, it was often a direct clash with the German and/or French police that triggered the final decision. The open and brutal cooperation of the French police in the arrests of Jews in 1942–44 contributed more than anything else to dispelling the last vestiges of trust in Vichy. Furthermore, this rising trend of clandestine activity within the Jewish community was connected to the developments within the resistance movements in French society. Several incidents relating to the Jews in the north and south will illustrate how they navigated between legality and illegality during the period of 1942–44.

On 28 January 1942, Darquier de Pellepoix, Vallat's successor, ordered André Baur to dismiss within two months all but 1 percent of the UGIF's foreign employees. The UGIF council knew by now what the consequences of such an act would be. The council considered offering its resignation rather than "ourselves to designate a part of our personnel, thus exposing them to measures that certain precedents have led us to anticipate."[51] During the following month, the council actively intervened with commissariat officials and with Röthke, Dannecker's replacement, and tried to reverse the order. When this proved unsuccessful, the council abandoned thought of resignation and pursued the negotiations until they

[51] Baur to Duquesnel, 4 February 1943, YVA, 09/6–2; council meeting was held on 2 February 1943, YIVO, RG 343, 131. See Marcel Stora to Rabbi E. Bloch, early February 1943, YIVO, RG 210, XXX1–24.

were allowed to keep about 20 percent of the foreign personnel.[52] But on the night of 17/18 March 1943 the Gestapo arrested some 60–80 foreign employees of UGIF who appeared on a list submitted to Röthke. The list had been fabricated in part, containing many incorrect names and wrong addresses, thus somewhat subverting Röthke's goal. Two months later, a commissariat official reported to Röthke that many of those Jews intended for deportation were in hiding and were continuing to receive salaries from UGIF.[53] The council had been promised by the commissariat that the employees would remain at their jobs until the end of March and upon dismissal would not be arrested. It is clear, however, that the council no longer took these promises at face value and arranged for many to go into hiding. At the same time that the council saved these employees, other Jews were placed in danger of deportation. Once again, UGIF North was entangled within its morally ambivalent structure. From its initial bold response of contemplating resignation, it came to accept a middle road that avoided jeopardizing its existence but dealt a fatal blow to certain Jews. Although it had made a tentative entry into the realm of illegality, it was far from accepting it as a way of behavior.

If the UGIF North was aware of the consequences—deportation to the unknown "East"—what prevented it from making a clear-cut decision? Was it simply the difficulty of a bureaucratic organization declaring its own demise or was it a matter of voluntary collaboration with the enemy? The events of summer 1943 suggest an answer. The Final Solution had been proceeding in France slowly, much to the anger of the Nazis. Only 55,000 Jews had been deported, a far cry from what France was expected to supply. In order to expedite matters, the Nazis decided to crack down on the Jewish community in June 1943. Part of this policy entailed new demands on the UGIF. These included the administration of the Drancy internment camp and responsibility for the "missionary plan"—that is, the plan whereby Jews would be encouraged voluntarily to join their family members interned in Drancy.[54] The UGIF council ac-

---

[52] On the extensive negotiations see Cohen, "Jewish leadership," pp. 177–80; cf. Szajkowski, *Gazetteer*, p. 11; m. Rajsfus, *Des Juifs dans la collaboration. L'U.G.I.F. (1941–1944)*, (Paris, 1980), pp. 158–60.

[53] See Billig, *Le Commissariat*, 1 : 384–85, 292–93. Cf. Rajsfus, *Des Juifs*, p. 161.

[54] See protocol of meeting between UGIF leaders and Nazi officials, 30 June 1943, YVA, 09/8–4; YIVO, RG 210, IV–4. See George Wellers, *L'Etoile jaune à l'heure de Vichy* (Paris, 1973), pp. 185–219.

cepted responsibility for administering Drancy in order to alleviate somewhat the fate of the internees. It rejected outright the diabolical "missionary project," for it entailed measures of a police character ("caractère policier") that were inimical to the UGIF's raison d'être.[55] The council's unanimous decision prompted André Baur to take a unique step. He asked the commissariat to arrange for him a private audience with the prime minister, Laval, in order that he might describe to him the deteriorating situation of the Jewish community.[56] This was the first and last time in the history of the UGIF North that its leaders decided to turn to the political arm of Vichy for help. Baur and the council still clung to a certain trust in Vichy's goodwill and believed that Laval would intercede with the Nazis. Baur's request went unanswered—or maybe it came in the form of his arrest some ten days later.[57]

These events illustrate the essential dilemma for the UGIF during the years 1943–44. Legality provided it with some hope of continuing its aid to the suffering community that still required its services. The council was convinced of the need to help the internees at Drancy. But the demand for outright collaboration with Nazi policies provoked open opposition, even though such a posture threatened the termination of the entire aid structure. From the summer of 1943, this would be the recurring issue for UGIF North, and it was thus never able to dispense totally with its legal framework.

The model of UGIF North well reflected the established elements of the community during the final phases of occupation. Another prominent model of Jewish behaviour that emerged was that of outright resistance. Resistance and rescue activity, in all their various forms, became a central force within the organized community, overcoming the differences between Eastern European Jews and native French Jews. A common purpose was reached, and nowhere was this more apparent than in the area of rescuing children.[58] By the fall of 1943 the more conservative agencies, affiliated with UGIF, and the Communist-oriented groups found themselves working together to disperse children in the north and south.

[55] Protocol of council meeting, 6 July 1943, CDJC, CDX–42.
[56] YIVO, RG 210, CVIII–5.
[57] See CDJC, CDXXX–41, XCVI. Baur met the commissariat official, Antignac, on 13 July 1943.
[58] Kieval, "Legality and Resistance," pp. 359–65.

Spurred on by the persistence of the French Resistance movement and the rapidly deteriorating fate of the Jews, these groups turned illegal activity into the distinguishing feature of French Jewry. The historical significance of their diverse activities lies not only in their success in saving thousands of lives, but also in pushing French Jewry's center of gravity away from the acceptance of Vichy toward its rejection. The peripheral groups had once again provoked the central forces in French Jewry to respond to their agitation.[59]

French Jewry had traveled a long road from its enthusiasm over France's declaration of war against Germany. The war years had brought untold disaster for many thousands of Jews in France but unleashed a myriad of responses from within the community. The divided community of 1940 appeared after years of suffering to share certain goals. French Jewry slowly overcame its confusion of 1940 and accepted a new raison d'être that was to leave its imprint on postwar French Jewry.

[59] See Michael Graetz, *From Periphery to Center. Chapters in 19th Century History of French Jewry* (Jerusalem, 1982), Ch. 10 (Hebrew).

PART 4

ANTI-SEMITISM

PATRICE HIGONNET

On the Extent of Anti-Semitism in Modern France

F EW JEWS lived in France from the Revolution to World War I, and nearly half of them resided in Paris. Before the 1930s, most Frenchmen probably had no sustained contact with compatriots whom they knew to be Jewish; anti-Semitism was not a critical issue in the public or private lives of Frenchmen. And yet, in recent years, the fate of Jews in France has become a touchstone for our understanding of modern French history as a whole. Anti-Semitism has become a critical representation of some fundamental aspects of French culture.

It is therefore of great consequence that the historiography of the subject has in recent years taken a sudden turn. Earlier work on the history of Jews in modern France started from a particular view of the French Revolution and of its republican sequels. The progress of assimilation was the leitmotiv of these studies. The French Revolution, "notre mère," had theoretically brought into being a civil society open to talents for both "ordinary" Frenchmen (like Picards or Normans) and extraordinary Frenchmen (Jews, Protestants, Alsatians, speakers of dialects). In that anticlerical republican synthesis, Catholic militants often felt excluded, but nearly everyone else felt symbolically encompassed. Discrimination in daily life was perceived as a gap, soon to be bridged, between the reality of French life and its republican matrix.

More recent work on Jews in France, however, has started from the other shore. Anti-Semitism is approached from its totalitarian consequence. Whereas assimilation was studied from its revolutionary origins, here the concentration camps are the critical fac-

tor; correspondingly, the new perception implies a diminished appreciation of the French Revolution and of its legacy.

An understanding of French anti-Semitism must start from an
appreciation of fundamental shifts in French historiography; it is
in that context that it will be considered here. It may be worthwhile to remember that the historiography of Jews today also has
an *air de famille* with the literature on another French religious minority, Protestants, as it was written in the eighteenth and nineteenth centuries. Today the history of the *religion prétendue ré-
formée* is not of burning interest. But it may be of passing interest
to remember that before 1900, the history of French Protestants
was a lively topic because it was read from the perspective of liberal defence of the republican state rather than from that of the
Protestants themselves. The focus of study then was set on the intolerance of the ancien régime, on Louis XIV and Bossuet rather
than on the origins, let us say, of La Banque Protestante. The Saint
Bartholomew's Day Massacre, the Revocation of the Edict of
Nantes, and the return of tolerance on the eve of the Revolution
were the critical landmarks of an interpretation whose emphasis
was political rather than social or cultural. *Comparaison n'est pas
raison*, but a point is to be made here, namely that the history of
religious minorities in France has been a protean field.

Recent work on France has emphasized the nonintegration of
Jews in French life. Revisionist historians have identified in French
Republican theory traces of what might be called the French Burk-
ean tradition. They highlight the numerous and savage attacks on
Jews that can be found in the writings of intellectuals from de
Maistre to Maurras; they dwell on the darker side of the French
national character. Sternhell, for example, explicitly connects the
strength in France of anti-Semitism with the weakness in that country of the liberal idea. "Anti-Semitism was one aspect of the great
revolt against the . . . core of the intellectual heritage on which Europe had been living since the eighteenth century. This very revolt
. . . brought about a convergence between antiliberal, antibourgeois nationalism and the variant of Socialism that, even while rejecting Marxism, remained revolutionary."[1] Anti-Semitic texts are
taken as the apex of an anti-Semitic *mentalité* that pervades the
culture as a whole.

[1] See above p. 132.

The emergence in our time of interpretations like Sternhell's, which emphasize the importance in France of *Blut und Boden*, is no surprise. Historians like Theodore Zeldin and Eugen Weber have underscored the artificiality, and by implication, the fragility of the French republican idea. If peasants were *made* into Frenchmen, it follows that their liberalism might just as easily be "unmade." Circumstances might turn Frenchmen back into peasants of a sort, illiberal, and anti-Semitic; and Vichy, one could suggest, did just that. Under the pressure of events, the superficiality of French republicanism was suddenly exposed; and with it, that of Jewish assimilationism.

Current cultural values reinforce the pessimism of the revisionists. In the Western world, the strength of nationalism is nearly everywhere on the wane. We are today more impressed than before by the survivals of ethnicity and more favorable to pluralism and cultural diversity. We insert our suspicion of uniformitarian bourgeois culture into our reading of the past.

Just how fragile the republican synthesis was will never be clear since it did collapse in a world war. It has always been known that liberalism in France had many enemies, some of them rightists, others leftists, and still others, after the 1890s, of a revolutionary conservative, fascistic kind. But it is also true that with the exception of a number of years that can be counted on the fingers of one hand, France since 1789 has been ruled by liberal centrists of the moderate left and right who did obey the rule of law. If Hitler had not come to power first in Germany and then in Europe, would the anti-Semitic Alibert ever have become minister of injustice? Would we know Benoist-Méchin's name? The setting of Céline's *D'un château l'autre* fascinates us precisely because the world that is described is, like its setting, so "boche-baroque."

In any case, few will deny that the French republican synthesis has had its antipluralist costs. Jews more than others have had to bear these costs. Since 1945, other groups as diverse as Catholics, feminists, homosexuals, and partisans of *l'Occitanie libre* have usefully reminded us of how narrow the French republican tradition was. And yet it is also obvious that this much criticized tradition had great strengths. Tens of thousands of Jews were successfully integrated into the national fabric. Captain Dreyfus's experience can be read in two ways. It was the overthrow of the republican state and not its intrinsic nature that led to the undoing of French

Jewry. Unlike Maurice Rajsfus, Yerachmiel Cohen in his admirable and judicious essay does not condemn the so-called "juifs dans la Collaboration" for placing their trust in their fellow Frenchmen, and he is right to withhold condemnation. The decision of the Jews who agreed to serve in the Union Générale des Juifs de France (UGIF) was anything but prudent. Their action, however, was neither ignoble nor historically absurd. Bernard Lazare has been singled out as one model of what Jews should have been. But one could also point to the example in the nineteenth century of Pissaro, the Rothschilds, Alphand, or Halévy; and in our own century to Bergson, Darius Milhaud, Max Jacob, Marc Bloch, Raymond Aron, Léon Blum, Pierre Mendès France, and Michel Debré.

The methods of revisionist historians can also be criticized. First, it can be said that the revisionists have mechanically assumed the deep popular resonance and obvious meaning of the well-known texts. But feminist criticism, for example, has attuned us to a more subtle reading of classic texts, and a similar approach could be followed here with profit. Second and more important, the revisionists have argued in a manner reminiscent of vulgar Marxism. They have moved rather unthinkingly from literary texts (taken at face value), to the supposed popular anti-Semitism, to the actions of the state. Embedded in their *discours* is the assumption that politics are a mere superstructure, and that one can move effortlessly forward and backward from politics to ideas to society.

But the secular experience of the French nation reveals precisely the reverse. As we know from Tocqueville (and many others), the continuity of the centralized French state has transcended all disruptions, including the revolutionary trauma of 1789–99. The French state, though limited in its scope, was nonetheless ubiquitous. The French bourgeoisie hid behind a national tariff barrier. The working class looked to nationalization as the means to social justice. The state affected literature and the arts. It interfered to support the family. It created a national linguistic community. It only grudgingly accepted the existence of private schools.

The resonance of anti-Semitic texts can also be questioned. For many French intellectuals, "Jewishness" became a code term for a category of destruction, at once horrifying and fascinating. This categorical structure often had limited relevance to their own lives: Degas, a friend of Halévy in fact, was a categorical anti-Semite in the abstract. Similar examples could be found for even the most frenetic anti-Semites, like Maurras or Rebatet. To infer that this intellectual and categorical perception of Jews had broad relevance for the population as a whole is bold indeed. French culture does have a persistent tradition of nihilism, necrophilia, and the cult of the violent and the irrational. But it is a commonplace that both bourgeois and popular French culture emphasize countervailing values of order, discipline, measure, and moderation. That the ravings of Léon Bloy or the deconstructionist nihilism of Blanchot have had intellectual appeal cannot be denied. Their relevance to the actuality of French life is very debatable.

In some respects, high culture, the shape of institutions, and the broad lineaments of popular French culture did indeed overlap. The centralization of the French state can rightly be seen as the expression, in part, of some deep-seated suspicion of cultural pluralism, a suspicion that subsumes anti-Semitism. But the centralized French state is also a distinct historical phenomenon that exists outside society, just as high French culture has as its root the ancient Cartesian distinction between the word and the world. The French state often follows its own trajectory, at once close to and removed from the other trajectories of French life, cultural, economic, or social. It could elicit unwavering loyalty, especially in critical times, as appears for example in Pétain's reply to what must have been an appalling letter written to him by the grand rabbin de France in late 1940. "L'obéissance à la loi est un des principes essentiels de tout Etat et une des conditions indispensables au redressement de la France. . . . Je suis heureux de constater que vous êtes animés de ces mêmes sentiments et je vous remercie de les avoir exprimés."[2]

It is historically suggestive that the three great religious pogroms of French history (the Saint Bartholomew's Day Massacre of Protestants, the September massacres of 1792 against Catholic priests, and the deportation of Jews in 1942–44) share certain characteristics. They all took place in moments of great social and political disruption, when silent majorities tend to go underground. Though not exclusively Parisian by any means, they nonetheless had a disproportionate Parisian component. All three events also were carried out by small groups of people, acting with the essential com-

---

[2] Maurice Rajsfus. *Des Juifs dans la collaboration: L'UGIF (1941–44) précédé d'une courte étude sur les juifs de France en 1939* (Paris: Etudes et Documentation Internationales, 1980), p. 66.

plicity or even the encouragement of the state. Very few Parisians, not to speak of Frenchmen, had anything to do with them.

The evidence at hand, the testimonials of the participants, the basic lineaments of French history all point to the importance of the state and to its isolation from social and cultural forms, themselves somewhat schizophrenic. Philippe Pétain was the last and the most derisory king of France, as his successor was its last crown prince. It is tempting to hate Laval's obedient prefects, or the police officials who kept their *fichiers* in good order. But such men were more heartless and efficient than specifically anti-Semitic. "Do not ask me," said Peyrouton, "if I am a Republican or an anti-Republican *fonctionnaire*. I am a *fonctionnaire*." It is paradoxical but also readily understandable that state worship should have climaxed in France on the collapse of the nation in 1940. Sudden disruption and unprecedented defeat heightened in Frenchmen the feeling that the state and even the army and its leader should be blindly obeyed.

Finally, it is of interest that an argument on the autonomy of the state and on the isolated nature of the French political *discours* is underscored by current trends in French historical writing. In a first step, during the 1950s and 1960s, historians of the *Annales* school moved away from economic and social history narrowly defined in order to focus on problems of *mentalités*. The old Marxist connection between economic structure and cultural superstructure was largely severed. In a second step, during the 1970s, historians like François Furet in his well known *Penser la Révolution* went one step further. Free-floating ideology became in this scheme the motor of political history. For Furet, it would be vain to reach back from the rantings of Robespierre to the opinions of provincial Jacobins. Political history is represented here as a house without windows, as a self-sustaining genre that is removed from broad social and cultural concerns. The analogy between revolutionary Terror and Vichy's anti-Semitism is a clear one.

The revisionist inquiry into the extent of anti-Semitism in modern France will profit from greater awareness of these gaps in French political consciousness. We need to find a constructive outlet and object for our outrage. A great crime has been committed, but, suddenly, there are no culprits, or those who are to be found are isolated and derisory. The ability to blame largely dissipates when attention is shifted away from society and toward the faceless state.

We must redirect our attention to the larger sets of attitudes that empower that state. In my view, the crime of ordinary Frenchmen in 1940–44 was not their anti-Semitism, but their passive conformity and their indifference to the plight of individuals—individuals who in this instance were Jewish. Their sympathy for Jews might have been greater if the categories of their psychic world had been differently arranged. But it is hard to say how much difference that would have made. Maurice Papon was content to persecute Jews under Vichy and to befriend them in later years. He is a man who deserves contempt, but I do not think that his actions can be understood in the context that Sternhell has laid out for us.

Comparaison n'est pas raison: Terror in 1794 was a defense of ideology whereas terror in 1943–44 *was* ideology. But the analogy to 1794 is still of use. Just as most Frenchmen and women in the earlier period were passive and often terrified observers of a political process they did not understand, so were Vichy and the German occupation largely superimposed on a passive population struggling to live from day to day. Though it may be true that the doctrinal terrorism of 1794 has antecedents in a prerevolutionary Rousseauistic impatience for pluralistic diversity, that mood was radically transformed, generalized, and dramatized by events that were anything but inevitable. Without doubt, the immediacy and horror of the death camps cannot be so readily accommodated; and raving anti-Semites did exist in France before 1940. Like all discourses that sever connections to a group ostensibly alien, this anti-Semitism did foster what Bergson has called the anesthesia of the heart. It encouraged a fatal passivity among Frenchmen, as it did in other countries, in America and in Britain. Frenchmen were encouraged by these ideologues in their indifference. But our perception today of revolutionary Terror de-emphasizes both personal motivation and simple cultural continuity, and so may our understanding of France, Vichy, and the Jews become less personal and textual.

PIERRE BIRNBAUM

Anti-Semitism and Anticapitalism
in Modern France

IN RECENT HISTORY, the Jews have been portrayed either as dangerous revolutionaries threatening the Western social order, as professional Bolsheviks intent on destroying the capitalist order,[1] or, on the contrary, as formidable financiers wielding an immense economic power and extending their control to all parts of the globe.[2] Whether they are perceived as violent Bolsheviks or, instead, as unscrupulous capitalists, the crucial point, for many hostile observers, is that the Jews, disregarding national borders, are active in all countries. According to this view, the Jews, a people long without a state, make light of national constraints and, by their fundamentally cosmopolitan strategy, maintain their own power.

From the ancien régime down to the contemporary period, the "myth of the bigwigs" ("le mythe des gros") has played a crucial role in the national ideology that structures French perceptions of social relationships. In opposition to *les gros*, the parasites, the "Two Hundred Families" or the "wall of money," all the *petits*— the have-nots, the pure, indeed, the people as a whole—are supposedly united in a common determination to reject those who are alien.[3] From La Bruyère to Stendhal, from Flaubert to Zola, from Maupassant to Claudel, throughout the history of French litera-

Translated from French by Jonathan Mandelbaum.

[1] See, for example, Robert Wistrich, *Revolutionary Jews from Marx to Trotsky* (New York: Barnes & Noble, 1976).

[2] Norman Cohn, *Warrant for Genocide: The Myth of the Jewish World-Conspiracy and the Protocols of the Elders of Zion* (London: Eyre & Spottiswode, 1967).

[3] Pierre Birnbaum, *Le Peuple et les gros: Histoire d'un mythe* (Paris: Grasset, 1979).

ture, the have-nots, the *sans-culottes*, the hungry, have struggled against *les gros*. Those "below," who inhabit the nether regions, have risen against the establishment, the "men at the top," those who "rule the roost."[4] *Les gros* have all the money; they are often bankers; and they are always fat. The people have waged a constant war on them: Joan of Arc rebelled against them; the crowds have stormed a succession of Bastilles; and, from 1936 to 1982, the Popular Fronts brought together the overwhelming majority of the populace, united against the infinitesimal minority of ruthless, domineering *gros*. The advantage of this oft told tale is that it ignores the internal conflicts in French society. Its use makes it possible to aim at the conquest of power by means of a catch-all strategy capable of uniting antagonistic social groups against an enemy all the more easy to demonize as he is supposedly alien to the people itself.

This myth has been perpetuated from the nineteenth century until today on both the far right and the far left: it effectively belongs to the French ideology. To this common denominator another element has sometimes been added, namely, the role attributed to the Jews in the international plot against the innocent populace. *Les gros* thus turn out to be the Jews, since they constitute a small group of cosmopolitan bankers who exploit every category of the population the world over—workers, peasants, artisans, small shopkeepers, and bosses alike. This distortion of the basic myth is, in varying degrees, a constant feature of recent French history.

During the latter half of the nineteenth century—a period in which France was becoming rapidly industrialized, huge fortunes were being amassed, and a succession of financial scandals broke—the moralizing denunciation of money led some commentators, such as Zola himself, to assert, "It is indeed Jewry as a whole, that stubborn and cold-blooded conqueror, marching toward the sovereign kingship of the world amid the nations it has bought one by one with its omnipotent gold . . . that rules the earth."[5] At a time when most Jews in France led a very modest and often even poverty-stricken existence,[6] the newspaper *La Croix*, which sold

[4] Ulrich Ricke, "Le Vocabulaire de la classification sociale dans la littérature française," *Langue française*, February 1971.

[5] Emile Zola, *L'Argent* (Paris: Livre de Poche), 483.

[6] Michael Marrus, *Les Juifs de France à l'époque de l'affaire Dreyfus* (Paris: Calmann-Lévy, 1972), chap. 3.

several hundred thousand copies daily, inveighed against specula-
tive capitalism in the following words: "Take away the Jew, and
capital will once again become a working tool, not a means for
speculation." Like the far left and the far right, La Croix attacked
those who came to symbolize les gros, namely, the Rothschilds; the
paper argued that "the handful of Jews who have swooped down
on our country must leave it, since the thirty-five million French
cannot do so."[7] During this very same period, Maurice Barrès
extolled Joan of Arc and cathedrals, attacked "cosmopolitan financial feudalism" and "Semitic high finance" (which was "grabbing public wealth"),[8] and, with Maurras, declared war on "anti-
France." The truth was that the "uprooted"—Barrès's déracinés—
included the Jews and not only the "stock market people." Barrès
joined ranks with the revolutionary right in a struggle in which
left-wing anti-Semitism, originally developed by Fourier, Proudhon, and Toussenel, compounded right-wing anti-Semitism. Both
varieties shared a hatred of the Rothschilds, symbols of the wealthy
exploiters—that is, the Jews. Drumont's La France juive systema-
tized this perception. The Blanquists and the Guesdists in turn regarded Captain Dreyfus as a symbol of the alliance between the
upper bourgeoisie and the Jews; in consequence, they adamantly
refused to support him.[9] The equation of Dreyfus with large-scale
Jewish capitalism, accepted from one end of the political spectrum
to the other, was even taken up by some members of the Jewish
working class, who attributed the anti-Semitism then prevailing to
the regrettable existence of "big Jewish financiers."[10]

Thus, by the end of the nineteenth century, the Jews were widely
regarded as the personification of les gros, who, in close collaboration with their cosmopolitan allies, exploited the entire French
people. This perception survived virtually unchanged into the interwar years and the Popular Front period. At the time, the Communist party and the left in general indicted the Two Hundred
Families, portraying them as new Bastilles to be stormed by the
people. The omnipresent theme of the struggle against the Two

[7] Quoted in Pierre Sorlin, "La Croix" et les juifs (1880–1899) (Paris: Grasset, 1967),
105, 110.
[8] Zeev Sternhell, Maurice Barrès et le nationalisme français (Paris: A. Colin, 1972), 233.
[9] See Zeev Sternhell, La Droite révolutionnaire (Paris: Le Seuil, 1978).
[10] Michael Marrus, Les Juifs de France, 284 n. 3.

Hundred Families relentlessly repeated for years and years was not in itself anti-Semitic but simply anti-capitalistic. No connection was made in either *L'Humanité* or *Regards* between large-scale capital and the Jews. Similarly, Francis Delaisi, in *La Banque de France aux mains des deux cents familles*,[11] and Augustin Hamon, in *Les Maîtres de la France*[12] (both authors wrote in the Communist press), studied the role played by the banking world as a whole without singling out the Jews.

Nevertheless one can observe the extent to which the Rothschilds, far more than any other bankers, were pilloried with striking frequency by *L'Humanité*, which printed a considerable number of caricatures of them.[13] Even if—unlike other currents of the French left—the Communist party cannot be described as anti-Semitic, it did resort to the language of the period. This sometimes gave rise to disturbing semantic perversions. The far right's denunciation of Léon Blum was echoed by the accusations of the Communist André Marty: "You, Blum, an intimate friend of the biggest cosmopolitan financiers, men who have won decorations for their plunder and theft—like Oustric, your friend." Somewhat later, Maurice Thorez himself proved no more reluctant to use such sinister vocabulary. On 16 February 1940, at a particularly tragic time for France, he referred to the Socialist leader as a "repugnant character," a "vile lackey of the London bankers," and "the jackal Blum," describing with horror "his fetid hypocrisy," "his reptilian contortions and hisses . . . his hands, with their long and clawlike fingers."[14] Thus, at a time when most of the Jews in France lived very modestly,[15] the Communist party leaders took up the equation between *les gros* and the Jews.

Yet only the far right, between the two wars, explicitly and persistently identified the two. The newspaper *Le Franciste*, for example, wrote, "We are a people, a race, a nation, say the Jews, and these foreigners are the masters of France."[16] In attacking plutoc-

[11] Paris, 1910; see also his articles in *La Flèche*, for example, in the 1 February 1936 issue.

[12] Paris: Editions Sociales Internationales, 1936.

[13] See for example *L'Humanité*, 27 July and 11 August 1935.

[14] Quoted in Annie Kriegel, *Le Pain et les roses* (Paris: Presses Universitaires de France, 1968), 237–38.

[15] David Weinberg, *Les Juifs à Paris de 1933 à 1939* (Paris: Calmann-Lévy, 1974), chap. 2.

[16] *Le Franciste*, 11 April 1937.

racy, the far right unfailingly identified it with the Jews. While joining in the condemnation of the power of big money, the far right identified the Two Hundred Families attacked by the Communist party with the Jews alone. For Céline, "there's no such thing as the Two Hundred Families . . . just one real, omnipotent, international family: the Jewish family, the great international feudal power that holds us to ransom, degrades us, and tyrannizes us." [17] In this heyday of the far right, there was no longer any hesitation. Ranging beyond the small group of "big Jews" who supposedly dominated France, open attacks were launched against all the Jews, now equated collectively and exclusively with *les gros* and regarded as foreigners open to every form of cosmopolitanism. As Céline put it, "people speak of the Two Hundred Families; one should speak instead of the Five Hundred Thousand Jewish Families that are occupying France." [18] The myth of *les gros* identified exclusively with the Jews reached its ultimate stage: this time, the connection between large-scale capitalism and cosmopolitanism was applied to Jewry as a whole.

After World War II, the myth was to lose some of its vitality. Nevertheless, it resurfaced during certain periods. For example, during the short-lived Poujadist movement, the dichotomy between "stateless financial powers [*les gros*]" and "ordinary folks [*le bon populo, les gars d'en bas*]" was revived. [19] *Fraternité Française* added, "Just try asking people with names like Isaac Mendès, Servan-Schreiber, or Ben Said to be French to the core." [20] Attacking degenerate foreigners and corrupters ("les métèques et les pourrisseurs"), Poujade called for a rebellion against those who "grow fat on the blood of all humble Frenchmen." [21] A latter-day manifestation of the influence of the *Protocols of the Elders of Zion*, this traditional accusation thus compounded the myth of *les gros*, giving it an overtly anti-Semitic and demonological character.

It should be observed that Pierre Mendès France, like Léon Blum before him, was singled out as a target for constant attacks. Ac-

---

[17] Louis Ferdinand Céline, *L'Ecole des cadavres* (Paris: Denoël, 1938), 235.

[18] Louis Ferdinand Céline, *Bagatelles pour un massacre* (Paris: Denoël, 1937), 141.

[19] See Dominique Borne, *Petits bourgeois en révolte? Le mouvement Poujade* (Paris: Flammarion, 1977).

[20] *Fraternité française*, 7 January 1956.

[21] Quoted in Stanley Hoffmann, *Le Mouvement Poujade* (Paris: A. Colin, 1956), 148, 158, 170.

cording to Poujade, Mendès France did not "have a single drop of Gallic blood in his veins."[22] For the far right, "Mr. Mendès France is determined to wipe out a considerable number of small and medium-sized firms"; consequently, "the horrible Israeli Mendès" had to be fought against since, "for lack of a governing family [*Aspects de la France* was and is a Royalist periodical], we must suffer two hundred plundering families."[23] Not to be outdone, some Communist party leaders who, as we have seen, had inveighed against Léon Blum in similar terms, returned to this anti-Semitic vein. Jacques Duclos, for example, in the corridors of the National Assembly, was alleged to have denounced Mendès France as a "timorous little Jew . . . shit without silk stockings."[24] Once again, the far right and the far left converged, combining anti-Semitism and anticapitalism.

But the times had changed, and this encounter took place only on very few occasions. When Georges Pompidou was elected president of the Republic after having worked, many years earlier, at the Rothschild bank, he was attacked primarily as "the banker within the State" who was handing the country over to "stateless France."[25] *Minute* too saw Pompidou as the servant of the Rothschilds, that is, of "the symbol of stateless money."[26] As for *L'Humanité*, it attacked "the one thousand stateless company directors who decide the fate of fifty million Frenchmen."[27]

At a time when France was living through a phase of intensive modernization, the Jews thus continued to be perceived as big capitalists who were undermining the moral health of French society. In rural areas, a spate of rumors accused even Jewish shopkeepers, intent on modernizing at all costs, of practicing the white slave trade by depraving innocent young French girls.[28] As a small grocer clearly explained:

I'm part of the neighborhood. I do people favors. I know my customers and their family situation. I know why Mademoiselle Camus pretends to

[22] Pierre Poujade, *J'ai choisi le combat* (Saint-Céré: Société Générale des Editions et des Publications, 1955), 116.

[23] *Aspects de la France*, 6 August, 25 June, and 8 January 1954.

[24] *Le Monde*, 29 October 1982.

[25] *Aspects de la France*, 26 April 1962, 28 February 1963.

[26] *Minute*, 29 May 1969.

[27] *L'Humanité*, 15 May 1969.

[28] See Edgar Morin, *La Rumeur d'Orléans* (Paris: Le Seuil, 1969).

have forgotten her purse at the end of the month. . . . It's true, a grocer is a friend. Just try asking the Jews who run the supermarket to worry about Mademoiselle Camus's financial problems at the end of the month. Those stores are just machines. We, instead, embody a certain France [*une certaine France*]. My father was wounded at Verdun. I was a prisoner in a *stalag*. I too have done my duty.[29]

While the myth of *les gros* was still current before May 1981, its most common version was that of monopolistic state capitalism as described by the Communist party; but this version was devoid of any anti-Semitic connotation. Similarly, during this period, the far right and the right seemed to have taken a more moderate line, and despite their occasional attacks on plutocracy, their anti-Semitism was distinctly less visible. In contrast, since the victory of the left-wing parties in the 1981 elections, the indiscriminate *amalgame* of Socialist-plutocrat-Jew has resurfaced. For the far right, the situation is clear: in a spontaneous return to the language of the 1880s or 1930s, it lashes out against "Mitterrand, Goldenberg and Co." as well as Jacques Attali, said to be setting up "royal-style social-ism" and even to have taken on the task of watching over the quality of "French cuisine," not hesitating to "taste its specialties even though the food isn't kosher." Another target is the "Mephistophe-lian" minister of justice, Robert Badinter. A caricature published at the time of the debate about identity checks shows the minister of the interior, Gaston Defferre, questioning Badinter: "Hey you there, strange-face! Second warning! Show me your identity pa-pers."[30] By 16 July 1981, *Rivarol* was denouncing "our Jewish ministers." While *Aspects de la France*, contrary to its earlier prac-tice, has avoided all anti-Semitic attacks, for *Rivarol*, Mitterrand "doesn't need to find himself in an electoral predicament to be the Providence of Shem's needy sons."[31]

In its relentless attacks on "social-plutocracy," *Rivarol* noted that, while the Jews voted for Mitterrand in 1981, they "are used to having to pack their bags in a hurry."[32] Similarly, at a demon-stration by police in protest against the assassination of two of their colleagues—a demonstration that degenerated into an anti-

---

[29] Michel del Castillo, "La Confession angoissée d'un petit épicier," *Réalités*, October 1960, 194.

[30] *Rivarol*, 22 April and 27 May 1982, 28 January and 11 March 1983.

[31] Ibid., 11 March 1983.

[32] Ibid., 17 December 1981.

government protest—one policeman described Robert Badinter as a "big bourgeois from a foreign country." [33] *Minute*, whose prose is so often Céline-like, has carefully avoided openly anti-Semitic criticism, even though its readers have been told that Robert Badinter and Jacques Attali are "practicing Jews," and that Pierre Mendès France, who belonged to "a secret and formidable people," was tainted by "the showiness of *L'Express*, its veneer, which barely concealed the parvenus of the [rue du] Sentier." [34]

In a total reversal of the notion entertained by a broad section of the left, the far right has come to equate *les gros* with the Socialists, whom they attack for their alleged connections with the forces of capitalism. For the far right, nothing better illustrates the power of the Jewish and Socialist plutocracy than the career of Pierre Mendès France. Thus, after stating that Léon Blum was "the lawyer for big capitalist firms," *Le Crapouillot* went on to say that Mendès France, a "*grand bourgeois*" and "business lawyer," a junior minister in Léon Blum's government in 1938, "was the connecting link between the generation of the Popular Front and that of the Congress of Epinay," [35] where the new Socialist party was born. Thus, over time, the myth remains the same: for the far right, whether during the Dreyfus Affair, at the time of Léon Blum, or in present-day France, the "masters" of France are the big Jewish capitalists acting in unison with the Socialist government, just as they were formerly supposed to be the faithful allies of international Bolshevism. Consequently, in the eyes of the far right, the plot has not changed.

The Socialist Party too, as in the days of the Popular Front, espouses the myth of *les gros* and is continually attacking the "wall of money," the "cosmopolitan bourgeoisie," the "money lords,"

[33] *Libération*, 4 June 1983. Similarly, according to Arnaud de Lassus, leader of the far right group Action Familiale et Scolaire, "four superpowers are colonizing France: the Marxist, the Freemason, the Jew, and the Protestant. They are symbolized by four ministers: Fiterman, Hernu, Badinter, and Rocard. . . . Badinter goes with Fiterman [as] Rothschild went with Marx" (Speech at the "Journée d'Amitié Française," Paris, 16 October 1983, quoted in *Le Monde*, 19 October 1983).

[34] *Minute*, 14 August and 23 October 1982. One can also ask oneself, according to Louis Pauwels, why "the Jack Langs, the Polacs, the Kahns, and the Levys" are incapable of talking about Hayek's thought and about liberalism—a curious list (*Le Figaro Magazine*, 16 January 1982). Pauwels was referring to Jack Lang, the minister of culture; Michel Polac, the producer of a controversial television talk show; Jean-François Kahn, a journalist; and Bernard-Henri Lévy, a philosopher.

[35] *Le Crapouillot*, October-November 1982, 20.

whom it accuses of trying to obstruct the Socialist experiment. But, as before, the party's denunciations are never tainted by anti-Semitism. The same cannot be said of the Communist party. While it too denounces the "wall of money" and "cosmopolitan capitalism" and regularly issues appeals to wage war on the "money lords," it does not hesitate to resort to the same arguments it used between the wars, and to stress the alleged links between international plutocracy, the Socialists, and the Jews. Before the two parties came to power together, and before the first round of the presidential elections of May 1981, the Communist party observed that "the Socialist party has already established ties with capitalism and with the State apparatus" dominated by "the tiny Giscardian caste." The Communists also frequently denounced "Claude Perdriel, a former employee of the Rothschild bank,"[36] and owner of *Le Nouvel Observateur*, the weekly that the Communist party regards as the mouthpiece of the Socialist party. For *L'Humanité*, the Giscardian clan had therefore "spun a web of connections with Socialist technocrats . . . to serve the interests of the very wealthy," and François Mitterrand himself did not hesitate to make visits to Washington and—yes—to Jerusalem.[37]

After the victory of the united left in 1981, necessity knew no law, and the Communist party ceased to refer to the Socialist party when attacking big capitalism. Nevertheless, it persisted in its prewar habit of singling out the Rothschilds as a special target. For example, after the nationalizations, "the Rothschilds are scheming" and "moving" to the United States.[38] As before, the Communist party continually voices its indignation at the misdeeds of the "wall of money" and analyzes the infamous doings of the "big" capitalists.

To be sure, the theme of the struggle against *les gros* is to be found in other countries, including both Britain and the United States.[39] Yet only in France has it reached such intensity; perhaps

[36] *L'Humanité*, 20 May 1980.
[37] Ibid., 3 March 1981; report by Georges Marchais to the Central Committee, ibid., 14 January 1981.
[38] Ibid., 10 and 11 July 1981.
[39] On Great Britain, see Claire Hirshfeld, "The British Left and the 'Jewish Conspiracy': A Case of Modern Anti-semitism," *Jewish Social Studies*, Summer 1981. Ferdinand Lundberg, *America's 60 Families* (New York, 1937) and Matthew Josephson, *The Robber Barons* (New York, 1934).

only in France is it such an enduring feature of both the far left and the far right. This simplifying and diabolical type of anticapitalism sometimes relies on a virulent anti-Semitism that equates, in a single accusation, the cosmopolitan character of big capitalism with the international dimension of Socialism. Consequently, the myth of *les gros* may have served as a common denominator for the various abortive attempts to impose Fascism in France.[40] The fact that the French state is so distinctly differentiated and institutionalized—the truth being that it is the state that is "strong," not *les gros*,[41]—may help to explain the failure of Fascism in France: by attacking large-scale cosmopolitan capitalism, at least ideologically, Fascism came up against a highly autonomized state that proved capable, before succumbing to the enemy from without, of resisting the enemy from within.

[40] See Zeev Sternhell, *Ni droite ni gauche: L'Idéologie fasciste en France* (Paris: le Seuil, 1983). The author illustrates this ambivalence of fascism in France but does not actually analyze the unifying role played by the myth of *les gros*. But see 280–81.

[41] See Bertrand Badie and Pierre Birnbaum, *The Sociology of the State*, trans. Arthur Goldhammer (Chicago: University of Chicago Press, 1983).

MICHAEL R. MARRUS

Are the French Antisemitic?
Evidence in the 1980s

THE MASSACRE in Jo Goldenberg's Paris delicatessen on 9 August 1982 has prompted many North American observers to ask: Is there an upsurge of antisemitism in France? Too frequently the response is simply presumed to be positive, without further ado. For it is often assumed that such spectacular attacks on Jews must represent the tip of an antisemitic iceberg, that behind them lies extensive and popularly supported anti-Jewish feeling. This essay examines both the assumption and the reality of French antisemitism today.

If one looks back, the shootings on the rue des Rosiers seem to fit a pattern of violence begun in 1978. That year explosions shattered a kosher butcher shop in Avignon, a Marseille synagogue, and the Paris headquarters of the Club Méditerranée, popularly associated with Jews through its founder and a chief executive. Then followed more bombings, including a murderous attack on a Jewish student restaurant in the Paris Latin Quarter, wounding twenty-six, an assassination attempt upon Nazi-hunter Serge Klarsfeld, and the killing of Pierre Goldman, a former hoodlum who became a best-selling Jewish writer. The most spectacular episode, until the rue des Rosiers incident, was a huge explosion outside the synagogue on the rue Copernic in Paris on Friday, 3 October 1980, exactly forty years after the issuing of the first comprehensive anti-

An earlier version of this article appeared in the *Jerusalem Quarterly*, no. 32, Summer 1984; it appears here by kind permission of the editors.

Jewish law by the government of Vichy France. Four people died, and nineteen were injured.

The blast on the rue Copernic seemed symbolic. Stunned by its violence, French Jews waited for an official condemnation. That evening Prime Minister Raymond Barre dropped his unfortunate phrase in a television statement condemning "this odious attack aimed at Jews attending the synagogue, and which struck innocent Frenchmen who were crossing rue Copernic." However intended, the distinction between the "innocent" French passers-by and the Jewish worshippers for whom the bomb was really intended outraged opinion and confirmed many in their view of antisemitism in high places. Despite spontaneous displays of popular revulsion against the crime in France, the government continued to stumble, giving signs of indifference. The next day a ceremony took place on the bombed street; no important cabinet representatives attended, and President Giscard d'Estaing was notably absent. Two police unions promptly declared that neo-Nazis had infiltrated the police. Interior Minister Christian Bonnet, stung by these charges, fell silent. Within days the weekly magazine *L'Express* commissioned a poll, which suggested that over half the adult French population believed that antisemitism was widespread in France.

Consistently with an important French tradition, intellectuals sprang into print with *prises de position*, addressing what had become the issue of the moment. In *L'Express*, Raymond Aron, the most prominent political theorist in France, counseled prudence and refused to conclude that the bombers were part of a rising tide of antisemitism. The hour was not Aron's, however; it belonged rather to the anguished analysts who were far more certain of such a link. Since Copernic such writers have expressed themselves more systematically, and have helped shape opinion about the present situation of Jews in France.

Perhaps the most widely discussed of these statements, *L'Idéologie française* (1981) by Bernard-Henri Lévy and *La République et les juifs* (1982) by Shmuel Trigano, reflected a broadly shared sense, however ill founded, that France had turned once more against the Jews. The photogenic and articulate Lévy, already known as a bright star of the anti-Marxist *nouveaux philosophes*, argued that a fascistic ideology dressed in the national colors marked French culture for close to a century, studiously ignored by analysts, yet remarkably influential. Behind current antisemitic episodes lay precisely this sinister and seductive national tradition. Trigano, for his part, took the rue Copernic bombing as his point of departure. To this young Jewish writer the republican order in France excludes *any* positive expression of Jewishness. Even in the remarkable Paris demonstrations of over 100,000 people denouncing the bombing he saw an inability to tolerate the Jew. The ecumenical character of the vast cortege, linking unionists of all stripes together with a broad range of political and public personalities, he somehow considered as a merely ritualistic French ceremony, one that buried the right of Jewish self-expression beneath a false front of collective action and agreement.[1] Such, as least, was the argument.

Across France, and certainly abroad, in North America, intellectuals and publicists issued similarly pessimistic evaluations. Writing in the *New York Times*, Flora Lewis described "widespread tremors of fear over what dark urges still lurk in many people's hearts." The historian Patrick Girard saw the Copernic outrage as the culmination of years of misgovernment and a profound weakening of the French moral fiber. "We are all guilty," he said. "This . . . is the inevitable consequence of the moral lapse that poisons the political life of this country. We are paying for years of recantation, petty acts of cowardice and large-scale compromises, of silence before assaults on human rights in the East as in the West."[2] In a flood of national self-recrimination, spokesmen of many persuasions linked antisemitism to powerful forces of the revived French right. Outside France, Jewish leaders denounced the bombing, to be sure, but also extended their evaluation to wholesale condemnations of France and the French, seen to be reawakening anti-Jewish feeling that recalled the wartime collaborationist regime of Vichy.

Another argument given wide currency at the time was that the French government's tilt away from Israel and toward the Arab states

[1] Trigano's convoluted argument deserves quotation in this context. "La manifestation enterrait Copernic au lieu de l'affronter et de le combattre. Elle avait bien sûr quelque chose de merveilleusement positif et que je ne tourne pas en dérision, que l'on me comprenne bien. Si cette manifestation ne s'était produite, la France aurait suffoqué et la situation juive aurait été bien désespérée; mais elle avait aussi quelque chose d'inquiétant dans son aspect de rite collectif sacré et narcissique, dans l'imaginaire qui la mouvait et semblait échapper à la maîtrise de sa finalité consciente." *La République et les Juifs* (Paris, 1982), 22.

[2] Patrick Girard, "Nous payons pour la mort d'un certain humanisme," *Cahiers Bernard Lazare*, November 1980, 5.

since 1967 had created a particularly favorable climate for anti-Jewish expression. Didier Bariani, president of the small French Radical party first declared this about rue Copernic, and the idea was repeated at the time by the Israeli prime minister.

After Copernic, however, the atmosphere seemed to improve notably. Elections in the summer of 1981 brought the Socialists under François Mitterrand to power, and with them hope for better relations between the French government and the Jewish community. Mitterrand was surrounded by Jewish advisers and associates. He reputedly took a dim view of the French police, who had failed to capture perpetrators of previous anti-Jewish outrages. On Israel he seemed particularly sensitive to Jewish concerns. His son, Jean-Christophe, has lived on a kibbutz in the Galilee, and he himself has long-standing ties with the Israeli Labour party through the Socialist International. Shortly after his election Mitterrand made a point of visiting Israel, the first European head of state to do so, and received an especially warm welcome. At the Hebrew University, where he was awarded an honorary degree, Mitterrand was lauded for his work in the French Resistance, his championing of Soviet Jewry, and what was called "his untiring efforts on behalf of mankind, the Jewish people, and the State of Israel."[3]

Then came the Israeli invasion of Lebanon in the summer of 1982. As the campaign escalated, rumblings from the Elysée Palace became more audible. The French government called pointedly for a halt to the Israeli advance before Beirut. In the European community, Mitterrand mobilized opposition to "the annihilation of the Palestinian people," and in one notorious remark, all the more clumsy for having been made in Budapest, compared Israeli attacks upon civilians to the Nazi wartime massacre at Oradour-sur-Glane. At home, the government-controlled television networks, strongly criticized for following an official line under the previous administration, were again accused of a sharply anti-Israeli bias.

Within French Jewry there were signs of disarray, as chunks of opinion broke away from a once solid block of support for Israel. Organized community institutions remained firmly behind the Israeli government, as did most French Jews, led by the chief rabbi of France, René Sirat, and community leader Alain de Rothschild. But for the first time since the creation of the Jewish state serious

[3] "French Leader's Efforts for Mankind Recognized," *Jerusalem Post*, 7–13 March 1982.

divisions opened. For many Jews the fighting created severe dilemmas. More than a hundred leading Jewish intellectuals protested against the war—including the respected philosopher Vladimir Jankélévich, who was later severely criticized for participating in demonstrations and publicly regretted having done so.

At the beginning of July came a call in Paris for negotiations with the Palestine Liberation Organization (PLO) from the much admired former French prime minister Pierre Mendès France, the late Nahum Goldmann, founder and former president of the World Jewish Congress, and its immediate past president Philip Klutznick, former U.S. secretary of commerce under President Jimmy Carter. Reporters avidly descended upon French Jewish personalities asking their opinions, and some of these drew distinctions unthinkable in previous Arab-Israeli wars.

With the siege of Beirut tension mounted. Criticism of Israel in the French media, especially newspapers, intensified sharply. There is little doubt that reporting of the conflict involved serious distortions and excesses, perceived by many Jews as reflecting deep-seated biases against the Jewish cause. On 12 July 1982, commemorating the fortieth anniversary of the huge roundup of Jews in Paris prior to their deportation and murder in Auschwitz, an emotional crowd heard Alain de Rothschild and Chief Rabbi Sirat denounce "a resurgence of racism and antisemitism during recent weeks," and argue the justice of the war waged by Israel for its right to exist.

Anti-Jewish incidents accompanied the heightened intensity of war abroad and bitter feelings at home. The terrorist attack in Goldenberg's was immediately preceded by a bombing at an Israeli bank in Paris and another at the now nationalized Rothschild Bank, as well as the machine-gunning of a car belonging to an Israeli diplomat.

But the methodical shootings on the rue des Rosiers on 9 August, leaving six dead and twenty-two wounded, surpassed all attacks on Jews in France since the end of World War II, not only in the scale of the bloodshed but also in cold-blooded ruthlessness. As with rue Copernic, there was a sudden outpouring of emotion and a denunciation of the government, the media, the police, and old traditions of French antisemitism. Abroad, commentators were quick to draw connections between the massacre at Goldenberg's and the murder of over 75,000 Jews by the Nazis during World War II, an operation carried out with the assistance of French collaborators.

Mitterrand himself was denounced as an assassin by an emotional crowd that gathered outside a memorial service for the victims. In an extraordinary statement Menachem Begin declared the following day that France was a country of "rampant antisemitism" and recalled the Dreyfus Affair at the end of the nineteenth century when cries of "Death to the Jews" echoed in the streets of Paris. If the French authorities would not put an end to these attacks, he said, he would call upon young French Jews to defend their own people—an ill-considered remark that was immediately disavowed by distraught French Jewish leaders.

Even to those who experienced this attack as a reenactment of rue Copernic there were unmistakeable differences in how public authorities responded to the two outrages. Giscard spent the weekend after rue Copernic hunting at a country estate; Mitterrand went to a memorial service at a synagogue near where the attack took place. Giscard's interior minister quickly refused to discuss the bombing in 1980 because of a police scandal; the current interior minister, Gaston Defferre, called attention to the international implications of the outrage, linking it to a renegade Palestinian group that had broken away from the PLO.

One need not accept Defferre's announced opinion, however, to see this bloody episode as part of a terrorist blitz, rather than as an expression of local hostility toward Jews. The French police have failed to stop not only antisemitic assassins, but others as well. Last March a terrorist bomb rocked the Paris-Toulouse express, killing five and injuring twenty-seven. In April, a huge car bomb exploded outside the offices of an Arabic-language pro-Iraqi newspaper, killing one pedestrian and wounding sixty-three others. The month preceding Goldenberg's saw more than one hundred terrorist incidents in France. An Armenian exile group set off an explosion near Notre Dame Cathedral wounding fifteen, and three days later another car bomb killed Fadel el-Dami, the number-two PLO man in Paris. There were also several dozen Corsican bombings, an attack on the apartment of Régis Debray (a radical writer advising Mitterrand) and a series of miscellaneous shootings and fire bombings. Attacks continued even after the rue des Rosiers killings, including more anti-Jewish bombs and an explosion outside the Iraqi embassy, credited to an obscure Iraqi opposition group. On 15 August 1982 came the destruction of the offices of the far-right weekly *Minute,* itself often accused of antisemitism and branded "fascist" by the political left.

Until the police uncover more hard evidence about the specifically anti-Jewish terror, it is hard to judge how much of it has been imported from abroad, and how much is due to local criminals. The problem is especially complex because evidence now suggests international cooperation among terrorist groups of very divergent political objectives.

My own feeling is that these antisemitic attacks do not derive from French issues but are rather an effort on the part of Middle Eastern terrorists to win political capital in the war against Israel by hitting at vulnerable targets. The Polish origin of the weapons used at Goldenberg's suggests such a conclusion and indicates links with other recent terrorist episodes in London, Vienna, Brussels, and Rome. No evidence, on the other hand, has connected anti-Jewish terrorism to any body of opinion in France. Whatever the causes of the current wave, a new tide of antisemitism in France does not seem to be one of them.

Consider how the present situation differs from the Depression years of the 1930s, when, all observers agree, France experienced an extraordinary rise of anti-Jewish feeling. In the 1930s antisemitism became a familiar coin of national politics in France, working its way into furious public debates on both social and intellectual issues, as well as the international crisis caused by Hitler. The present situation contrasts markedly with those years.

Since the press has been identified by some as the most important factor behind the current violence, it is useful to compare its past and present references to Jews. Coloring the anti-Jewish image of the Popular Front era was a seemingly endless production of newspaper articles denouncing a Jewish peril in tones that approached hysteria. Paris alone had thirty-four dailies at the beginning of the thirties, and the right and far-right press represented far more than their strength in the country at large. "It is no exaggeration," according to the respected political analyst René Rémond, "to say that the Frenchman, even if he voted left, most often read a newspaper of the right that leaned more and more toward fascism."[4]

The popular press, always more politically focused than similar papers in North America or Britain, printed grotesque caricatures of Jewish personalities; the weekly *Gringoire*, with its circulation of about 500,000 making it by far the most widely read of its type, could at times rival *Der Stürmer* in its antisemitic enthusiasm. It requires some imagination to appreciate the malice with which Jews were portrayed by inexpensive, mass-circulation newspapers of the time, reaching a huge audience.

The most outrageous antisemitic charges were detonated by the journals of the far right, blasting the Jewish prime minister Léon Blum, who took office in 1936. Before the passage of the Marchandeau press law of 1939 it was possible for journalists openly to denounce the Socialist leader as inaugurating a Jewish takeover of France. "It is as a Jew that one must see, conceive, hear, fight and destroy this Blum," wrote the influential Charles Maurras in the *Action française*; the same newspaper regularly described Blum's government as "le cabinet du Talmud."[5] Maurras himself called openly in 1935 for the assassination of enemies of France like Blum (he favored using a kitchen knife), in an article for which he was briefly imprisoned; two years later Maurras was elected on the first ballot to the Académie Française and thus solidified his position in the world of French letters.

Whatever one thinks of the French press in the 1980s, its tone is light years away from such incendiarism. Indeed, there is not a single newspaper today that openly expresses antisemitism, and I know of no serial publication of any sort that attacks Jews in this way.

Concerns have been expressed in France about a consolidation of newspaper ownership and control in the hands of the right, notably in the person of the dynamic Robert Hersant, a friend and ally of Giscard who was allegedly a wartime collaborator and antisemite. Hersant now owns the important daily, *Le Figaro*, with

[4] René Rémond, *La Droite en France, de la première restauration à la Ve République* (Paris, 1963), 229.

[5] Joel Colton, *Léon Blum: Humanist in Politics* (New York, 1966), 195; Eugen Weber, *Action Française: Royalism and Reaction in Twentieth-Century France* (Stanford, Calif., 1962), 374.

three-quarters of a million readers, controls the much weaker *France-Soir*, and perhaps a fifth of the other titles around the country. His empire also extends to the weekly *Figaro-Magazine*, run by two stars of the new right, Alain de Benoist and Louis Pauwels. But there is not a trace of antisemitism that I have seen in these papers, which regularly run columns by Jewish writers and are probably more pro-Israel than many North American equivalents.

Jews generally feel more uncomfortable with the imperious and authoritative *Le Monde*, largely controlled by its own editorial staff, and since 1969 a voice on the left. *Le Monde* has been a resolute supporter of Third World causes of many sorts, including some dubious ventures like the Pol Pot regime in Cambodia, and it is perhaps not surprising that its editorial line sometimes runs strongly against Israel. Here too, I see no antisemitism. The open forum for articles run by the paper has sometimes caused minor storms in the Jewish community, as with the space provided to the late Wladimir Rabi, a long-time critic of the French Jewish establishment, but I believe the charges of *mauvaise foi* on the Jewish question to be utterly wrong.

Consider only one example of alleged press antisemitism. A major row broke out in the autumn of 1978 when *L'Express* published an interview with an unrepentant Louis Darquier de Pellepoix, Vichy France's murderous commissioner-general for Jewish affairs in 1942–44, who recently died in exile in Madrid. Given the platform of a major weekly news magazine, Darquier denied the Holocaust and defended his role in the persecution of Jews in France. Whatever the wisdom of publishing the piece in the first place, it seems clear that the interviewer, Philippe Garnier-Raymond, firmly intended the article as an exposé, a needed reminder of the French role in the Nazis' destruction of Jews. The compiler of an earlier book that highlighted some horrors of French collaboration, he laced his interview with refutations of the odious Darquier, who could hardly have been happy with the final result. In a letter to *Le Monde* Raymond Aron and Jean-François Revel spoke for *L'Express* when they protested their original intention "to bring to light this pathological dimension of the human spirit that is racism, just as one brings to light a cancerous tissue."[6] Debate thereafter turned upon the wisdom shown by *L'Express* in pub-

---

[6] "Une lettre de MM. Raymond Aron et Jean-François Revel," *Le Monde*, 1 November 1978.

lishing the article, and upon secondary issues such as the failure of the government to pursue Darquier and other war criminals. Antisemitism in contemporary France was hardly the issue.

The most recent accusations against the French press relate to its treatment of the war in Lebanon, arguing that a sharp bias against Israel created a climate ripe for antisemitic assassins. As the writer Claude Lanzmann bluntly declared, "it is words that have killed at Goldenberg's." Without rehearsing the sins of the French press, it seems obvious to me that these charges have been strongly exaggerated in the heat of the current controversy over the war itself. Doubtless the press has been guilty of sensationalism in portraying destruction wrought by Israeli actions, and doubtless there have been excesses and distortions. But to leap from these to sweeping charges of antisemitism is to cross a mighty gap. And then to claim that this is the foremost cause of the violence—when throughout Paris bombs are exploding for a variety of causes—strains credulity to the limit. For the moment, the hypothesis seems doubtful and in any case impossible to prove or disprove.

It also helps to see a highly opinionated French press in its context. North Americans engaged in analyzing French newspapers should beware of applying their visions of balanced reporting to French journals, whose tone derives from quite different journalistic traditions. The pitfalls will be especially great when focusing on a single issue. Paris-based Jane Kramer put the point well in a recent *New Yorker* article. "No one here expects the press to be objective, or even fair. English and American newspapers seem strange to the French, because they serve no persuasive purpose as the French understand it. A Frenchman reads the paper to corroborate his prejudices, or he reads many papers and makes a sort of collection of prejudices. He is not much interested in information without a strong attitude attached to it."

Further reminiscent of the 1930s for some is the apparent ideological renovation of the far right—the so-called *Nouvelle Droite*, which emerged in 1979. This group is seen in direct intellectual lineage to the extreme antisemites of the Popular Front era, then associated with wildly anti-Jewish publications like *Je suis partout*.[7] This already evanescent Paris fashion plainly lacks both the brilliance and the originality of its 1930s counterpart, and it seems

[7] See I. R. Barnes, "Intellectual Processes on the French Far Right," *Patterns of Prejudice* 16 (January 1982), 3–12 for an example of this kind of reasoning.

obvious that Jews are not on the new rightists' agenda. The closest that these paragons of "European civilization" (their umbrella organization is GRECE, or Groupement de Recherches et d'Etudes pour la Civilisation Européenne) come to the matter is their wholesale opposition to nothing less than the entire Judeo-Christian tradition, so large a target that even the most keen manage to avoid seeing Jews at the center of the world's ills. Alain de Benoist, a key figure in this crowd, actually has some nice things to say about Jews in his *Les Idées à l'endroit* (1979), a basic book for the movement. Benoist denounced racism and xenophobia, while expressing concerns about decadence, open immigration, and the idea of human equality. However uneasy Jews and others may justifiably feel about this frequently muddled concoction, laced with what Eugen Weber calls "a heroic subjectivism," there is nothing whatever to match the 1930s obsession with Jews seen in writers like Céline, Robert Brasillach, or Pierre Drieu La Rochelle.

Far more preoccupied with Jews are the professional deniers of the Holocaust, those who spend their time organizing and writing about the nonexistence of the massacre of European Jews during World War II. Looking back to the masterworks of the late Paul Rassinier, now famous internationally as a patron saint of the anti-Holocaust cause, these polemicists have had wide media exposure in France, partly through the efforts of the irascible Robert Faurrison, a literature professor, who defended his position in a celebrated court case recently. A strange assortment of political bedfellows have joined this movement, including representatives of the far right, of course, but also some from the far left, such as the sociologist Serge Thion. To date the influence of these champions of fantasy remains unclear, and it is difficult to judge the degree to which their campaign draws upon antisemitism, contributes to it, or reflects traditional French attraction to a sharp polemic, however grotesque its formulation.

Neo-Nazis, of course, exist in France as in practically every Western industrialized society. These are people who sneak out at night to spray antisemitic slogans on the walls of the *Métro*, and who occasionally do much worse: it seems likely that such fanatics have been behind at least some of the violent anti-Jewish incidents in Paris over the past few years, including bullets sprayed at the synagogue on the rue de la Victoire, the Holocaust memorial in the Marais quarter, and several Jewish schools. The problem remains.

Perhaps more ominous than the existence of these deviants has been the apparent lack of energy shown by the French police in cracking down on the malefactors. Despite a degree of police power under Giscard that outraged civil libertarians, French authorities have appeared unwilling or unable to make headway against the far right. This failure has been ascribed to an old association, going back to the Vichy period and the time of the Algerian War, of the French police with neo-Fascist diehards; the role of the police in protecting the state against the far left following the events of May 1968 has been seen as another possible explanation of the failure. Whatever the cause, the police seemed extraordinarily indulgent toward such plainly Fascist and antisemitic bodies as he Fédération d'Action Nationale Européenne (FANE). In the week before the rue Copernic bombing *L'Express* devoted a long article to neo-Nazi groups and asked in a headline, "Are the police infiltrated by the extreme right?" Several policemen's associations claimed precisely this in the autumn of 1980 as we have seen, pointing to some thirty officers, former militants of the now dissolved FANE. It was also reported that extremist elements had penetrated the corps of bodyguards about President Giscard himself. According to a Harris poll taken immediately after the rue Copernic bombing, 57 percent of those surveyed believed that the French police had not done enough to combat neo-Nazism.

With Mitterrand came changes that may have helped unwittingly to encourage terrorism of all sorts, especially that of the far left. Attentive to calls from civil libertarians and supporters of a variety of revolutionary causes, the Socialist government granted asylum to foreign political extremists, notably some accused Basque terrorists, and liberalized police procedures. A Gaullist-established police unit was recently dissolved. Police morale reportedly fell. By the summer of 1982 this laxity had become notorious: just before the Goldenberg's shootings the judge investigating the Aldo Moro assassination in Italy complained that France lagged severely behind other European countries in the war against international terrorism.

In the wake of the Goldenberg's *attentat* Mitterrand swung sharply against extremist groups—much as Léon Blum did in 1936 when faced with an upsurge of political violence. In a rare television interview, given a few days after the rue des Rosiers murders, Mitterrand announced the creation of an anti-terrorist police unit with a new junior minister in charge, tighter border surveillance, the expansion of security forces, and a crackdown on the use of diplomatic cover for violent groups—the latter a pointed move against certain Arab governments' representatives. Unlike opinion in the 1930s, however, when the political opposition shrieked bitterly at the dissolution of local Fascist leagues by Blum, opinion now seems solidly behind the president.

As in the 1930s, recent antisemitic agitation seems to coincide with a much discussed wider climate of xenophobia, in which recent immigrants to France are frequently blamed for a variety of sins. Jews are not the most prominent newcomers, as they were in the Popular Front era, nor do they bear the greatest degree of hostility. Indeed, I would argue that the singling out of other groups has drawn much attention away from Jews, so that popular anti-Jewish feeling has diminished as other, more visible targets have appeared.

Statistics provide the background. France now has twice as many Jews as in the 1930s, about 700,000, making this the fourth largest Jewish community in the world—after the United States, Israel, and the Soviet Union. Well over half of this population came from Tunisia, Morocco, and Algeria since the late 1950s, profoundly changing the face of Judaism in France, ultimately contributing to both a striking Jewish renewal and a marked pluralism within the Franco-Jewish world.

Parallel to this Jewish influx was a huge wave of immigration of other groups, destined to meet the strong demand for labor generated by a remarkable postwar economic revival, beginning in the early 1950s. Immigration soared to well over 100,000 per annum in the next decade and declined only with the worldwide economic slump after 1973. By 1975, when Giscard blocked the further importation of workers, there were about 4.5 million foreigners in France, more than double the number present in 1960. Some two million of these were Algerian, Tunisian, or Moroccan Arabs or Berbers, who outnumber Jews in France by about three to one.[8] But unlike the Jews, most of whom could legally remain in France, the North Africans and other immigrant workers had only pre-

[8] Statistics on foreign workers are conveniently found in Gary P. Freeman, *Immigrant Labor and Racial Conflict in Industrial Societies: The French and British Experience, 1945–1975* (Princeton, N.J., 1979).

carious rights of residence. With economic recession, they were no longer needed or desired.

The French experience is similar to that of other European states that relied heavily upon foreign workers during the spurt of economic growth in the 1960s, notably Switzerland and West Germany. As in those countries, the 1970s saw governments of poorer countries attempting to expel the unskilled, manual workers who now constituted an embarrassment to their hosts, threatening to be a charge on the public purse, a source of intractable social problems of integration, and a potential source of unrest. Giscard hoped to induce these workers to return home, but relatively few took the bribes that were offered. Foreigners still constitute about 10.5 percent of the work force in France, with the bulk of the newcomers terribly housed and concentrated in menial jobs that the French find unacceptable.

Until the mid-1970s there were few public objections in France to the presence of so many outsiders. Despite the long and bloody experience of war in Algeria, moreover, remarkably little tension existed between North African workers and the rest of the French population. Surveys showed that North Africans were unpopular, to be sure, but attitudes toward them, as well as toward other foreigners, showed signs of softening as time went on.[9] With the economic downturn of the last decade, referred to in France as "the crisis" these days, opinion hardened. Unemployment in September 1983 stood at 9 percent, extremely high by French standards, and foreigners have found themselves readily blamed for taking the jobs of Frenchmen and imposing unfair burdens on social services. Together with such accusations have come the familiar fantasies, half-truths, and ill-concealed resentments, energizing French traditions of xenophobia and racism.

During the 1981 presidential election campaign politically sensitive Communist mayors in the Paris "red belt" shocked many by their open appeal to such sentiment, an indication of how deeply rooted it was among certain groups of voters. (Significantly, not one political party and not one politician hoisted the banner of antisemitism.) The pattern was repeated during the nationwide municipal elections in the spring of 1983, with a vitriolic campaign orchestrated mainly by the far right. Voting results suggested

[9]Ibid., 275.

that such appeals had a significant impact. Arab workers in particular were victimized, far more so than Europeans or blacks from
such former French colonies as Senegal and Martinique. Prejudice
in France has always been less color-conscious than in Ango-Saxon
countries, and it is perhaps understandable that in times of trouble
hostility toward outsiders should focus upon the largest and poor-
est minority—in this case North African Muslims—which has the
most vulnerable and marginal role in economic and social life. Bitter memories of the Algerian conflict may, oddly enough, now be
playing a more serious role in relations with North Africans in
France than they did in the 1960s.

As the issue of foreign workers became more heated, government crackdowns and police repression seemed at times to encourage group tensions. Once Giscard's efforts to repatriate them appeared to falter, officials took sterner measures, including forcible
expulsions without possibility of appeal—leading to several causes
célèbres in 1980. Some expellees turned out to have been born in
France and never to have seen their supposed country of origin;
others seem to have been deported for transparently political reasons. Civil libertarians and political critics understandably referred to government action as racist. Police regularly raided immigrant neighbourhoods looking for foreigners whose papers were
not in order. Gangs of working-class toughs took matters into their
own hands, and violent clashes resulted with "les bicots," the de-
risive term for North Africans in France. Militants of the far right,
including neo-Nazis, took up the anti-immigrant campaign, and as
Edouard Roditi pointed out recently the antisemitic and the anti-
immigrant activism often merged in industrial suburbs or school
playgrounds.[10] In response, civil rights organizations traditionally
associated with the defense of Jews such as the League for the
Rights of Man and the International League against Racism and
Antisemitism mobilized on behalf of Arab immigrants, the most
frequently attacked group of foreigners.

Only recently has there been a change in government policy, and
it is too early to tell whether this will affect public opinion. Under
Mitterrand the government took a conciliatory line, halting summary expulsions and granting amnesty to some 100,000 alien
workers illegally in France, thus regularizing their status. This

[10] Edouard Roditi, "Antisemitism in France," *Midstream*, November 1980, 9–14.

move, one should add, went sharply counter to the policies of other European governments faced with similarly large communities of foreign workers. Officials now openly criticize the "racism" exhibited by the previous administration and recommend a more open, humane approach to outsiders. Foreigners can now form their own associations without following cumbersome application procedures, and receive more consideration from civil servants. Opposition spokesmen, however, have attacked these moves sharply and will not let the issue of foreign workers cool. At the moment, the government has been forced to retreat somewhat on immigration matters, a sign that opinion remains quite hostile to aliens. The current call to crack down on foreign political activists clearly reinforces this tendency.

Despite the heightened climate of xenophobia, however, surveys of opinion in France suggest strongly that anti-Jewish feeling has been decreasing steadily since the end of World War II and thus has not been seriously affected by recent group tensions such as I have described. The polls tell an interesting story.

In France, as in many countries, the high degree of antisemitism immediately after the defeat of Hitler was shockingly evident. One study by the respected Institut Français d'Opinion Publique (IFPO) in 1946 showed that close to half of the population (43 percent) did not believe that a Frenchman of Jewish origin was as French as any other Frenchman. This key question, also posed with respect to Bretons, Alsatians and Corsicans, was submitted again in 1966 and 1978. By 1966 the proportion having doubts about the Frenchness of French Jews declined to 19 percent and by 1978 was only 9 percent. Significantly, more of those surveyed in 1978 were dubious about Corsicans (11 percent) than about Jews. The 9 percent who hesitated to include Jews fully within the national community also seems less shocking when we learn that 8 percent felt similarly about Alsatians, and 4 percent about Bretons. The weekly *Vendredi Samedi Dimanche*, which commissioned the most recent poll, headlined the finding "Frenchmen Display Slightly More Anti-Corsican Feeling than Antisemitism."[11]

Other surveys tend to corroborate the IFOP studies. The Louis

[11] *Vendredi Samedi Dimanche*, 16 February 1978. For a detailed analysis of the IFOP survey of 1966 see Doris Bensimon and Jeannine Verdès-Leroux, "Les Français et le problème juive: Analyse secondaire d'un sondage of l'I.F.O.P.," *Archives de sociologie des religions* 29 (1970), 53–91.

Harris Institute asked a sample immediately after the Rue Copernic bombing whether various categories of persons were thought "too numerous" in France, repeating an investigation done in 1977. While this poll suggested a slight diminution of intolerance, almost half of the population surveyed felt that there were too many "foreigners in general," and slightly more registered this sentiment for North Africans. Some 28 percent felt that there were too many blacks from Africa, 16 percent that there were too many Spaniards. Twelve percent said that there were too many Jews, and 6 percent that there were too many Corsicans. In both 1977 and 1980 Louis Harris posed a similar question to that of IFOP in an effort to gauge the strength of antisemitism (In your opinion, is a Jew as French as another Frenchman?) and yielded similar results: there was a marked decline from 22 percent in 1977 to 10 percent in 1980 who responded negatively. (Notably, however, just over half the population believed just after the bombing that antisemitism was fairly widespread in France.) IFOP also registered a clear reduction over the period 1966 to 1978 of those who would avoid having a Jewish president of the Republic (from 50 to 24 percent), a Jewish son- or daughter-in-law (from 37 to 16 percent), or a Jewish boss (from 32 to 13 percent).[12]

However interpreted, these results suggest a marked diminution of antisemitism in France, as most commentators on these surveys have agreed. In 1966 IFOP asked how respondents defined *themselves* on this question, and 9 percent openly avowed antisemitism while 85 percent rejected it. In 1978, when the question was last asked, 5 percent declared themselves antisemites and 90 percent did not. These results would approach those of other Western democracies, I would think. And while one must be cautious about the import of such findings, given that an anti-Jewish climate may well be the work of a minority, the general trend seems unmistakable. Although serious group tensions remain in France and seem even to have increased over the last decade, hostility toward Jews has declined among the vast majority of Frenchmen.

Students of antisemitism sometimes make the error of assuming that people are normally preoccupied with Jews. But there is no law of nature that requires Jews to be so prominent in terms of in-

[12] *L'Express*, 17 October 1980.

terest, sympathy, or antipathy. One can well imagine an opinion survey administered, say, in the year 2000, when most respondents would have not the slightest idea *what* they thought about Jews or antisemitism. We are far from this situation today, I hasten to add. Nevertheless, it seems clear to me that group prejudices in France, as distinct from terrorist outrages, have tended over the past decade to fasten upon other objects than Jews.

There is no doubt, on the other hand, that a hard core of anti-Jewish feeling persists in France, and Jewish history provides ample enough grounds to judge how dangerous such fanaticism can be. Antisemitism, moreover, has proven to be extremely volatile, capable of sudden growth in times of national collapse, for example, or perhaps some spectacular new crisis in the Middle East, in which Jews might find themselves once again on the firing line of national debate.[13] A low score on an opinion poll hardly buries antisemitism forever.

At present, however, we seem to be left with the spectacle of a gradually reduced intensity of popular antisemitism, alongside a violent flurry of anti-Jewish activity. The latter has confused many observers, I think, who immediately link present outrages, the persecution of Jews under Vichy, and the rich French traditions of antisemitism. Yet terrorism has a life of its own, independent of such antecedent conditions; they are unnecessary for those who scrawl "Death to the Jews" on walls, desecrate cemeteries, or kill indiscriminately. The evidence I have discussed, admittedly circumstantial, suggests that the most recent, dramatic manifestations against Jews in France are the work of such groups of criminals.

Ultimately, and on a day-to-day basis, the well-being of Jews as well as other minorities in France depends upon a strengthened climate of tolerance, a greater willingness on the part of Frenchmen to accept that which is different. French tradition has for a very long time militated against difference, and until recently intellectuals, politicians, and civil servants tended to unite in celebration of a unitary system of language and culture. Associated with the march of reason and progress since the times of the Revolution and Napoleon, this fundamental condition of French life quickly revealed its other face: an intolerance of that which stood apart from

[13] I have surveyed this problem in "The Theory and Practice of Anti-Semitism," *Commentary*, August 1982, pp. 38–42.

official definitions of the national community. France's republican heritage thus called for the thorough assimilation of all disparate elements, including Jews. Only now are there signs that this tradition is eroding, giving reasonable grounds for hope that in time conditions for all minorities will improve.

The Socialist majority in France today manifests significant uneasiness with the highly centralized structures of the Fifth Republic, frequently associated with an overly rigid, excessively managed society. Continuing what was so tentatively begun under Giscard, or some would say in 1968, the new regime has taken steps toward a real devolution of authority and planning to all levels of local government, to local institutions of various sorts, and to regional interests. In embryo, we might even say, is a more flexible, less bureaucratic, more pluralistic society. To be sure, other forces pull in the opposite direction—the great mountain of bureaucracy and entrenched interest, a natural bias toward statism in Socialist tradition, and the need for strong central direction to achieve many Socialist objectives, such as equalizing wealth and opportunity. Time will tell whether decentralizing tendencies mature, and no one should assume that such vast transformations can occur overnight.

Taking the measure of these new impulses at the end of his second long book on France, John Ardagh sees the French as drawn hesitantly toward "a gentler society, less hectically ambitious, with more accent on leisure, quality of the environment, local self-help, and the warmth of local community." [14] For those who know France this temptation will seem a strange preference indeed for *la grande nation*. And it may seem odd even to consider this possibility when the carnage of a new massacre of Jews is fresh in all of our minds. But the decline of popular antisemitism in France may also seem bizarre to those who expect French history to be constantly repeating itself. The question remains open.

[14] John Ardagh, *France in the 1980s* (Harmondsworth, England, 1982), 654.

PART 5

EMANCIPATION REEXAMINED

SHMUEL TRIGANO

From Individual to Collectivity: The Rebirth of the "Jewish Nation" in France

S INCE 1978, French Jewry has been experiencing a crisis in its relationship both to French society at large and to itself. The publicity it has enjoyed in the mass media—in a country where Jewish topics had been taboo since World War II—is evidence of this phenomenon. This development is to be viewed as a fact— the resurgence of the "Jewish question" in the collective conscious- ness in the late 1970s. The gradual, continuous, and as yet un- finished process can be variously interpreted. Of course, the most immediate explanation is to see it as the consequence of Israel's heroic saga, enacted in its several wars (most notably since 1967). In this respect, the Yom Kippur War of 1973, and the election of Mr. Begin in 1977 stand out as turning points, for as Israel's star waned it was inevitable that the "negative"—and in any case am- biguous—images of the Jew should resurface.

But the new situation can also be explained by specifically French social parameters. The existential (but not theoretical or political) crisis of Jacobin centralism favored the "pluralization" of France and the emergence of a plural French identity. At a time when re- gionalism was being asserted by a variety of groups, and "differ- ences" were being championed (women and homosexuals), the Jews were the last group within the French nation to be confronted with their self-image. This is understandable, for they had been the first to be obliged to be "more than the others"—to be "French" above all else. The last symbol of France one and indivisible disap-

Translated from French by Jonathan Mandelbaum.

peared with the exaggerated "Judaization" of the French *israélites*. Among the other purely French—and more circumstantial—explanations, one is of particular importance: the resurgence of an ideological and belligerent right (the *Nouvelle Droite*) in the desert of French ideology, especially in the context of the enfeeblement of Socialism and the depreciation of Marxism. For the opposition to "Judeo-Christianity" is one of the major arguments of the *Nouvelle Droite*.[1] The emergence of this "new right" is a development whose importance is only just beginning to be appreciated. Today, the new right is ideologically structuring the right as a whole—now in opposition—by providing it with the veneer of modernity and sophistication that had hitherto been lacking in its confrontation with a Socialist party populated with intellectuals.

Toward the end of Giscard d'Estaing's presidency, the Jewish community found itself the focus of a contest between the right and the left. The *Nouvelle Droite* was ideologically inclined to challenge the reputedly Jewish features of the West, despite its denials of anti-Semitism. As for the left, it felt that the Jews constituted an electorate that had to be won over[2] by defending the Jewish experience as the ultimate recourse of democracy.[3] In an indistinct manner, the Jewish experience became once again a medium for a nationwide debate in France; old collective attitudes were revived, but this time they were expressed in an indirect language that lent itself to confusion. On the threshold of a new phase of its identity, the collective consciousness rediscovered the Jew as the archetypal "republican man" and latched onto him as the last vestige of a bygone world,[4] while looking with anxiety to the future.

But, in the last analysis, while all these explanations carry undoubted weight, it is the evolution of the Jewish community itself, of its structures and mentality, that seems likely to provide the decisive explanation for the topicality of the "Jewish question" in France. Indeed, it is on this basis that one can best understand the

[1] See my article in *Le Monde*, 1 September 1979, "C'est le Juif qui est en question."

[2] Thus the Socialist party seems to have supported the Renouveau Juif movement, whose sole program was a vote of censure against Giscard d'Estaing. This was confirmed by the statements of its leader, H. Hajdenberg, in support of the Socialists at the time of the presidential election.

[3] See the intellectual debate on the Jew and democracy analyzed in my book *La République et les juifs* (Paris: Les Presses d'Aujourd'hui-Gallimard, 1982), 136ff., "Les mirages du Juif médiatique."

[4] Ibid., 88ff., "Fin de France."

intersection and integration of the three levels—the "international" level (Israel's wars), the national level (the state of French society) and the Jewish level (changes in the community)—that may be distinguished in the interpretation of the position of the Jewish community today.

The charter of Jewish life in France since the Revolution—contrary to the ancien régime, in which the Jews were regarded as a "corporate body"[5] or "Jewish nation"—treated the Jews as individuals and not as a collectivity. Henceforth, it was as individuals, what is more, as abstract individuals, not as specifically and publicly Jewish individuals, that Jews obtained civic rights. The public and historical status previously enjoyed by the Jewish nation—despite its being confined to its ghettos and deprived of all recognition—was now lost, indeed banned. "For there can be no equality where differences exist,"[6] proclaimed Jewish representatives at the National Assembly. It was unconstitutional to suppose that "the Jews [have] either the capacity or the right to band together into a corporate body, and neither this right nor this capacity can be vested any longer in any group of citizens—for all citizens are now only individuals."[7] The famous statement of the Comte de Clermont-Tonnerre sounds as an ominous warning.

But, it will be said, the Jews have their own Judges and laws. . . . The Jews must be refused everything as a Nation; they must be granted everything as individuals. . . . They must be refused legal protection for the preservation of the so-called laws of their Judaic corporate body. They must constitute neither a political body nor an order within the State. They must be citizens individually. But, it will be said, they do not want to be. Well, if they do not, then let them say so, and in that case they should be banished. One cannot accept a society of noncitizens within the State and a nation within a nation.[8]

The abstract nature of the Jew's new individuality deserves to be

[5] For example in A. Ravel and A. D. Milhaud, "Observations pour les juifs d'Avignon à la Convention nationale," in *La Révolution française et l'émancipation des juifs* (Paris: Editions d'Histoire Sociale [EDHIS], 1968), 5 : 13.

[6] Quoted in ibid.

[7] "Rapport fait par Saladin, au nom d'une Commission spéciale composée des représentants Grégoire, Chappuy, Couvot, Beyts et Saladin," 7 Fructidor Year VII (24 August 1799), in ibid., 8 : 13.

[8] "Opinion du comte Stanislas de Clermont-Tonnerre, député de Paris," 23 December 1789, in ibid., 7 : 8.

singled out for attention, in that the Jews recognized as citizens were no longer seen as Jews. The citizen embodied in the Jew no longer corresponded to the Jew embodied in the citizen. The system governing this abstraction and dehistoricization of the Jew is simple, for the Jews "are men like us; they are men first, Jews afterward."[9] The same principle (abstract and universal mankind) that allowed the founding fathers of the Republic to view the Jews as men led them, in a perfectly logical manner, to ignore and obliterate the Jews among men (Jews and non-Jews), to cease to recognize the Jews among the men they were emancipating. Henceforth, both the Jewish nation and the Jewish individual were—in theory and in their official sociopolitical depiction—erased from the history of the Republic.

This definition of the citizen as applied to the Jew underwent an objective evolutionary process, an (almost logical) shift, from the earliest days of "modern" France. The very structure of the republican conceptualization of the Jew was pregnant with such a possibility: the fragile paradox that constituted the identity of the Jew was bound to come undone, separating the two elements it combined—the Jew and the citizen.

This republican paradox of the Jew could be stated as follows: the Jew is a man, but man is not Jewish/a Jew. The interplay of man and Jew was a two-pronged mechanism. What served to grant the Jew his emancipation served to deny him his Jewishness in emancipation. This dialectic was set in motion by a shift from the singular to the universal and vice versa, in the negative mode:

1) The (abstract) Jew is an (individual) man (like you and me; it is as an individual that we recognize him in his private relationship to us: he is like one of us).

2) (Abstract) man is not an (individual) Jew: mankind, in its universal state, cannot be embodied in a particular man—a Jew. At this point, the Jew has changed his identity. He is now a citizen.

The paradox is resolved through the following syllogistic argument:

1) All Jews are men—the criterion of generosity (let us recognize them then!).

[9] Abbé Grégoire, "Apologie des Juifs," in ibid., 4: 108.

2) Not all men are Jews—the criterion of universality (let us cease attributing excessive importance to them!).

3) Jews are only men (they are not entitled to any more recognition than other men, and, while men, they are nothing "more" than that).

One could visualize the logical argument above by the following diagrams:

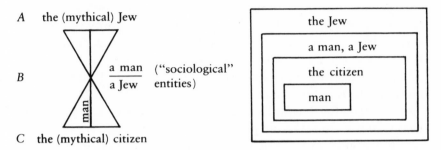

A   the (mythical) Jew

B $\dfrac{\text{a man}}{\text{a Jew}}$ ("sociological" entities)

man

C   the (mythical) citizen

the Jew

a man, a Jew

the citizen

man

LEVEL B (the particular, the embodiment of the abstract) serves here as the key for the transformation of A into C—for the subsuming of the Jew by the citizen. The individual recognized in the act of emancipation serves to remove Jewish individuality from the process.

A and B conflict: the mythical Jew versus the assertion that he is like all other men.

B and C conflict: the Jew-like-the-others (that is, a Jew), *because* he is like the others, is only a citizen. In other words, his distinctiveness (like that of other men) is once again negated, and—since it is asserted, in the same logical process—this means that his identity is mythified once more. He becomes *the* citizen par excellence, the glorious and shining counterpart to the obscure and negative "Jew" (*the* Jew) the assertion of whose distinctiveness had provided a way out of the anti-Jewish impasse of the ancien régime (departing from the myth to arrive at the sociological reality). Thus the original situation had come full circle. We have here an example of a conceptual revolution (the recognition of the Jew) that failed and took a bad turn. Waged around the central concept of "man," [10] which allowed the transition from *the* (mythical) Jew

[10] Ibid., 108: "For a long time now, it has been repeated that they are men like us; they are men first, and Jews afterward."

to *a* man and from *a* Jew to *the* (mythical) citizen, this mental revolution failed in its recognition of Jews in history; it refused to uphold their specificity in the dialogue, obliterating it instead by a
return to myth (*the* citizen).

Despite the (Jewish) citizen's new, luminous appearance, the
positive myth (the citizen) that served to mask the negative myth
(the Jew) continued to be haunted by the demons of the latter. For
it was *a* Jew—the individual (and identity-conscious) Jew, the Jew
who persisted in his Jewish distinctiveness—who was to become
something of a challenge to *the* citizen, the only entity that others
were willing to see in him. It was *a* Jew who was to undermine
from within the conceptual clarity of *the* citizen.

Such a (twofold) logical construct was bound to lead to a twofold expectation regarding the Jew.

In *the* Jew, the Jew and the citizen were joined; in *a* Jew, these
two entities were locked in perpetual combat. *A* Jew would always
have to provide impeccable proof of his status as universal *citizen*,
but in this display the figure of the eternal and demonic Jew would
always loom. On the one hand, *a* Jew had to embody the new man,
the conceptual clarity of the Republic: it was in each individual
Jew that *the* Jew—a paragon of the ancien régime—had to be
crushed in order to ensure the triumph of *the* citizen, the new man.
But, on the other hand, as it was *the* Jew that had to be transformed if the Republic was to be victorious, it was *the* Jew en-
shrined in each individual Jew who came to be seen as the sharpest
antithesis of the citizen. The Jew thus represented the *Janus bifrons*
of the Republic—at once *the* citizen, the man of the Revolution,
and *the* Jew, the man of the ancien régime; at once a proof of the
Revolution's success and a threat to that success. Hence the Jew symbolized both France's absolute negative entity (the anti-Republic)
and her absolute positive entity (the Republic par excellence).

This dual approach to the Jews is fully discussed in texts of the
revolutionary period. Accordingly, some speak "in praise of Jews"
by depicting them as peaceful and bucolic beings, akin to "the Noble Savage," whose integration into French society was expected to
bring economic recovery and increased commercial activity. Paradoxically, by "freeing" the Jew from his curse—symbolized most
notably by commerce and usury—the aim was to "win over to
France an industrious and trading nation that can only vitalize, increase, and revive trade, and attract an abundance of wealth to the

kingdom." [11] Thus, behind the Jew-as-citizen, there loomed, from the outset, the hydra of international "plutocracy." The revolutionaries dreamed of Noble Savages and expected traders. Similarly, they preached the disappearance of the Jew qua Jew in history by invoking the historical entity of the Hebrews and, in addition, their experience in Palestine: "The Jew, in and of himself, is suited to all arts and crafts, to all the functions exercised by citizens. His stay in Palestine is factual proof of this potential." [12] The densest Hebrews would make perfect Frenchmen.

Through the man/nature dialectic, which had made it possible to recognize all men and all Jews, the mythical entities of the Jew and the citizen were easily reversed:

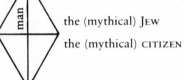

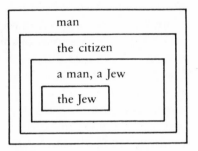

The mythical level became the prism mediating between *a* Jew and *a* citizen, with all the attendant risks of ideological perversion. Henceforth, the two triangular constructs ignored each other, failed to communicate, and overlapped. The dialectical mobility of the first construct was replaced by a mythical rigidity in which concepts overlapped and no longer interacted.

Every man (every Jew) could henceforth be suspected of carrying within him the (mythical) Jew—the antithesis of man/the citizen.

The far-reaching dimension on the national scale of the "Jewish system" developed by the Revolution must be noted. Indeed, from the very outset, the entity of the Jew, because of its being mythified, involved far more than the Jews themselves; indeed, it shaped French society's self-image. "The question of the accession of the Jews to citizenship in France is related to the whole of the various elements that are to compose the majestic edifice of the Constitu-

[11] "Assemblée des représentants de la commune de Paris," 24 February 1790, in ibid., 6:11.
[12] Abbé Grégoire, "Apologie," 99–100.

tion." [13] "The National Assembly cannot fail to consider that the request submitted to it today concerns the whole of the political system that must henceforth govern France. . . . When it is a matter of taking in, of incorporating another people into one's own, how could one fail to consult the French people?" [14]

Thus the Jewish question coincided with the question that modern France put to itself concerning its identity, its structure, and its relationship to its history. This was not so much the question posed to France by the existence of Judaism as the question posed to France by itself. The tangible and pervasive effect of this all-embracing phenomenon was later confirmed by the fact that at the end of the nineteenth century [15] as well as at the end of the twentieth century, [16] anti-Semitism constituted the only channel of communication between the far left and the far right, the only possible form of consensus between them. It was the very framework within which the two extremes of the system could coexist, and thus the integrating element tht enabled the system to survive. This is what Barrès meant in speaking of anti-Semitism as a "means of national reconciliation." Such a perspective allows us to measure the immanent pervasiveness of the Jewish entity in the Republic. The structure of the Jewish question in modern France could be defined as the interplay arising from the contradiction between the particular and the universal, "nations" and the state, the concrete and the abstract, the ancien régime and the Republic, man and the citizen, the Jew and man, the Jew and the citizen.

This unresolved "play" (in the same way one says "there is some play") in the structure of the republican edifice underlies the Jewish question in modern France, for it is through the Jewish entity that it has been most fully displayed, crystallized, and formalized.

At regular intervals, and in keeping with the very (inter)play we have analyzed schematically, the French collective consciousness has quite naturally persisted in regarding the Jews (individuals and citizens) as a particular and specific collectivity. Defined as individuals, the Jews have been portrayed as a collectivity in the collec-

---

[13] "Assemblée, ..." 24 February 1790, 9.

[14] "Opinion de l'évêque de Nancy, député de Lorraine," *La Révolution française*, 7:6.

[15] In particular, anti-Semitism drew the far left close to the far right.

[16] For instance, former "leftists" such as Serge Thion have adopted positions closer to the far right via anti-Semitism (or rather anti-Judeo-Christian-ism).

tive imagination of the past two centuries, although this dimension, of course, has never acquired ideological and constitutional legitimacy.

At the dawn of modern France, a process was thus set in motion that eventually led to the collectivization of the Jews—despite the fact that such a phenomenon was ruled out by the logic of the one and indivisible Republic. This irrepressible tendency of the republican system to turn the Jews into the very entity that the system forbade them to become could be likened to the psychoanalytic logic of the return of the repressed. Two sets of processes explain this tendency: three processes engendered by the system, or rather by its dysfunction (these may be termed intrasystemic processes), and two processes that disturbed the coherence of the system and originated outside it (extrasystemic processes).

In the first category, we can distinguish, to begin with, the effect of a "logic of suspicion," in that the Jews had openly and genuinely renounced their collective dimension—the texts are there to prove this [17]—so that it could be ascribed to them only as an unspoken and covert phenomenon. This suspicion was to crystallize the basic archetype of anti-Semitism in the Republic, the "Jewish plot," which was naturally regarded as international: as they were suspected of forming a nation and thus of being alien to France, the Jews could threaten France only from without by obeying interests external to France, even as they threatened it from within. Consequently, this was an abstract, diffuse, insidious, monstrous, and worrying threat. Here too, we can discern the pattern of the particular (the specific Jewish nation, external to France) and the universal (the hidden, abstract, unsuspected—and thus omnipresent—Jewish nation within France), organized into a within/without scheme. The myth of the Jewish plot was to be dressed up in every ideological color—plutocratic, Masonic, Bolshevik, internationalist, capitalist, Semitic, and so on. This logic of suspicion, although propounded in the name of republican individualism (the Jews were accused of no longer being individuals) led to a "massification" of the Jews in the collective imagination, which, at this level, understandably patterned its notions about the Jews on the modes of "myth."

Another process of collectivization of the Jews may be discerned

---

[17] See my analysis and the quotations in *La République et les Juifs*, 99ff., "Le Franco-judaïsme aux abois."

in the anti-Semitism that prevailed in the years prior to World War II, and especially in its juridical institutionalization by the Vichy regime. Although citizens of the Republic, in an individual and abstract capacity, the Jews *qua Jews* were *collectively* deprived of their citizenship and collectively removed from the French nation. One could hardly designate in a more effective manner the collective Jew present in the French citizen. Such an experience was bound to affect the modes in which Jews identified themselves with the French nation; it left indelible marks both on the Jews who had been singled out as Jews and on the collective consciousness.

A final process of collectivization of the Jews in the contemporary period can be related to the underground workings of the dialectic of the particular and the universal, this time applied to French society at large. Changes in sociocultural categories, particularly after May 1968, have gradually conferred a de facto "republican" legitimacy on "groups" (described two centuries ago as "factions"), lobbies, "differences," sectional claims, and so on. Ecological organizations, women's groups, socioprofessional categories, regional and minority cultures, sexual "minorities" (such as homosexuals)—have all become social, political, and cultural actors (at times aggressive ones), so much so that the old, authorized actors—essentially the political parties—have come to be regarded as obsolete in the collective consciousness. The impact of May 1968 has in effect pulverized the dogma of the abstract universality of politics and brought about the triumph of the particular. In an ideological setting of this sort, the citizen can no longer define himself with reference to the universality of the state, but with reference to his own specificity and family—or collectivity. Hence the concept of collectivity has acquired a sociopolitical standing in the Jacobin Republic, even though—and therein lies the problem of the contemporary age—this de facto evolution has not yet been given a de jure formulation. In this transitional situation, it is thus inevitable that by virtue of their very citizenship the Jews should evolve in unison with the society in which they live, and that they should rediscover and elaborate a collective Jewish identity.

But we can also discern two extrasystemic processes, pertaining to the historical evolution of the Jewish condition, that have fostered the collectivization of the Jews.

First, there is the resurgence of Jewish messianism in France. The question of messianism was crucial to the discussion of whether

Jews should be granted civic rights. It was the ultimate cause of perplexity that subsisted in the minds of those who wondered whether Jews could become Frenchmen: "Can he cease to weep when he remembers Zion, or, if he does not forsake the hope of rebuilding the Temple in Jerusalem, how much credence should we lend to his promises?"[18] "The notion that they will one day triumph over their enemies, as they await a messiah . . . has been the basic factor militating against the incorporation of the Jews into the nations that have taken them in."[19] "A tribe . . . whose eyes are constantly turned toward the common fatherland, where its scattered members will one day be reunited, a tribe that in consequence can forge no solid links with the land that bears it. . . ."[20] And it is this messianism that the Jews explicitly abandoned. "They await the messiah but they await death with an even greater certainty,"[21] declared Zalkind Hourwitz—to whom Léon Blum replied two centuries later that "their Messiah is nothing other than the symbol of eternal justice."[22]

The nineteenth-century *israélites*, for their part, forged, by way of substitution, a Judeo-French republican messianism: "The age of the Messiah was ushered in by this new society, which replaced the old Trinity with another trinity . . . Liberty! Equality! Fraternity!"[23] Zionism—a resurgence of the "Jewish nation" and "proof" of the fortunate historical continuity of the age-old hope that the exiles would be reunited in Zion—was to challenge these predictions. At a very early stage, Zionism was perceived by French Jews as a challenge, most notably because its political scheme, international in scope, clashed with their similar scheme and their claim that, having been emancipated by the great Revolution, they were the elder sons of world Jewry. But the challenge ran deeper still, for Zionism once again defined the Jew as a nation and a specific entity. The founding of the State of Israel, as well as the repercussions

[18] "Rapport édité par M. Vion, conseiller référendaire en la chancellerie du Palais et membre du commissariat de district de Saint Germain l'Auxerrois," *La Révolution française*, 6:19.

[19] "Dissertation . . . lue à la commune de Paris, par M. Vieillard . . . commissaire du comité de Saint Roch," in ibid., 6:3.

[20] "Opinion de l'évêque de Nancy, député de Lorraine," in ibid., 7:3.

[21] "Apologie des Juifs," 77.

[22] "Nouvelles conversations de Goethe avec Eckermann," in *L'Oeuvre de Léon Blum* (Paris, 1954–55), 1:267.

[23] Maurice Bloch in "La Société juive en France depuis la Révolution," *Revue des Etudes Juives* 48 (1904):41.

of the dangers facing Israel and of its victories, only materialized in flamboyant guises what already existed in embryo by the late nineteenth century. This phenomenon, by revitalizing Jewish messianism, very gradually revived the notion of a collective reunion with Zion, the "national" horizon of Jewish existence, the idea of a Jewish collectivity.

The second process, which pertains to the internal evolution of the community, was triggered by the massive influx of North African Jews in the 1960s, for this influx upset the individualistic and denominational outlook of metropolitan French Jewry.

The primary factor was a quantitative one. For the first time, French Jewry was endowed with "masses,"[24]—a change that significantly modified its image and identity. But, most important of all, North African Judaism (although possessed of long-standing French nationality, in the case of Algerian Jews) did not correspond, historically and above all behaviorally, to the individualistic and abstract definition of the Jew in France.

There are several explanations for this phenomenon. First, because of its relatively late encounter with the modern West, North African Jewry had remained closer, especially in objective terms, to traditional community life (this is evidenced by its life-style, family relationships, continuity of customs, and so forth). More important, however, this encounter with the West—in the event, with a colonizing power—occurred outside metropolitan France, with consequently diminished and less sudden effects. Both the ambiguous citizenship granted to North African Jews (thanks to Adolphe Crémieux) and the uncertain status of the Algerian territories (colonies and *départements*) intensified this experience. In addition, the integrative dimension of a monolithic French society was lacking: the setting was outside metropolitan France; there was a distinct Muslim and oriental tonality, characterized by the coexistence of several ethnic groups, religions, languages, and cultures. In such circumstances, the relationship with French culture—a link that had become crucial to Algerian Jews—could only be "abstract" and intellectual in its very essence, which is not to say that it was not deep or authentic. Finally, for the generations of the exodus of 1962, the break with an age-old life-style constituted a revolutionary experience. There is no doubt that, prior to the exodus, the

[24] According to most estimates, the size of the Jewish community doubled between 1956 and the 1970s.

assimilation process was about to reach the point of no return for the younger generations—the ones that are making themselves heard twenty years later, in the 1980s. Exodus and uprooting have disrupted that process for a very long time to come, just as, with more negative effect, they have forever destroyed the identity of the fathers. In short, North African Jewry—with its assertive and ostentatious mode of identification, its very extroverted and expansive psychological character, and its patterns of cultural and family behavior—by achieving an uninhibited synthesis with French culture, restored a full measure of reality and vividness to the notion of a Jewish collectivity.

A similar situation (the sudden emergence of an assertive variety of Judaism within France's "symbolic" Jewry) had already occurred in the prewar years, when Eastern European Jews (who—as the result of a different process of "modernization" and Westernization—also had a collective notion of Jewish life) immigrated into France. The ensuing crisis had led French Jews to adopt attitudes of rejection and dissociation in order to preserve the consensual framework of their individual and abstract citizenship. Today, however, such a reaction would be impossible, not only because of the magnitude—indeed, the numerical superiority—of the new "immigration" (a somewhat paradoxical one, since it took place between French *départements*—namely, Algeria and *la métropole*) but also because of the fact that North African Jewry is not "foreign," either by its language, its culture, or its status. The crisis of the Judeo-French system today is thus more radical, for the system cannot resolve the crisis by rejecting the "immigrants," the disturbing intruders: they are French. The crisis of the system has no solution outside the system, and the latter must therefore absorb the crisis and transform itself.

The crisis of the traditional Judeo-French system thus involves restoring a collective dimension to Jewish life and identity in France.

This new development—within a framework that has remained unchanged as far as ideology, institutions, and official practice are concerned—is accompanied by a series of divergent modes of sociopolitical and cultural behavior, which vividly demonstrates the gap between words and action.

Objectively speaking, it is undeniable that the behavior of French Jews today is collective in nature. There are numerous signs of this, first of all at the institutional level. The founding of the Conseil Représentatif des Institutions Juives de France (CRIF) in 1943, during the Resistance, marked a turning point in that French Jewry, for the first time in history, set up a collective representative body that conferred a collective dimension on the community—even if within very narrow limits. Furthermore, in its charter of 25 January 1977, the CRIF stated that it recognized Israel as "the foremost expression of the Jewish Being." The establishment of the Fonds Social Juif Unifié also put an end to the *israélite* identity, for it was the first time that a Jewish institution was created with secular aims (social, cultural, and so on) and not with the aim of organizing religious worship. Even the Consistory is affected by this trend: its objectives are now domestic, and no longer international and "universalist" (as was the case with the Alliance Israélite Universelle in the nineteenth century); today, it increasingly refers to itself as the chief rabbinate, Israeli style. In the statement made by the chief rabbi, René Sirat, on the occasion of his investiture, the community is depicted almost as a state or nation. "I would say that in the Jewish community of France there also exists a legislative power, a judicial power and an executive power [namely, tradition, the rabbinical tribunal and the rabbinical council, which must] gradually [become] the government of the French rabbinate and [which] assumes its responsibilities through a system of great ministries."[25]

Many signs point to the collective dimension acquired by Jewish life in France during the Fifth Republic: mass gatherings of several hundred thousand Jews ("Les Douze Heures pour Israël"—"Twelve Hours for Israel"); Jewish demonstrations; slogans such as those calling for a "Jewish vote" at election time; Jewish voices speaking up on the occasion of every major event; the phenomenon of local Jewish radio stations everywhere in France; the resurgence of a Jewish "culturalism" based more on Sephardic and Ashkenazic nostalgia (one speaks now of Jewish cultures) than on the Jewish tradition; and the revival of philosophical reflection concerning Judaism.

But this objective change has not yet spread to ideological discourse or to the level of awareness with respect to events. The transformation of French society has not yet reached the insti-

[25] *Agence Télégraphique Juive* (Paris), 9 January 1981.

tutional phase. Apart from the regional reform enacted by the Mauroy government, the French political class and French political culture remain Jacobin. To a certain extent, the establishment of regional powers represents a re-creation of Jacobin centralism at the regional level. This is obviously the case with the reform of public education, a decisive sector as regards political culture.[26] Regionalism is an administrative reform; it has not yet become a form of political culture. This applies as much to the political sphere as to the various regional movements disappointed by the regional reform.

A fortiori, Jacobinism is even more powerful when it concerns the Jews. When left-wing politicians list the constituent elements of the French nation, they mention the Corsicans, the Bretons, and others, but never the Jews. Similarly, the Giordan report (on "Cultural Democracy and the Right to be Different"),[27] while displaying a certain recognition of Jewish culture, does so with such a misunderstanding of history that the consequences are disastrous. After two centuries—or, in the case of some, one century—of French citizenship, the Jewish community is included in the cultural category of "second-generation immigrants from North Africa" and classified in a subcategory comprising the Armenian and Gypsy communities—both of which, incidentally, together with the Jewish community, are described by the minister of culture as "communities taken in" by the French community.[28] This hesitation between abstract, absolute citizenship and historical, "national" citizenship—between universal citizenship and special citizenship (for if one is a citizen, one enjoys the same status, even if it dates from yesterday, as those who have been citizens for twenty centuries, without any implication of having been "taken in" or not! There are no guests or minorities)—is a good illustration of the fact that the new situation has not yet been formalized either politically or sociologically, that it is at variance with the ideological consensus in France, and that it is censored in its manifestations by the internal coherence of the system.

This censorship is most in evidence in the official discourse and everyday consciousness of French Jewry, which are characterized

---

[26] See interview with Edgar Faure on university reform, *Le Monde*, 17 May 1983, 11.

[27] See my analysis in "Quelle place pour la culture juive dans la France de demain?" *L'Arche*, 310, January 1983.

[28] *Le Monde*, 10 November 1982, 18.

by the community's indecision with respect to its new condition and identity. Here, the discourse does not correspond to reality, or rather it does not correspond to it in a coherent manner. On the one hand, the discourse perpetuates the republican concept of the Jew, the ban on a Jewish collectivity, while on the other hand it asserts the existence of that collectivity in a paradoxical and untimely way. For example, the CRIF, in the very charter in which it proclaims its collective representativeness, warns against regarding it as "a partisan pressure group"; at the same time it occasionally denies itself the right to intervene in whatever way in French political life (except as far as anti-Semitism is concerned). During the 1981 election campaign, the *grand rabbinat de France* announced that its "unvarying position" is "not to intervene, in any manner or form, or at any time, in the electoral sphere." [29]

The hiatus that has developed between behavior and discourse— a hiatus that shows through in the ambivalence of the discourse itself—does have some roots in institutional structures. The most obvious sign of this is the low rate of Jewish participation in the life of Jewish institutions [30]—a phenomenon that can also be attributed to the lack of sociopolitical congruence between representative circles and the community at large (as regards socioprofessional categories, ethnic origin, age, and tangible strength). This is due no doubt to the fact that the CRIF represents only associations in which metropolitan Jews of the pre-1962 years were fairly active, whereas such institutionalized associational practices were unfamiliar to the newcomers, who had their own community networks. But there are other points of intrainstitutional attrition that reveal the hiatus in question, such as the conflictual relationship between the Consistory and the Fonds Social Juif Unifié, both competing for exclusive representation of the community in its dealings with the authorities. The repercussions of this rivalry are perceptible at both the national and local levels, with respect to questions of precedence and organization.

Thus the behavior of Jews and the objective features of their con-

---

[29] *Le Monde*, 16 April 1981.

[30] In 1980, 24,000 households (of the 180,000 Jewish households in France) contributed to the fund-raising campaign of the Appel Unifié; but all households having contributed even as little as Fr. 10 are counted as donors. The figure for 1981 is 23,500 donors and for 1982 (the year of the "Peace for Galilee" campaign), 32,000.

dition have changed too rapidly in relation to the constitutional framework and sociopolitical categories that govern the expressions of Jewish life in France (but nothing says that this framework and these categories will change). Consequently, Jewish manifestations in terms of collectivity are of an unhewn, unconceptualized, and unformalized character. We are dealing with a form of behavior, a mentality; this is still a far cry from a policy or an attempt to construct an identity. That is why the problem raised by the sudden appearance of these manifestations within the established framework is repressed, minimized, and obliterated in the collective discourse and consciousness—a reaction that does little to quell the attendant unease. Quite the contrary, the sense of scandal is accompanied by the perception of a disturbing oddity, of an insoluble mystery that will perhaps, some day, prompt a recourse to conspiracy theory explanations. Whatever is in store for the future, the present situation is yet another rearrangement of the pattern of the particular and the universal, this time illustrating their growing separation and their disconnection.

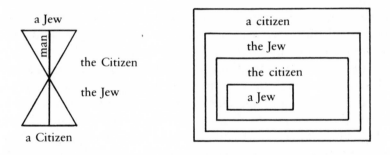

A Jew seems to appear alongside *the* citizen in a conflictual relationship, while in *a* citizen (which is what a Jew is) looms the disturbing figure of *the* Jew. Particularity (a Jew, a citizen) is present at both ends; that is, the conflictual relationship is very concrete and not confined to the ideological level. It is mediated by the mythical levels (*the* Jew, *the* citizen), which are connected in a reversed and contradictory manner. A Jew no longer leads on to *the* Jew, but to *the* citizen, in a conflictual mode. Similarly, *a* (Jewish) citizen leads on to *the* Jew in a contradictory manner.

The elements of the Judeo-French system are no longer assembled in a single, integrated relationship.

Jewish discourse is characterized not only by the denial of the collective Jewish dimension, but also by a positive, assertive, and militant theme: the defense of Zionism and the State of Israel, a theme that corresponds to a formal political commitment of the community vis-à-vis the authorities. "On the eve of 5743, they [the Jews] reassert their indestructible attachment to the cause of the people and State of Israel, and express their absolute trust in them," proclaimed the chief rabbinate after the war in Lebanon[31]— one of innumerable statements of this kind issued by all the Jewish institutions. And it is indeed at this level that the ambivalence becomes blatant. We have seen this in the case of the rabbinate, in the previous quotation (see note 29). We can also see this in the words of the leader of Renouveau Juif. The instigator of the "Jewish vote" campaign declares in the same breath: "I've chosen France . . . if I had chosen Israel, I would be there today. My reaction now is as much that of a Frenchman as that of a Jew"; "The Zionist movement should take the place of a Jewish political movement . . . if we want to defend Israel effectively, it is at the political level that we must struggle."[32]

How is one to interpret this positive and paradoxical theme, which is all the more astonishing as it has no logical and linear foundation in the discourse and in the community that convey it? This untimely appearance of an apologetic Zionism has raised a problem of interpretation, in that this form of Zionism is as exaggerated in gesture and speech as it is insignificant in reality (it has prompted neither an aliyah nor a revival of Hebrew). But the psychological explanation usually provided for it is inadequate (complexes, hysteria, neurosis). How could the locus of the most baroque ambivalence of French Judaism be an expression of the absurd?

It is not enough to divorce a social event from its social context on the grounds that one cannot understand it. One must therefore grasp it fully in its ideological and sociological dimension. Every phenomenon must be understood primarily in its own terms. And one can understand the logic of this particular phenomenon only by putting it back in the context of the French system (instead of abstracting it from reality and interpreting it according to another

[31] Statement of 12 September 1982.
[32] *Le Monde*, 26–27 October 1980; *Dialogue*, 4 (February 1981).

methodology), by seeing it as the effect of a system—in other words, by interpreting as a whole, with the greatest possible coherence, all the elements we have listed:

—the official, individual framework of Jewish identity

—the unconscious, self-censored assertion of the existence of Judaism as a collectivity

—the declarative negation of this collective dimension in France by the official community

—the total commitment to Zionism

All these elements are contradictory and negate one another.

Far from being a zone of absurdity at the heart of the Judeo-French edifice, *community Zionism* appears, on the contrary, as the ultimate and most meaningful synthesis of this system.

In a country where it is impossible to proclaim the existence of a Jewish collectivity, Judeo-French Zionism seems to be the most grandiose and powerful means of reiterating the assertion of a "Jewish nation" in France. The statement is made here and now in France, but through the prism of a distant and future entity, an identity situated three thousand kilometers away, in short, an identity whose presence is obtained at the price of its own absence.

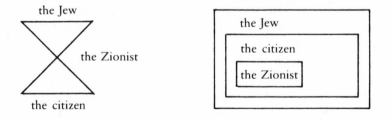

In this ideological configuration, the particular and objective dimension (*a* Jew, *a* citizen) disappears. Only the myths are present, which is a sign of the increased precariousness of the Jewish condition. What is more, it is the Zionist concept that mediates between the myth of the Jew and the myth of the citizen. The Zionist fuses *the* citizen and *the* Jew into a single whole, as can be observed in the very widespread notion that Zionism is supposed to embody democracy and the West at the heart of a "fanatical" Middle East. This phenomenon was strikingly confirmed after the great demonstration in Tel Aviv following the Sabra and Shatila massacres: Israel, previously a "monster," was now extolled as a model for European democracies!

Thus Judeo-French Zionism, so implausible in certain respects, comes across as the most rigorous and effective rationalization to date of the structural ambivalence of Jewish life in France. This variety of Zionism contains a metaphor (in the etymological sense of a "transfer" and in the figurative sense of a "poetic image") of Jewish existence in France, or rather a synthesis of the impossibility of a collective Jewish life in France and the persistence of that life in France.

We thus come to the paradoxical idea that, in order to assert their collective presence in France, the Jews resort to Zionism and are led to identify themselves with a state that is foreign to the French people, as if the only way for Jews to exist in France were for them to be elsewhere.

Why Zionism? First, the remoteness of the affirmative symbol makes the assertion of Jewishness in France tolerable (especially as the criterion of territoriality, which goes hand in hand with republican citizenship, is indirectly perpetuated through the invocation of *Eretz Israel*). But, more important, Zionism glorifies the "national" Jewish dimension and comes as a reply—two centuries later—to the price paid by the Jews for their civic rights: the abandonment of Jewish messianism.

The recourse to Zionism may also be informed by another logic: that of the Revolution, of the time when champions of the Jews called for equal rights by citing Jewish achievements in Palestine as proof of their sociability and their capacity to become French citizens. Zionism here takes on an assimilationist value (Israeli soldiers and peasants prove to the Diaspora Jew that he can be a good citizen—in the Diaspora. This is a matter of image and de facto recognition). It could be argued that, by giving substance to a republican vision, this form of Zionism is capable of satisfying the system's most crucial requirement: the normalization of the Jews (obtained at the price of their being mythically provided with a territory), a prerequisite for their integration into French society.

Today, however, this brand of Zionism seems to be characterized instead by a centrifugal impulse. The more awkward the community's status in French society, the more it will resort to Zionism, to a reference point outside the system, in order to assert itself in France. The greater the number of maverick groups, or groups that feel marginalized, within the community, the more these groups will turn to the ideology that is antithetical to this marginalization:

Zionism. Thus one can better understand the meaning of the very powerful commitment to Zionism voiced by the Sephardim or by the Renouveau Juif in its quest for power. These groups are obliged to situate themselves outside the system (via Israel) in order to assert themselves in France. Zionism consequently appears as a destabilizing factor and a force of challenge within the community.

But perhaps Zionism as defined by the revolutionary ideology of 1789 (a factor of integration and assimilation) also remains valid. If so, the paradox of the community's discourse would be open to a new interpretation. It could be argued that a twofold Zionist strategy is at work: a combination of the integrationist and assimilationist Zionism professed by the community's officials and the revolutionary and subversive Zionism of the masses. The encounter between the two may be responsible for a fundamental misunderstanding at the heart of the structure and crisis of the Jewish community. Both the representative elites and the masses—according to this interpretation—are Zionist, but each side reads Zionism differently. This would explain why the masses repeatedly accuse the elites of lukewarm feelings toward Israel, and, conversely, why the elites feel guilty over this issue[33] or, occasionally, voice their anger (when they brand the masses as fanatics). French Jews are overwhelmingly (witness the "Twelve Hours For Israel" and more sporadic demonstrations) centrifugal Zionists while their elites tend to be centripetal Zionists, even if, since the war in Lebanon, one can observe a radicalization of their discourse in a centrifugal direction—in short, a change in Zionist strategy.

For the moment, at any rate, the major effect of the Zionist phenomenon is integrative. In other words, the community's Zionist commitment has a strictly intra-French value. To begin with, in concrete terms, while Zionism has become, on certain occasions, a mode of political expression for the Jews (the "Jewish vote," supposedly determined exclusively on the basis of questions involving Israel), it would be easy to show that this vote is guided by strictly Judeo-French questions and interests, but that it represents nonetheless a reality specific to Jews. Thus the Jewish vote is the expression of a diffuse pattern of Jewish political behavior, which resorts to Zionist themes to assert the Jewish presence in France. It is precisely this recourse that makes for its diffuse character.

[33] See the words of a high-ranking official of the CRIF after the rue Copernic bombing, quoted in *La République et les Juifs*, 154.

The strategy of community Zionism is an integrative one, destined in the first instance for internal use. Zionism of this sort serves as an ideological melting pot for the resurgence of the Jewish nation *in France*. This commitment—which, in addition, has all the attractiveness of a moral and historical struggle for liberation, in short, of enthusiastic exaltation—enables the community to build itself by gathering together its members, mobilizing its forces, organizing itself, and setting up networks of legitimacy and authority.

This mobilization of the community has been achieved only by the use of an extra-French referent. At this level, Zionism plays a strategic role for external use. It is the only ideological structure that allows both the Jewish community and French society to rationalize, and thus to escape from, the impasse to which the elements of the situation lead. According to this tacit contract, the Jews can assert themselves—since there is no alternative—but they must make that assertion three thousand kilometers from France. The community's Zionism has become a modus vivendi for the Jews and for France, enabling the Jews to affirm the existence of the "Jewish nation" objectively while remaining within the official framework—in which this statement is forbidden. At the same time, it allows French society to ignore this intra-French statement officially, by ascribing it to a bizarre and exotic sentimental passion (and not a rational idea) peculiar to French Jewry: Zionism. But this objective can be attained on only one condition: this form of Zionism must be humanitarian, lachrymose—it must keep a low profile. For the system to function, Israel must be right; consequently, the community is continually led to defend an Israel that is weak and under attack, even when, as during the war in Lebanon, Israel displays an unchallenged and activist military might. What could be termed ideological blindness actually plays a very precise ideological role. The community clings to the only ideological rationalization of its present situation in France because it cannot provide any other.

Thus we are led, paradoxically, to a definition of Jewish existence *in France* via a "shift," a metaphor. This shift occurs in the sphere of symbolic geography—which says a lot about the (Jacobin) territorial referent of French citizenship and culture, and also about the impossibility for Jews to have a French territorial referent. This territorial criterion is present even in the Giordan report (referred to above), which, in its most earnest effort to recognize minority cultures (and consequently Jewish culture), is obliged to resort to the concept of "*nonterritorial* linguistic and cultural minorities."

The Zionist metaphor of French Jewry thus immediately situates the existence and identity of the community on a second level—an abstract and immaterial symbolic level. Community life therefore has an innate tendency to become an empty stage set, a shadow theater. Everything "here" is expressed in the words of "over there." This is the very definition of allegory—a form of discourse that says one thing while saying another. In this case, the shift in terminology occurs between the Jewish sphere and the Zionist sphere.

Consequently, the community's relationships to itself and to the authorities are built on a system of symbolic signals: everyone is actually talking about the same thing (the Jews in France) while ostensibly talking about something altogether different (Israel). And the astonishing thing is that, without ever being entirely taken in, everyone understands one another. Zionism has become the communication medium between the Jews and French society at large. When the community wishes to secure recognition from the authorities, the CRIF sends a delegation to meet with the president of the Republic and the representatives of the political parties before every election. When the political parties want to woo the Jewish electorate, they announce their program for Israel. When President Mitterrand visited Israel, he felt he had fulfilled his obligations toward the Jewish electorate as far as its intra-French interests were concerned. When the community voiced its opposition to the conference on Palestine, originally scheduled to be held at UNESCO headquarters in Paris in August 1983, the president of the Jewish community of Strasbourg, Jean Kahn, declared that the event could trigger "an oubreak of anti-Semitism in France. . . . If the conference takes place one year to the day after the rue des Rosiers attack, the Jews of Europe will come to Paris to demonstrate, and this could result in breaches of public order." [34] The surprising connection made between the international conference and the predictable attack on Israel on the one hand and an anti-Semitic explosion accompanied by a violent Jewish reaction on the other is very questionable in its appearance, but it is rich with significance for us. Attention should be drawn here to a new and very

[34] *Le Monde*, 19 March 1983.

meaningful feature, the forecast of a violent reaction by the Jews, which is a good indication of the assertive dimension of Jewish existence (a collective existence, since a demonstration is involved), even though this assertion is justified—almost apologetically—as a reaction to anti-Semitism (the negative profile once again).

In another context, when Menachem Begin called on Jewish youth to engage in self-defense and French newspapers devoted their editorials to this violation of national integrity, all parties concerned understood the issue at stake. Without going into the question of the "audacity" of the Israeli prime minister, who indeed transgressed the rules of international courtesy, and without taking into account the objective aspect of the event, one can observe that here too, the discourse used has a secondary meaning, which essentially relates to the collective differentiation of French Jewry. For the notion of self-defense leads to the notion of a group at odds with a surrounding group, and this differentiation is seen, of course, as expressing a crisis in the Judeo-French consensus, as an attack on France's national integrity. Begin's words materialized a diffuse feeling of apprehension in the collective consciousness and came as a fulfillment of the expectations and needs of the Judeo-French system itself.

Thus community Zionism is a vehicle for the strongest possible assertion of Jewish nationhood in France, but it is also its greatest burden, for it involves the Jewish community in a symbolic transfer that cuts it off from its presence in France.

In actual fact, community Zionism preserves and gives a new lease on life to the old republican image of the Jew by integrating into the system the very disturbance that had affected it throughout the process we have described. With this ideological structure, we come to a conservative stasis of the system defending itself against its own dislocation. Community Zionism is the last phase. This restructuring once again isolates the historical Jew from France and recognizes an abstract type of Jew, no longer the *israélite* but the Zionist Jew, who is, on the face of it, the concrete antithesis of the *israélite*. A sign of the times! *Israélitisme* today is necessarily Zionist-French in that the two ideologies ratify the absence of the Jew in France and, more generally, in history. The matrix of the two ideologies is indeed the same. The only difference between them is that an abstract nationalism has taken over from an abstract religious denomination, but the structure and consequences are the same.

A tangible sign of this absence is to be found in Jewish institutions, where, unlike the lower and middle ranks, the governing circles are still composed of "old French" and *israélite* members, with as yet very few Jews from North Africa (the executive committee of the CRIF, elected in April 1983, was exactly one-fourth North African Jews, not counting the still vacant seats allotted to the Zionist movement). These elites continue to direct the community along well-defined lines that are far from corresponding to its new state, in that the policy being implemented (especially in the cultural and educational spheres) fails to meet the needs recently created by the community's change of character.

This discrepancy between reality and official discourse—an inescapable consequence of the practical handling of metaphorical identity—accounts for the apparent confusion currently besetting the community. There are serious analysts (adducing opinion polls as evidence) who predict a dire fate for the community, and equally serious analysts who describe it in the paradisaic terms of a golden age. This confusion points to the transient character of the present phase. The very structure of the system contains the seeds of its own decay. The contradictory interplay between the two poles brought together in the allegory is designed to lead the system to its breaking point, not so much for the simple reason that the discourse runs counter to objective reality as because the discourse itself, in its social and symbolic effect, contains the elements of its own invalidation.

The truth is that the communication medium—community Zionism—used by the community (and French society at large) is problematic. Furthermore, the use of Zionism as a basis for building the identity of a *French*—and exclusively French—Jewish community is fraught with uncertainty, both from the point of view of French society as a whole and from that of the community itself, not to speak of the weaknesses inherent in an ideological construct such as this.

As far as French society is concerned, the uncertainty is obvious, for the Zionist theme can lead to a powerful revival of the conspiracy theme. All the factual prerequisites for this are already assembled. Both the reconstitution of collective Jewish existence and the self-censorship and censorship that prevail in relation to it are magnified by the open and objective display of a collective form of behavior and by the feeling that it has been publicly recognized. This creates a "safety clause" that frees the inhibitions of the collective French consciousness in the face of renewed public suspicion toward the Jews; this clause also neutralizes the community's potential awareness of the problem. The very nature of the Zionist ideology reinforces the conspiracy theme by specifically referring to a Jewish collectivity, the "Jewish nation." This entity is glorified in the full splendor of nationalism and given a political organization. Furthermore, it is endowed with international ramifications through the agency of the Zionist movement, whose impact is, in this case, directly and assertively intra-French.

All the factors at work in the community's predicament—determined, it must be recalled, by its setting—tend to foster an attitude of suspicion. Against the background of what amounts to a collective pattern of behavior, the official negation of this same behavior by the community's leaders, coupled with the open and total commitment to Zionism, provides very strong grounds for an attitude of suspicion, despite the protestations of all parties concerned. In truth, this outcome is inherent in the logic of the system—a system so confined and so precariously balanced that it leaves the door open to very few alternatives, for the law of scarcity (the Jews are scarce) governing the system is very rigid. Consequently, the positive misunderstanding (the collective assertion of Judaism in France via Zionism) that has enabled French society under the Fifth Republic to live in peace with the Jewish community (and vice versa) could well degenerate into a tragic negative misunderstanding under the pressures of the system.

But the precariousness of the medium is also due to another factor. Although community Zionism is an instance of pleading one's own case, it makes reference to a very concrete theater of operations: the Middle East conflict. The situation of a community that has adopted a Zionist stance will thus depend on the turn of events in the Middle East and will be vulnerable to the slightest reversal. Both the setbacks and excesses (such as victories) of Israeli policy have a direct impact on the community.

In this respect, the war in Lebanon will have lasting consequences. Behind the media descriptions of the conflict loomed the oldest stereotypes of anti-Semitism.[35] But it was particularly the tragic affair of the Sabra and Shatila massacres that came as a confirmation of the fragility of the French consensus over the Zionist basis of the community's collective identity. We are judging here not the veracity of the facts but the ideological and systemic effect of the discourse. The moment Israel is no longer "right," the moment Zionism loses its humanitarian character and Jewishness its lachrymose tinge (because of Mr. Begin's radical discourse or the horror of the massacre), the entire Judeo-French edifice collapses, and the community feels—rightly so, given the nature of the system—that its very existence is threatened when Israel, whatever its share of responsibility for its actions, loses its legitimacy. Community Zionism is a system that works in a vacuum and bears little relation to reality outside France. In such a system, in which the community defines itself through Zionism, any attack on Zionism—which is rarely distinguished from the policy of Israeli governments—is perceived as an attack on the community, even if that is not objectively so. Such is the logic of the ideological system. That is why, in a no less apparently irrational manner, community spokesmen have desperately tried to preserve the myth, even to the point of rejecting the findings of the Kahane Commission's report.[36] This reaction was their way of rightly defending the integrity of their identity in France; it had very little to do with outside reality, or even with Israel. Another proof of the predominance of the criterion of the lachrymose Jew, a Jew accepted out of humanitarian compassion and reduced to an abstract, ahistorical, and ethical myth, is provided by the total reversal of Western opinion after the decision to set up the commission of inquiry in Israel. It was a surprising turnaround—from a condemnation of Israel to unstinting praise. A self-accusatory Israel, proclaiming its guilt (even if, objectively, this behavior obeyed a very different logic), was perceived through the prism of the Judeo-French system in strict accordance with the notion of the lachrymose Jew and especially with the abstract notion of the Jew, who is supposed to embody in the absolute a moral ideal whose incarnation is known to be impossible in the world of mankind. The status quo was thus

---

[35] See my article in *Sillages* (French-language quarterly of the World Zionist Organization), Fall 1982.

[36] See for example *Le Quotidien de Paris*, 16 February 1983.

restored, and the community regained its French legitimacy. The myth was saved, the Jew of the Republic given a new lease on life: the Jew was no longer overstepping the bounds prescribed by the Republic.

It will be observed here that the republican notion of the Jew is still very much alive in 1983. During the war in Lebanon, the republican syllogism was spontaneously applied (for it is a part of the common ideology) to the question of the genocide:

1) All Jews are men, therefore we recognize them/We recognize the gravity of the genocide, and we sympathize.

2) But not all men are Jews/There have been other, equally devastating genocides (Cambodia, Biafra, and so on).

3) The Jews, while they are men, do not exist as Jews/The Jews do not have the exclusive privilege of suffering; consequently, the genocide of the Jews is one of a number of genocides (it is made banal) (variant: there was no genocide); therefore the Jews are not entitled to preferential treatment or to special consideration: they will be treated like the others (which always means—in this language—worse than the others, as if to make up for the opposite excess and the guilt that prevailed earlier).

It is this ideological schema that informed the collective consciousness and the media [37] during the war in Lebanon. This event, furthermore, saw the unconscious reactivation of the worst patterns of medieval anti-Judaism, which have survived with surprising intensity well into the modern age.

Is one therefore to speak of a possible rebirth of anti-Semitism in France? The aim here has not been to imply that the Republic is anti-Semitic, but to show that it *can* engender anti-Semitism. In this respect, our analysis indicates that all the prerequisites for such a resurgence are assembled, although (it should be stated) it has not yet actually manifested itself,[38] except in an abstract manner during the war in Lebanon. The credibility of this hypothesis has been confirmed by the economic, social, and political crisis and by the wave of xenophobia directed against the great number of North African immigrants, an animosity that was forcefully ex-

[37] See, for example, the leftist paper, *Libération*, during that period.

[38] Certain anti-Semitic books such as Bernard Granotier, *Israël cause de la 3e guerre mondiale?* (Paris: L'Harmattan, 1982) may herald such a trend.

pressed during the campaign for the municipal elections of 1983. Generally speaking, the Jews occupy a very precarious symbolic position in the Republic of the 1980s. In an increasingly region- alized France, the system inescapably leads the Jews to appear as the "last Frenchmen of France," unlinked to any specific portion of French territory, with no other moorage point than France "one and indivisible"—France as an abstract and total idea. Logically, as we have seen, the Jew, in his positive embodiment, is called upon to witness to the republican idea, to France's unity, and to the uni- versality of citizenship—all the more so when these values are no longer attested to concretely by the French people as a whole.[39] And what if the Republic's ultimate guardians, the witnesses to the sacred republican entity, began to act in unison with society and their fellow citizens? The Jewish entity serves here as a revealing sociological indicator of French society.

The opinion polls that have measured the extent of anti-Semi- tism are subject to caution as regards their methodology and their reliability. The crucial methodological question is to decide what is meant by the notion of anti-Semitism. The word is so trite as to have lost all meaning. It is clear that the anti-Semitism of the 1930s is indeed dead. But, in the meantime, the nature of Jewish identity has also changed. Today there is no doubt that the assimilationist *israélites* are totally accepted, but the same does not apply so easily to the "Jews" and their aspirations toward a visible and positive existence, at once collective, cultural, and historical. The "histori- cal Jew" continues to pose a problem serious enough to account for the building of the complex ideological edifice examined here, whose sole purpose was to cope with that figure within the econ- omy of the system. As the Jew has turned into a positive figure, the reaction of intolerance toward him has of necessity taken forms other than "anti-Semitism": it no longer feeds on the social imagi- nation but takes the shape of a concrete and objective situation, of a concrete social fact, on a par with the new, social, and concrete (albeit as yet unconscious) dimension of Jewishness in France. The social fact is the impossibility of a Jewish collectivity being ac- cepted in France; the possible revival of "anti-Semitism" will take the shape of a refusal of this collective dimension. Depending on whether one defines the Jew in old terms or in modern terms, the

[39] See *La République et les Juifs*, "Les derniers Français de France."

results of an opinion poll on anti-Semitism will of course be totally different.

As regards the community's strategy, the medium of Zionism involves a negative feedback. The metaphorization of collective existence irresistibly leads to its being dematerialized. The community's identity symbol places it manifestly "elsewhere." Consequently, Jewish existence is quite naturally desubstantialized. The center of the community does not lie within the community itself. This is true not only at the psychological level but also at the practical, institutional level, with the predominance in many spheres (cultural, educational, and communal in particular) of the great international Israeli-based and Israeli-run Jewish institutions. For a good number of its needs and decisions, the community is dependent on these institutions, which do not always have an accurate perception of its reality and which, above all, tend to centralize and ossify the spontaneous processes occurring inside the community.

The political nature of the identity myth (Israel as a political entity to be defended in a narrowly partisan political context) engenders a paradoxical process of overpoliticization and underpoliticization. Overpoliticization, because the community's life and consciousness focus exclusively on Israeli politics. As an immediate consequence, the community becomes fragile. Thus the debate in the community centers on the sole principle underlying the consensus: political Zionism. But community Zionism lends itself to a misunderstanding between centrifugal Zionism (that of the masses) and centripetal Zionism (that of the ruling spheres). This misunderstanding makes the community vulnerable to its unconscious internal contradictions, not to speak of the non-, anti-, or a-Zionist Jews inside the community, who are in conflict with it chiefly over this question. In this connection one may note that the controversy centers on a non-French question (Israel), which is a way of preserving the objective integration of the community at the French level. The paradox persists at this very level: one could say that despite its divisions, the community enjoys a high degree of internal cohesion.

This is also a situation of weakness because a genuine community cannot be built on a foundation as superficial and abstract as a political myth. Politics belongs to the outside world. The life of a community, a fortiori of a Jewish one, is basically made of a very deep cultural exchange, not of a partisan political debate—least of all one that takes place at second remove. This debate has created a total ideological vacuum in a community that has been overideologized (by political Zionism). The natural corollary of this de facto situation is a loss of cultural identity: Jewish culture is disappearing rapidly and giving way to a journalistic, event-oriented form of knowledge. As a result of all these phenomena, the community is underpoliticized. Here again we find the dual profile and dual logic of French Jewry. Zionist-centered overideologization effectively produces an ideological vacuum that is perceptible if one considers the community in its relationship to itself. In the writer's experience of various Jewish communities in France today, the average French Jew is indifferent to the community itself and totally unconcerned by the positive construction of a community in France, whether in the cultural and educational sphere or in the (intra-French) political sphere.[40] The impression of a renewed creativity and commitment in the community since the late 1970s is to be interpreted, naturally, in the context of the Judeo-French paradox. Admittedly, there is a certain vitality, but it is neutralized by the system in which it manifests itself. This applies as much to the new literary and philosophical creativity—which I have called media Judaism[41] and which I regard as a reformulation of nineteenth-century Franco-Judaism—as to the dynamic phenomenon of "Jewish radio stations." The case of these radio stations is very telling, for the community has found them to be an appropriate vehicle for a revival that is accompanied by an absence. They constitute a medium at once all-encompassing, reaching out to every Jewish home, and symbolically uniting the community, while incapable of uniting it in practice; a medium for an abstract, fictive community; a medium so extraordinary that it consists entirely of Israeli songs and Israeli news, thus affording the opportunity of truly releasing one's psychological tension: the joy of being in Israel—at home.

It is symbolic that the Cercle Gaston Crémieux (a non-Zionist group) should have been the only Jewish organization to react *officially* to the Giordan report (by holding a symposium); yet this does not mean that its officials were any more aware of the inevitable marginalization that the argument contained in the report entails for the Jewish community. The question of culture, of defin-

---

[40] See my article "Communauté en péril!" *L'Arche*, June 1983.
[41] See *La République et les Juifs*, "Les mirages du Juif médiatique."

ing Jewish existence in France, clearly fails to mobilize the French-
israélite governing circles in the official institutions. Apart from
the struggle against anti-Semitism, the community has no notion
of its existence in France. The narrowly political advocacy of Israel
reduces the community's role in domestic French political life. And
this underpoliticization is further aggravated by the nature of the
community's narrowly political commitment to Israel, for the community, in this case, acts as an intercessor vis-à-vis the French authorities. It does not act politically in the sphere of power (because
in any case the issue at hand is an extra-French problem) but tries
to exercise an influence *on* the authorities, in the manner of the
"Court Jews" of the eighteenth century. This is an archaic relationship to politics (and even a form of political ignorance) that confirms the community's political heteronomy and its feeling of help-
lessness. From the standpoint of the French political class, such an
"inconsequent" type of behavior (but it is only outwardly so) causes
the community's Zionist commitment to be viewed as a psychological problem affecting the Jews—an anxiety, a vague sentimental expectation with no concrete intra-French dimension (and
there are logical reasons for such an interpretation, for French policy toward Israel is not a decisive issue as far as strictly domestic
affairs are concerned); similarly, the community denies itself the
possibility of political action in the domestic area, thus losing
much of its political credibility there.

To sum up, the metaphorization of the Jewish community leads
inexorably to its losing touch with itself, to its losing its sense of
reality, to its extraterritorialization—and all of this can spell the
disappearance of the "historical Jew." Consequently, the door is
open to a marginalization of the community (isolation within the
nation's body politic, obsolescence and delegitimization of community life, atomization, incompatibility between community and nation, heteronomy, and so on).

Thus the community's communication medium proves to be very
fragile, because of the diversity of the elements that it organizes
into a highly complex and sophisticated pattern. In order to survive, such a structure requires a great, constant, and sustained ex-
penditure of energy to preserve its equilibrium. The community
seems to lack sufficient resources to achieve this, because of the
narrowness of the system in which it participates. In other words,
the difficult position of equilibrium and isomorphism now reached

by the system through the agency of the Zionist metaphor is very
ephemeral indeed. It represents the system's last determined effort
to survive in a phase where the preconditions for equilibrium are
increasingly harder to guarantee.

What can such a crisis lead to? The future will depend on the
behavior of two variables: (1) an independent variable, the pressure of the system on the community (a pressure that is a combination of two secondary variables: the state of French society and developments in the Middle East), and (2) the community's strategy,
which, at present, is a dependent variable, for it is totally determined by the pressure of the system. Metaphoric Zionism represents a rationalization of the current stalemate and bears witness
to the passivity of the community element. It is a spontaneous and
mechanical product of the system. If we go back to the diagram
of our systemic analysis, with some alterations, we obtain the
following:

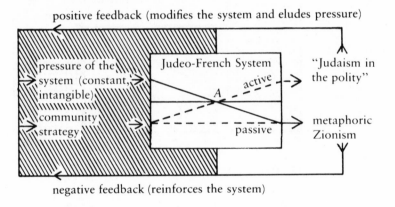

positive feedback (modifies the system and eludes pressure)

pressure of the system (constant, intangible)

community strategy

Judeo-French System

active

A

passive

"Judaism in the polity"

metaphoric Zionism

negative feedback (reinforces the system)

▨▨▨ primary environment (the givens of the system)

☐ secondary environment (the products of the system, re-
introduced into the environment of the system)

A critical crossover point in the system (intersection of the two
variables)

If the state of French society and the political situation in the
Middle East worsen, this spontaneous community strategy (the
metaphor) will, unwittingly and automatically, put the community
itself in jeopardy. If, instead, the strategy has changed in the meantime—if, that is, the community has actually devised, in a rational

and political manner, an intra-French and autonomous strategy, a "Judaism in the polity"—then the break will not occur. But this is still to assume that the pressure of the system (particularly the variable relating to French society, which seems to us the more decisive of the two subvariables) will decrease, either by itself or under the effect of a new approach to the problem by the community—an approach that would alter the premises of the debate by defusing their potential explosiveness. This is another way of saying that the margin for transforming the community's strategy from a dependent into an independent variable is narrow. In the short term, it does not seem that these two conditions (for avoiding a breakdown of the system) will obtain.

One could schematize the relationship between these variables as follows:

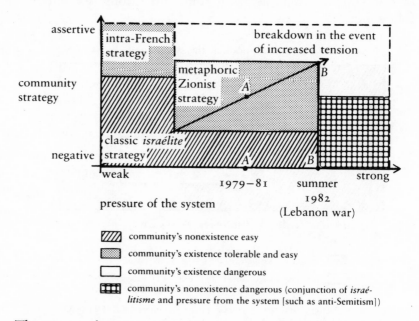

The greater the pressure and the more assertive the community's strategy, then the more perilous the interrelationship between the community and French society.

Of course, as we have seen, the evolution of the Jewish community in France and of its condition is of interest in its own right. But the analysis of this phenomenon has far broader implications. As the first Jewish community in Europe to have been directly emancipated, by the great Revolution, it stands as a prototype and a laboratory for modern Jewish existence. It was within the framework of this community that the profile of modern Jewish identity was developed. It is possible and logical that the crisis of this model (a crisis that, for all the reasons examined above, seems to us to be clearly present in these final years of the twentieth century) may undergo its most significant development in its initial setting and perhaps lead to a new configuration of Jewish existence in the modern or "postmodern" world. The crisis of the very man—the Jew—who was meant to represent the quintessence of modern man abounds in lessons of universal import, which shed light on the structure of the crisis of modern citizenship. In this wider crisis, the rise of ethnicity and "differences" today poses a radical challenge to the democratic system by revealing its critical impasse: the difficulty of finding conceptual space for the particular within the reputedly rational and universal modern state—and thus, conversely, the failure of the system's philosophy of the universal.[42] Democracy welcomed its Jewish citizens less as Jews than as abstract men, a fortiori less as a people than as anonymous individuals to whom it gave a new filiation.

The post–World War II process appears increasingly as a radical turning point in the development of modern Jewish citizenship in the democratic countries of the Diaspora—a development whose future course is impossible to predict. In point of fact, back in the late nineteenth century, political Zionism came as the Jewish response to democracy's insensitivity toward Jewish existence and especially as a reaction to the most unexpected form of anti-Semitism, the form that develops in democracies. In this respect, the Zionization of the Diaspora can be seen in a new light, as a reiteration of the nineteenth-century Jewish reaction (i.e., the beginnings of Zionism) to the first disappointments with democracy. There is, however, a single and major difference. Zionism has become an introverted creed, centered on the Western Diaspora, and no longer an extroverted one, centered on the creation of a state in the Middle East. The same situation is thus repeated without the hope of a potential outcome. The Zionization of the Diaspora has thus no doubt made its mark upon the century, with all the consequences

[42] See ibid., chap. "La Démocratie: Par delà 1789."

that this involves. If the Diaspora Jews, in order to live as Jews in the Diaspora, are obliged—on account of democracy's insensitivity to their existence as Jews—to resort to the myth of a Jewish state (Zionization) without access to the prerogatives of such a state (that is, by not emigrating to Israel), then they are doomed to confinement, to being ghettoized inside Western democracy.

This situation does not yet obtain in the early 1980s. Nevertheless, the present phase heralds the large-scale revival of the "Jewish nation," of the Jewish people, at the heart of Western democracy—which has never been ready to admit it for the past two centuries. This development takes the form of an astonishing ideological phenomenon: the recourse to Zionism in order to affirm a Diaspora existence. In this respect, Zionism is not the ideology of French Jewry alone. It is the ideology of French society as a whole. This phenomenon is the product of the democratic system and of the French system.

In its internal significance, the value of the ideological phenomenon can be precisely defined if one interprets it according to Durkheim's laws of collective ideation.[43] By asserting itself as a mythical, romantic, and quasi-messianic supercommunity (Zionism's Israeli nation), the Jewish community establishes its collective identity in France. The supercommunity is neither the real community nor the ideal community, but the community psychically affected by a state of social hyperanimation, of social ferment. Creating a society, Durkheim tells us, always involves a ferment that stems from a state of exaltation that grips a physically and qualitatively concentrated society. In this psychic state, the society's self-image affects all the ways in which the society is present to itself. Here, the ferment is of course the struggle for and defense of Israel, activities in which the community reaches its maximum state of physical and qualitative concentration and its most intense state of ferment. This movement produces an image, and this ecstatic image of the community is a Zionist one. Through this image, Jewish society asserts itself (in France via Israel) by negating itself (in France, since it uses the medium of Israel); it achieves unity via dualization (the community is united in *France* around Israel).

[43] Henri Desroche, "Retour à Durkheim?," *Archives de Sociologie des Religions* 27 (1969): 79–88.

In conclusion, I must outline, for the sake of greater clarity, the methodological base of the approach that I have applied here. My theoretical intention was to reintroduce the Jewish view of things into sociological and historical analysis (in this case, the point of view of the existential Jewish community on its history within French society). This runs implicitly counter to official ideology in modern Jewish historiography, and the history of anti-Semitism can in no way substitute for Jewish history. We have to recognize Jewish existence as a total sociohistorical fact, so that the final level of analysis of Jewish history and society is always that of the Jew considered as a collective agent in history and society. Far from treating Jewish existence as the sediment of outsiders' perceptions, we have to restore to its full dimension the Jewish view of the world's existence and of the Jewish people's existence.

Remarks on Trigano

S HMUEL TRIGANO's paper is a remarkable essay. It can be read in
two ways. As a document, reflecting the recent transformation
of the Jewish community in France, and the challenge to the Jacobin tradition by the more militant elements of this community
(mainly, those who had to uproot themselves from North Africa),
Trigano's paper is invaluable. As a set of statements about French
history and about the present condition of what might be called
Franco-Jewish relations, it is, however, far more questionable. I
will discuss it by commenting first on what he says about the past,
and later on his views of the present. But I cannot help remarking
at the outset that this brilliant attack on the "republican system"
with its fondness for abstractions (the citizen, the nation) and its
somewhat parochial universalism, is itself written in a style that
shows the power of assimilation of the system: abstractions, ele-
gant plays on words, a formidable amount of intellectualization
(reinforced by various diagrams), a gift for arresting (albeit, at
times, opaque) formulas—these features of the paper are also the
characteristics, dazzling and exasperating, of French academic culture. Rarely has an assault on a system, a plea for collective differentiation, been staged so completely in the manner of and according to all the canons of the enemy.

There are two points in Trigano's account of the Jacobin system
that deserve a rebuttal. The first is explicit. He presents this system, which "reduces" men to what is supposedly common to them,
i.e., citizenship, and which eliminates their concrete and particu-
laristic features in order to retain only their civic essence, as if it

had been aimed at depriving Jews of their Judaism; and therefore as a repression. But historically, it was meant by its authors as an emancipation, and felt as such by the Jews. Moreover, insofar as it was a war machine against the specific features of any group, it was aimed at the Catholics, that is, at the Church and at all those—in a country that was far from dechristianized—who accepted the political dogmas of the Church. Trigano's history of France curiously ignores the central event of modern French history, the struggle between the lay state (with its Rousseauistic philosophy) and the Catholic Church—a struggle in which the lay crusaders were often joined by Protestants and Jews. The ban on Jewish "corporations" was a small aspect of the ban on all corporations (*loi le Chapelier*), another measure aimed at emancipating all those whose status had been frozen in the guilds and castes of the old society, as well as at freeing trade and enterprise. What the Republic needed in order to triumph was not the transformation of *the* Jew (Remember how small the Jewish minority was!) but the taming of *the* Catholic; to argue that it was *the* Jew who appeared as the greatest obstacle to *the* citizen is quite extraordinarily ahistorical. "The absolute negation of France (the anti-Republic)" was the *clerical*, not the Jew. And if the Jews are not treated like Corsicans and Bretons today, it is because the issue of the rights of religious or cultural groups cannot be raised without the whole Catholic question arising once again. (The same tendency to exaggerate the importance of the "Jewish question" reappears in the passage where Trigano calls antisemitism the only link between the far left and the far right, their only consensus: as if the condemnation of the modern bourgeois order, nostalgia for certain aspects of prerevolutionary society, and above all anticapitalism, had not provided a far broader common ground.)

A second point in Trigano's analysis is implicit. The political-ideological "construction" of citizenship, the Jacobin abstraction, is presented as if it had been totalitarian: as if it had wiped out, or had at least been intended to wipe out, all group particularities. Interestingly enough, this is an accusation that was usually hurled at the republican system by those very antisemites of the left and right, a Proudhon and a Maurras, who were pleading for decentralization and the rights of smaller communities. The myth of the Jewish plot, presented by Trigano as the inevitable effect of the "logic of suspicion," that is, of the fear that the Jews were, after all, not truly citizens, happened to flourish mainly among people who did *not* accept the Jacobin philosophy and who denounced it either in behalf of pluralism, or because it tried to exorcise the reality of class oppression through bourgeois formalist abstractions: people who either saw the Jews as foreigners (whereas the republican system saw in them "only" French citizens), or excoriated them as dissolvents of the traditional social order and values (along with other dissolvents such as the industrial bourgeoisie). In reality the totalitarian "potential" of the republican system was never realized, for two reasons. First, it remained unacceptable to a large part of the French political class and public, on the right and on the left: the "right to be different" was claimed by Catholics (reactionary or liberal) as well as by syndicalists. Secondly, this potential never existed. To be sure, the Jacobin concept of citizenship was broad, since it extended to cultural life (as the not yet ended battle for and against private schools demonstrates). But it never covered the sphere of economics and social life: as long as associations and interst groups did not challenge the law, they could always prosper and proliferate. To find in the system that sees only man in the citizen the sole and oppressive reason for Jewish assimilation in nineteenth-century France is to provide a very simplified reading of a complex process. It leaves out a notion—nationalism—that is, to be sure, one of the chief features of the republican system yet exceeds it by far, and that operated as a magnet and a constraint in every important European country. Trigano's history is as French-centered as the French history he denounces. If there was no Jewish "community" in modern France, it was not because official France forbade it: it was because of the same processes, official and unofficial, deliberate and mechanical, that turned—to use the title of Eugen Weber's book—peasants into Frenchmen, or, elsewhere, Bavarians into Germans, Neapolitans into Italians, Welsh miners into British Socialists.

Trigano's analysis of the present raises three important issues. One is that of French antisemitism today. He does not say much about it although he recognizes that one should not exaggerate its importance. But he makes two remarks that deserve some discussion. One concerns the importance of the new right; the other deals with the way in which the media presented the invasion of Lebanon by Israel. I think that one should not exaggerate the importance of the new right: it certainly does not provide the "ideological structure" of the current opposition. The latter is made of two groupings, one of which—the Union pour la Démocratie Française (UDF)—is a mishmash of traditional French conservative liberalism and of Christian democracy, while the other—the Rassemblement pour la République (RPP)—is a mix of Gaullism and political opportunism. The lofty racism and anti-"Judeo-Christian" philosophy of an Alain de Benoist float far too high in the sky to provide structure to politicians; at most, the new right's (mis)use of biology and ethology in behalf of antiegalitarianism lends itself to exploitation against the "Socialo-Communist" brand of egalitarianism: no more, no less.

As for anti-Jewish feelings and movements in France, one has to distinguish four strands. One is properly antisemitic and based either on religious or on social arguments (the two kinds were merged by Drumont). The social bases of this traditional antisemitism of the far right and of the left have been largely destroyed; the ideologies of these factions have also been transformed, on the right because of the radical shift in the Catholic Church's worldview, on the far left—to put it bluntly—because other scapegoats have displaced the Jewish bogeyman. A second strand, powerful in the 1930s, was xenophobia; today it expresses itself powerfully again—but against immigrant workers and foreign students, not Jews. A third strand can be called antipluralistic; the Jacobin hostility to "differences"; as Trigano recognizes, there is, today, an "existential crisis" of Jacobinism, and the pressures toward decentralization, for the recognition of cultural diversity, etc., have not weakened yet. Fourth, there is hostility to "dual citizenship." It is not new: the French right, and at times also the Socialists, have charged the French Communist Party with being a foreign agent. What is relatively new is the suspicion that the French Jewish community might practice dual allegiance to France and to the State of Israel (it is not Zionism as such that is an issue). But this does not mean that every criticism of Israel's policies should be seen as more or less hidden antisemitism: often it is no more than dismay at policies of force and occupation used by former victims of oppression, no more than sympathy for the underdog (however marred by romanticization of terrorism); no more than the criticism many Israelis have made of their own government's behavior.

However, the hostility to dual citizenship brings one to the second issue raised by Trigano: the French Jewish community's relation to Israel. Trigano repeatedly describes what he calls French "community Zionism" as a kind of compensatory phenomenon: since France prevents "the assertion of a Jewish community," this community "transfers" its will-to-exist to Israel, projects itself abroad: Zionism (in Trigano's debatable use of this term) thus becomes "the only ideological structure" that allows the French Jewish community and French society to rationalize and to get out of their dead end. Once again, *French* society and *France*'s political ideology are held responsible for a collective attitude of Jews that is characteristic not only of French Jews but of American Jews just as well: Zionism as a "metaphor," Israel as the focus of hopes, fears, and exaltations of Jews living among the gentiles, these are facts of life both in a Jacobin, unitary nation such as France, and in the pluralistic United States. And yet nobody in the United States would analyze these facts as evidence of the "impossibility of Jewish collective existence" there. Once again Trigano's analysis is too French-centered, French-obsessed; and just as, in his discussion of the past, he left out all the "assimilationist" factors other than the Jacobin system (and tended to assimilate antisemitism with it), here he leaves out those features common to Jewish communities living far from Israel, in a large number of Western countries, that explain what he calls the "overideologization in Zionism": this "renaissance that accompanies an absence" is not a purely French phenomenon at all. In fine French fashion, he interprets in ideological terms and as "the product of the democratic and of the French systems" an event that is far more complex and requires a delicate analysis of the Jewish condition today.

The reason why he chooses his interpretation is strategic. Trigano wants the French Jewish community to stop, so to speak, alienating itself through Zionism, and to begin asserting itself in France, as a real community; indeed he wants it to build its own society. A third and most fundamental issue is thus raised, but not resolved in the paper. *De quoi s'agit-il?* What are to be the relations between this Jewish society and France? Trigano seems to be calling for the politicization of the former (it should "act politically in the sphere of power" rather than "exert influence on power": French abstractions and distinctions sometimes obfuscate rather than enlighten); cultural concerns are not sufficient. To behave as a political community only in matters concerning Israel, he says, means to condemn oneself to "ghettoization" within Western democracy. What exactly does he want? He talks about rewriting Jewish history from the viewpoint of the Jew as collective actor, about recapturing a Jewish perspective on the Jewish world and people. The only concrete implication that makes sense is the notion of *a* Jewish people, with its own institutions and will. But what is to be the political forum of this people? Will each "national" fragment have to demand the right to establish its own political institutions within the nation where it lives? *Cultural* autonomy can be granted to nonterritorial groups, but, in all Western democracies, the basis of political organization—centralized or decentralized, unitary or federal—is territorial.

I will not discuss here the notion of *a* Jewish people. (I agree with the reservations presented recently by Raymond Aron in his *Memoirs.*) Let us assume that there is such a people. Will any nation accept the solution that can be read between the lines of Trigano's essay: literally, a binational constitution? And if he is right in suggesting the total incompatibility between the French republican system and "Jewish difference," would not such a solution lead to the demise of that abstract notion of common citizenship that Trigano, to be sure, deplores but that provided French Jews with a protection against persecution, with a legal shield against their enemies (who, I repeat, were often those of the French democratic state)? Would it not vindicate all the antisemites who propagated the myth of the Jewish plot and the "logic of suspicion"?

Like many founders of new nations, Trigano is rewriting the history of his people, in order to fix the blame for past fiascoes on the people's oppressors or deniers. But the founders of new nations could at least build on the genuine nationalism, or will-to-independence, of their followers. Can those French Jews who now proclaim their common identity and criticize with some contempt past assimilation as cowardly abdication or self-hatred, really secede while remaining French? And do they want to go so far? Maybe Trigano's work should be read above all as a consciousness-raising exhortation. But intellectual and political leaders have a duty to tell their followers exactly where they want to go, and to be clear about the chances, the costs, and the risks.

DAVID S. LANDES

Two Cheers for Emancipation

N O ONE who writes about Jews and Jewish life in the Diaspora over the last two thousand years can fail to recognize that it has been on balance an unhappy experience and that Jewish survival has been something of a miracle. Not a divine miracle necessarily, though some would claim that; rather a man-made miracle, the result of a tenacious (some would say obstinate) faith and hope and an inexpugnable sense of identity and self-worth. Non-Jews have often seen this self-esteem as an outrageous pretension to chosenness—the more unacceptable, even intolerable, as it usually clashed with outward signs (dress, manners, speech) of what was defined as higher civilization. Observant Jews have no trouble with such scorn; they are armed by the very fact of their observance. For nonobservant, assimilating Jews, however, the slings of contempt and offers of "improvement" have always posed a painful dilemma—the prospect of salvation, but only at the price of rejecting one's roots, one's parents, one's family, one's own self.

This price has varied with time, place, and person. In societies of quasi-universal religious affiliation, a Jew could "pass" only by apostasy—often an act of demeaning self-repudiation. In Christian Europe, it was sometimes easier to allow the children to be baptized into the majority faith: they could handle the change more easily, unless they took the tenets of the Church so seriously as to fear for their parents' salvation. (This transgenerational route was particularly characteristic of Protestant areas, say, northern Germany in the early nineteenth century. In some Catholic lands this option was precluded by the refusal of Church authorities to allow Christian children to remain with Jewish parents. But one does find unintended transgenerational shifts in the case of children baptized without the parents' knowledge or consent and then removed from their care. The best-known example is the infamous Mortara affair in the mid-nineteenth century; and an unknown number of similar cases arose in connection with the rescue of Jewish children in World War II.) Or the children might marry out, breaking the line of descent and opening a new chapter paradoxically built on remembering to forget.

Over the centuries, by one route or another, willingly or compelled by force, millions of Jews left their faith and people. These losses—by murder, abduction, constraint, defection, conversion—constituted a continuous if irregular hemorrhage, for the Jews were prevented by law and custom from compensating their losses by propaganda and proselytism. Indeed so severe were the penalties for apostasy from Christianity, which fell on convertor and convert alike, that the Jews instituted inhibitions on proselytizing that constituted a prohibition. These inhibitions remain in effect to this day. Marriage and love are not seen by Orthodox Jews, in contrast to Christian churches for example, as valid reasons for conversion to Judaism. This self-restraint in turn has only reinforced the Jewish reputation for clannishness.

The so-called Enlightenment of the eighteenth century sharply reduced the price of defection. It devalued religious faith in general, putting old beliefs in doubt and proposing new faiths of a more pallid, less demanding, more "rational" character. The non-doctrines of the varieties of deism—the looseness or absence of theology, the abhorrence of dogma, the emphasis on an obvious, "reasonable," "natural" morality—made these new faiths ideal vessels for those who wanted to leave the "outworn" confines of Judaism for more spacious opportunities. A Jew who could not abide the thought of a trinitarian faith or believe in divine incarnation or transsubstantiation could live with God the Great Clockmaker or the all-purpose deity of the Unitarians and Universalists.

Following hard on these intellectual and ideological explorations (experiments?), the French Revolution offered the political vision of a national collectivity freed of religious identification and hence open to participation by people of all faiths (or no faith). Enlightenment and Revolution combined to offer the Jews of France, still living as an organized community within the larger Catholic society, the chance to be Frenchmen like other Frenchmen. This implied the dissolution of those communitarian structures and attitudes that separated the Jews from their neighbors. Specifically, the position of the Jews as a nation living in the midst of the French nation could not be allowed to continue.

This offer was seen by non-Jews as a great benevolence, an act of emancipation. Indeed many opposed it as too good for the Jews, perceived as hopelessly benighted, unregenerate, and (to use the Catholic term) perfidious. The Jews in turn were inclined to see their new status as a liberation from old ways and constraints, an entrance ticket into a world of much wider economic and intellectual opportunity. The extraordinary success of Jews and people of Jewish extraction in a wide array of public and private activities—and this in the face of persistent prejudice and hostility—in the period that followed is testimony to the talent previously bottled up by segregation, imposed and self-imposed. On that point, one has only to recall that Jews were once thought unsuited to mathematics. Of course: if the best brains of a population are steered into theological disputation, it will not produce many mathematicians. But it will turn out some sharp theologians.

In the matter of Jewish emancipation, then, France set the example. (The only places to anticipate this development were some of the colonies of British North America.) Hence France's reputation among Jews as a land of special hospitality and enlightenment. This was particularly true of those Jews who were already caught up in the process of assimilation and cultural "evolution"; even the wealthiest and most privileged had the sense that they would be better off in France; and so, from the early nineteenth century, such names as Rothschild, Fould, Erlanger, Eichtal, Heine, and Gunzburg enter French society and history. As for the French Jews themselves, they, like Jews in the United States, cherished their good fortune and offered their love without measure to their new Zion. At the limit, one has a letter like that of this young Jew, dead on the field of battle, to Charles Maurras no less:

Born to a Jewish family, I have felt myself completely detached from Jewish tradition, completely French. It has been enough for me to be a good Frenchman and to be logical with myself, to adopt the doctrines of the Action Française in all their implications. When the time comes for you to read these lines, which are to reach you only if I die, I shall have definitively acquired, by mingling my blood with that of the oldest families of

France, the nationality that I lay claim to. Thanks to you, I shall have understood the necessity and beauty of this baptism.[1]

Emancipation had its price, though. It implied in the long run the assimilation of the Jews to their neighbors' manners, values, eventually their beliefs—or lack of belief. Not in principle, to be sure: Jews would continue to be Jews at home and in the synagogue, Frenchmen everywhere else. In practice, however, many of the traditional rules of Jewish observance had been devised to sustain Jewish separateness and identity (the dietary laws, for example), and now separateness had to go. The Jews had been emancipated, but not Jewishness.[2] The record shows that French Jews found it increasingly difficult to reconcile the rules of their faith with the opportunities and requirements of civil education and achievement. And when the two considerations clashed, the Jews—even their rabbis—tended to sacrifice the Law to social, political, and business success. One example: Sabbath school attendance. Given the highly selective character of French schooling and the conditions of access to power and the professions, ambitious Jewish families had no choice but to send their children to the public schools and hence to Saturday classes.[3] Some of them tried to reconcile this necessity with their religious beliefs by asking their children not to write—an impossible and unenforceable constraint. In the end, the educational system operated to sever the Jewish child from observance; and while parents (and grandparents) may have deplored this, they viewed it as a necessary (or desirable) avenue of promotion, in other words, of happiness.[4]

[1] R. Gross, *Enquête sur le problème juif*, p. 43, cited in Pierre Aubéry, *Milieux juifs de la France contemporaine à travers leurs écrivains* (Paris: Plon, 1957), p. 298.

[2] This was the German formula; but it was equally applicable in France. See Jacob Katz, "German Culture and the Jews," *Commentary* 77, 2 (Feb. 1984), 57.

[3] One may ask why the Jews did not establish religious day schools offering classes in secular subjects of a quality comparable to those of the best lycées. It might have been done, although it would have solved the problem only up to the level of higher education. There would still have been the necessity of accommodating to Saturday classes in the *grandes écoles*.

[4] The practice persists to this day, in spite of the growing adoption of the five-day week and the long weekend. Saturday classes continue, but only for half a day and on a less serious level than regular weekday classes. Thursday is free. Educators explain that five days of class in succession are too much for little children; that they need a mid-week break. If you want a lively debate, try to explain to a group of French people, Jewish or non-Jewish, that the institution of Saturday classes is objectively anti-Jewish. Most Frenchmen cannot even understand the issue.

The historical record shows that the Jews of France had fair warning of the tacit assumptions underlying their emancipation and the reservations held by many of their non-Jewish compatriots. Napoleon himself, for all his carefully cultivated reputation as legatee of the Revolution and propagator of its ideals, was not ready to accept the legislation on Jewish citizenship. In 1806 he summoned an assembly of Jewish *notables*, with a view to mobilizing Jewish leadership for a program of self-improvement, inspired of course from above. It is no accident that the questions (challenges) posed focused on such issues as intermarriage and so-called usury. Would the Jews be ready to become like other Frenchmen, to melt into French society at large? And would they deal in business with gentiles as with their fellow Jews? Many, perhaps most, non-Jewish Frenchmen would have responded no to both these questions. Napoleon himself was surely not unrepresentative: "It is necessary to consider the Jews a nation and not a sect, for they are a nation within a nation. I should like to prevent them, at least for a certain length of time, from taking mortgages; it is too humiliating for the French nation to find itself at the mercy of the vilest of all nations."[5]

The representatives of the Jewish communities made reassuring reply. This was not easy, not only because Napoleon (and his agent Molé) wanted answers that were at variance with Jewish law and custom, but because the Jewish representatives were themselves divided on how much to concede to what was defined as good citizenship. Some saw this as an opportunity to escape from Judaism and were ready to promise anything; others saw this as the death of the community and wanted an unambiguous reaffirmation of the *halachah* (law, commentary, interpretation, tradition, custom—the Way). The result was a compromise that was also an evasion. Thus on intermarriage, the response pointed out that a Jew who married a non-Jew remained a Jew. While Jews were forbidden to marry idolators, Christians (who worshipped the God of heaven and earth) were not considered to be in that category; and although Jewish law would not permit a religious sanctification of mixed marriage, the Jew who entered into such a union civilly would still be a Jew.

[5] In April 1806 to the Conseil d'Etat. Cited in Frances Malino, *The Sephardic Jews of Bordeaux: Assimilation and Emancipation in Revolutionary and Napoleonic France* (University of Alabama Press, 1978), pp. 68–69.

The result of this hunger for acceptance was galloping consumption. In the century following the Revolution, the bulk of the older Jewish communities of the southwest and the Comtat Venaissin simply melted into the larger population. They intermarried, moved, abandoned religious rites and customs. A small number resisted, but over a period of generations, their very fewness was an invitation to disappearance. It was easier to sustain the faith in Paris, where there was a growing Jewish community, hence a critical mass. But people went to Paris to rise in the economic and social scale, and ambition is the handmaiden of assimilation. Only the reservoir of eastern Jews, in Alsace and Lorraine, kept the community going, and they were hardly more wed to tradition than the Sephardim. They were slower to change because many of them still lived in rural villages under conditions of social segregation and diffuse opprobrium (and occasional violence) that recalled an older regime. But as they too were caught up in the process of urbanization and assimilation, they followed the same *cursus*, fifty or eighty years later. The history of the Debré family may serve as archetype: grandfather Simon, come from Alsace to serve in Paris as *grand rabbin*; son Robert, an outstanding physician, *professeur de Faculté*, freethinker (?), host to guests of all persuasions; grandson Michel, a Catholic, prime minister to de Gaulle and a spokesman for his president's anti-Israel policies. Patrice Higonnet includes Michel Debré among his examples of succcessful French Jews. Jews would not consider him Jewish, except in a genealogical sense that is usually denoted as racist and appropriately deplored.

For many, Jews and non-Jews, this gradual incorporation of the Jewish population into the French body social has been viewed as a good thing, as *civilisation* at work. But there were *accidents de parcours*: the Damascus blood libel in the 1840s; the Mortara kidnapping under Napoleon III—and these showed the tenacity and latent virulence of anti-Jewish sentiment. To be sure, both of these *affaires* originated outside of France and could be dismissed as extraneous; but their resonances within France hinted at the persistence of an older, prerevolutionary anti-Jewish mythology. No one could have taken the blood libel seriously who was not sensitized by a millennium of Christian demonology; and no one could defend the kidnapping of Edgar Mortara except in the context of the Catholic doctrine of salvation. To be sure, there were representations by the French government (and others) to the papal authorities asking for the return of the Mortara child to his parents. These reflected not only a humanitarian concern for the sanctity of the family and human freedom, but also the special diplomatic ties of France to the new, anti-Papal Italy. But good French Catholics understood and accepted the Vatican position, which was not simply an adventitious response but was rather inscribed in a centuries-old tradition of forced and unwitting conversion followed by seizure and sequestration. The issue was to arise again in the France of the 1940s and 1950s with regard to Jewish children saved by baptism. The *cas classique* was the Finaly affair (1952–53), eventually decided in favor of the children and their Jewish relatives (the parents had died in an extermination camp); but this was only because republican France was not the Papal States and civil law prevailed against a massive conspiracy. In the meantime, the salvationist position received widespread public support, to the tune of arguments that went back to the Middle Ages.

More troubling was a tenacious hostility to Jews as economic exploiters and profiteers. This was a theme endemic to Alsace-Lorraine, where Jews were often creditors to a peasantry that found no one else ready to incur the risks of crop loans. And it became a matter of national saliency when Jews moved to Paris and came to play a disproportionately important role in banking and state finance. These were the decades of railway promotion, stock market speculation (usually designated by the pejorative term *agiotage*), increased recourse to limited liability (in French: limited responsibility); also of new fortunes won in *coups de bourse* and other fortunes lost. Jews were prominent in this *brassage d'affaires* and took much of the blame for what many perceived as a socially subversive pattern of get-rich-quick and beggar-thy-neighbor. The Rothschilds in particular, seen as kings of the Jews, became symbols of monopoly and the target of the vilest vituperation. Much if not most of this criticism came from the left of the political spectrum—from such socialists as Fourier, Toussenel (*Les Juifs, rois de l'époque*), Proudhon, and Marx (for what his influence mattered). As Zeev Sternhell has amply demonstrated, this anti-Semitism of the left became a constant of the French political equation, persisting into the twentieth century in spite of explicit condemnations—one more example of the failure of formal doctrine to dominate or suppress deep social attitudes.

Such lapses on the part of what many are wont to perceive as "the good guys" have occasioned embarrassment and given rise to explanations (excuses) of uncommon sophistry. Many have taken refuge in metaphor: it is not the Jews as Jews who were being attacked; it is simply that the name *Jew* (*juif*) had become a symbol of huckstering and exploitation. To be sure: the pejorative connotation of words allow and encourage their use as generic labels going beyond their original specification. Yet such extension in no way diminishes their libelous impact, and the equation of *Jew* and *Jewish* with an array of despised or deprecated characteristics constituted a collective slander and targeted the group for opprobrium or worse. Contrary to the children's aphorism ("Sticks and stones . . ."), the bad word *can* harm: *notat et designat . . . ad caedem unum quemque nostrum.* Populist anti-Semitism was the socialism not only of fools but of villains. This much even the most assimilative Jews understood; and they called themselves *israélites.*

The anti-Semitism of the right, relatively quiescent in those middle decades, revived after 1870. At bottom it was, as always, religious—hence learned in childhood and retained as a conscious or subconscious premise available for activation in later life. But now a new component was added, namely racism. This new secular theme logically stood in direct opposition to the older anti-Judaism, which was correctable by conversion. In practice, Jew haters were quite capable of nourishing both forms of hatred simultaneously, which is precisely what one would expect of an attitude that is felt rather than thought and finds its justifications wherever they come to mouth.

The intellectual source of the new anti-Semitism was an increasingly popular racial interpretation of human history, building partly on ethnographic and philological speculations, partly on post-Darwinian derivations of evolutionary theory. The central theme was the interaction of higher and lower human groups (races), marked off by inherited physical characteristics (hair color, eye color, head shape, etc.) and such cultural manifestations as language. By no coincidence, many of these schemas consigned the Jews (and often Semites in general) to the lower category of those defined as unattractive, incapable of higher or finer sentiment, even dangerous. Thus Michelet, who contrasted the "peoples of light" (India, Persia, Greece) to the "peoples of twilight" (Egypt, Syria, the Jews). (One should be grateful, I suppose, that he spoke of twilight and not of darkness.) An amusing—though not funny—by-product of these racist lucubrations was the need—for some at least—to reconcile the new paradigm with the requirements of religion. What to do with Jesus? Ernest Renan ("the Semitic race, compared with the Indo-European race, really represents an inferior combination of human characteristics") solved the problem by pointing out that the population of the Galilee was of mixed origin; besides, by definition the Savior had none of the faults or defects associated with Semites.[6]

The attraction of such paradigms for anti-Semites lay not only in the pseudo-scientific justification they offered for preexisting prejudice, but in the obstacle they posed to Jewish attempts to "pass." No longer would conversion to Christianity constitute an entry ticket. No longer would good speech, the right tailor, proper manners and all the other manifestations of breeding and citizenship suffice to erase the biological stain. Edouard Drumont understood the stakes: in 1896 he promoted a competition for the best essay on the theme, "Of practical means of arriving at the annihilation of Jewish power in France, considering the Jewish danger from the point of view of race and not of religion." Maurice Barrès also: "That Dreyfus is capable of betrayal, I infer from his race."[7] A Jew was a Jew was a Jew.

To put things in context, one must recognize that the racist version of anti-Semitism took hold more in Germany than in France, where genetic prejudices foundered on the national conviction that *la civilisation française* could redeem anyone, of any color. And indeed, French scholars have stressed this distinction between the two countries by way of extenuation: the French, they argue, have never adopted the implacable view that Jews are inherently, irredeemably bad, and their blood so powerful as to corrupt any mixture (Pierre Chaunu: "Drumont is not Hitler"). The French version was rather one of Jewish obstinacy—"It takes a lot of water to baptize a Jew"—and resistance to change over a period of generations. Conversion to Christianity was at best a step in the right direction, at worst an insincere maneuver. When Victor Hugo—no

[6] For some of these racist observations by otherwise estimable scholars, see Alain Guichard, *Les Juifs* (Paris: Bernard Grasset, 1971), p. 62.

[7] Ibid., pp. 63–64. At a higher level, of course, a Jew could never "make it," could never fool a real expert. Thus De Gaulle—who we are assured was not an anti-Semite—to Ben-Gurion regarding the Frenchness of Edmond de Rothschild: "Cet homme n'a jamais parlé français." From an article by Ben-Gurion in *L'Actualité* (a Gaullist review), cited ibid., p. 233.

anti-Semite he, but a poet who understood his public—wanted to characterize the apostate Jew Deutz ("German"), the man who betrayed the Duchesse de Berri, he went right to the heart of the matter: the man was a venomous fraud.

> Ce n'est même pas un juif. C'est un païen immonde.
> Un renégat, l'opprobre et le rebut du monde,
> Un fétide apostat, un oblique étranger.

And he cursed him, with a curse whose resonance is immediately comprehensible in terms of anti-Jewish demonology.

> Sans qu'un ami t'abrite à l'ombre de son toit
> Marche, autre juif errant! Marche avec l'or qu'on voit
> Luire à travers les doigts de tes mains mal fermées!

Two developments gave force to this harder form of anti-Semitism —in France as elsewhere. One was the apparent rapidity and ease of Jewish assimilation into an increasingly secular society. For anti-Semites (who, I fear, like the poor, "shall never cease out of the land"), there is nothing so vexatious as the thought of the disappearing Jew, the Jew who pretends (no question of sincerity in such matters) to become a Christian (Frenchman) like everyone else.

For such Jew haters, in other words, the very success of the assimilative process is a provocation. We have no French statistical data on economic performance by religion, but there is good reason to believe that Jews did disproportionately well in business and trade. Some of them, moreover, were only too pleased to show their success by the pomp and luxury of their house and table, and Christian guests sometimes returned their hospitality by denouncing their materialism and *gaucherie* to all who would listen. Some of these wretched exercises in social mockery, like the Chateaubriand report on a Rothschild dinner in London, have passed into what we would now call literature. No less vexatious was the growing and disproportionate success of Jewish students in an educational system that selected by anonymous, competitive examination.[8] Julien Benda, for example, argued that the heightened anti-Semitism that preceded the Dreyfus Affair was due to Jewish self-assertion and ambition. "The triumph of the Reinachs in the *concours général* seems to me one of the essential causes of the anti-Semitism

---

[8] Note that some areas of power and privilege were preserved from "invasion" by retention of oral examinations: thus the *inspection des finances*, the *cour des comptes*, and the *internat des hôpitaux* in Paris.

that would explode fifteen years later. Whether the Jews were aware of it or not, such successes were perceived by the other French as a provocation by people who, having just come in, announce, 'That's what we are, and you'll see.'"[9]

The other and possibly more important factor was the immigration into France of Jews from Eastern Europe. In the late nineteenth century the flow was not large, indeed was tiny by comparison with the flood that came to America. But France is smaller, and the Jews who came concentrated in Paris, as elsewhere in Berlin, Vienna, London, New York. An anti-Semite would say that homeopathic doses were enough: once a body social has been sensitized, even a small quantity of an allergenic substance can provoke a massive reaction. Here was an echo from a forgotten (and for many Jews, repressed) past: the Eastern European Jews looked different, talked different, ate different. It goes without saying that the resident French Jewish population—these people who had just spent a century emancipating themselves from their past—were not overjoyed to be reminded of their cousins and antecedents. The best the French Jews thought they could do for these unfortunate coreligionists (testimony to the fact that Jews could be, and were in their great majority, very poor) was to send them somewhere else— to Palestine maybe, or the United States of America. But that was more an expression of preference than a realistic policy. In the meantime, anti-Semites were not slow to rub their noses in the "oriental" connection; thus Edouard Drumont, writing in *La Fin d'un monde* (1889) about Heinrich Heine (alias Henri Heine): "The exquisite poet, the refined Parisian, is indeed the brother of the dirty kikes, the Galician kikes with their curly forelocks who, come together for some ritual murder, laugh with one another while, from the open wound of the victim, there runs pure and crimson the Christian blood for the sweet bread of Purim." The text is an appalling but not unrepresentative sample of the mélange of medieval and modern, Christian and racist demonology, that marked the anti-Semitism of the late nineteenth century. And that, of course, is the point. The Jew was damned if he was, damned if he wasn't; at once too French and too foreign; blamed for copying and blamed for being different—in short, blamed for being Jewish. Careful scholars make it a point to distinguish among varieties of

[9] Aubéry, *Milieux juifs*, pp. 107–8, citing Benda, *Jeunesse d'un clerc*, p. 44.

anti-Semitism, and such distinctions are no doubt intellectually useful; but in anti-Semitic practice, all arguments were (and are) good and were changed and mixed as needed. Nothing is abandoned; *tout est bon.*

The Dreyfus Affair, then, burst on a Jewish community in turmoil and confusion. The great majority of the Jewish establishment looked for someplace to hide, tried to bury its head and shame, sought to avoid getting involved (Charles Péguy: "They ask for, they seek only silence. All they ask is to be forgotten"). Dreyfus himself, it is clear, embodied the same reaction—a poor focus for commitment and loyalty. But the swell of anti-Semitic anger and hatred made it hard for anyone to remain distant and indifferent. Drumont, Barrès & Company whipped up opinion and played the treason card (who were these Alsatian Jews anyway but Germans, hence born traitors?). The anti-Semites of the Catholic right wrapped themselves in the cloak of patriotism and made the Jews whipping boys for all the ills of modernism, secularism, Jacobinism, and (if I understand Pierre Chaunu correctly) the genocide of the Vendée and the legacy of the Revolution.[10] And on the left, the same old *rengaine* of Jews and Mammon, Jews and hucksterism, Jews and profiteering and exploitation, was played to a fare-thee-well. Only the courage of a few (Zola, Jaurès) belatedly saved the honor, such as it was, of the "progressive" forces; and not because Dreyfusards particularly understood the crime and outrage of anti-Semitism, but because it was borne in on those who thought a little that the prosecution (persecution) of Dreyfus was the rallying point for antirepublican elements, for all the enemies of a nonclerical (anticlerical) society and the heritage of 1789.

In the decades that followed, French anti-Semitism was somewhat subdued, discredited by the debacle of Dreyfus's exculpation. It had invested too much in the Affair, and now its discomfiture was commensurate. But anti-Semitism did not disappear—not while children learned it with their catechism, while Charles Maurras and his "integral nationalists" made it a staple of their propaganda, while populists continued to exploit the old myths of Jewish mammonism. And then the interwar years, bringing a new surge of Jew-

[10] See the discussion in Université de Paris-Sorbonne, Institut de Recherches sur les Civilisations de l'Occident Moderne, *L'Antisémitisme: hier et aujourd'hui* (Paris: Colloque 1983), p. 48.

ish immigration from Eastern Europe, reawakened old fears and revulsions. Here was a revival of the earlier shock of the late nineteenth century, but *en plus grand*. The new immigration was bigger, more salient, in large part owing to the closure of the United States. When the thirties brought their tale of depression, unemployment, and woe, this influx of foreigners became indigestible. The French, it is said, are given to xenophobia. Be that as it may, the 1930s witnessed a *flambée de xénophobie*, of involuntary returns of immigrant workers to such homelands as Italy and Poland, of denunciations of *métèques*, of barriers to admission of the ever larger stream of political and religious refugees. France was not very different in these respects from other West European countries; but it was perhaps more strident in its hostility, which represented a break with a long-established tradition of hospitality.

As earlier, the influx of "oriental" Jews with un-French ways proved acutely embarrassing to the established Jewish community. Jews who had spent generations learning to fade into the background felt once again compelled to justify their Frenchness. The list of Jewish complaints against the newcomers reflected this inner turmoil and unhappiness; also a profound gap in *Weltanschauung*: Why did they have to be so noisy and visible? Why did they insist on using several languages in the same sentence ("Jamais hat es so viel geployvet auf Paris")?[11] Why were they ready to see anti-Semites around every corner? Why were they always interested in knowing whether someone was Jewish or not? All of this made the Jewish establishment that much more anxious to prove itself to the non-Jewish population around, as David Weinberg's study of the Jewish community of Paris amply demonstrates.

The divisions within the Jewish community could only weaken its response to the graver dangers that ensued. The German victory and occupation and the establishment of a regime that brought with it an agenda of anti-Jewish measures—a program of native *cru* that needed no stimulus or reminder from the German occupier but drew rather on decades of anti-Semitic *pourriture*—caught many Jews unprepared, trapped in the web of deeply cherished loyalties, expectations, loves. It is not easy to come to terms with a threat to a century and a half of rights and entitlements: witness the readiness of many Jews, fled to the south in June 1940,

[11] Which recalls the prostitute's line in one of Edith Piaf's songs: "Liebling, komm dors mit mir."

to return north after the armistice, confident in the justice and protection of French law. The consequent uncertainties and mistakes
contributed to a massive catastrophe, which fell primarily on those
immigrant Jews who had not yet been admitted to citizenship or
whose citizenship was, in the French idiom, *de fraîche date*. In
retrospect, apologists for the French wartime performance have
sought to mitigate the guilt by arguing that someone had to go, so
the French saved their own Jews and delivered the others. Statistically this is undoubtedly true, as any good *chi* test will show. But
it is not at all clear that the distinction was qualitative so much as
temporal. The aliens went first; Vichy did not have time to deliver
the rest.[12] When the final results were tallied, it was found that
half the alien Jewish population was sent off in sealed cars, some
80,000 men, women, and children (the children were delivered
even before the Germans asked for them); and that of that number
almost none returned. The survivors in France owed their lives to
chance, to friends, to confusion, to clandestine help, to money—
above all, to the limits of power in time of war, political revolution,
invasion. We are talking of only four years from the defeat of 1940 to
the landing in Normandy. The French record, on balance, proved
better than that of most of occupied Europe, though not so good as
that of Italy, say, or Denmark or Bulgaria.[13] It fell far short, though,
of what France had been led to expect of itself or what the world
expected of it.

Which brings me to the heart of the historiographical problem:
precisely because France has long stood for the highest political

[12] Some French Jews, of course, did go, among them the family of Jules Isaac, coauthor of
the most popular history textbook (Malet et Isaac) of the interwar years. It was this experience that led Isaac, who like most assimilated French Jews had more or less forgotten (but
does one ever forget?) his Jewishness, to rethink his identity and write a number of major
works on Jews and anti-Semitism, in particular *Jésus et Israël* (Paris: Albin Michel, 1948)
and *Genèse de l'antisémitisme* (Paris: Calmann-Lévy, 1956). Cf. Rabi (pseud.), *Anatomie
du judaïsme français* (Paris: Les Editions de Minuit, 1962), pp. 183–86.

[13] In all fairness, the Danish community was much smaller than the French and the task
of rescue proportionately easier. As for Bulgaria, the pattern was similar to that of France: a
readiness to deliver non-Bulgarian Jews (from the newly annexed territories of Thrace and
Macedonia, for example) and a delaying action on the others. The success of this delaying
action, however, owed much to the active intervention of the Christian hierarchy in Bulgaria, which made public protest against the proposal to turn the Jews over to the Germans.
The head of the Church, Archbishop Kiril, went so far as to send the king a telegram
(March 1942) saying he placed his conscience ahead of loyalty to the crown and that, if
deportation were attempted, he would lie down on the rails in front of the trains carrying
Jewish victims. World Jewish Congress, *News and Views* 8, 2 (Nov.-Dec. 1983), 4–5.

ideals, because it has seen itself and been seen as a model for other nations, because those who write French history almost invariably love their subject—for these and other reasons, the story of French anti-Semitism is very problematical, hard to live with, and hard to reconcile with one's emotions. Jews and non-Jews have preferred not to talk about it, in the hope perhaps of avoiding thorny issues or of letting sleeping dogs lie: thus Chastenet, who found it possible in his "standard," multivolume history of the Third Republic (his entry ticket into the Académie Française) to write about Boulangism without any reference to its anti-Semitic populism; or Eugen Weber, who managed the more difficult trick of discussing the Dreyfus Affair without mentioning the word *Jew*.[14] Much of the criticism of Sternhell's work, in my opinion, reflects similar motivations: he should have left well enough alone.

It is useful to draw up a catalogue of these nuances, mitigations, reticences, exculpations, and misgivings. In the literature on the subject and in some of the papers in this volume, we are told, among other things:

—that the Jews constitued only a tiny minority of the French population; and that in much of France there were so few of them that one can safely say the inhabitants had never knowingly seen one—as though anti-Semitism needed personal contact and experience to flourish;

—that manifestations of anti-Semitic feeling, as in the Dreyfus Affair, were never more than local, hence implicitly limited in meaning and impact, "a storm in an urban teacup" (to cite Weber again)—some teacup! Paris, perhaps;

—that most Frenchmen did not read the anti-Semitic diatribes diffused by such papers as *La Croix* and *La Libre Parole*; though Paula Hyman and Zeev Sternhell point out they sold for pennies and in the hundreds of thousands, circulations far greater than those achieved by the "respectable" press;

—that such poisons as were disseminated never really affected readers, who bought these newspapers for other reasons;

—that these doctrines were really of German origin and never

[14] Eugen Weber, *The Nationalist Revival in France, 1905–1914* (Berkeley and Los Angeles: University of California Press, 1959), pp. 21–23. The version presented here is somewhat different: "Antisemitism plays a seminal role in the Affair, but the Affair is not really about Jews." Weber, "Reflections on the Jews in France," above, pp. 23–24.

authentically French—though one could hardly be more French than Barrès ("les Lorrains ont la France dans les tripes"); what's more, French anti-Semitic propagandists, by comparison with their German counterparts, were uncommonly eloquent and, by "talking a better game," were able to exert an influence on the "best" as well as the "worst" people); and

—that however much anti-Semitic extremists may have called for persecution, the French state, French law, French justice were there to protect the rights of the Jews—as of all other Frenchmen; while on the other hand,

—that anti-Semitic actions, as in World War II, were the work of the French state rather than the French people, and that much that was done was done by functionaries following orders (more "banality of evil");

—that the failure of French society in World War II to defend the Jews against the crimes of Vichy and the German occupier was due, not so much to anti-Jewish feeling, as to indifference—the indifference of the hard-pressed, single-minded, self-interested would-be survivor;

—that anti-Semitism was essentially an aberration, never legitimate—though only a Jew could think that it was not *salonfähig* in the politest non-Jewish circles;

—that one must distinguish among varieties of anti-Semitism, and the French variety was not the worst by a long shot; specifically, the French never produced the kind of bloodthirsty Jew killer the Germans found at home and in Eastern Europe;

—that one should distinguish between ideological anti-Semitism on the one hand and personal relations on the other: some of the most rabid anti-Semites managed to have Jewish friends (Degas and Halévy, Barrès and Léon Blum); and a final comfort,

—that French anti-Semitism, such as it is, is part of a larger xenophobia (nothing personal), and that, if anything, the French dislike some other national and religious groups—Arabs, for example—more than they dislike the Jews.

All of this, by way of putting things in context, of attending to nuances, of being historic (rather than "ahistoric," a sin newly discovered by nonhistorians for the purpose of criticizing those they disagree with)—in short, of saving a certain image of civic idealism and benevolence. And that image is also true—as those Jews who came to France as to a haven understood full well. We have here one of those all too common dilemmas of historical interpretation where both sides are right: everything depends on premises and point of view. Those whose admiration and love for France require purity of motive and perfection of comportment will find this edulcoration truthful and necessary. (There are also those who love France even when she falls short.) Others will see them as an exercise in special pleading. If I may indulge myself in a truism: these shadings surely made a difference to some survivors; they did not make enough difference to save the victims. The survivors remain to testify to their own good fortune; the victims are not there to summon witnesses and engage attorneys. So the historian must assume the task. One thing is clear: whatever the nuances, no French Jew could walk this kind of spiritual and social calvary unscathed. And that is true of Jews elsewhere as well: every Christian country has had its history of anti-Semitism.

Problematical as the interpretation of French anti-Semitism may be, the inverse aspect of the relationship is even harder to come to terms with (see the Trigano-Hoffmann exchange). This is the pull of French assimilation, the readiness of France to absorb outsiders, indeed the pressure it exerts on them to give up those characteristics, spiritual as well as material, that separate them from the rest of the population. For the Jews, as we know, this was an implicit condition of emancipation, and the Jews themselves perceived it as an opportunity to build a New Jerusalem. Now in our own time, new attitudes have come to the fore and compelled a reconsideration of this process. For the first time, really, minority groups in France (Bretons, Basques, and Provençaux as well as Jews) have challenged the Jacobin consensus by asserting a *droit à la différence*. The North African Jews, more than their predecessors, have been ready to be publicly Jewish, to vote Jewish, even to disagree with the state about issues of foreign policy. (The only precedent that comes to mind here is the Catholic resistance to the pro-Italian, anti-Papal policy of Napoleon III.) For those who now assert the right to be both French and Jewish—Jewish not only individually in religious matters, but as an identified group—the very virtue of France as a country of welcome and refuge for the oppressed, the very *mission civilisatrice* that France has always taken such pride in, has come to be seen as a silent, almost insidious form of oppression.

Such a view goes against the grain. It puts in doubt precisely those characteristics of French society and civilization that have always been deemed the most generous and forward-looking, and by the same token challenges a universalistic credo that many would consider far more enlightened than group loyalty or chauvinism. One cannot help being reminded of the surprise that liberal, "open-minded" non-Jews feel when they declare readiness to see their children marry Jews, only to see the offer rejected: how ungrateful! how benighted! To say nothing of illiberal non-Jews; listen to Pierre Poujade defending himself against charges of racism: the real racists, he argues, are "the Jews who, for generations, have refused Christian marriages!" And in an attack on Pierre Mendès France: "Since 1700 and some, you've never allowed yourself to marry a Dupont, but always some cousin within a small circle. The Mendès family has never allied itself with a Poujade or a Durand: that's racism, that's what we mean by a state within the state!"[15] In other words, we have here a classic *dialogue de sourds*: Jews (or any comparable minority) tend to see exogamy as a threat to group identity and survival, whereas the enlightened representative of the majority sees it as a gesture of welcome and a way of eliminating those particularities that are a barrier to civilized intercourse.

Meanwhile the immigration from North Africa has substantially increased the size of the French Jewish community, to the point where it is now the fourth largest in the world. The North African Jews, it is often remarked, are different from earlier immigrants in that many were already French citizens and spoke French before their arrival, hence had less difficulty in acculturation. On the other hand, they really feel Jewish, and their devotion to and joy in religious observance has revitalized a community that had largely lost its spiritual raison d'être. They also cherish their membership in a Jewish people, sometimes to the point of putting it ahead of all else. The reasons for this group loyalty are to be sought in the character of North African society, which was characterized by strong vertical cleavages along linguistic, ethnic, and

---

[15] Cited by Béatrice Philippe, *Etre juif dans la société française* (Paris: Editions Montalba, 1979), p. 385. The French has been cleaned up: "Depuis 1700 et quelque, vous n'avez pas été foutus de vous marier. . . ."

religious lines. In this unfused amalgam, the Jews, for all their French citizenship, held a problematic place between Muslim Arabs and European *colons*. The former continued to cherish age-old prejudices against outsiders whose very quickness to embrace French *civilisation* was perceived as an implicit rejection of the host society; while the Europeans held them at arm's length and provided a fertile field for the ugliest forms of anti-Semitic propaganda. So the Jew was in but never of the body social. This kind of segregated status is of course characteristic of societies that define membership particularistically rather than territorially or nationally, and in this respect, the Jews of Algiers were no different from the Jews of Warsaw, Łodz, Czernowitz, or Jassy, to say nothing of the rural *shtetlach* scattered throughout Eastern Europe. To be sure, their condition in Algeria, where they enjoyed the privilege of citizenship, was significantly better than in the Pale or Moldavia, where the state made anti-Semitism an instrument of public policy and connived at persecution and violence. So great was the difference and so well did the Jews of North Africa understand it, that no sooner was independence in prospect than they cleared out. If they entertained any illusions about the possibility of staying and flourishing in the Muslim successor states, their neighbors soon dispelled these by giving vent to long repressed hostility or to new, anti-Israeli attitudes easily transmuted into *attitudes anti-israélites*.

When these Jews came to France, then, they brought with them a pride in being French—they had made a choice—but also an aggressive, reactive pride in being Jewish. They were not like the resident French Jews, whether of old Alsatian stock or East European. Some of these had been confirmed in their Jewishness by their wartime experience; but many had not and systematically refused any attempt to inculcate in them a religious or ethnic consciousness. Indeed many survivors of the war and occupation—even of the camps—drew the conclusion that enough was enough, that they and their children must somehow disappear as Jews. There was a wave of name changes, of intermarriages, of baptisms, of deliberate refusal to circumcise, so that their sons should not some day be betrayed by the mark of the covenant—in short, a rush to the exits. By way of contrast, the North African Jews were more like the parents and grandparents of these disheartened, disaffiliated Ashkenazim—like those immigrants of the twenties and thirties who had brought to Paris the keen sense of group identity and distinctiveness that had enabled them to survive as Jews in Eastern Europe. So once again, one had within the Jewish community a reenactment of the war between Frenchness and foreignness, between universalism and particularism, between the Jacobin sense of unitary nationalism and a minority's commitment to separateness and pluralism. In Belleville and the Marais, European Jews moved out and made way for the newcomers, whose manners and manner offended them. Some Sephardic immigrants resisted intermarriage with Ashkenazim—and of course, vice versa. Nor was it easy for the old-timers to understand the willingness of North African Jews to flaunt their religion and intrude group considerations into national politics. The notables had long practiced the policy of *shtadlanut*—quiet, behind-the-scenes negotiation via friendly powers and intermediaries. The newcomers, on the other hand, were ready to take to the streets and make Jewish interests a voting issue, thereby raising the specter of double allegiance. There is no dirtier term in the Jacobin (patriotic) political vocabulary.

But this time the conflict was muted by the lessons of experience: after the debacle of the thirties and World War II, the Jewish establishment was concerned not to divide a community that needed all the solidarity it could muster. The older community moved to share synagogues, revenues, and power with the new; while the older leadership learned to change tone and style to accommodate the more outspoken stands of the newcomers. All of which has led some observers to speak of a major change in the character and agenda of French Jewry, raising its self-awareness and shifting it in an activist direction.

That may be, though it would be premature and hazardous to predict a permanent transformation. The collaboration between older and newer Jews cuts both ways; while the growing economic and social success of the newcomers will almost surely erode an earlier sense of separateness—just as it did with previous waves of immigrants. What the older generation wants is not necessarily what it gets. One has only to attend a holiday service in the great Sephardic synagogue in the rue des Tournelles to see the changes under way: the grandmothers, many of them still in dark, shapeless sacks that cover them from head to toe, piously attentive, lips moving in prayer and eyes taking everything in; the mothers, symbols of their husbands' success, decked out in jewels and finery, locks carefully coiffed and features painted, chattering animatedly throughout the service; the daughters, some of them in miniskirts, bright red lipstick and dark eye shadow, dangling over the balcony to watch the young men below, in and out of the synagogue all day long. How long before they too melt into the larger population, see their children lose their faith or, worse, change their faith and inter-marry? Man proposes, but time disposes.

Meanwhile, as Michael Marrus points out, anti-Semitism in France is now not nearly as bad as it used to be. In the years imme-diately after the war, the Jewish returnees were often subjected to disagreeable evidence that sufferings and losses had not earned them a respite from hatred. Daniel-Rops told them, in a book that sold 700,000 copies (*Histoire sainte: Jésus en son temps*), that in the cosmic balance sheet the Holocaust was some kind of repara-tion for the murder of Jesus. Those who had been robbed of prop-erty and homes found it hard to persuade the spoliators to aban-don their spoil. New right-wing sheets and tracts appeared to renew the lies and slanders of yesteryear. And every poll showed that the French people had in fact been influenced by old myths and new propaganda to perceive the Jew as the eternal outsider if not enemy. Such feelings have now abated, and although anti-Semitism persists (where does it not?), it is less salient and oppres-sive, also less respectable, than it once was. The strenuous effort by the Catholic Church to expunge those elements of the liturgy that embodied and thus promoted anti-Jewish sentiments has been both sign of and summons to this moral progress.

And what of tomorrow? Is the improvement permanent? If it were, would that hasten the assimilation and disappearance of French Jewry? Or is there now a large enough Jewish community and one committed enough to its own identity and interests—to the survival of Israel, for example—itself to survive in this most absorptive of cultures? Can France change and become a pluralist society? Does it want to? Will it have to?

These are not easy questions to answer, because they concern the future and one's answers come as much from the heart as the head. The easiest thing, perhaps, is simply to assume continuity (*plus ça change, . . .*), and that would imply a resumption of as-similation. Jean-Paul Sartre wrote that it is the anti-Semite who creates the Jew, and that, come socialism, there would be no more anti-Semites; hence presumably no more Jews. As well wait for the Messiah. But even if there were no socialism, the Jews have their own impulses. It is almost unthinkable in France, for example, that in the event of intermarriage between Jew and gentile, the gentile partner should convert to Judaism. And that in itself tells volumes.

Besides, France itself is almost irresistible. The saying has it, "*Wie Gott in Frankreich. . . .*" It is not clear that even God could long refuse the privilege and pleasure of becoming a Frenchman.

Some people (including some who mourn the extinction of the least animal species and would give life and fortune to save the snail darter) would see in the disappearance of French Jewry a great advance toward an ecumenical world of undifferentiated humanity. Others would weep at the loss. And the world—all of us—would be poorer.

PART 6

HISTORIOGRAPHY

GEORGES WEILL

French Jewish Historiography:
1789–1870

THE HISTORIOGRAPHICAL analysis of the history of Jews in France from the Revolution to the mid-nineteenth century is no easy task. The late historian François Delpech, who attempted such an analysis ten years ago, defined the difficulties involved: the complexity of the revolutionary and imperial period, filled with events that continue to provoke heated controversies; gaps in the source material, scattered among a number of archives; misconceptions about Jewish history in the official historiography; lastly, the challenge to assimilation—indeed, to the very notion of emancipation—by various schools of thought.

The quarrels between historical schools and their impact on French historians have been masterfully recounted by Delpech in his paper at the conference on *Les Juifs et la Révolution française* held in Paris in 1974. His study actually goes up to the July Monarchy and surveys the (very scanty) historiography of that period. Examining the contemporary literature, he contrasts the arguments advanced in favor of Enlightenment ideas, the work of the Constituent Assembly, and the supporters of the Napoleonic reforms with the arguments of the counterrevolutionaries and anti-Semites. He then looks at the debates that followed the publication in 1928 of Robert Anchel's famous book, *Napoléon et les juifs*. Delpech calls for a more open-minded approach by French historians (both Christian and secular) to Jewish distinctiveness and, above all, for a better understanding of Jewish history.[1]

Translated from French by Jonathan Mandelbaum.
[1] François Delpech, "L'Histoire des juifs en France de 1780 à 1840," in Albert Soboul and Bernhard Blumenkranz, eds., *Les Juifs et la Révolution française* (Toulouse, 1976), 3–46. For an understanding of the background to this discussion the author refers the

Delpech's call does not seem to have been heeded by French academics, who, on the whole, remain as indifferent as before to marginal cultures and faithful to the unitary view of their nation's history.[2] A few examples will suffice to illustrate this. In a work published twelve years ago on the history of Paris during the Revolution, Marcel Reinhard devoted several passages to Jewish life in the capital. Although he discussed the role of Zalkind Hourwitz and the lawyer Godard, he failed to mention the succession of votes on the Jewish question taken at the National Assembly.[3] The volume in the same series devoted to imperial Paris (by Jean Tulard) leaves a more favorable impression: the history of the Jewish community in Paris is dealt with briefly, but on the basis of an up-to-date bibliography.[4]

Paul Leuilliot, otherwise an extremely scrupulous historian, fell into another trap when discussing the Jewish problem in post-Napoleonic Alsace. By underscoring complaints about usury—complaints that would tend to prove peasant indebtedness in Haute-Alsace—he emphasizes the persistence of anti-Jewish attitudes. While his doctoral thesis has the merit of following the texts of the period closely, the same cannot be said of the strange hodgepodge that results in volume 7 of the *Nouvelle Histoire de la France contemporaine*, despite its being the work of two eminent specialists. The authors get Leuilliot's figures wrong and revive—after a fashion—the negative image of the Alsatian Jew. The other volume in this series make hardly any mention of developments concerning the Jews during the Revolution and the Empire.[5]

Finally, Paul Gerbod's otherwise distinguished volume on Euro-

---

reader to Annie Kriegel, *Les Juifs et le monde moderne: Essai sur les logiques d'émancipation* (Paris, 1977); and "L'Assimilation à la française, à propos d'un livre de Patrick Girard [*Les Juifs de France de 1789 à 1869* (Paris, 1976)]," *Nouveaux Cahiers* 45 (Summer 1976): 43–48. Also David Feuerwerker, *L'Emancipation des juifs en France: De l'Ancien Régime à la fin du Second Empire* (Paris, 1976).

[2] F. Delpech, "Les Juifs en France et dans l'Empire et la genèse du grand Sanhédrin," in *Le Grand Sanhédrin de Napoléon* (Toulouse, 1979), 1–26.

[3] Marcel Reinhard, *Nouvelle Histoire de Paris: La Révolution (1789–1799)* (n.p. [Paris], 1971); Frances Malino "Zalkind Hourwitz: juif poloanais," *Dix-Huitième Siècle* 13 (1981): 79–89.

[4] Jean Tulard, *Nouvelle Histoire de Paris: Le Consulat et l'Empire (1800–1815)* (n.p. [Paris], 1970).

[5] Paul Leuilliot, *L'Alsace au début du XIXe siècle: Essai d'histoire politique, économique et religieuse (1815–1830)*, 3 vols. (Paris, 1960), esp. 3 : 233–46; A. Jardin and A. J. Tudesq, *La France des notables*, vol. 2, *La Vie de la nation (1815–1848)* (Paris, 1973), 123–24.

pean religious history in the Nouvelle Clio series features several passages on the Jews: a brief account—with inaccuracies and omissions—of the problem of anti-Semitism in Europe, based (for France) on an outdated book by Malte-Brun; a highly inaccurate account of the Diaspora from a purely demographic point of view; a reference to contemporary Jewish thought in connection with Vatican II; and a mention of the founding of the Alliance Israélite Universelle.[6]

This sampling of authors is not exhaustive. One could easily find other examples, even very recent ones, of the superficial character of certain statements on Jewish topics and the casual way in which some otherwise highly regarded historians deal with Jewish history in France.[7]

A balanced and comprehensive coverage of French Jewish history in the period 1789 to 1870 was attempted by François Delpech in the two chapters he wrote for the *Histoire des juifs en France*, published in 1972. These pieces remain the best and most useful surveys of the subject. A useful supplement is provided by the third part of Simon Schwarzfuchs's work on the Jews of France, which sheds new light on still relatively unexplored events pertaining to the internal evolution of French Jewry and to religious problems.[8]

Béatrice Philippe's book, which, like Schwarzfuchs's, spans twenty centuries of Jewish history in France, can usefully be consulted for the post-1789 period. Written in a lively, incisive style and solidly documented, it provides a brilliant patchwork of historical, documentary, and literary texts and represents a very successful effort in its genre.[9]

A Centre Nationale de la Recherche Scientifique (CNRS) research team directed by Bernhard Blumenkranz has drawn on Pari-

[6] Paul Gerbod, *L'Europe culturelle et religieuse de 1815 à nos jours* (Paris, 1977).

[7] Witness François Furet's reviews—motivated, quite rightly, by the best of intentions—of the Diaspora series, reprinted in his *L'Atelier de l'histoire* (Paris, 1982), 273–90 (trans. into English by Jonathan Mandelbaum as *In the Workshop of History* [Chicago, 1984]). For another, and very academic, view of the Jewish problem, see the discussion that followed Georges Wormser's talk, "La Création du Consistoire central des israélites," in *Français israélites* (Paris, 1963), 17–46.

[8] F. Delpech, "La Révolution et l'Empire" and "De 1815 à 1894," in *Histoire des juifs de France* (Toulouse, 1972), 265–346; Simon Schwarzfuchs, *Les Juifs en France* (Paris, 1975).

[9] Béatrice Philippe, *Etre juif dans la société française, Du Moyen Age à nos jours* (Paris, 1979; paperback ed., 1981).

sian archives and libraries for a vast compilation of documents concerning the Jews from the sixteenth century to the present. This work can be regarded as an introduction to the sources.[10]

The fifth volume in the *Publications of the Diaspora Research Institute* series of the University of Tel Aviv is devoted to France. The work of Mme Neher-Bernheim, this volume contains 116 documents ranging from the mid-eighteenth century to the Second Republic and concerning the whole of France. While following a chronological order, the work emphasizes socioprofessional structures, demography, public opinion, and the transformation of the communities. Rather than a synthesis—always very difficult to achieve when dealing with so long a period—this is an abundant and varied collection of documents.[11]

Léon Santener, director of the Editions d'Histoire Sociale, issued facsimile reprints of fifty-six previously unobtainable literary and political texts concerning emancipation (originally published between 1787 and 1806); the minutes of the Sanhedrin meetings were also similarly reproduced as an annex to the proceedings of the 1977 conference on the subject.[12]

The many books, articles, and studies by the late Zosa Szajkowski, particularly his bibliographical studies, deserve mention here. Roland Marx's research on Alsace during the revolutionary period, however, replaces Szajkowski's work on that region.[13]

The best general study of the events surrounding the emancipation, both on the Jewish side and in the National Assembly, has been provided by Gerard Nahon in a paper delivered at a conference at Haifa in 1975. Not only does it include a full bibliography, but it sheds new light on the conflicts between Portuguese-origin Jews and Jews from eastern France.[14]

[10] B. Blumenkranz, *Documents modernes sur les juifs (XVIe–XXe siècles)*, vol. 1, *Dépôts parisiens* (Toulouse, 1979).

[11] Renée Neher-Bernheim, *Documents inédits sur l'entrée des juifs dans la société française (1750–1850)*, 2 vols. (Tel Aviv, 1977) (offset).

[12] *La Révolution française et l'émancipation des juifs*, 8 vols. (Paris, 1968); *Le Grand Sanhédrin*, 153–220.

[13] Roland Marx, *Recherches sur la vie politique de l'Alsace prérévolutionnaire* (Strasbourg, 1966); *La Révolution et les classes sociales en Basse-Alsace* (Paris, 1974); "Les Juifs et l'usure en Alsace: réflexions sur un mythe," *Saisons d'Alsace*, n.s., no. 55–56 (2nd quarter 1975): 62–67; and "La Régénération économique des juifs d'alsace à l'époque révolutionnaire et napoléonienne," in *Les Juifs et la Révolution française*, 105–20; Fernand L'Huillier, *Recherches sur l'Alsace napoléonienne* (Strasbourg, 1947), 519–49.

[14] Gérard Nahon, "Separades et ashkenazes en France: La Conquête de l'émancipation

Jacques Godechot's paper at the 1974 Paris conference on the French Revolution challenges the authenticity of Bonaparte's "appeal," issued during the Syrian campaign of 1799; his opinion tallies with that of Simon Schwarzfuchs, who also argues that the text was apocryphal, despite its having been mentioned in the official *Moniteur*.[15]

The Jews of Paris have been studied in a recent article, overlooked by Reinhard, which provides interesting information on the socioprofessional structure of this almost entirely Ashkenazic community, 80 percent of which consisted of small shopkeepers. For Marseille, there is a study of the famous Bacri firm, whose brokerage activities were indirectly at the origin of the conquest of Algeria.[16]

The only narrative history of the Jews in Paris during the revolutionary period remains that of Léon Kahn, published as long ago as 1898.[17] Because of the density of its Jewish population and the complexity of local problems, Alsace remains central to studies concerning Jewish history of the revolutionary period. Roland Marx deserves credit for having integrated the Jewish question into the broader historical context, first in his work on political life in Alsace from 1787 to the end of the Directory, and later in his book on social change in Basse-Alsace during the Revolution.[18] The sometimes tragic fate of Alsatian Jews during the Revolution and under the Terror has been examined by several authors, including Paul Hildenfinger, E. and M. Ginsburger, and Rodolphe Reuss. The career of Cerf-Berr, one of the most active militants in the cause of the emancipation of Ashkenazim in eastern France, has been studied in several recent articles by Renée Neher-Bernheim, Robert Weyl, and myself.[19] A useful supplement to these studies is provided by Robert Weyl's articles on the "préposés de la Nation

---

(1789–1791)," in Myriam Yardeni, ed., *Les Juifs dans l'histoire de France* (Leiden, 1980), 121–45.

[15] Jacques Godechot, "La Révolution française et les Juifs (1789–1799)," in *Les Juifs et la Révolution française*, 47–70.

[16] Liliane Hagège, "Les Juifs dans la section parisienne 'Beaubourg' pendant la Révolution française," *Archives juives* 6 (1969–70): 42–50; Françoise Hildesheimer, "Grandeur et décadence de la maison Bacri de Marseille," *Revue des etudes juives* 136 (1977): 389–414.

[17] Léon Kahn, *Les Juifs de Paris pendant la Révolution* (Paris, 1898).

[18] See n. 13.

[19] G. Weill, "Les Juifs d'Alsace: Cent Ans d'historiographie," *Revue des etudes juives* 139 (January-September 1980): 81–108.

Juive d'Alsace," and the history of Rosheim and the Rosenwiller cemetery.[20]

There are few recent articles on Metz and Lorraine, apart from the paper by Tribout de Morembert at the 1974 conference on the Revolution. The Lunéville community has been studied by Mlle Job.[21]

In contrast, the question of the Jews of Bordeaux has been re-examined in a totally new perspective by Frances Malino in her study of the origins and growth of the Portuguese community of the city from 1550 to the end of the Empire. Malino's study is impeccably documented; it should be supplemented by her other publications, which deal with the diary kept by Abraham Furtado during the Terror and with his role at the meeting of the Sanhedrin in 1807 (see Malino's paper at the 1977 conference on the Sanhedrin).[22]

For Avignon and the Comtat Venaissin, we now have the excellent dissertation by René Moulinas. The end of the *carrières* (Jewish streets) and the dispersion of the *comtadin* Jewry have also been discussed by Armand Lunel in his history of Provençal Jewry in the inimitable manner of this appealing author, belatedly awarded the Prix National des Letres. The Jews of Nice have been dealt with in a brief study by Hugues-Jean de Dianoux.[23]

Simon Schwarzfuchs's book on the Napoleonic period deals with the entire range of issues connected with Napoleon's policies and

---

[20] Robert Weyl, "Les Préposés généraux: Organisation civile et religieuse des juifs en Alsace (1648–1793)"; and "Les Juifs à Rosheim," in Freddy Raphaël and Robert Weyl, *Regards nouveaux sur les juifs d'Alsace* (Strasbourg, 1980), 17–45, 87–132.

[21] Henri Tribout de Morembert, "Les Juifs de Metz et de Lorraine (1791–1795)," in *Les Juifs et la Révolution française*, 87–104. Françoise Job, "Les Communautés israélites de l'arrondissement de Lunéville au début du XIXe siècle," *Archives juives* 9 (1972–73): 19–27, 43–51; 10 (1973–74):44–52; 11 (1975):11–16, 61–65; 14 (1978):11 (on Jacob Brisa, deputy to the Assembly of Notables).

[22] Frances Malino, *The Sephardic Jews of Bordeaux: Assimilation and Emancipation in Revolutionary and Napoleonic France* (University, Ala., 1978), trans. into French by Jean Cavignac as *Les Juifs sépharades de Bordeaux: Assimilation et émancipation dans la France révolutionnaire et impériale*, Cahiers de l'Institut Aquitain d'Etudes Sociales, no. 5 (Bordeaux, 1984); "'Mémoires d'un patriote proscrit', by Abraham Furtado (1793–1794)," in *Michael* (University of Tel Aviv) 4 (1976):74–162; "Furtado et les juifs portugais," in *Le Grand Sanhédrin*, 49–66; and "From Patriot to Israelite: Abraham Furtado in Revolutionary France," in J. Reinharz and D. Swetschinski, eds., *Mystics, Philosophers and Politicians: Essays in Honor of Alexander Altmann* (Durham, N.C., 1982), 212–48.

[23] René Moulinas, "Les Juifs d'Avignon et du Comtat," in *Les Juifs et la Révolution fran-*

their repercussions in Europe. Schwarzfuchs examines Napoleonic reforms in such a way as to demystify a reputedly explosive subject, paving the way for a reappraisal of the consequences of the decision to convene the Sanhedrin and to set up the consistories. Schwarzfuchs also exposes certain enduring apocrypha and puts the role of notables and rabbis in proper historical perspective.[24]

The best recent detailed studies of the Napoleonic period have been published as part of the 1977 Paris conference on the Sanhedrin. Chief Rabbi Charles Touati has carefully examined the Sanhedrin's decisions in the light of rabbinical law. David Sinzheim, president of the Sanhedrin and France's first chief rabbi, has now found a biographer in Rabbi Alexis Blum. The small Jewish communities of the Bouches-du-Rhône (essentially offshoots of the Comtat community) and that of Nice have been thoroughly studied by Françoise Hildesheimer. Lastly, Mme Neher-Bernheim and E. Revel-Neher have produced an original study on the themes of Judeo-imperial iconography, whose symbolism is evocative of the new Caesar's pride.[25]

In a study that deals with the ancien régime but also provides solid guidelines for research into the early nineteenth century, Gerard Nahon recommends a systematic effort to locate the rolls of the *déclarations de noms des israélites* of 1808, still often kept in town halls. These records constitute the logical starting point for a methodical census of the Jewish community during the Empire. The same author also calls for more extensive use of demographic sources along the lines of what Françoise Hildesheimer has done for Marseille and the Côte d'Azur.[26] Moché Catane published a short article on the circumstances of the founding of the Strasbourg consistory, which also contains an interesting discussion of the per-

---

çaise, 143–82, and *Les Juifs du Pape en France* (Toulouse, 1981); Armand Lunel, *Les Juifs du Languedoc, de la Provence et des Etats français du Pape* (Paris, 1975); Hugues-Jean Dianoux, "Les Juifs de Nice et la Révolution française," in *Les Juifs et la Révolution française*, 183–90.

[24] Simon Schwarzfuchs, *Napoleon, the Jews and the Sanhedrin* (London and Boston, 1979).

[25] Charles Touati, "Le Grand Sanhédrin de 1807 et le droit rabbinique," in *Le Grand Sanhédrin*, 27–48; Alexis Blum, "Sinzheim, le porte-parole des Ashkenazim," in ibid., 118–31; Françoise Hildesheimer, "Population et personnalités juives du Sud-Est," in ibid., 67–85; Renée Neher-Bernheim and Elisabeth Revel-Neher, "Une Iconographie juive de l'époque du Grand Sanhédrin," ibid., 132–48.

[26] S. Posener, "Les Juifs sous le Premier Empire," *Revue des etudes juives* 93 (1932): 192–214; 94 (1933): 155–56; Gérard Nahon, "Démographie des Juifs de France au

sistence of Jewish settlements in northern Alsace into the mid-nineteenth century.[27]

For the period of the Restoration and after we now have Phyllis Albert's major study of French Jewry from 1815 to the end of the Second Empire, based on extensive research into unpublished and printed sources and covering broad and hitherto unknown aspects of demography, the institutional growth of the consistories, and the political, social, and religious struggles that marked nineteenth-century French history. She reasserts the valuable role of both rabbis and notables. Albert establishes a thematic infrastructure encompassing the administrative, legal, moral, and cultural issues that dominated the history of the period.[28]

David Cohen's dissertation on the Jews under the Second Empire comes closer to the French academic tradition, since it is largely taken up with biographical studies, an examination of government policies, and history at the departmental level. This work contains a wealth of information—treated with a painstaking attention to detail—regarding the social and economic evolution of French Jewry, charities and educational schemes, official careers, government response and attitudes. The final result, however, is somewhat diminished by problems in presentation and by the author's excessive concern to demonstrate the political, civil, economic, and intellectual integration of the Jews into French society.[29]

XVIIIe siècle: Etat des questions et des sources," paper delivered at the 8th International Congress of Jewish Studies, Jerusalem, 1981, to be published in the monograph series of the Division of Jewish Demography, Institute of Contemporary Jewry, Hebrew University of Jerusalem (I thank Mr. Nahon for kindly allowing me to consult his paper, which contains an extremely up-to-date bibliography and was most useful to me in preparing this survey).

[27] Moché Catane, "Les Communautés du Bas-Rhin en 1809," *Revue des etudes juives* 120 (1961): 321–43.

[28] Phyllis Cohen Albert, *The Modernization of French Jewry: Consistory and Community in the Nineteenth Century* (Hanover, N.H., 1977). On the "civic and moral education" mission entrusted to the consistories, see F. Delpech, "Du catéchisme impérial aux premiers catéchismes juifs: Le Projet de catéchisme impérial israélite de Joseph Johlson," in *Mélanges André Latreille* (Lyons, 1972), 117–29; Roger Kohn, "Les 'Bordelais du Nord': Le Consistoire israélite de Nancy et les idéaux d'émancipation (1809–1813)," *Annales de l'Est* 33, no. 4 (1981): 291–320. The quarrel over the extension of the Montmartre cemetery in Paris, a possible cause of the reform of 1844 concerning the recruitment of notables, is discussed by Renée Neher-Bernheim, "L'Effervescence provoquée par les problèmes de sépulture des Juifs de Paris sous Louis-Philipppe," in *Michael* (University of Tel Aviv) 4 (1976): 248–72.

[29] David Cohen, *La Promotion des juifs en France à l'époque du Second Empire (1852–*

Cohen's relatively optimistic findings concerning the integration of civil servants ought to be modified in the light of the survey conducted by J-P. Roger, R. Martinage, and P. Lecocq on the careers of thirty Jewish magistrates of the nineteenth century. The survey suggests that, while no career problems can be discerned during the July Monarchy, the same does not apply to the following period, when religious origin often affected promotion. The hierarchy, however, was firmer in its support of Jewish magistrates at the time of the Dreyfus Affair.[30]

Michael Graetz has published an important book and several articles (most of them in Hebrew) on the history of ideas in the eighteenth and nineteenth centuries and, in particular, on Joseph Salvador, Feuerbach, Moses Hess, and Saint-Simonianism.[31]

Other aspects of the vast area explored by Michael Graetz have been treated in the context of economic, social, or literary history. One such topic is the prodigious rise of James de Rothschild, who, together with his sons, was a towering figure in nineteenth-century France. The late Bertrand Gille's gigantic history remains unfinished, but it already gives some idea of the power of the French branch of the family.[32] More accessible to the general reader, although possessing qualities as a scholarly summary, is Jean Bouvier's book, reissued in 1967. A biography of James de Rothschild was published recently by his great-great-granddaughter, Anka Muhl-

---

1870), 2 vols. (Aix-en-Provence and Paris, 1980); "L'Image du juif dans la société française en 1843, d'après les rapports des préfets," *Revue des etudes juives* 136 (1977):163–69; and "Une Etonnante Initiative des juifs de France sous Napoléon III," ibid., 134 (1975):210–13.

[30] Jean-Pierre Royer, Renée Martinage, and Pierre Lecocq, *Juges et notables au XIXe siècle* (Paris, 1982), 148–61. This chapter also discusses Algerian Jews, who were often hired as representatives of the law (*auxiliaires de justice*). In this connection, Crémieux's influence during his two spells as minister of justice seems to have been decisive. Jonathan Helphand, "French Jewry during the Second Republic and Second Empire (1848–1870)," Ph.D. diss., Yeshiva University, 1979 (microfilm).

[31] Michael Graetz, *Periphery and Center: From Saint-Simon to the Foundation of the "Alliance Israélite Universelle" (1820–1860)* (in Hebrew) (Jerusalem, 1982); "Une Initiative Saint-Simonienne pour l'émancipation des juifs," *Revue des etudes juives* 129 (1970): 67–84; "French Jewry in the Nineteenth Century," in *Emancipation and Enlightenment in Central and Western Europe (1789–1880)* (Tel Aviv, forthcoming); "'Rothschild, roi des juifs': L'Impact d'un mythe au XIXe siècle," paper delivered at Haifa conference on "Myths in French History," 1981 (forthcoming); and "Le 'Juif marginal' et la dynamique de la renaissance juive au XIXe siècle," in *Aspects du sionisme: Théorie—utopie—histoire* (proceedings of a conference held in Paris, 1976) (n.p. [Paris], n.d. [1982]).

[32] Bertrand Gille, *Histoire de la maison Rothschild*, 2 vols. (Geneva, 1965–67).

stein, who provides some new information drawn from family archives that were thought to have been lost, as well as an up-to-date genealogical tree.[33] It should be noted that the earlier works on the Rothschilds remain useful and that no satisfactory biography exists of the philanthropist of the family, apart from an essay on his role as colonizer by J. Margalith.[34]

Phyllis Albert, in a recent article, examines the hitherto largely neglected problem of reformist tendencies in nineteenth-century French Judaism. Her study shows that liturgical reforms, initially advocated by certain notables, were taken up by scholars and academics, and later by some rabbis, but that the consistories, by limiting changes in the organization of worship to a minimum, remained conservative, even as they disarmed the champions of innovation or removed them from positions of responsibility.[35]

Doris Bensimon-Donath was the first to apply new computer techniques to the sociological study of French Jews. While these quantitative analyses are undoubtedly useful, they can in no way substitute for the in-depth inquiry into human phenomena that ought to be one of the historian's major tasks.[36]

The problems concerning Jewish population growth are well known to specialists of the eighteenth century, but few studies deal with the later period. In an article devoted to the fertility of French Jewish women in the nineteenth century, Paula Hyman has argued that the birth rate of the Jewish population of eastern France, in particular of the Bas-Rhin, was noticeably higher than that of the rest of the local population. This interesting but geographically restricted investigation deserves to be carried further.[37]

[33] Jean Bouvier, Les Rothschild (Paris, 1960; reprinted 1967); Anka Muhlstein, James de Rothschild (Paris, 1981).

[34] J. Margalith, Le baron Edmond de Rothschild et la colonisation en Palestine (Paris, 1957). This work must henceforth be supplemented by Simon Schama's excellent book, Two Rothschilds and the Land of Israel (London, 1978), which provides a detailed study of Baron Edmond's role in the economic development of Ottoman Palestine.

[35] Phyllis Cohen Albert, "Ethnicity and Jewish Solidarity in Nineteenth-Century France," in Mystics, Philosophers and Politicians; and "Non-Orthodox Attitudes in Nineteenth-Century French Judaism," in F. Malino and P. Cohen Albert, eds., Essays in Modern Jewish History: A Tribute to Ben Halpern (East Brunswick, N.J., 1982), 121–41.

[36] Doris Bensimon-Donath, Socio-démographie des juifs de France et d'Algérie: 1867–1907 (n.p. [Paris], 1976) (offset).

[37] Paula Hyman, "Jewish Fertility in 19th-Century France," in Paul Ritterband, ed., Modern Jewish Fertility (Leiden, 1981), 78–93.

Except for Alsace, provincial studies are sparse. The Alsatian Jews' way of life has been studied by Freddy Raphaël in a series of articles subsequently collected in two volumes. Although primarily based on a sociological approach, some of these studies, on such topics as peddling, festivals, and popular life, provide a sensitive evocation of the atmosphere of Alsatian villages. The problem of conscripts trying to avoid military duty by a form of piety based on popular beliefs and naive mysticism is treated convincingly, and Raphaël's conclusion on the matter would corroborate Phyllis Albert's arguments about Jewish solidarity.[38]

Robert Weyl has studied the history of the Rosheim community (Bas-Rhin) up to the war of 1870. His various articles on Alsatian Jewry, concentrating more on the ancien régime and the Revolution, also touch on the nineteenth century and discuss various topics hitherto disdained by some historians: popular and liturgical art, gravestone symbolism, and synagogue architecture. Another example of a local monograph—this one even gives the genealogy of extant families—is provided by Salomon Picard and Chief Rabbi Bloch in their history of Grussenheim, a small village of the Haut-Rhin Ried, the only remaining traces of whose Jewish population (over three hundred before 1914) are a street and a local cemetery.[39]

The Judeo-Alsatian dialect has attracted a number of researchers. Apart from the older but still useful studies by Chief Rabbis Emmanuel Weill, Simon Debré, Honel Meiss, and A. Zivi, one should consult the pamphlet by Louis Uhry, which contains a good linguistic introduction, an index, and comparison tables.[40]

Six Alsatian synagogues were equipped with organs from the mid-nineteenth century on; these have been inventoried by Meyer-Siat. The enduring *querelle de l'orgue* would deserve to be studied once again.[41]

---

[38] Raphaël and Weyl, *Juifs en Alsace* (Toulouse, 1977) and *Regards nouveaux sur les juifs d'Alsace*; F. Raphaël, "Les Juifs d'Alsace et la conscription au dix-neuvième siècle," in *Les Juifs et la Révolution française*, 121–42.

[39] Joseph Bloch and Salomon Picard, *Grussenheim* (n.p. [Colmar], 1960).

[40] Louis Uhry, *Un Parler qui s'éteint: Le Judéo-alsatien* (Paris, 1981); on the other studies mentioned, see my article in *Revue des etudes juives* 139 (1980): 105, n. 79; R. Matzen, "Vieux Dictons, proverbes et adages judéo-alsaciens," *Saisons d'Alsace*, n.s., no. 55–56 (2nd quarter 1975): 158–78; and "Le Judéo-Alsatien et les hébraïsmes alsaciens," ibid., 189–206.

[41] Meyer-Siat, "L'Orgue dans les synagogues d'Alsace," *Archives juives* 8 (1971–72):

The few studies on other regions are listed by David Cohen in his bibliography (2:854−9). I shall content myself with referring the reader to that work. It should also be pointed out that several recent studies exist—in printed or typewritten form—concerning the Jews of Bordeaux, Dijon, Lyon, Nice, Marseille, and Versailles.[42]

The history of the Jews of Lyon has been treated by Delpech in a brief study that looks at the financial and administrative difficulties facing this small community, which grew from fifteen families in 1789 to fourteen hundred persons in 1870, and obtained its own consistory in 1857. The author discusses the role of the controversial Heymann de Ricqlès, inventor of the synthetic mint alcohol that bears his name—a product almost as popular in France as Coca Cola.[43]

The journal *Archives israélites* has published in several installments a study by Françoise Job of the Lunéville community since the Revolution, certain sections of which deal in some detail with the Napoleonic period.[44] An inventory of pre-1945 synagogues in the department of the Moselle has been prepared by P. Meyer.[45]

Few biographies are available.[46] On the Reinach family, among whose members were the three famous brothers Joseph, Salomon,

---

7−8; and "Les Orgues Wetzel dans les synagogues d'Alsace," *Saisons d'Alsace*, n.s., no. 55−56 (2nd quarter 1975):245−49.

[42] See David Cohen, *La Promotion des juifs*, 854−57. E. Houth and Gérard Nahon, "La Communauté israélite de Versailles," *Revue de l'histoire de Versailles et des Yvelines* 59 (1971):39−65; Nathan Levy, "Historique du cimetière israélite de Versailles," *Archives juives* 7 (1970−71):51−55.

[43] F. Delpech, "La Seconde Communauté de Lyon (1775−1870)," *Cahiers d'histoire* 13 (1968):27−66; Robert Biltz, "L'Affaire Charleville," *Archives juives* 4 (1967−68):39−41 (discusses Rabbi Charlerolle's dispute with Ricqlès); Robert Biltz and Jean Kohn, "Ricqlès, la menthe forte qui réconforte!" *Amicale philatélique France-Israël* 29 (1981), no. 300:843−55; no. 301:958−76; Louis Herbay, "Un Point de vue lyonnais sur la situation des Israélites de France," *Archives juives* 8 (1971−72):18−21.

[44] See no. 21.

[45] P. Meyer, "Synagogues anciennes de la Moselle," *Archives juives* 17 (1981):19−33.

[46] S. Posener, *Adolphe Crémieux*, 2 vols. (Paris, 1933−34); G. Weill, "L'Abolition du serment *More Judaico*," *Daguesh* 1 (March 1979):95−100 (on the role of Chief Rabbi Isidor); Jacques Eisenmann, "Zadoc Kahn: Le Pasteur et la communauté," *Nouveaux Cahiers* 41 (Summer 1975):20−40 (excellent; concentrates on the late nineteenth century, but also describes the early career of Zadoc Kahn, who became chief rabbi of Paris at the age of thirty in 1868). On the candidacies for the post of chief rabbi of France in 1846, Jonathan Helphand, "Une Lettre de Marchand Ennery," *Archives juives* 16 (1980):30−35, and Roger Kohn, "A propos d'une lettre . . . ," ibid. 18 (1982):32. On these questions, see also the forthcoming articles by J. Helphand, David Cohen, and others.

and Theodore, we now have Corinne Casset's recent Ecole des Chartes thesis.[47]

Richard Ayoun's *mémoire de maîtrise* (master's thesis) on Chief Rabbi Mahir Charleville is a good example of the possibilities of the biographical method. In an area closer to literary history, Joe Friedman has published a biography of Alexandre Weill, an unjustly forgotten publicist.[48]

The founding of the Alliance Israélite Universelle in 1860 marked both the culmination of an ideological process and the advent of a new political force whose influence remains very largely to be explored, whether in Europe itself or in the Mediterranean countries where it played its major role. By the adoption of the liberal and positivist ideas of the French school, the Alliance was, in a certain sense, the first universalist-leaning Jewish organization. Its history is becoming more familiar, and a number of studies in progress are gradually providing a clearer picture of the various facets of its activity.[49]

The periodical *Archives israélites*, which contributed decisively to the shaping of the mid-nineteenth century Jewish intelligentsia, has been studied by Béatrice Philippe.[50]

A posthumous work by Z. Szajkowski on Jewish schools in France since the Revolution has recently been published.[51]

The history of Algerian Jewry, long dependent on old and often biased works, is now fortunately enjoying the same revival of interest as North Africa in general. The Ben Zvi institute in Jerusalem and the University of Provence have joined forces in an attempt to give new impetus to a field where research is still hampered by the

[47] Corinne Casset, "Joseph Reinach avant l'affaire Dreyfus," in *Positions des thèses soutenues par les élèves de la promotion de 1982 pour obtenir le diplôme d'archiviste paléographe* (Paris, 1982), 51—55.

[48] Richard Ayoun, *Mahir Charleville* (Paris, 1973) (typewritten); Joe Friedmann, *Alexandre Weill, écrivain contestataire et historien engagé (1811—1899)* (Strasbourg and Paris, 1980).

[49] Georges Weill, "Charles Netter ou les oranges de Jaffa," *Nouveaux Cahiers* 21 (1970): 2—37; "Emancipation et humanisme: Le Discours idéologique de l'Alliance Israélite Universelle au XIXe siècle," ibid., 52 (1978): 1—20; and "The *Alliance Israélite Universelle* and the Emancipation of Jewish Communities in the Mediterranean," *Jewish Journal of Sociology* 24, no. 2 (December 1982): 117—34; see also no. 31 above.

[50] Béatrice Philippe, *Les "Archives Israélites" de France, de leur création en 1840 à février 1848* (Paris, 1975) (mimeographed).

[51] Zosa Szajkowski, *Jewish Education in France, 1789—1939*, ed. Tobey B. Gitelle (New York, 1980).

lack of centralized and easily available sources. The overview provided by Richard Ayoun and Bernard Cohen, although still very incomplete from a historian's standpoint, does constitute a useful supplement to Robert Attal's bibliography, itself regularly updated. Other studies, such as those by Simon Schwarzfuchs and Michel Abitbol, permit a more accurate assessment of the French institutions in Algeria.[52] In spite of certain initial investigations, much remains to be done. Research on North Africa is certainly the area where cooperation between archivists, librarians, scholars, community leaders, and notables would be the most desirable.

In the course of this essay I have tried to give some idea of the range of the more noteworthy publications of the past decade, while emphasizing the major trends in the historiography of modern France. Although these trends are influenced by widely differing historical schools, one can nevertheless point to certain dominant themes.

In the first place, one problem continues to attract the attention of all these schools, whatever their ideological leanings—the problem of emancipation. By granting civil and political rights to the Jews as *individuals* and not as a *nation*, the members of the Constituent Assembly went beyond the notion of simple tolerance and paved the way for a new experience, which, despite major failures, such as the Dreyfus Affair and the Vichy regime, still continues.

A second controversial issue is the ambiguous relationship that developed, from the First Empire onwards, between the French Jewish community and the new administrative and religious structures imposed by the state. The conservative spirit and routine-mindedness of the consistories set up by Napoleon had difficulty adjusting to the social dynamism of the nineteenth and twentieth

[52] Michel Abitbol, ed., *Communautés juives des marges sahariennes du Maghreb* (Jerusalem, 1982); other conferences listed in Richard Ayoun and Bernard Cohen, *Les Juifs d'Algérie: Deux Mille ans d'histoire* (Paris, 1982), 237–38; Robert Attal, *Les Juifs d'Afrique du Nord* (Jerusalem, 1973), with supplements in *Sefunot* (1980–); André Nouschi, "Observations sur la démographie historique des juifs algériens," in *Les Juifs dans l'histoire de France*, 165–75. Several papers on Algeria were delivered at the Sénanque conference on "Relations intercommunautaires juives en Méditerranée et en Europe occidentale," 11–13 May 1982 (proceedings to be published by the Université de Provence). On the Central Consistory's role in Algeria, see: *Nouveaux Cahiers* 29 (Summer 1972), special issue, "Algérie"; Simon Schwarzfuchs, *Les Juifs d'Algérie et la France (1830–1855)* (Jerusalem, 1981); Gérard Nahon, "Le Consistoire israélite d'Oran et le décret du 16 sept. 1867," *Michael* (University of Tel Aviv) 5 (1978):98–129.

centuries—hence the ideological and intellectual tensions perceived by many historians, tensions that partly explain the failure of reform movements and the growing success of assimilation.

Recent historiography has taken a very keen interest in these hitherto relatively neglected problems. The work of historians such as Albert, M. Graetz, Schwarzfuchs, Helphand, and David Cohen offers an opportunity to reassess the role of the leaders of modern French Jewry.

Thirdly, one must cite a number of studies—narrower in scope but guided by novel approaches—that lay the groundwork for an examination of the changes in nineteenth-century French Jewry. Such changes include the development of communities in Alsace, Lorraine, the southwest, and the southeast; the immoderate growth of Paris; the accession of the Algerians to the French religious and administrative sphere; Jewish participation in social and political life; the impact of demographic problems; the process of economic integration; and the attempts to foster Jewish schools. These studies ought to enable us to arrive at a better definition of the true nature of assimilation.

My fourth and final point will be more critical, but it is no more than a rehearsal of the wish voiced by François Delpech ten years ago. It is not unreasonable to hope that French historians will consent to take greater precautions when dealing with the Jewish problem, and that they will be less casual in discussing issues that, albeit marginal, are a constituent element of France's national culture. Jewish historians, for their part, ought to refrain from polemics. As Simon Schwarzfuchs has so effectively pointed out, French Jewry, obliged to find solutions to difficult problems of adjustment, created distinctive structures and adopted modes of thought whose imperfections did not prevent them from playing their role in the life of the nation.

PAULA E. HYMAN

French Jewish Historiography
since 1870

FRENCH JEWS were the first to be emancipated but among the last to have their postemancipation history written. Only in the past two decades has there emerged a significant historiography concerned with the political, social, cultural, and institutional development of the French Jewish community within the context of the larger French society. While much of this new historiography has focused upon the critical periods of the Revolution and the Napoleonic era, when the conditions of Jewish integration into France were elaborated, it has also begun to explore the past century of French Jewish life, shaped by internal migration, war and its consequences, and successive waves of immigration.

The early acquisition and success of emancipation in France deterred the writing of French Jewish history in the modern period for at least two reasons. The polemics attending the emancipation struggle had made it clear that after their acceptance as citizens Jews were expected to retain no special group identity other than a religious one. Nor was their behavior expected to deviate in any noticeable way from that of other Frenchmen. Berr Isaac Berr, the Nancy *maskil*, faithfully expressed the mood of the time when he wrote in his 1791 *Lettre d'un citoyen*, "It is indispensable to abandon that . . . sense of community or corporate group with regard to all civil and political aspects not inherent in our spiritual laws; we must be only individuals, Frenchmen occupied with true patriotism and the general welfare of the nation; willing . . . to be-

come useful to our fellow citizens."[1] Hence to all intents and purposes, the message of emancipation was that the history of French
Jews as a distinctive minority had come to its conclusion with their
momentous change in civil status.

Since French Jews were emancipated before they were acculturated, they were, for the most part, spared the long struggle to justify themselves that German Jews endured for the better part of a
century. For German Jewish intellectuals, in particular, that struggle
provoked a painful self-consciousness that was often translated
into historical consciousness. While French Jewish critics were impelled to compose essays on the need to institute social reforms
among the Jewish masses of Alsace-Lorraine, they had the good
fortune to know that their legal status did not depend upon their
abilities at persuasion. Moreover, Jewish intellectuals in France,
unlike their colleagues across the Rhine, could make their careers
within the university without confronting their Jewishness every
step of the way. Thus, the psychological and social pressures that
stimulated the writing of Jewish history in Germany were muted in
France.

By the end of the nineteenth century and the beginning of the
twentieth, scholars did begin to address themselves to the end of a
separate Jewish group experience in France by investigating the
process of emancipation during the revolutionary and Napoleonic
years. The past century of French Jewish history has attracted attention only recently. In part, this avoidance of the recent past reflected the difficulties of conducting research when relevant archival material was closed. Yet pragmatic considerations were not the
determining factor. Since modern Jewish history was not a recognized field and since French Jews were deeply immersed in French
culture, French scholars of Jewish origin (for example, Marc Bloch)
tended to apply their talents elsewhere.

Only as the premise that emancipation brought a particularist
Jewish history to a close fell into disfavor, did scholars begin to
study the events of the most contemporary period. Thus, it has
been Eastern European Jewish immigrants to France in the interwar years and the post-Holocaust generation in France, North
America, and Israel who have created an extensive literature on

[1] Berr Isaac Berr, *Lettre d'un citoyen, membre de la ci-devant Communauté des Juifs de
Lorraine, à ses confrères à l'occasion du droit de Citoyen actif, rendu aux Juifs par le décret
du 28 Septembre 1791* (Nancy, 1791).

nineteenth- and twentieth-century French Jewry. Because the ideological constraints on the study of modern Jewish history survived
longest in France, much of the historiography on modern French
Jewry has been produced by North American and Israeli scholars.

Even before the emancipationist ideology loosened its grip on
French Jewish intellectuals and scholars, some works of historical
interest dealing with the post-1870 period appeared. Commissioned by the *Jewish Quarterly Review* in 1891, Rabbi S. Debré
provided a sober historical overview of the Jews of his own time,
including an assessment of the inroads of assimilation and the impact of the loss of the Jewish heartland of Alsace-Lorraine upon
France's Jewish community.[2] Indeed, the gradual erosion of traditional Jewish culture in Alsace-Lorraine, followed by the German
conquest of the provinces, stimulated interest in recording and preserving the Jewish folklore of the region. That impulse, visible as
early as the 1860s, reached its fruition with the publication of
Léon Cahun's *La Vie juive* in 1886.[3] Illustrated with lithographs by
Alphonse Lévy, the volume celebrated the intense love of Ashkenazi
French Jews for their provinces of origin as well as a rural way of
life that was fast disappearing even within those provinces. This
concern for demonstrating the continuity of Jewish settlement on
French soil was reflected also in the publication of books and articles on the history of local Jewish communities, particularly
in Alsace-Lorraine, but elsewhere as well.[4] A similar type of pride in
the Jewish community's institutional achievements also prompted
the writing of histories of major Jewish educational, cultural, and
philanthropic organizations, such as the Alliance Israélite Univer-

---

[2] S. Debré, "The Jews of France," *Jewish Quarterly Review* 2 (April 1891), pp. 367–435.

[3] Léon Cahun, *La Vie juive* (Paris, 1886). See also the stories of Daniel Stauben (Auguste Widal), *Scènes de la vie juive en Alsace* (Paris, 1860) and G. Stenne (Daniel Schornstein), *Perle* (Paris, 1877), as well as Alexandre Weill, *Ma Jeunesse* (Paris, 1870), *Braendel* (Paris, 1860), and *Couronne* (Paris, 1878).

[4] Among the many studies, see M. Ginsburger, *Der Israelitische Friedhof in Jungolz* (Gebweiler, 1904); *Die Juden in Rufach* (Gebweiler, 1906); and *Les Juifs à Ribeauville et à Bergheim* (Strasbourg, 1939); Maurice Bloch, *L'Alsace juive depuis la révolution de 1789* (Gebweiler, 1907); Honel Meiss, *Choses d'Alsace. Contes d'avant guerre* (Nice, 1913) and *Traditions populaires alsaciennes à travers le dialecte judéo-alsacien* (Nice, 1928); and S. Debré, *L'Humour judéo-alsacien* (Paris, 1933). Concern for expressing local patriotism and tracing the experience of Jews under French rule in Alsace-Lorraine was stimulated as well by the German conquest and occupation of the province. See Elie Scheid, *Histoire des juifs d'Alsace* (Paris, 1887).

selle and the Ecole Rabbinique de France.[5] Often rabbis, firmly attached to the local community or institution, pioneered in this filiopietistic historiography.

While the Dreyfus Affair stimulated a vast literature, much of it polemical, it did not lead French Jews to reflect upon their own recent history. France's Jewish community had marked with enthusiasm the centennial of the French Revolution and trusted in the security offered by a century of undisturbed citizenship. As nationalism in France became the province of the right, the Jewish community continued to adhere to a French nationalism tied to the ideology of the Revolution. Troubled by the resurgence of anti-Semitism during the 1880s and after, some French Jews presented analyses of the causes of the rise of the new movement.[6] Interest in anti-Semitism, however, did not challenge the regnant myth of the absence of a postemancipation Jewish history in France. On the other hand, a number of intellectuals, most prominent among them Edmond Fleg and André Spire, embarked upon a lifelong investigation of the meaning of Jewish identity and the sources of Jewish culture. In their poems, novels, essays, and, in Fleg's case, translations as well, they brought issues of Jewish concern and aspects of Jewish thought to a French audience.[7]

The interwar period witnessed the first appearance of contemporary Jewish historical literature in France. The Eastern European Jewish immigrants who had settled in France maintained the ethnic conception of Jewish identity that was deeply rooted in the Eastern European milieu. The scholars of that community considered no aspect of the political, social, and cultural experience of the Jewish community beyond historical investigation. Thus,

[5] See, for example, Léon Kahn, *Histoire de la communauté Israélite de Paris*, vol. 1–3 (Paris, 1884–87). Narcisse Leven, *Cinquante Ans d'histoire: L'Alliance Israélite Universelle*, 2 vols. (Paris, 1911); Jules Bauer, *L'Ecole rabbinique de France* (Paris, 1930): A. Navon, *Les 70 Ans de l'Ecole Normale Israélite Orientale (1865–1935)* (Paris, 1935).

[6] See, in particular, Isaïe Levaillant, "La Genèse de l'antisémitisme sous la troisième république," *Revue des Etudes Juives* (hereafter *REJ*) 53 (1907), pp. lxxvi–c, and Bernard Lazare, *L'Antisémitisme, son histoire et ses causes*, 2 vols. (Paris, 1894).

[7] Both Fleg and Spire became Zionists in the wake of the Dreyfus Affair. Among Fleg's many works are *Ecoute, Israël* (Paris, 1913), *Pourquoi je suis juif* (Paris, 1928), *Israël et moi* (Paris, 1928), and *Anthologie juive* (Paris, 1923). See also André Spire, *Versets: Et vous riez—Poèmes juifs* (Paris, 1908), *Quelques Juifs et demi-juifs*, 2 vols. (Paris, 1928), and *Souvenirs à batons rompus* (Paris, 1962). The series of books of Jewish interest that Fleg edited at Editions Rieder was the predecessor of similar series currently published by Calmann-Lévy and Albin-Michel.

Solomon Posener, an acculturated Russian Jewish immigrant, published important articles exploring the social consequences of the Revolution for France's Jewish population as well as a major biography of the most significant Jewish political personality in nineteenth-century France, Adolphe Crémieux.[8] By the 1930s such figures as Zosa Szajkowski (S. Fridman), A. Menes, and M. Dobin had published seminal studies of their own immigrant community in France, its occupational structure, and its development of a vibrant labor movement.[9]

Reflecting the impact of Eastern European Jewish historiography, these scholars, with the exception of Posener, published their work in Yiddish, often in the pages of the *YIVO Bleter*, and thus wrote for an international Jewish academic audience of Eastern European provenance. The culmination of a decade of their work was the publication, by the YIVO Institute in New York in 1942, of a two-volume collection of essays entitled *Yidn in Frankraykh*.[10] This work reveals a broadly conceived interest in the history of the Jews in modern France. Based on documentary sources, the articles deal with Jews and the French Revolution, the Revolution of 1848, the Paris Commune, and the Dreyfus Affair, as well as the institutional structure of Paris Jewry in 1939 and the early legislation of the Pétain government. Thus, while episodic in structure, the volumes conceptualize an ongoing modern Jewish historical experience in France that transcends political regimes and even the different origins of the individuals comprising French Jewry. They also locate the Jews within a French context, for they draw upon

[8] S. Posener, *Adolphe Crémieux*, 2 vols. (Paris, 1933–34). An English version, translated by Eugene Golob, was published by the Jewish Publication Society in 1941. See also his articles: "Les Juifs sous le premier empire," *REJ* 90 (1931), pp. 9–27; 93 (1932), pp. 192–214; 94 (1933), pp. 157–166; and "The Immediate Economic and Social Effects of the Emancipation of the Jews of France," *Jewish Social Studies* (hereafter *JSS*) 1 (1939), pp. 271–326.

[9] One early study in French of the immigrant Jewish working class was M. Lauzel's *Ouvriers juifs de Paris* (Paris, 1912), which focused on the cap makers. See also M. Dobin, "Di professies fun di yiddishe emigrantn in Pariz," *YIVO Bleter* 4, 1 (August 1932), pp. 22–42, and "Yiddishe imigrantn arbeter in Pariz, 1923–1928," ibid. 3, 4–5 (April-May 1932), pp. 385–403; A. Menes, "Yidn in Frankraykh," ibid. 11, 5 (May 1937), pp. 329–55; and Zosa Szajkowski [S. Fridman], *Etudn tsu der geshikhte fun ayngevanderter yiddishn yishuv in Frankraykh* (Paris, 1937); "Fun yiddishn arbeter-leben in Pariz," *Di Yiddishe Ekonomik*, May-June 1938, pp. 232–49; [S. Fridman], *Di professionelle bevegung tsvishn di yiddishe arbeter in Frankraykh biz 1914* (Paris, 1937).

[10] *Yidn in Frankraykh* (ed. E. Tcherikower), 2 vols. (New York, 1942).

French sources and periodization as well as internal documents of the Jewish community.

While the impact of this work upon the postwar community of Franco-Jewish scholars was limited by its publication in Yiddish (and abroad), its appearance heralded a new conception and legitimation of contemporary Jewish history in France. According to this vision, French Jews, though acculturated and integrated within France, continue to manifest social, economic, political, and cultural as well as religious characteristics that merit scholarly investigation.

The development of an extensive French Jewish historiography concerned with the period after 1870 is of recent vintage. It has been fueled by the rise to maturity of Jewish historical studies on a university level throughout the world and by the impact of the Holocaust and the establishment of the State of Israel upon the most recent generations of Jewish scholars.

Because it partakes of the currents of modern historical scholarship and of modern Jewish consciousness, the recent literature on the past century of Jewish experience in France has sought to locate France's Jewish community within two contexts: that of French history and that of comparative Jewish history. Thus, the literature has focused on the relationship of the Jews of France to the larger society and to the state, with particular attention to the impact of such key political episodes as the Dreyfus Affair, World War I, and the rise of the Vichy regime; on the acculturation and communal and socioeconomic development of successive waves of Jewish immigrants—from Alsace, Eastern Europe, and North Africa; and on the changing forms of Jewish identification and participation within French society.

If the French Jewish community could take pride in its early emancipation and easy process of assimilation into French culture and society, the resurgence of anti-Semitism in the 1880s and 1890s, capped by the painful episode of the Dreyfus Affair, challenged the complacency of French Jewry.[11] Because the Affair rocked

---

[11] French anti-Semitism has received less scholarly attention than the German movement. Robert Byrnes's study of nineteenth-century anti-Semitism, *Anti-Semitism in Modern France* (New Brunswick, N.J., 1950) has yet to be superseded. For the period of the Dreyfus Affair, Steven Wilson's massive new book, *Ideology and Experience: Antisemitism in France*

French politics for a decade and seems to presage the grim events of the 1930s and 1940s, it has attracted the attention of critics and scholars seeking to understand the place of anti-Semitism within French and European politics and the social position and self-perception of French Jews. Already in 1935 Léon Blum had used the Dreyfus Affair as a weapon in his attack upon the politics of the Jewish bourgeoisie of the interwar years.[12] In 1942 Hannah Arendt first presented her thesis on the failure of Jewish leadership in modern times and the centrality of anti-Semitism for understanding the nature of the modern state by focusing upon the Dreyfus Affair and the political blindness of the Jewish notables.[13] While castigating the self-deception of the Jewish establishment, she also brought to public notice the political wisdom of the dissenter from the establishment position—the pariah who based his political stance upon an assertion of his Jewishness—in this case, Bernard Lazare.

Arendt's evaluation has proved influential. Indeed, Michael Marrus, whose *Politics of Assimilation: French Jewry at the Time of the Dreyfus Affair* remains the classic study of the subject, has acknowledged his debt to Arendt's thesis.[14] Marrus depicted the political quietism of the consistorial leadership as a direct consequence of the acceptance of the terms of emancipation. Newcomers to French culture and eager for acceptance into French society, the spokesmen of French Jewry trumpeted the congruence of French and Jewish values and hence became incapable of reacting when specifically Jewish interests were threatened. Like Arendt, Marrus

---

at the time of the Dreyfus Affair (Rutherford, N.J., 1982) explores the social, political, and ideological dimensions of anti-Semitism in France. On the ideological and political development of the anti-Semitic right, see Eugen Weber, *Action Française* (Stanford, Calif., 1962); René Rémond, *La Droite en France: De 1815 à nos jours* (Paris, 1963); Robert Soucy, *Fascism in France: The Case of Maurice Barrès* (Berkeley and Los Angeles, 1972) and *Fascist Intellectual, Drieu la Rochelle* (Berkeley, Calif., 1979); and Zeev Sternhell, *Maurice Barrès et le nationalisme français* (Paris, 1972); *La Droite révolutionnaire 1885–1914: Les Origines françaises du fascisme* (Paris, 1978); and *Ni droite ni gauche: L'Idéologie fasciste en France* (Paris, 1982). On Catholic anti-Semitism, see Pierre Sorlin, *"La Croix" et les Juifs (1880–1899)* (Paris, 1967) and Pierre Pierrard, *Juifs et catholiques français: De Drumont à Jules Isaac (1886–1945)* (Paris, 1970).

[12] Léon Blum, *Souvenirs sur l'Affaire* (Paris, 1935).

[13] Hannah Arendt, "From the Dreyfus Affair to France Today," *JSS* 4, 3 (July 1942), pp. 195–240. She expanded her thesis in *The Origins of Totalitarianism* (Cleveland, 1951), pp. 98–120.

[14] Michael Marrus, *The Politics of Assimilation: French Jewry at the Time of the Dreyfus Affair* (London, 1971).

also devoted considerable attention to that maverick anarchist-Zionist Bernard Lazare as an exemplar of an alternative vision of Jewish politics and identity. Where the Jewish notables resolutely refused to acknowledge the political potential of anti-Semitism and to formulate a defense policy, Lazare saw clearly that anti-Semitism was no atavism, but a real threat to the acceptance of Jews as French citizens. (Ironically, the marginal Lazare, the subject of a comprehensive biography by Nelly Wilson,[15] has the distinction of being the single most written-about Jewish personality in turn-of-the-century France).

In his exploration of the meaning of community to a diversified French Jewish population, Marrus also sketched the socioeconomic contours of France's Jewish population and signaled the importance of Eastern European immigrant Jews as a growing challenge to the politics of assimilation. In both these areas Marrus's work has stimulated further research.

Making innovative use of census data, marriage, death, and army recruitment records, Doris Bensimon-Donath has constructed a sociodemographic portrait of French Jewry, with special emphasis on Paris, in the period 1870–1914.[16] While noticeably lacking in historical context, this rich sociological study provides us with our first precise data on the occupational structure, nuptiality, mortality, geographic and social mobility, and residence patterns of French Jewry. Bensimon-Donath underlines the important role of migration, both internal and international, in the development of the French Jewish community. The growth of the Jewish community of Paris, whose increasing dominance of French Jewish life is one of the central demographic and institutional facts of the modern period, was entirely dependent upon in-migration. In 1872, for example, only 17 percent of the Jewish population of Paris was native to the city. In that year immigrants from Alsace-Lorraine and from Western and Central European countries accounted for the majority of Paris's Jewish residents. On the eve of World War I increasing immigration from Eastern Europe ensured that the foreign-born comprised close to half of the city's Jewish popula-

[15] Nelly Wilson, *Bernard-Lazare: Antisemitism and the Problem of Jewish Identity in Late Nineteenth-Century France* (Cambridge, 1978).

[16] Doris Bensimon-Donath, *Socio-démographie des juifs de France et d'Algérie: 1867–1907* (Paris, 1976). For an earlier demographic study, see Michel Roblin, *Les Juifs de Paris* (Paris, 1952).

tion. Concerned with general processes of social change, Bensimon-Donath points out that in their geographic mobility and level of ur-banization French Jews surpassed the rest of the French population.

With respect to other social indices as well, Bensimon-Donath compares French Jews with their non-Jewish fellow citizens. In patterns of family formation, for example, French Jews did not differ appreciably from the larger population. They were, however, considerably more literate and more likely to choose commerce, white-collar salaried positions, and the free professions as their path of upward social mobility. In all areas immigrant Jews of Eastern European origin lagged behind the native-born population.

As Eastern European, and to a lesser extent North African and Levantine, immigrants made their way to France, they became by the inter-war period the majority of France's Jewish population. Indeed, the historiography reveals that French Jewry has been recast, time and again, by successive influxes of immigration.[17]

Charlotte Roland's *Du ghetto à l'occident* was the first postwar study devoted to the acculturation of Eastern European Jews to France. Sociological in its approach, it surveyed immigrant Jews and their offspring living in the Belleville neighborhood of Paris. Roland charted changes in values and sociological characteristics between the generations as well as the decline of Belleville as a distinctive Jewish quarter. This study was a snapshot in time, which captured one moment in the life of an immigrant population but neither traced the development of the community nor evaluated its place within the entire album of French Jewry.[18]

My own work, *From Dreyfus to Vichy: The Remaking of French Jewry, 1906–1939*, focused on the institutional, cultural, and po-

---

[17] Because France has not been seen, nor perceived itself, as a nation of immigrants, the general historical literature on immigration to France is far less extensive than is the case for the United States. And many of the early sociological studies and political science essays on the subject are distinctively negative in tone. Jewish historians, however, have been aware of the centrality of immigration in the development of the Jewish communities of France, England, South Africa, Canada, Argentina, Mexico, and, of course, Israel, as well as the United States. The international dimensions of Jewish migration in the modern period make possible a comparative analysis of the impact of different host environments upon Eastern European Jewish immigrants and of the consequences of immigration for the institutional and cultural development of each Jewish community. For the most recent survey of the literature on Jewish immigration, see Lloyd Gartner, "The Mass Migration of European Jewry" (Heb.), in his *Migration and Settlement in Israel and among the Nations* (Jerusalem, 1982) pp. 343–83.

[18] Charlotte Roland, *Du ghetto à l'occident* (Paris, 1962).

litical impact of Eastern European immigrants upon the French Jewish community as well as upon the internal development of the immigrant settlement. It suggests that the xenophobic and all-embracing nature of French culture, even in its liberal definition, placed limits on the types of self-definition and communal development available to Jews in modern France. Indeed, because of French animus against foreigners and their own reluctance to engage in politics, native French Jews appear to have been less willing to come to the political defense of immigrant Jews than were the native Jewish elites of England, the United States, and Germany.

While native Jews asserted their claim to leadership of the entire Jewish population in France, the two communities influenced each other. Immigrant Jews availed themselves of the philanthropic and educational facilities administered by the native Jewish community and accepted acculturation as an inevitable process. Yet the immigrants challenged the hegemony of the consistorial elite over communal affairs along with its quietistic political stance. Taking for granted the legitimacy of Jewish politics, the immigrants created a vigorous labor movement, participated actively in leftist politics, and developed cultural Zionism within France. In the first four decades of this century they infused new ethnic and political elements within the public life of French Jewry and created a pluralist definition of Jewish identity. Whether such pluralism would have won legitimacy within French society remains open to question.[19]

Concentrating on the critical decade of the 1930s and the social and political challenges it posed to a divided Jewish community, David Weinberg analyzes the impact of the Nazi threat upon native and immigrant Jews alike and the futile efforts each group made to unite in the face of growing political pressures.[20] In *A Community on Trial* Weinberg demonstrates that the different political responses to the threat of anti-Semitism generated within the native and immigrant camps stemmed from conflicting views of Jewish identity. Yet he also places the political developments within the

[19] Paula Hyman, *From Dreyfus to Vichy: The Remaking of French Jewry, 1906–1939* (New York, 1979).

[20] David Weinberg, *A Community on Trial: The Jews of Paris in the 1930s* (Chicago, 1977). A French translation appeared first as *Les Juifs à Paris de 1933 à 1939* (Paris, 1974). For a study of German Jewish refugees in Paris in the same period, see Walter Peterson, *The German Left-Liberal Press in Exile: Georg Bernhard and the Circle of Emigré Journalists around the Pariser Tageblatt–Pariser Tageszeitung* (Ph.D. diss., State University of New York, Buffalo, 1982).

Jewish community—from the Jewish Popular Front in the immigrant quarter to the emergence of a nativist right-wing movement among the French Jewish elite—squarely within the French political scene of the 1930s. The political fragmentation of French Jewry in many ways paralleled the split of the French polity into two hostile camps. Moreover, the xenophobia that flourished in France in the 1930s in part accounts for the antipathy of native French Jews toward their immigrant coreligionists. Exploring the seething cauldon of Jewish politics in Paris, by then the home of two-thirds of French Jewry, Weinberg presents a poignant and incisive portrait of a heterogenous Jewish population in flux.

North African immigrants have written the latest chapter in the long saga of immigration as the source of Jewish vitality within France.[21] Since the arrival of some 250,000 Jews from North Africa primarily in the years since 1956, they have retraced many of the steps taken by their immigrant predecessors of different geographic origin. Yet in some ways the North African immigrants were unique. Unlike their Central and Eastern European predecessors, their acculturation to French language and civilization preceded their migration. Many—most notably those from Algeria—were already French citizens. Moreover, they were drawn not from the lowest social classes but often from the middle and upper ranks of the community. Finally, their patterns of settlement have been more diversified than was the case with earlier Jewish migrations.

The historical impact of the North African Jewish community upon the institutional, cultural, and political life of French Jewry has yet to be written. While sociological studies of the adaptation of these immigrants have been undertaken, they have not addressed the ways in which the unique characteristics of the North African Jews have shaped their process of integration nor the ways in which that process has resembled, or differed from, the experience of earlier waves of Jewish immigrants.

---

[21] On the Jews of North Africa, see André Chouraqui, Les Juifs d'Afrique du Nord: Marche vers l'occident (Paris, 1952). An English version was published under the title Between East and West: A History of the Jews of North Africa (Philadelphia, 1968). Simon Schwarzfuchs, Les Juifs d'Algérie et la France (1830–1855) (Jerusalem, 1981); Michel Ansky, Les Juifs d'Algérie du décret Crémieux à la Libération (Paris, 1950); Doris Bensimon-Donath, Evolution du Judaïsme marocain sous le Protectorat français, 1912–1956 (Paris, 1968); Michel Abitbol (ed.) Judaïsme d'Afrique du nord au XIXe—XXe siècles: Histoire, société et culture (Jerusalem, 1980); and Michael Laskier, The Alliance Israélite Universelle and the Jewish Communities of Morocco (Albany, 1983).

Based upon a survey questionnaire and interviews conducted in 1966–67, Doris Bensimon-Donath's *L'Intégration des juifs nord-africains en France* provides the most comprehensive information on the socioeconomic attributes, self-perception, and attitudes of North African Jewish immigrants ranging in age from 15 to 45.[22] Bensimon-Donath finds that the economic and social integration of this group has been largely successful and far surpasses the economic mobility of their countrymen who settled in Israel—a conclusion confirmed by Inbar and Adler's comparative study of Moroccan brothers who emigrated to Israel and France.[23] She also notes that Westernization and decline in traditional religious observance preceded the migration of these Jews to France.

While the outward signs of integration into France are striking, both Bensimon-Donath and Inbar and Adler point to evidence of psychological and social insecurity among North African Jewish immigrants in France. For example, fully 71 percent of those under 25 in Bensimon-Donath's sample were considering or had considered emigration, primarily to Israel. Despite little personal experience of anti-Semitism, these Jews had not, at least by the early 1970s, definitively cast their lot with France.

As for their Jewish identity, Bensimon-Donath records that North African Jewish immigrants and their children retain a strong sense of Jewishness that combines both religious and ethnic elements. While they are far more traditional in religious behavior than the rest of the French Jewish population, a large minority is no longer traditionally observant. As Inbar and Adler reveal, in comparison with their Israeli cousins, the second generation in France manifests much greater discontinuity in religious and social values. Both sociological studies speculate that the process of integration within France may lead to a rapid erosion of Jewish religio-cultural practice and identity. Such a forecast, however, rests in part upon assumptions that assimilation is a unilinear process and that a vigorous ethnic identity and a high level of religious observance are not consonant with modernity. Recent developments among other Jewish communities, however, as well as among other ethnic groups

[22] Doris Bensimon-Donath, *L'Intégration des juifs nord-africains en France* (Paris and the Hague, 1971).

[23] Michael Inbar and Chaim Adler, *Ethnic Integration in Israel: A Comparative Case Study of Moroccan Brothers Who Settled in France and in Israel* (New Brunswick, N.J., 1977).

throughout the world suggest that particularist identities may survive the impact of modernization.

No less influential than immigration in the experience of French Jewry in the twentieth century has been the period of World War II. The Vichy regime's revocation of emancipation as well as its collaboration in the deportation of 25 percent of France's Jewish population challenged popular notions of the receptivity of France to its Jewish residents. It also raised questions about the ideological predispositions and behavior of the French bureaucracy, elite institutions, and the masses. Moreover, the conditions of the Holocaust years led to the establishment of Jewish institutions that have remained important in the postwar period.

Like other communities that fell victim to Nazism, French Jewish survivors of the Holocaust felt impelled to memorialize their dead and record their own resistance. Thus, as early as 1947 the Centre de Documentation Juive Contemporaine, the major research institute and archive on the Holocaust in France, published an account of the activity of Jewish organizations in France during the war years; the immigrant Jewish left likewise recorded its exploits in a bilingual volume.[24] While many of these early works were essentially memoirs unfiltered by time or the perspective accorded the academic observer, they remain useful sources for current historians.[25]

Other early works reflected systematic historical investigation of specific aspects of the Holocaust years. Léon Poliakov was one of the first historians to analyze the status of Jews under Nazi occupation and the evolution of the policy of Nazi Germany and its allies.[26] Joseph Billig's study of the General Commissariat for Jewish Affairs pioneered in the rejection of the thesis that Vichy anti-Semitism was made in Germany; rather he argued that Vichy's anti-Jewish policy was a product of indigenous French anti-Semitism,

[24] L'Activité des organisations juives en France sous l'occupation (Paris, 1947); Combattants de la liberté (Paris, 1948).

[25] See, for example, the accounts of Jacques Lazarus, Juifs au combat: Témoignage sur l'activité d'un mouvement de résistance (Paris, 1947) and Anny Latour, La Résistance juive en France (1940–1944) (Paris, 1970). Most useful of this genre are David Knout, Contribution à l'histoire de la résistance juive (Paris, 1947) and Joseph Weill, Contribution à l'histoire des camps d'internement dans l'anti-France (Paris, 1946).

[26] Léon Poliakov, La Condition des juifs en France sous l'occupation italienne (Paris, 1946) and L'Etoile jaune (Paris, 1949).

neither imposed nor inspired by the Nazis.[27] Finally, in an article and the introduction to his historical gazetteer, Zosa Szajkowski posed questions about French responsibility for Vichy policy and about the attitude of the consistorial notables to the establishment and functioning of the UGIF (Union Générale des Israélites de France), the central organization imposed upon French Jewry in late 1941 by the Nazis. Szajkowski suggested that the Consistory's antipathy to the UGIF reflected its long-standing opposition to any secular definition of Jewishness, to organizations that challenged its supremacy, and to cooperation with immigrant Jews.[28]

With the opening of new archival material, rich and sophisticated analyses of French policy and Jewish behavior during the Holocaust have appeared. Adam Rutkowski has made available new information on the activity of French Jewish organizations, both legal and underground, in the years 1940–44 by publishing documents from the collection of the Centre de Documentation Juive Contemporaine.[29] In his recently completed doctoral dissertation and in a number of articles, Yerachmiel (Richard) Cohen has written a comprehensive study of Jewish policy in France during the Holocaust and has located the development of that policy within the framework of general French responses to Vichy and to the German occupation.[30] Avoiding the easy and fashionable but unhistorical indictment of the Jewish notables,[31] Cohen analyzes

[27] Joseph Billig, *Le Commissariat général aux questions juives, 1941–1944*, 3 vols. (Paris, 1955).

[28] Zosa Szajkowski, "The 'Central Jewish Consistory' in France during World War II," *Yad Vashem Studies*, vol. 3 (Jerusalem, 1959), pp. 173–86; and *Analytical Franco-Jewish Gazetteer* (New York, 1966).

[29] Adam Rutkowski (ed.), *La Lutte des juifs en France à l'époque de l'occupation* (Paris, 1975). Other new books on the Holocaust period include S. and B. Klarsfeld (eds.), *Die Endlösung der Judenfrage in Frankreich: Deutsche Dokumente 1941–1944* (Paris, 1977); *Eglises et chrétiens dans la IIe guerre mondiale* (Lyon, 1978); and G. Wellers, A. Kaspi, and S. Klarsfeld (eds.), *La France et la question juive 1940–1944: La Politique de Vichy, l'attitude des églises et des mouvements de résistance* (Paris, 1981).

[30] Yerachmiel (Richard) Cohen, *The Leadership of French Jewry during World War II* (Ph.D. diss., Hebrew University of Jerusalem, 1981). See also his "French Jewry's Dilemma on the Orientation of its Leadership: From Polemics to Conciliation, 1942–1944," *Yad Vashem Studies*, vol. 14 (Jerusalem, 1981), pp. 167–204; "Towards a History of the Establishment of the UGIF in Northern France" (Heb.), *Yalkut Moreshet* 30 (November 1980), pp. 139–56; "A Jewish Leader in Vichy France, 1940–43: The Diary of Raymond-Raoul Lambert," *JSS* 43, 3–4 (Summer–Fall 1981), pp. 291–310; and his review essay "Vichy and the Jews" (Heb.), *Zion* 47, 3 (1982), pp. 347–65.

[31] In this vein, see Maurice Rajsfus, *Des Juifs dans la collaboration: L'U.G.I.F. 1941–1944* (Paris, 1980).

the split among the Jewish leadership with reference to the UGIF and describes the evolution of a policy of cooperation between the Consistory and the UGIF and between native French and immigrant Jewish circles.

As Cohen illuminates the stages of Jewish responses to Vichy and the Nazi occupation, so Michael Marrus and Robert Paxton, in their definitive study, lay bare the development of Vichy policy and public reactions to it.[32] In an earlier book on Vichy, Paxton paid considerable attention to Vichy's anti-Jewish policies and their rootedness in French ideology and the political circumstances of the late Third Republic.[33] Here Marrus and Paxton expand this thesis, pointing to a continuity between the antiforeigner legislation of the late 1930s and Vichy's anti-Semitic laws. They also provide a mass of evidence, much of it new, to argue persuasively that Vichy's anti-Semitism was not simply in imitation, or anticipation, of Nazi goals but served Vichy's own needs, both political and ideological. While the Jewish survival rate in France was among the highest in Nazi-occupied Europe, they reject the notion that Vichy sacrificed foreign Jews in order to protect French citizens. They do, however, indicate that Vichy's leaders differentiated between foreign Jews and Jewish citizens on a number of occasions, even if they were ultimately unwilling to risk German displeasure by withholding Jews of French citizenship from deportation.

In addition to analyzing the policy of Vichy's leadership toward the Jews, Marrus and Paxton also attempt to plumb French public opinion regarding Vichy's anti-Jewish measures. Making careful use of prefects' reports, they show a widespread indifference on the part of the French populace to the situation of the Jews and an acceptance by much of the elite institutional structure, such as the churches, of Vichy's philosophy. However, they also reveal that the mass deportation of Jews in the summer of 1942 initiated a period of disenchantment with Vichy's anti-Semitic program, promoted passive resistance among many Frenchmen, and ultimately undermined Vichy's legitimacy. The willingness of individual Frenchmen as well as some clerics to warn Jews of impending

[32] Michael R. Marrus and Robert O. Paxton, *Vichy France and the Jews* (New York, 1981). A French version, with an appendix containing documents, appeared first: *Vichy et les juifs* (Paris, 1981).

[33] Robert O. Paxton, *Vichy France: Old Guard and New Order, 1940–1944* (New York, 1972).

arrest as well as to hide Jews contributed to the relatively high survival rate of Jews in France. Thus Marrus and Paxton, while ranking Vichy among the most collaborationist of regimes, present a complex portrait of attitudes and policies toward Jews in wartime France.

If we have learned much about Vichy's anti-Jewish policies and Jewish responses to them, in both organizational and military spheres, we have yet to explore fully the impact of the Holocaust upon French Jews and upon Jewish-gentile relations within France. It is likely that the more frequent Jewish-Christian dialogue in the postwar years as well as the more assertive political stance of contemporary French Jewry is, at least in part, a consequence of the Holocaust.

As the largest Jewish community in Western Europe, as a community with roots deep in French soil and yet comprised in large part of individuals transplanted from elsewhere, French Jewry has begun in the past two decades to reflect on its situation and to invite the scrutiny of others. Some of that reflection has been cast in a scholarly tone; much of it has been the province of journalists and essayists.[34] The very proliferation of philosophical, sociological, and historical treatises on the condition of Jewishness suggests the emergence in recent years of new possibilities of Jewish identity and activity in France.

The parameters of Jewish identity in modern France were first delineated in 1957, when Pierre Aubéry published his lively analy-

---

[34] French Jews are still less predisposed to historical research than to philosophical and sociological analysis and speculation upon the nature of the Jewish condition. There has been a spate of writing in this vein in France in the last two decades, and particularly in the past five years. Worthy of note are R. Misrahi, *La Condition reflexive de l'homme juif* (Paris, 1963) and André Neher, *L'Existence juive* (Paris, 1962) and *L'Exil de la parole* (Paris, 1970). Albert Memmi's classic two-volume essay, *Portrait du juif* (Paris, 1966) and *La libération du juif* (Paris, 1966) reflect the author's experience in North Africa as well as his confrontation with modernity in its French guise. See also Annie Kriegel's *Les Juifs et le monde moderne* (Paris, 1977) and Bernard-Henri Lévy, *Testament de Dieu* (Paris, 1979). Shmuel Trigano's stimulating polemical analyses of the failure of Jewish modernity and his delineation of new paths for Jews to follow vis-à-vis modern society find expression in his *Le Récit de la disparue* (Paris, 1977); *La Nouvelle Question juive* (Paris, 1979); and *La République et les juifs* (Paris, 1982). Alain Finkielkraut has also contributed to the discussion of the contemporary Jewish condition with his *Le Juif imaginaire* (Paris, 1980) and *L'Avenir d'une négation* (Paris, 1982). See also, Richard Marienstras, *Être un peuple en diaspora* (Paris, 1975).

sis of Jewish self-consciousness in twentieth-century France.[35] In particular, Aubéry dissected the powerful impulse among Jews toward complete assimilation into French culture and society and their consequent reluctance to take political positions as Jews. Yet he pointed out that the objective situation of Jews in this period—because of the experience of anti-Semitism and the antagonism of the right to Jewish emancipation—as well as the political heritage of Jews of Eastern European origin pushed Jews to vote heavily for parties of the left, thereby reinforcing their image as corroders of French tradition. Still, the dominant message that Aubéry proclaimed, and that Rabi affirmed in his historical essay, *Anatomie du judaïsme français,*[36] several years later, was that French society, so suspicious of Jews as the symbol of the foreign, promoted their assimilation as the sole legitimate mode of interaction between the minority group and the majority population. If the suspicion was never completely eroded, France had the distinction of offering the rewards of high office and prominence within the cultural realm to Jews who learned well the lesson of assimilation but were unwilling to pay the price of baptism.

Although virtually all Jews living in France today are French by virtue of their cultural formation, they have retained a refractory particularism that has manifested itself in current historical literature as well as in political demonstrations. Bernhard Blumenkranz, through the Commission Française des Archives Juives, has accorded scholarly recognition to the study of Jewish particularism in modern France by commissioning and publishing a series of volumes that encompass the totality of French Jewish history, and not merely its medieval or Revolutionary facets.[37] The scholarly activity of Blumenkranz and his colleagues has also stimulated research and teaching of Franco-Judaica at French universities. Similarly, Calmann-Lévy's Diaspora series has brought to the French

[35] Pierre Aubéry, *Milieux juifs de la France contemporaine à travers leurs écrivains* (Paris, 1957).

[36] Rabi (pseud.), *Anatomie du judaïsme français* (Paris, 1962).

[37] The Collection Franco-Judaica, under Blumenkranz's direction has published the following volumes of interest to students of modern French Jewry: *Bibliographie des juifs en France*, ed. B. Blumenkranz (Toulouse, 1974); *Histoire des juifs en France*, ed. B. Blumenkranz (Toulouse, 1972); *Les Juifs et la Révolution française*, ed. B. Blumenkranz and Albert Soboul (Toulouse, 1976); Freddy Raphaël and Robert Weyl, *Juifs en Alsace: Société, culture, histoire* (Toulouse, 1979); and *Le Grand Sanhédrin de Napoléon*, ed. B. Blumenkranz and Albert Soboul (Toulouse, 1979).

public not only classics of Jewish thought but also new commentaries upon Jewish texts and interpretation of the modern Jewish experience in France.[38]

Dominique Schnapper's recent sociological study, *Juifs et israélites*, locates these phenomena of a resurgent Jewish particularism within a broad perspective. Schnapper delineates several ideal-types of Jewish identification and behavior (or, better, *mentalités*) in contemporary France: observant Jews, whose identity is rooted in a religious metaphysic; militants, who espouse their Jewishness primarily in politico-national terms, through their activity on behalf of (or occasionally against) the State of Israel; and *israélites*, who continue the previously dominant mode of assimilation combined with avowal of a Jewish identity weak in content. (Here Schnapper points out that today's *israélites* are more conscious of anti-Semitism and less likely to wave the patriotic flag than were their predecessors of earlier generations).[39]

Schnapper links this pluralism of modes of Jewish identity in France, and particularly the reassertion of a religious or ethnic Judaism, to the transformation of advanced industrial society. While the uniformity and homogenization of life-styles produced by industrial societies stimulate a search for new forms of individuality and rootedness, including the rediscovery of ethnic or religious particularity, advanced industrial societies also provide the leisure time, economic sufficiency, and educational opportunities vital for the quest. Indeed, Schnapper concludes that only when it is based upon an intellectually vigorous social group will the reassertion of particularity survive in modern times. In this regard, French Jews appear to be in an especially advantageous situation. Their social class and Jewish heritage predispose them to take advantage of higher education and to engage in intellectual endeavors. Thus Schnapper dismisses as no longer valid the finding derived from past experience that upward social mobility and access to secular

---

[38] Calmann-Lévy has published the previously cited works of Marrus, Weinberg, Girard, and Marrus and Paxton, in addition to books by Hannah Arendt, Isaiah Berlin, Gershom Scholem, Nahum Goldmann, David Lazare, and André Neher. The series relies heavily upon the translation of foreign scholarship.

[39] Dominique Schnapper, *Juifs et israélites* (Paris, 1980). An English translation was published in 1983 by the University of Chicago Press. It should be pointed out that Schnapper underestimates the Jewish consciousness and activity of at least some segments of those who defined themselves as *israélite* in the nineteenth and early twentieth centuries.

culture weaken Jewish consciousness. In the contemporary period, they may very well provide the means for the reinvigoration of Jewish identity.

An overview of the years since 1870 indicates that this has been a century of discontinuity for French Jewry. True, the communal institutional structure established by Napoleon remains in place (though supplemented and transformed by the separation of Church and state), and recurring patterns of migration and acculturation can be discerned. Yet, the actors in the drama have changed, as has the script. The emergence of a Sephardic majority among the Jews of France brings a new cultural tone to Jewish life, both religious and secular, as well as a new cadre of leadership. At least some French Jews now succeed in combining a high degree of religious observance with social and cultural integration. The ethnic and political aspects of Jewish identity, for so long denied legitimacy within French society, have now become the modal forms of Jewish self-expression in France.

Index